for Arnold

tenacious pursuer
of truth

Alex Dallas

One World Emerging?

ONE WORLD EMERGING?

Convergence and Divergence in Industrial Societies

Alex Inkeles

 WestviewPress
A Division of HarperCollinsPublishers

Published in 1998 in the United States of America by Westview Press, 5500 Central Avenue, Boulder, Colorado 80301 2877, and in the United Kingdom by Westview Press, 12 Hid's Copse Road, Cumnor Hill, Oxford OX2 9JJ

Library of Congress Cataloging-in-Publication Data
Inkeles, Alex, 1920–
   One world emerging? : convergence and divergence in industrial
societies / Alex Inkeles.
      p.   cm.
   Includes bibliographical references and index.
   ISBN 0-8133-3397-0 (hardcover)
   1. Social history—1945– . 2. Social change. 3. Social
institutions. I. Title.
HN17.5.I528 1998
306'.09—dc21   97-46434
                                                                   CIP

The paper used in this publication meets the requirements of the American National Standard for Permanence of Paper for Printed Library Materials Z39.48-1984.

10   9   8   7   6   5   4   3   2   1

for Bernadette

CONTENTS

TABLES AND FIGURES

Tables

Figures

PREFACE

Massive forces driving social change are surging through the world, increasingly reaching into what had been the most inaccessible and remote corners of the globe. Since the mid–nineteenth century, industrial production, technologically sophisticated agriculture, popular education, mass media and electronic communication, high-speed transportation, and science-based research and development have transformed Europe and most of North America. Even as Russia turned to socialism and Communist rule after World War I it nevertheless built into its system all the elements in this list. In Asia Japan led the way in the first half of the twentieth century, but in the second half many others joined the mainstream while in some respects Japan moved to the position of world leader.

Other nations of Asia, notably India and China, have only in modest degree joined this world revolution, and still others, such as Burma and Vietnam, are, for the present at least, operating in a largely premodern mode. This is also the case for many parts of South America, and even more so for most of Africa. One of the great unknowns is whether or not those nations now outside the mainstream, particularly in Africa, can be brought within it as effective members of the modern world community. Making that possible is surely one of the greatest challenges facing humanity in the twenty-first century.

To give structure and coherence to the enormously complex process that constitutes the modern world revolution, I emphasize the theme of *convergence,* both in institutional structures and in popular attitudes and values.

Although its elaborations and ramifications can become extraordinarily complex, the basic idea is very simple. We start with the assumption that some human needs and aspirations are more or less universal. At the individual level these include health, material well-being and the means to achieve it, some degree of personal security, reasonably stable and satisfying patterns of interpersonal relations, and some form of community. At the national level they include various forms and degree of power, autonomy, prestige, and territorial integrity.

In the modern world most governments and the vast majority of individuals have apparently concluded that most of these goals are more fully and effectively attained to the degree that one adopts and develops a standard set of institutions: factories, schools, mass media, airlines, universities, hospitals, banks, and perhaps most important of all, institutes and science centers for generating new basic knowledge. Related processes, such as the decrease in family size and the aging of the population in industrial nations, stimulate the adoption of other institutions such as social security and old-age pension schemes. The increasing proportion of women working outside the home, and related developments, lead to the elaboration of service institutions such as fast food sources and commercial laundries. And so it goes.

All this means that increasingly all industrial nations, and others aspiring to become industrial, come to have the same array of institutional patterns, toward which array they *converge*. Some get it all, some understand or can develop only part of the array. Some utilize these institutions well, some less well, and some very poorly indeed. There is much room for variation, and seeking the reasons for it will keep large numbers of social scientists and commentators well occupied for many years to come. But such variation does not deny the main effect of a *general* movement toward a common set of institutions. Moreover, the test of effectiveness in reaching stated goals, and the competition with others joined in the same interlocking international system, together create additional pressure to refine and reorganize particular institutions, and even the whole array, in accordance with principles that come more and more to be widely accepted, thus giving further impetus to the process of convergence in institutional structures across national boundaries.

The second realm of convergence involves the movement of national populations away from whatever had been their diverse indigenous cultural patterns and toward the adoption of attitudes, values, and modes of daily behavior that constitute the elements of a more or less common world culture. In this process almost every aspect of life is influenced, and in many instances profoundly changed. The realms affected range from the most personal and intimate, as in how one finds a spouse and the role of love in that search, to the more abstract, as in conceptions of what makes for happiness and a good life. In between these poles a host of attitudes, values, and ways of living are shaped in increasingly comparable ways as styles of clothing and modes of dress, tastes in popular music, and even preferences in food come to be internationalized and relatively homogenized. At the core of all these changes, in many ways the key element in the whole process, is increasing individualism, the creation for each person of a distinctive identity separate from that of clan, family, and even nation. But this freedom from communal and collective control and dominance is not attained without its costs, expressed in part in painful isolation and in part in the loss of social control over behavior. These outcomes in turn stimulate both individual and community efforts not only to compensate for lost social values but also to stop or even to reverse the process of social change.

The forces that move people to these new uniformities are numerous and their action and interaction complex. Whole schools of sociological research are dedicated to advancing the claims of one source and mode of influence over the others. Broadly speaking, they may be divided into two sets. One stresses the importance of forces *external* to any nation that spread, perhaps even force, their influence in many places and consciously *manipulate* the lives of many peoples. The other emphasizes processes *internal* to each population as it adjusts to new institutions the experience of which *spontaneously* encourages certain modes of response similar to those of the populations in other nations confronted by essentially the same conditions of life.

Frequently cited as centrally directed sources of great influence external to the nations and peoples of the world are powerful Western countries and especially the United States, international organizations such as the United Nations at the world level and the Pan-American Health Organization at the regional, packaged and standardized entertainment of the sort dispensed by Disneyland and most notably Hollywood, multinational corporations such as the Coca-Cola Bottling Company in the case of consumer preferences and behavior, and Wall Street and the New York stock market in the case of finance.

To explain the impact of these external forces advocates of their importance rely on theories of diffusion and models of power and influence. Those who stress the internal and spontaneous forces rely more on ideas about human adaptability, on the common tendency toward imitation, and on theories of learning. Although we may assume that there are outcomes that can be relatively unambiguously attributed either to outside influences or spontaneous internal adaptation and learning, in most situations both external forces and internal psychosocial processes have been at work in complex interactions. One of the major challenges for the social scientist is to identify and weigh the relative contribution of different influences, external and internal, on the outcome of any particular instance of convergence in different national populations.

However, we should not fall into the error of assuming that convergence—however powerful a tendency it may be—has or will surely occur in any given realm or that it will sweep up in its current each and every population. On the contrary, our experience is replete with instances in which whole nations, or major subgroups within countries, resist the influences impinging on them, and make major efforts to preserve and enhance their cultural distinctiveness. In extreme cases the leaders of a nation may attempt to cut their population off from outside contact almost entirely. Thus in the late eighteenth century and much of the nineteenth China and Japan followed a "closed-door" policy. In the twentieth century both Communist Russia and China sought to isolate their people for various long periods. Indeed, the Chinese officially labeled foreign films, books, and ideas as "bourgeois pollution." Less extreme but comparably motivated have been the efforts of the *Académie Française* to prevent the infusion of English words into the French language.

Religious leaders seem especially sensitive to tendencies toward convergence and often spearhead massive campaigns of resistance to the forces that shape the emergent common world culture. They not only strive to inoculate their immediate congregations against such influences, but frequently seek to co-opt the coercive powers of government to enforce on everyone under its authority conformity to the ideas and practices of a singular religious vision. A striking example is the effort of some Islamic leaders to replace existing secular legal codes and substitute the *sharia*, a religious legal code, as *the* law of their country. In a comparable but less comprehensive move, the Orthodox rabbis of Israel have secured the exclusive right to control marriage and divorce in that country, placing this whole realm outside the framework of normal governmental control. And the Roman Catholic Church continues its absolute rejection of most forms of birth control and all forms of abortion. Starting from quite different ideological premises, all manner of conservation movements, including "Green" political parties, seek to mobilize antigrowth sentiment opposed to the seemingly insatiable and deeply destructive demand for nature's resources that the new world order generates.

These are examples of resistance written large. They are matched by hundreds of instances of individuals and communities whose history is written too small to be much noticed but who nevertheless in myriad ways devise their own special strategies for preserving their distinctive institutions and ways of living and believing.

Whether these forms of resistance to what has been termed "the acids of modernity" can stem the tide and even turn back the engulfing sea that drives the forces of convergence into every corner is surely problematic, as indeed is the extent and the depth of the convergence process itself. It is the task of social science to help us to recognize, and so far as possible to understand, the full power as well as the limits of the massive forces of social change that have been loosed on the world in recent historical time and will continue to shape its character well into the twenty-first century. The challenge is formidable, but the responsibility is compelling. At least I have deemed it so, and so have found myself returning to grapple with it in various ways and in different forms through most of the fifty years I have been active as a sociologist concerned with the analysis of social systems. This book is a record of my long-term and continuing engagement with the issue of convergence and divergence in industrial societies. Previously shared only with professional colleagues who read social science journals, these pieces will now, I hope, find a wider audience among scholars in other fields as well as among students and that part of the general public concerned to understand better the social forces that seem to have us all in their grip.

I have organized the volume into five parts. Part 1 provides the general perspective that orients the enterprise as a whole. In these chapters I try to clarify the different meanings of convergence and other key concepts, such as parallel change, to suggest how convergence might be measured and to illustrate both its pervasive scope and its limits. I point to language, religion, and legal systems as examples of social forms and expressions that seem most able to resist the pressures toward convergence.

Part 2 explores the convergence process at the level of the largest unit of social organization, namely, the nation-state. As political and economic systems, both Soviet Russia and Communist China adopted distinctive forms of organization that set them apart from the great majority of industrial and newly industrializing nations. It would be a serious failure of judgment not to acknowledge the facts of totalitarian control of all aspects of life and the great price in lives lost and wealth squandered under the various forms of political coercion and forced economic development that the leadership of these countries inflicted on their peoples. At the same time, it would be a serious denial of historical and sociological evidence not to recognize the extent to which first Soviet Russia and later Communist China increasingly introduced the array of institutions—ranging from the modern school to the modern army—that we have identified as part of the complex of institutions on which the world's nations are converging. In the process they have lost much of their distinctiveness, becoming increasingly recognizable as industrial societies.

India, by contrast, adopted the forms of democratic government and preserved a high degree of freedom for individuals and communities, but otherwise sought to minimize industrialization and maintain a village-based agricultural and handicraft economy. But in the last decade of the twentieth century India also increasingly opened itself to the outside world and adopted more of the institutional pattern characteristic of advanced industrial societies. Anticipating the future of these nations, I argue that "the transformative power of modern institutions is so great that the response of the people to them will be very much alike regardless of the population's cultural starting point or the larger socioeconomic context in which they are located."

In Part 3 I shift the focus to concentrate on specific institutions and institutional complexes, in particular the school and the family. Marriage and family relations are a central element in every society. No other institution is more often treated as the key repository of custom and as the embodiment of distinctive cultural values. Indeed, if marriage and family patterns can be shown to converge, then it might be argued that no other institution can hope to escape the pressures for the adoption of new modes of interpersonal relationship. We do indeed find much evidence of profound change and of resultant convergence in the way in which marriages are arranged, in residence patterns, in fertility rates, and in many other matters. But there are clearly areas in which convergence is resisted. For example, the proportion of women who work after marriage varies greatly from country to country even when the nations compared have similar levels of industrialization and urbanization.

Educational systems show a higher and increasing degree of uniformity across national boundaries. Something like the family as we know it has existed from earliest times, and as a culture pattern it is everywhere deeply ingrained and complexly linked to many other elements of any given culture. The school is a social unit developed only in relatively recent times, and it is much less likely to have distinctive deep roots in the various local cultures in which it now operates. This permits it to be adapted to outside influence more readily, and also to be changed more easily in accord with technological imperatives. We are therefore not surprised to find that it manifests very marked convergent tendencies in such characteristics as class size.

Part 4 places emphasis on process, even while acknowledging that process cannot always be understood apart from the institutions in which it is manifested. In the realm of social stratification it is clear that occupations are assigned almost exactly the same prestige in all industrial nations. Whether this results from an earlier process of convergence or reflects some more fundamental human propensity remains an open question. The emergence of such common standards can in part be explained by the extraordinary growth of communication links, especially electronic, which increasingly open every part of the world to the flow of a standard set of ideas and images.

But to receive an idea is not necessarily to accept it, as our study of the world's constitutions reveals. Many features of national constitutions are copied from those of the first nations to have written constitutions, but the borrowing is selective. Our survey of the guarantee of due process in the world's constitutions over a 100-year span shows very little evidence of convergence on a common standard. This supports our assumption that national legal systems tend to follow distinctive paths much determined by their origins and history.

In the last part of the book we move from institutions to individuals, looking to their attitudes and values, their preferences and tastes, and their behavior in the course of carrying on daily life. Here too we must acknowledge the evidence of persistent differentiation across national lines. Hence the proportion of the population that feels itself to be "happy" varies greatly from one industrial country to another, and it is notable and sobering that as nations become richer their populations do not become happier. Yet in general it is in this realm of the individual response that we find the most extensive and pervasive evidence of convergence. The social order common to industrial societies produces a structure of responses in the citizens of most nations that is strikingly similar from one country to the next. And as the new order of industrialization, urbanization, mass education, and mass communication spreads to other parts of the world, as it has most recently to Asia and the Pacific Rim, so too the ideas, values, and behaviors we recognize as modern and postmodern come increasingly to be adopted and expressed by the individuals who come in contact with these new institutional influences. In many instances these changes have been so deep and pervasive as to lead the social scientists who reported them to characterize them as "nothing short of phenomenal."

Of course the end of the story, if we can assume it will ever have one, is not yet written. Whether the tidal sweep of modernization will raise all boats while swamping and burying those too tied down to rise remains an open question. The seawalls and levees built here, there, and everywhere by those who would conserve and preserve their distinctive traditions and cultural forms may hold. Indeed, the whole process might be reversed by some great force not yet identified. However, I think it more likely that the forces making for a more unified and homogeneous world will prevail, and that in fifty years, if I could be here to write the same book, it might be possible to drop the question mark from the title *One World Emerging?*

To get even this far I have had to rely on the help and cooperation of many individuals and institutions. The authors who worked with me on the several chapters that were collaborative efforts are acknowledged in the opening-page footnotes of those chapters. In the same place I have identified the foundations and research institutes that were particularly important sources of support for certain of the studies I undertook. What has been most valuable was the freedom to explore and experiment outside the constraints of an externally imposed research agenda, a privilege which my position as Senior Fellow of the Hoover Institution granted me through the good offices of its recent and current directors, respectively, Glenn Campbell and John Raisian. No less important was the stimulus of many Hoover colleagues, particularly Seymour Martin Lipset, Thomas Metzger, and Larry Diamond, whose continuous engagement with me on the issues I address in this book did much to reduce error and sharpen the focus of my effort. When it was all written, and even as it was rewritten, three superbly intelligent and incredibly efficient assistants, Gloria Spitzer, Karen Gough, and Basia Mecinski, got it all into the computer and out to the publisher.

Alex Inkeles

One World Emerging?

Part One

GENERAL PERSPECTIVES

one

THE EMERGING STRUCTURE OF WORLD SOCIETY

In the second half of the twentieth century, laymen and professional intellectuals alike have frequently expressed the sense that the relationship of all of us, all humankind, to one another and to our world, has been undergoing a series of profound changes. We seem to be living in one of those rare historical eras in which a progressive quantitative process becomes a qualitative transformation. Even when, in more sober moments, we recognize that we are yet far from being there, we have the unmistakable sense that we are definitely set off on some new trajectory, and that we are not merely launched but are already well along toward an only vaguely identified destination. The widespread diffusion of this sense of a new, emergent global interrelatedness is expressed in numerous ideas, slogans, and catch phrases that have wide currency, such as "world government," "the global village," "spaceship earth," "the biosphere," and the ubiquitous cartoon of a crowded globe with a lighted fuse protruding from one end, the whole labeled "the world population bomb." Although the pervasiveness of the response to this emergent situation certainly tells us that *something* is happening, its diversity highlights our confusion as to exactly *what* it is that is happening.

Reprinted with permission from Alex Inkeles, "The Emerging Social Structure of the World," *World Politics*, Vol. 27, No. 4 (July 1975), 467–495.

Obviously the issue is one that is going to occupy us for a long time to come. Indeed, it is of such fundamental significance that our future welfare, perhaps our survival, will depend on our ability initially to understand and subsequently to guide the processes of change in which we are caught up. Consciousness and concern about this process at the community and national levels has become so widespread as to be commonplace and even banal. But it should give us pause—perhaps it is even cause for alarm—that so little attention is being paid to the problem of social change at the global level, at least when one expresses the amount of that attention as a proportion of the time the world's specialists in sociology and political economy spend on other scientific problems and issues. Moreover, such attention as the issue gets is usually sporadic, the methods applied eclectic, the data of dubious validity and reliability, and the "mode of analysis" casual and unsystematic. It will require a great and concerted effort over many years to rectify our inadequacies in this regard. Of the several tasks that lie before us, it seems to me that one of the most critical, especially at this early stage in our work, is that of clarifying our basic concepts. It is to that end that I plan to devote a large part of this chapter. I shall also make a few forays into the empirical realm, not so much as to make a convincing case about the facts as to illustrate and test the usefulness of some of the conceptual distinctions I feel it important to introduce.

A Set of Basic Concepts and a Historical Excursus

If we are moving toward a new condition, it will be helpful to have some sense of what that condition may be. Otherwise it is logically impossible to tell whether or not we are indeed more closely approximating it. Some reflection on the matter makes it immediately apparent that there is not one single end state toward which we may be moving but rather that there are several. Moreover, we should also recognize that we *start* not from one position but in fact from several, depending on the unit of action from whose perspective we view the situation. Some brief excursions into definition and a clarification of basic concepts are therefore indispensable to further discourse on the matter.

Basic Concepts

What is most distinctive about the problem before us is that it moves us beyond even the largest customary unit of social analysis, namely the nation-state, to focus on the entire human population of the globe. Of that population, and of the social units into which it is organized, we are asking: What kind of sociocultural system did it constitute in the past, what character does it have in the last quarter of the twentieth century, what are its current emergent properties, and what will be its probable future characteristics?

Given this perspective, we might well have framed our investigation in the terms common to the analysis of social systems as large and complex as the nation-state. Thus we might inquire into the structure of stratification among the units; the nature, if any, of the overarching legal system; the social consequences of the economic subsystem; and the extent of shared values, norms, and behavioral dispositions. Although this approach would be legitimate, and no doubt revealing, I have chosen instead to rely on a different set of concepts that I feel is better suited to dealing with the distinctiveness of the problem at hand. This set of categories seems less to presume that the world does indeed share what can meaningfully be described as "*a system of social action*." At the same time, it does not exclude consideration of the important themes such as stratification and the sharing of norms.

Autarky.   Autarky exists when a set of people share a more or less completely self-contained and self-sustaining sociocultural system. The condition does not necessarily assume physical isolation, although such isolation is often associated with autarky. Rather, to meet the test of autarky, a system should be such that if all other forms of human and social life were suddenly to disappear, the remaining system would have a high probability of continuing to propagate itself in much the same form it had before the cataclysm overtook everyone else. This condition is most easily met by small and isolated communities—for example, tribes living on isolated Pacific atolls or high mountains. Mere isolation, however, is not enough to guarantee the condition of autarky. A particular type of social structure and economy is essential. A group that depended on other tribes for a basic commodity of life such as salt or for an indispensable and unsubstitutable instrument for gathering food such as a trap, or was obliged regularly to come together with others to permit exogamous marriages, would to that degree be less able to satisfy the requirement of autarky. Thus an Eskimo family wandering in a full isolation for months across the arctic wastes in search of food is not an autarky, since functions critical to maintaining the long-term system of action of the group require that its members periodically come together with other similar physically isolated families to exchange brides and perform certain religious and communal services essential to the continuation of the sociocultural system of the tribe. An Eskimo tribe as a whole, however, might well qualify as an autarkic social system.

Although small and isolated groups with simple social systems and primitive economies may predominate among autarkies, such systems are also found at the other end of the scale of size. Units at the level of the nation-state may achieve a high degree of autarky. Thus Japan, Soviet Russia, and Communist China, at various periods in their history, more or less totally sealed their borders and strove to achieve complex goals of social reorganization while relying almost exclusively on resources and ideas internal to their respective sociopolitical systems.

Interconnectedness, Dependence, and Interdependence.   Moving away from autarky, we encounter various degrees of interconnectedness and dependence. The terms refer to similar but not identical conditions. *Interconnectedness* refers to the volume or frequency of communication, interaction, or exchange between two sociocultural systems. It is most often expressed in the exchange of goods and services, that is, in trade, as when tribes living in the hills may grow tea that they exchange in regular markets for rice grown by culturally distinct tribes living in the lowland valleys.

Substantial interconnectedness suggests and may lead to but is not a sufficient condition for *dependence*. Dependence refers to reliance on an item of exchange that is more or less indispensable to the survival of the system or systems engaging in the exchange. A system experiencing such dependence would to that degree be unable to achieve or maintain autarky.[1]

In a system of exchange, however, the implications of the exchange are not the same for all the units participating. The salt given by system A in exchange for the jade beads of system B may be vital to the physical continuity of B, whereas the beads may easily be replaced in A by some other means of ornamenting the dress used in tribal dances. A and B are therefore interconnected but not interdependent. B is dependent on A, but A is not dependent on B. To illustrate from the contemporary world, Japan and the United States each manifest an extremely complex pattern of interconnectedness with other countries. In the case of the United States, however, the means are available for continuing the current American system basically intact without relying on these ties. Japan, not possessed of domestic sources of coal and iron ore, to say nothing of oil, could not possibly continue as a major industrial producer without its external trade. Japanese interconnectedness is therefore also extreme dependency, whereas U.S. interconnectedness, while extensive, is manifested by a system that is, overall, so autonomous as to have high potential for attaining a condition of autarky.[2]

Integration and Hegemony.   *Integration* is a step beyond interdependence. It represents a condition in which formerly autonomous units have more or less permanently surrendered vital functions to another, more extended unit while still retaining a substantial number of other vital functions. Integration may therefore apply to only a given institution, to a subset of institutions such as the economic or political, or to a series of major institutional complexes. Thus two neighboring states may adopt a joint customs arrangement with regard to third parties and suspend such formalities for all goods passing between the two states, while each yet maintains a separate parliament, executive, police force, tax system, and the like. For example, the princely states of India after independence were largely, although not totally, integrated into the new national state while retaining some degree of distinctness. In time we may expect this integration to become complete, and these units of the system will become indistinguishable from all the other subdivisions of the Indian state.

Integration may, of course, be either voluntary or imposed. Thus the total integration of the colonies in the former British Empire was, with few exceptions, a result of the imposition of force, whereas the participation of most of the ex-colonies in the Commonwealth was largely voluntary, perhaps because it involved a lesser degree of integration. Integration imposed by force may be treated as a special case, designated as *hegemony.* This was the predominant mode of integration in the past, and its history has not run its course, although we may hope that voluntary integration will be the predominant mode in the future.

Convergence. Integration sometimes presupposes and often leads to similarities in political form, in social organization, or in cultural patterns, but such similarities are neither a necessary nor a sufficient condition for integration. Where social units start from diverse positions on some scale of organization, sociopolitical structure, or culture and then move toward some more common form on the given dimension, the process is labeled *convergence.* Just as integration may occur without convergence, as in the relations of an imperial center and its colonies, so convergence may occur without any substantial degree of integration. Thus the Soviet Union and the United States may become more alike in their urbanization, dependence on scientific research and technological innovation, and development of a delinquent subculture among the *jeunesse dorée,* without any substantial movement toward greater integration of the two political systems. The complexity of the convergence issue is explored in depth and illustrated in detail in the next chapter.

A Historical Excursus

Having elaborated our basic set of concepts, at least in preliminary form, we should now test their serviceability. Ideally, one would apply this test to a number of historical periods, such as prehistory, the era of Greco-Roman dominance, the medieval period, and the premodern world scene. I restrict myself here to a single application, in this case the earliest relevant period, namely, prehistory.

Before undertaking this exploration, however, it seems appropriate to pause long enough for one general note of caution concerning the severe limits on our ability to generalize, which constrain us the moment we move from the nation-state or the culture region to the global level of analysis.

Throughout much of recorded history, different areas of the world were at quite different stages of development, especially as far as the levels of technology and of political integration are concerned. The Earth was divided into a series of different worlds, each with its own character as a subworld. Moreover, for much of human history some of these subworlds were in total ignorance of the existence of each other. Great Incan and Mayan empires rose and fell without having any awareness of Europe, just as Europe was totally unaware of those empires. Of course it is precisely the fact that such complete isolation and insulation is no longer possible that distinguishes the modern era. Knowing that, however, does not settle for us the question as to whether, in dealing with such periods, it is really appropriate to treat the world as one unit, or as a series of discrete subworlds, for each of which we need to test, separately, the extent to which the elements within it enjoyed autarky, were independent, converged on a common model, and so on. It seems both more consistent with our theoretical orientation and more consonant with practical constraints to maintain a focus on the world as a single system. Applying our concepts to the prehistorical period, approximately between 10,000 and 5,000 B.C., we may say the following of the world at that time:

Autarky was extremely high, which is to say of course that dependence was very low. Hunting and gathering, herding, and limited agriculture permitted relatively self-contained, self-supporting communities.

Interconnectedness was minimal. Most groups had contact only with immediately adjacent groups; exchange was limited to a small number of less than vital commodities; interchange of persons, customs, ideas, and technology was extremely selective. Although pottery, animal husbandry, and some cultivated plants gradually diffused, the norm seemed to be total avoidance of engagement where possible, and sporadic, brief, and limited engagement where unavoidable.

Integration was rarely the outcome of such connections as were established. Populations were often nomadic or in other ways in motion, which reduced the temporal length of contact between groups below the term optimal for integration. In addition, the groups coming into juxtaposition were often extremely disparate, as illustrated in a later historical period by the relations between the settled, cliff-dwelling, almost "urban" Hopi, and nomadic herders such as the Navajo. The barriers to the integration of such groups were very great. Moreover, limits on the technical capacity of rulers, above all with regard to communication, minimized the prospect of establishing political *hegemony,* and hence further reduced the attainment of other forms of integration.

Convergence. It is a curious feature of the prehistorical period that despite maximal autarky and minimal interconnectedness and integration, convergence was quite substantial. Probably the most important manifestation of the similarity that most societies displayed in that period was in their level of technology. That technology, in turn, evidently established constraints that influenced institutional patterns, thus ensuring the existence of certain very broad similarities in the social organization of late Stone-Age and early Bronze-Age societies.

Our image of the standing of the prehistorical period on the seven dimensions of our analytic scheme, reducing our characterization of each to a key word or phrase, may be summarized as follows:

Autarky	High
Interconnectedness	Minimal
Dependence	Extremely limited
Interdependence	Virtually none
Integration	Virtually none
Hegemony	Minimal and sporadic
Convergence	Considerable similarity in technology; modest in other forms of culture

Once we move into the historical era, we quickly discover how difficult it is to avoid being ethnocentric. For example, if we elect to represent early history by the period from 200 B.C. to A.D. 200, the temptation for an individual in the European historical tradition is to treat it automatically as the era dominated by Greek culture and the Roman Empire. From the perspective of an Asian, however, it might more appropriately be seen as the period of the flourishing of the great Han dynasties. Going either back or forward, the specific actors would change, but the pattern would remain the same. The tendency for vast parts of the global population to become organized in great territorial hegemonies marks a sharp break dividing the historical period from prehistory. These hegemonies were generally concentrated in, although not absolutely limited to, distinct, even if broad, culture areas and were generally organized and dominated by a particular dynamic subgroup within the area. They were possible only after widely diffused, settled agriculture made available large surpluses of grain and labor. But they depended at least as much on technological advances such as irrigation, improved navigation at sea, systems of imperial roads such as those built by Darius for the Achaemenid Empire, and the development of cavalry and a reliable bronze or iron sword. Equally critical was the development of new forms of political and military organization, including the means for collecting and allocating the surplus food and human services that became available.

Within the limits of each of these subworlds, and notably within the area of Roman dominance, *autarky* was greatly reduced, *interconnectedness* and *interdependence* became much more extensive, and despite a high degree of cultural diversity in the hinterlands, a *convergence* toward a common metropolitan culture was strongly manifested.

In the global system as a whole, however, the tendencies were different. The characteristic of the world system was that it was multicentered. Each of the major subworlds, such as Rome and China, manifested a high degree of *autarky*. *Interconnectedness* between the major subworlds was relatively minor, limited to a few trade routes carrying mainly specialized commodities, particularly luxury goods not at all vital to the economy or to the social structure of either party to the exchange. In brief, neither dependence nor interdependence was manifested between these subworlds. Finally, *divergence* rather than congruence was the norm in the elaboration of social and cultural forms. In this era, each of the subworlds greatly elaborated forms of stratification, of architecture and art, and of religion, starting from different points and following principles of internal coherence that moved them in ever more divergent directions. The phrase "a typical resident of the world" is a much less meaningful concept when applied to this period than it was when applied to the prehistorical era.

We have come forward partway through history, although by great leaps and bounds, with at least some basis for concluding that our small repertoire of concepts provides a reasonably serviceable instrument for characterizing the global social system at any one time. Thus assured, we may turn to our analysis of the current modern period, which is to be the main object of our analysis.

The Recent Modern Era

At some point after the medieval period in Europe, the world entered upon a new and unprecedented era of interconnectedness. No precise moment or event can claim unambiguous priority in defining the start of this era; appropriate candidates might be Marco Polo's visit to Asia in the last quarter of the thirteenth century or Columbus's discovery of the New World at the end of the fifteenth. In any event, after a slow beginning lasting several hundred years, the rate of interchange among individuals, institutions, and societies began to grow at an exceedingly rapid rate.

In characterizing the modern era, one is greatly tempted to see a relatively sharp break with much of what had gone before in human history. To the Western imagination, this temptation is reinforced by the image of the Dark Ages, exaggerated perhaps, but on the whole correctly perceived as one of stagnation and even retrogression on many dimensions of human endeavor. But even if we use as our standard the centuries that witnessed the remarkable burgeoning of the Roman Empire, we must be struck by how little that was fundamentally new was added to knowledge or to humankind's stock of basic resources. The Romans may have been great innovators, but they were mediocre inventors. And of this small set of inventions they sometimes took but little advantage, as in the case of the water-wheel.[3] By contrast, what is archetypical of the modern era, and in particular of the industrial system, is the great flood of new materials, techniques, knowledge, and institutions, coupled with an explosive growth in the production and diffusion of people, goods, services, ideas, and relationships. In many respects the facts are staggering.

Probably the most dramatic changes have come about through the growth of population. Thus the modern era, although representing less than one-tenth of 1 percent of the time humans have been on the earth, has produced about one-quarter of all the human beings who have ever lived.[4] Not only are the numbers vastly larger, but also per capita consumption has increased enormously. As a result, the world's supply of nonreplenishable resources is being consumed at an exceedingly high rate. We may fault D. H. Meadows et al. and the Club of Rome on one or another of their projections, but it is difficult to disprove their contention that in many respects the modern era has become the era of exponential growth.[5] Such growth is one of the most fundamental facts of our time. To deny it is ridiculous, even though embracing it uncritically is foolish. Social reality is much too complicated to permit one to summarize it in a single statistic or to represent it adequately by a single concept. That becomes fully apparent when one examines some of the evidence bearing on the issue of the interconnectedness of the modern world.

Interconnectedness

A very large number of indicators may be drawn on to prove that the national institutions and populations that comprise world society have been very rapidly increasing the degree of their interconnectedness over the last half century. Among many indicators of this trend, we may point to the following:[6]

University-Level Students Abroad.   The number of students studying outside their own country approximately doubled between 1960 and 1969, rising from 239,000 to 477,000. This continued a pattern that had been in evidence at least since 1950. Over that longer period of time, the annual increase in the number of students studying abroad was in excess of 7 percent per year.[7]

Foreign Mail.   Between 1938 and 1970 the volume of foreign mail sent and received by forty reporting countries increased almost seven times. The annual rate of increase was some 6 percent per year.[8]

International Telephonic and Telegraphic Communication.   Closely paralleling the pattern manifested by the mails, a marked increase is shown in the frequency of electronic communication across national boundaries. The number of telegrams sent abroad in 1970 was more than two and a half times that for 1938, indicating an annual increase rate of 3 percent per year.[9] Moreover, there was a much higher rate of increase in the frequency of international telephone calls, conservatively estimated at 15 percent per year in the decade of the 1960s.[10] Putting all the evidence together, we may safely assume that the total of international wired and wireless exchanges combined has increased at a rate sufficient to ensure at least a doubling every decade. These trends are further elaborated and discussed in Chapter 9.

International Tourist Travel.   From 1954 to 1970, the twenty-six main "tourist-receiving" countries experienced a surge from 26 million to 106 million visits, indicating an increase of about 8.7 percent per year. This did not come about merely because the affluent were flooding the more exotic corners of the globe. For example, in this same period the interchange between Europe and the United States, accounting for a large part of all tourism, also increased at a rate in excess of 7 percent per year.[11]

World Trade.   Commerce between nation-states increased tenfold between 1938 and 1969. In each of the three decades it more or less doubled, indicating an annual increase of approximately 7 percent.[12] Increases expressed in value terms, as these are, should perhaps be discounted to allow for inflation. But even expressing the value of world trade in constant 1963 prices, the three-decade period still yields an annual rate of increase of about 5 percent.[13]

Direct Capital Investment Abroad.   Data for the United States, the most readily available, show a change in the annual rate of investment from about 1 or 2 billion dollars from the 1946–1952 period to 3 billion by 1963, and then to 8 billion by 1971. Even allowing for inflation, the amount of such investment clearly at least doubled within the last decade.[14] Data on the rest of the world, still being studied, are expected to show comparable patterns.

International Nongovernmental Organizations (INGOs).   From around 1850, when some five or ten INGOs were founded in each quinquennium, the number founded rose to over 300 per quinquennium by 1950. From 1954 to 1968 the rate of increase in the total number of such organizations was about 5 percent per year.[15] Moreover, a study of the congresses and conferences sponsored by these organizations would presumably show an equal and more likely a higher rate of participation by groups and individuals than is indicated when participation is measured on the basis of the number of "organizations" involved.

International Governmental Organizations (IGOs). In general, membership in such organizations increased substantially after World War II. In the United Nations, for example, the rate of membership increase from 1945 to 1970 was 3.6 percent per annum; for the United Nations Educational, Scientific, and Cultural Organization (UNESCO) it was 6.4 percent. Some of the specialized organizations, such as the General Agreement on Tariffs and Trade (GATT), underwent an annual membership increase of over 10 percent.[16]

Caveats and Conclusions. The pattern manifested in these figures is unmistakable and indeed rather remarkable in its consistency. Over a wide range of systems of exchange we find evidence for rapid acceleration in the development of ties linking nations, their institutional components, and the individuals who populate them. The abundance and complexity of the networks that interconnect the world's population are, and have been for some time, growing at a phenomenal rate. With some variation according to the specific indicator used, recent decades reveal a general tendency for many forms of human interconnectedness across national boundaries to be doubling every ten years.[17]

Obviously there are many quite serious defects in the available data, which it will take us a long time to correct. There are also some anomalous findings that may be hard to explain. In addition, summary figures on average rates such as those given obviously must conceal a great deal of variation in the degree to which different nations and people are participating in this increased interconnectedness. The variation is by no means obvious; indeed, there are some marked surprises in store for anyone who will carefully examine the detailed statistics.

For example, not wealth but the size of the population best predicts the dependence of countries on foreign trade. The proportion of gross national product (GNP) represented by trade rises from a mere 10 percent in countries of more than 100 million to almost 80 percent in countries of less than 1 million.[18] In the utilization of telegraphic communication directed abroad, the less developed countries have actually been gaining markedly on the more developed, since their rate of increase of the use of such means of communication was 4.3 percent, against 2 percent for the advanced countries, between 1938 and 1970.[19] There is also a contrast between tourists, who mainly come from the wealthier countries, and students, who are mainly sent abroad to study by poorer countries. Only a relatively small proportion of the student body of the wealthier countries studies abroad.[20]

All these anomalies, if such they be, surely have sensible explanations, and could be discussed at length.[21] Some of these issues will indeed be further dealt with later in this chapter. The main point, however, is that these complexities do not gainsay the main thrust of the data.

Faced, then, with the evident facts of such rapid growth of interconnectedness, one must inevitably wonder what the long-term implications of this process will be. Can and will the expansion of connectedness go on indefinitely? If not, what are the limits on further expansion? And, whether the expansion continues or must come to a halt at some more or less definable point, what will the resultant world system be like?

First, we should acknowledge the obvious fact that worldwide connectivity cannot continue to grow indefinitely. Indeed, for some forms of interchange we can specify absolute ceilings and practical limits on further expansion. For example, the increase in membership in the United Nations from 1950 to 1970 was clearly determined by a set of unique historical circumstances. Even if a number of the currently less well integrated nations were to break up into several separate sovereign states where only one existed before, the earlier rate of increase in UN membership would not be sustained. By contrast, there is no obvious limit on the rate of participation by individuals and subgroups in international nongovernmental organizations. Since there are billions of people who do not yet participate in any way, and much more involvement is possible on the part of those already active, we could well have a doubling of participation every decade for a very long period indeed. Overall, the situation is evidently complex, with objectively defined limits balanced against forces making for probable long-term increases.

The case of university students studying abroad illustrates the complexity of the issue. First, we must acknowledge that there is obviously a theoretical point beyond which it would become impossible to maintain the high rate of increase in study abroad that the world experienced in recent decades. It is equally obvious, however, that with only 2 percent of all university students studying abroad, we are very far from reaching that theoretical limit.[22] We may well wonder, therefore, if more practical considerations do not hold some promise of stemming the tide.

We can, indeed, identify certain forces that should act, over time, to reduce the number of students studying abroad. As we shall see below in the discussion of dependence, the tendency to send university students abroad to study is related to the availability of domestic training facilities. In very small countries, such facilities will most likely always be limited to a few important fields. In the larger national communities, however, a greater number of places over a wider range of subjects is likely to become available within the country as each increases its wealth and develops a fuller array of domestic institutions for advanced training. Indeed, it is precisely because the wealth and the institutional resources of almost all countries are increasing, however much less rapidly and less equitably than we might hope, that we can expect most countries to find it possible, in time, to train their students at home.

The attainment of this stage of development by most of the currently less developed countries could lead the *proportion* of students studying abroad, and in time perhaps even their *absolute* number, to become stabilized, and the numbers and proportions might even begin to decline absolutely. Such trends can actually already be observed in specified fields, such as engineering and medicine, which, with each passing year, account for a smaller percentage of the students studying abroad.[23]

However, the issue is complicated by the prospect that as countries increase in wealth, the students who now go abroad out of necessity may increasingly be replaced by those who go to foreign countries because it is presumed to be "broadening." That has been the chief reason for study abroad by the more affluent, and there are no grounds for assuming that the idea will not also appeal to those whose higher income is of more recent vintage. In other words, if the supply of discretionary income keeps up with or surpasses the diminution in the pressures of practical necessity, a decline in the proportion of students studying abroad may be quite long in coming.

Having now acknowledged the observed, the practical, and the theoretical limits on indefinite exponential growth, my impression is nevertheless that many indicators of interconnectedness have no obvious saturation point. In any event, most indicators are very far from having reached the point at which growth must stop. On the contrary, the fact that on many indicators the less developed countries show a tendency toward acceleration in the rate at which they become connected to the outside world gives reason to assume that the trends noted earlier still have much momentum.[24] Most of the indicators I have identified respond to the growth in wealth. And wealth, however unevenly distributed, is increasing in *most countries,* and in some *segments* of all countries. We may therefore confidently expect the next thirty, and perhaps the next fifty, years to be characterized by the increasing interconnectedness of the world population.

Interdependence

Interconnectedness may suggest but does not necessarily define interdependence. Dependence exists where a service, commodity, or resource obtained from abroad is relatively vital and not easily substitutable. Interdependence exists where there is a relatively equal or balanced exchange of such goods. If country A has good coking coal and country B has ore, and each makes its own steel, they are interdependent in the steel-making process. If capital is in surplus and can find no profitable investment in C, whereas D has rich and potentially profitable resources and no capital, an exchange between them may also indicate a basic interdependence. How much of the observed interconnectedness reported in the preceding section also represents some approximation of this type of interdependence cannot be stated with precision. Indeed, one may easily be misled into assuming that all increases in interconnectedness also mean increased interdependence, when they actually represent nothing of the kind. Take, for example, the exchange of students among countries. As noted earlier, the *number* of students studying abroad has been rising by over 7 percent per year. The absolute number of interconnections will therefore double every decade. To assert *interdependence,* however, we should be able to show that such exchanges serve functions not permitting ready or efficient substitution. Alas, that assertion cannot be made, since of the world's university student body fewer than 2 percent study abroad. It is clear, therefore, that despite steeply rising *interconnectedness* in absolute numbers, most countries are *not* linked with others in a system of interdependence as far as the education of university students is concerned.[25]

There are probably many other forms of exchange and interconnectedness that also do not involve a substantial element of interdependence. Take, for example, the tourist flow between the more developed countries. For many years Japan was the favorite goal for American tourists to Asia, even though few Japanese came to the United States. Then, in a short span of time, the number of tourists coming from Japan to the United States, and particularly to Hawaii, rose from about 15,000 to over 300,000 annually.[26] This counterflow perhaps was some slight help in adjusting the balance of trade between the United States and Japan. Beyond that, however, the exchange of several million tourists between these two countries can hardly be assumed to have been terribly important to the life of either. We had interconnectedness without interdependence.

Nevertheless, the world does offer a number of examples of true interdependence, which provide some basis for asserting that there has in recent decades been a real increase in that phenomenon. Probably the best example—certainly the best-documented case—is that of world trade.

Nations, especially nation-states, are driven to trade by the limits on autarky and by the demands of efficiency. It is the rare nation indeed that can find within its boundaries all the material it needs, and it is the exceptional producer who can find a large enough market within one nation's population to permit an efficient scale of production. The contrast with the task of educating students is striking. Belgium can educate virtually all of its university students at home, but within the confines of its limited territory it can find but the smallest part of the material necessary to operate a modern industrial civilization, and only a tiny market for its industrial output. Hence Belgium must trade so extensively that such trade amounts to three-fourths of its GNP. That is of course a rather high proportion, but not unusual. Of seventy-nine countries tabulated by Taylor and Hudson for 1965, the median proportion of GNP represented by trade was 34 percent.[27] In sharp contrast, students studying abroad represented only 4 percent of all university enrollees in the median case for 119 countries.[28]

But what of the future? Will this particular kind of interdependence in trade increase? Since small nations are more forced to trade, and since more and more of the new nations are in the category of "ministates," one might expect the importance of trade relative to GNP to rise. One would be led to the same conclusion on the basis of the increasing industrialization of the world, since industrialization seems to be a great stimulus to trade.[29] There are of course countervailing trends that might work against the success of this reasonable prediction. For example, national economic policies increasingly apply pressure for import substitution, fostering the manufacture of products within the country in which they are to be sold. In one way, that means less international trade. However, this practice may reduce one type of import only to require another—the assembled automobile, previously imported whole, now being replaced by imports of steel, rubber, copper, chrome, and the like. It turns out, somewhat to our surprise, that the available data for seventy-nine countries show very little recent change in the median proportion that trade represents of GNP—the figures being 37 percent in 1959 and 34 percent in 1965.[30] This reflects a very high degree of interdependence.[31] By contrast, consider the situation in earlier times. Certainly the Roman era was impressive for the bulk and variety of commodities exchanged, yet how sobering it is to realize that in the first century B.C. the number of caravans annually crossing from China to Europe via Russia was perhaps one dozen each year.[32] Even allowing for more extensive commerce by sea, external trade must have represented a negligible proportion of GNP in these systems.

Beyond trade, it is likely that the national science establishment of all countries would be seriously hampered, and might indeed be rendered relatively sterile in all but the largest nations, were it not for the continuous interchange of ideas and personnel among the several countries important for scientific production. Some great literature would probably continue to be produced by authors and some vital new paintings by painters if we cut off all international contacts among creative artists around the world, but a substantial case can be made for the critical role that such exchange plays in stimulating and sustaining innovation and vitality in aesthetic creation.

In science, as in trade and capital flows, the giants, such as the United States and the USSR, are probably least interdependent with the world system; curiously enough, though, it is precisely these two giants that seem most consistently and forcefully to impinge on the development of all the rest of the world.[33]

Dependence

If the earlier example of tourist exchanges between the United States and Japan had involved Jamaica, Mexico, or Spain rather than Japan, the matter would have appeared in quite a different light. This would not be because the tourism would mean more for the United States, obviously, but rather because it would be so much more vital for the countries receiving the tourists.[34] Exchanges vital to one partner but of relatively casual significance for a second define situations of dependency for the former.

In the nature of the case, the poorer or so-called less developed countries most often find themselves in the position of such dependency. Curiously, the situation most commonly cited to illustrate such dependency—that in which these countries seem limited to selling raw materials in exchange for finished industrial products from the advanced countries—is more nearly a situation of interdependence than of strict dependence.[35] Nevertheless, there is plenty of evidence of the pervasive dependence of the overwhelming majority of the less developed countries. They are dependent on the more advanced countries for all manner of more sophisticated machinery, including complex machines of war; for scientific knowledge of all sorts and the related training of specialists in a host of fields; for the technical and organizational know-how vital to large-scale, complex productive enterprises; and for the investment capital essential to purchasing, borrowing, renting, or otherwise employing those resources.

Again, the situation may be vividly illustrated by the statistics on students sent abroad to study. In 1968 fewer than 1,000 students went from North America to study full time in South America, but more than 10,000 made the trip in the opposite direction. For Asia the contrast was even more dramatic, since 63,000 students came from Asia to North America, compared to only about 1,000 North Americans studying in Asia.[36] These exchanges are wildly disproportionate not only in absolute numbers but also in terms of the ratio that students studying abroad represent of all university students enrolled at home. Fewer than 1 percent of North American students study abroad, and slightly more than 1 percent of European students. By contrast, Africa and the Arab states were, as late as 1968, obliged to send 15 and 19 percent, respectively, of their students abroad for university-level education.[37] It is evident, then, that many of the smaller and poorer nations are heavily dependent in this respect.

The dependency is all the more obvious if we examine particular fields, especially the scientific and technical. For most of the youths from the advantaged countries the act of going abroad is an indulgence; they usually could do as well at home. For comparable students from the less developed countries going abroad may be an absolute necessity—the only way to obtain the desired training. This is reflected in the distribution of specialties chosen by students studying abroad. In 1966 almost two-thirds of all North Americans studying abroad took "arts" subjects, whereas some 55 percent of students from the developing countries were studying the more applied and critical fields of science, engineering, medicine, and agriculture.[38] The dependence is more evident still when we consider the contribution that study abroad makes to the supply of critically needed specialists in the composition of their respective professions in certain countries. Thus in 1966 some 28 percent of Africa's science students were obtaining their training abroad, as against a mere 0.3 percent of North American students of science seeking their training abroad.[39]

Integration

Increasing interconnectedness and high levels of interdependence might well be expected to serve as preconditions, even as stimulants, for increasing integration. In actual fact, the extraordinary increases in interconnectedness and interdependence that humankind has experienced since World War II have not been reflected in any really substantial increase in the integration of national states into a united world political system. While the growth curve for interconnectedness has been exponential, the curve for integration has been at best linear, and many more conservative observers would insist that it be shown as more-or-less flat, with a few small peaks to reflect events such as the creation of the European Economic Community or other regional agencies.

Even these organizations are of course extremely limited in their powers. As for the agencies of the United Nations and of UNESCO, though they serve extremely valuable functions in setting standards, gathering statistics, and channeling aid, most have in fact not succeeded in securing the surrender of virtually any important function or other element of sovereignty from the individual nation-states. Indeed, the multiplication of nation-states, including island ministates, emerging as new sovereignties out of the elements of dissolving colonial empires, had by 1970 brought us to a condition such that the degree of integration of the world system was probably substantially less, on balance, than it had been in 1900. There is therefore not much basis for challenging the assessment of Philippe de Seynes, the UN undersecretary for economic and social affairs, who asserted that as late as 1972 we still lived in "an almost anarchical world community with a mosaic of states as yet bound together only by the most general notion of solidarity and with an international system in which the area of clearly recognized common interests is still small [and] the possibility of central planning immediately conjures up new uncertainties, specifically the fear of manipulation by the powerful."[40]

The Main Elements of Convergence

We now come to the consideration of convergence, an issue that seems to be particularly vexing to social scientists. Much of the difficulty of dealing with this problem stems from the failure to distinguish with sufficient precision the different elements of a very complex situation. A minimum list of such elements should include the following:

1. Modes of production and patterns of resource utilization
2. Institutional arrays, forms, and processes
3. Structure and patterns of social relationships
4. Systems of popular attitudes, values, and behavior
5. Systems of political and economic control

Since these elements not only may change at different speeds but also may actually move in opposite directions, the prospects for seemingly contradictory conclusions are substantial. The following summary position on the issues may be offered:

1. *Modes of Production and Patterns of Resource Utilization.* In this respect the general movement is unmistakable and often seems almost inexorable. Indeed, the key to all other issues in the convergence debate may lie precisely here. Marion Levy proposes that we judge modernization by the propensity to utilize inanimate sources of power. By that standard all nations are certainly converging toward a common model, albeit at enormously different rates. The uses of power may, however, be only a crude indicator of a more fundamental process—that of increasing dependence on science and the resultant technology. This conception permits us to appreciate the importance of objects utilizing little power, such as transistors and desk computers, as well as the significance of the chemical-biological revolution symbolized by inoculation and "the pill" in human biology, and by miracle rice, insecticides, and fertilizers in agriculture.

Different societies may play quite different roles as producers of new knowledge of this sort, and they may differ greatly in the speed with which they more or less fully adopt and utilize the products of new technology. Nevertheless, the increasing dependence of all societies on that technology and its products, and the incorporation of all peoples into the network of their influence, is unmistakable. Electronic communication, scientific medicine, rapid transit, and computerized record keeping are a few of the outstanding examples of this wide diffusion.

2. *Institutional Arrays, Forms, and Processes.* One of the hallmarks of modern or developed societies is the presence of a fairly standard array of institutional structures and the wide diffusion of the forms and processes characteristic of their operation. The key element in the transformation that so many societies are experiencing consists in increasing differentiation and specialization, arising as a response to steady technological change and growing human interconnectedness. This process of differentiation leads to the burgeoning of new institutions. Within these new institutions, in turn, rational-technical bureaucratic forms of administration tend to diffuse and come to predominate.

Medieval society could reasonably be encompassed by reference to the state, the church, the military, the town and its special classes, the manor, and the peasant villages. In modern society we confront, by contrast, a vast array of institutions previously unknown or existing in only very rudimentary form, but each now fully elaborated, with its own character and special forms. The king's chancellery becomes a host of government ministries; the pursuit and dissemination of knowledge move from being a subordinate concern of the church to become the specialized responsibility of a vast array of academies of science, research institutes, universities, and schools; and so on, across many other realms encompassing medicine, law, insurance, trade, production, recreation, and leisure. Furthermore, within all these newly elaborated institutions there is a strong tendency to establish rational bureaucratic modes of organization.

The process is of course full of vicissitudes, and in many cases what is actually achieved by way of developing an efficient organization is very far from the Weberian model or the canons set by the Harvard School of Business Administration. Neither should one ignore countermovements designed to increase decentralization and to minimize bureaucratization, tendencies that I cannot pause to discuss. Nevertheless, the main thrust toward bureaucratization and the rationalization of administration is not to be denied. In substantial degree the world *is* being cast in the Weberian mold.

3. *Structure and Patterns of Social Relationships.* I have in mind here such cultural and structural subsystems as the kinship system, the class structure, and the patterning of leisure-time activity. The basic issue for convergence theory is to assess how far the increasing similarity in modes of production and their associated institutional forms and processes encourages the development of concomitant similarities in sociocultural subsystems. Substantial and rather convincing documentation is available (as I demonstrate in Chapter 7), indicating that worldwide family patterns are converging on a norm common to urban-industrial societies.[41] There is equally extensive evidence to sustain the argument that the stratification systems of all large-scale complex societies have come to resemble one another in many essential respects.[42] Although the facts are less well documented, a case can probably also be made for convergence in the use of leisure within comparable segments of urban-industrial societies.[43]

Of course all of the facts and alleged facts need to be critically assessed. In addition, the same mode of analysis should be extended to other features of the cultural subsystem, such as religion, to ascertain how far, if at all, comparable tendencies may be discerned there. Certainly we must anticipate that there will be some aspects of the cultural systems shared by particular national and subnational populations that will be completely—and others at least relatively—immune to standardization, despite strong pressure exerted by other elements of the social system. On balance, however, I see no way to deny that some elements of the cultural system of national populations are manifesting a considerable tendency toward convergence as the nations move along the continuum leading them to the status of advanced industrial societies.

4. *Systems of Popular Attitudes, Values, and Behavior.* In 1960, in a paper called "Industrial Man" (reproduced in this volume as Chapter 11), I demonstrated that in a variety of realms there was a similar *structure* of attitudes and values manifested by the population of a diverse set of developed and developing countries.[44] It is important to stress that the similarity was not in the *average* opinion but rather in the *distribution* of opinion across the stratification system. The populations were alike only in that the structure of opinion in all cases was similar, with certain views and orientations becoming either more or less frequent as one went up or down the scale of education, occupational prestige, and the like. The theoretical explanation for these patterns was that the differentiated life experience of people in different strata of large-scale complex societies generated a standardized differentiation of response. This idea was subsequently tested more systematically in my cross-national research on individual modernization. There I was able to demonstrate, quite unambiguously I believe, that in six quite diverse developing nations each increment of increasing contact with modern institutions moved people a corresponding degree along a composite scale of modern attitudes and values.[45]

I read this evidence as arguing strongly that as human life experiences become more alike, attitudes, values, and basic dispositions will also become more alike. However, this should not be interpreted to mean that *all* people will become psychically alike. Clearly, if the theory I enunciated is correct, people will not all become alike so long as there are patterns of social differentiation *within* national populations. Moreover, the fact that people may become more alike should not obscure the fact that their having started from quite different initial positions may still leave them quite dissimilar even after they have moved a substantial distance toward some common norm.

Finally, it should not be forgotten that I posit movement toward a common attitude and value norm only with regard to certain specific qualities—as identified by the syndrome of individual modernity—and in response only to selected features of modern industrial and organizational experience. There are clearly many other realms of attitude and value that are independent of the industrial organizational complex common to advanced nations. The influence of cultural traditions or national history may more strongly affect attitudes concerning democracy, social distance, and stratification. Hence the attitudes of the citizens of Australia and England on these issues may be widely divergent despite the fact that the two nations share the same broad cultural tradition and that both qualify as modern complex societies. The features held in common by the two societies are evidently less effective in influencing the attitudes in question than are the facts of the pioneering tradition in Australia and the low status origins of the original settlers there.

5. *Systems of Political and Economic Control.* I have in mind here the nature of the state and the organization and distribution of power along with the mode of its exercise. It is over this dimension that the greatest disagreement, and perhaps the greatest misunderstanding, has been manifested in the course of the debate about convergence. The Soviet system persisted in its main form for almost fifty years beyond the predictions of those who asserted that the Soviet and the American systems were going to converge on some common position.[46] Indeed, the steady divergence of China from the Soviet Union, so far as concerns the sharing of a common socioeconomic system, must give pause to those who assumed that, at least within the so-called socialist half of the world, a common social order would surely be emerging. Outside the socialist world the situation is comparable. Despite an extraordinary degree of *decentralization,* the United States continues to display most of the standard attainments of modernity that are also manifested by an equally *centralized* France, with the system of each in fact having had its origin in premodern times.

Therefore, anyone who insists that the emergence of a common standard of economic and political organization for modern nation-states is inevitable must be prepared to acknowledge that this outcome can only be expected to arrive after a span to be calculated in centuries rather than decades. And, I fear, he must be prepared to face a very difficult task in specifying whether the common system that will presumably emerge will be more like that of the United States or that of the Soviet Union, or some variant altogether distinct from these.

Some will argue that all these models that focus on the nation-state are obsolete and urge us to recognize the multinational corporation as having transcendent significance in its impact on the existing modes of political and economic organization of the world system. They see this new form of social organization as exercising economic power on a scale of magnitude and coordination so great as to make its heads more powerful than any set of national rulers—indeed, to make them the cadre of a new form of world government. Against this image, however, one must balance the evidence of continuing and effective exercise of the power of the state in forcing such entities to adapt their policy to national interests or else suffer a set of consequences that can go as far as exclusion from the territory of a given state and even, ultimately, total confiscation.

All this is not to say that there is no process truly common to all the states of the modern world. I believe there is. That common feature is the growing power of the state to control the lives of its citizens. That process is of course most dramatic in those parts of the world where a central state apparatus was previously either weak or nonexistent. I believe, however, that the same tendency is also manifest in countries such as the United States that have a long history of organized government but in which we are experiencing a new tendency in the progressive penetration of systems of central control into more and more aspects of individual life.[47] Whether this is a long-term trend toward which all humankind is converging, or whether the process is reversible in countries that attain a sufficiently high degree of development, I find very difficult to decide.

Conclusion

To sum up my position on the convergence issue, there is evidence of a strong tendency for all nations to move toward increasing utilization of modes of production based on inanimate power, resting in turn on modern technology and applied science. Managing this type of system as well as coping with the new demands that populations impose for special goods and services encourages the elaboration everywhere of new institutional structures that are highly specialized in function and characterized by standardized modes of nominally rational technical bureaucratic procedure. These new productive arrangements, and the patterning of institutional forms intended to deal with them, rather consistently foster the incorporation of the population into new roles and patterns of role relationships; in turn, the latter directly or indirectly shape the structure of human relations in matters of class, kinship, leisure, and the like. This new structure of relations is in part produced by and in part induces new attitudes and values, forming the complex or syndrome we may identify as modern and postmodern.[48] This in turn brings the individuals occupying similar statuses in different societies much closer than was commonly the case in earlier times.

All of these processes, however, are subject to countervailing and contradictory trends that greatly mute the force of the tendency toward the emergence of a uniform world culture. One of the most important of these brakes on the process of homogenization lies in the distinctive cultural traditions that different national populations bring to the contemporary situation, and in the array of historically determined institutional arrangements with which they enter the contemporary era. These traditions and forms seem remarkably adaptable, and a high degree of variability in economic and political arrangements seems compatible with the management of a modern industrial society. Finally, despite the uniformity of the pressures and the consistency of the trends we observe, we should not lose sight of the enormous range over which the world's nation-states are spread on the various dimensions of development. Unless some unforeseen event causes the advanced nations to halt their further development while the others catch up, we can count on a very large amount of diversity throughout the world for at least another century.

two

CONVERGENCE AND DIVERGENCE IN INDUSTRIAL SOCIETIES

Are the industrialized nations moving toward a common social structure? Can we say what the forms of this emergent sociocultural system are like? Can the speed of convergence in different institutions be specified? Are there realms more resistant to change? More important, are there ways in which the systems are becoming not more, but less, alike—that is, is there evidence of divergence? What accounts for such convergence as we do observe as well as for resistance to change and for the divergent tendencies?

These questions have obvious intrinsic interest for anyone at all concerned about social processes in the contemporary world. They present a particular stimulus—and a challenge—to those professionally interested, as historians or social scientists, in the theory of social change in large-scale systems. They have important ideological implications, as the idea of convergence, like that of modernization, is perceived by Marxists as a challenge to their orthodox theory of societal evolution. Finally, these questions have political implications, both with regard to the challenges that any nation's domestic policy may expect to meet and for the prospect that the next decades will witness the increased integration of nations in larger and more comprehensive unions.

Reprinted with permission from Alex Inkeles, "Convergence and Divergence in Industrial Societies," in *Directions of Change: Essays on Modernization Theory and Research*, ed. Mustafa O. Attir, Burkart Holzner, and Zdenek Suda (Boulder: Westview Press, 1981), 3–39.

Before we reach any conclusions and draw out their implications, we must pass through a long process of defining terms, settling on indicators of change, discovering the available facts, and assessing such evidence as we may uncover. Some would argue that the only proper way to conduct an inquiry such as this is first to go through those preliminary steps before attempting to say anything by way of conclusion. Against this quite reasonable position we may argue that it will help sharpen our focus if, as we examine the wide range of issues to be considered, we bear in mind at least some tentative estimate of where we think the inquiry is leading. I shall therefore set down in relatively unqualified terms, and without amplification, some of the hypotheses with which I began this investigation and which I am still prepared to entertain after an initial period of fairly systematic study.

It should be understood that I am talking about tendencies, correlational patterns if you wish, and not about social laws. In the nature of the case, there will be many exceptions to any proposition I offer. Even a strong correlation, so long as it is not a perfect one, allows many cases to fall off the main line. Such exceptions are, of course, legitimate foci of interest. Under some circumstances, they may even be critical. My inclination, however, is to search for evidence of regularity, to see whether there are any relatively general patterns in the process of social change experienced by the advanced industrial countries, and to try to understand the divergent cases in the light of what we have learned about the general pattern.

A Set of Hypotheses and Propositions

1. The industrial societies of the world are converging on a common social structure.

2. The pace of this convergence was greatly accelerated in the 1960s and 1970s, and except where "ceiling" effects operate, this heightened rate of congruent change will be maintained in the 1980s and 1990s.

3. Although some slowing of the rate of change may be anticipated, it will continue to be high in relation to the period before World War II.

    a) The rates of social change depend in part on rates of economic growth, and these may be expected to be lower in the next decade—at least in the more industrialized countries.

    b) "Ceiling" effects limit further change in realms where very high levels of congruence have already been attained. This is especially true in the case of countries culturally more homogeneous and economically highly advanced, as in the case of those in the European Economic Community (EEC).

4. The convergence process is highly differentiated, proceeding at very variable rates in different realms of the sociocultural system. One

might say that the central and distinctive task of systematic inquiry in this realm is to establish which subsystems change at what rates. A preliminary assessment of such differences in the rate of change in five realms, such as "system of political and economic control," was presented in Chapter 1.

5. Insofar as they come to share a common structure, or are subject to common forces of change, the industrial countries increasingly share the same set of social "problems," among them marital instability, juvenile delinquency, redundancy of university graduates, and the decay of the inner city.

6. There probably are regular sequences through which the process of convergence moves across the major components of the social system.

   a) One of the most common sequences should show change initiated in the economic system followed by changes in demographic patterns, in primary relations, and in popular attitudes and values.

   b) Such sequences are unlikely to present themselves in exclusively linear fashion—feedback loops seem inevitable.

7. Some sequences of change may be historically conditioned. In European development, marked demographic changes generally followed upon important changes in food supplies or in occupational, residential, and related patterns of living. In the recent history of developing countries, however, precipitous and critical changes, notably in death rates, were in effect "imported" with virtually no change in antecedent sociocultural conditions.

8. If regular sequences can be established, their existence will support the assumption that causal connections can be established between the elements involved in these sequences. A convincing case can be made that changes in the occupational structure cause changes in family patterns. By contrast, although certain family patterns may impede changes in occupational structures less than will others, it seems unlikely that changed family patterns cause significant changes in the general occupational structure.

   The replacement of farming and handicraft production by industrial plants and service industries that separate the place of work from the place of residence makes the siesta increasingly impractical and leads to the continuous workday. By contrast, the introduction of the siesta into an industrial society, if we can imagine it, would not succeed in forcing abandonment of the continuous workday in factories, although it might affect offices and most likely would influence the hours of business in shops for consumers.

9. Many, perhaps most, of these causal sequences operate independently of the specific national context in which they occur; that is,

they operate in both nominally socialist and capitalist systems. Soviet ideology was ineffective in preventing the development in the USSR of a prestige hierarchy based mainly on education and occupation, almost identical with that in other industrial countries. It was equally unsuccessful in preventing cross-generational mobility from being determined mainly by parental education and occupation. And it lost the battle to prevent the spread of the consumer ethic in the Soviet population.

10. Even if they do not follow the same developmental sequences, industrial nations will converge at the same point on many dimensions. For example, in the United States, the extensive diffusion of primary schooling may have run well ahead of industrialization, whereas in England, the sequence was reversed. Nevertheless, in common with other modern systems, both countries came to have close to 100 percent of school-age children enrolled in primary schools. Similarly, the tertiary sector of the labor force grew at a much slower rate in the USSR than in comparable nonsocialist countries, while the proportion in the secondary sector grew at a considerably faster rate. Yet as the Soviet system matures, the relative proportions in these sectors may be expected to come more into line with the general European pattern, although the sequence for arriving at those points will have been different.

11. We cannot establish unambiguously whether the *main* motor driving the industrial nations to common forms of social organization is technical change or value change. The growth of scientific knowledge and the continuous elaboration of technical innovation carries its own powerful social imperatives. At the same time, we must acknowledge that technical rationality is itself a value. More important, perhaps, is the fact that technical rationality cannot sustain itself, but rather depends on a broad base of social support.

   It may be argued that what actually drives the system is the wide acceptance of a set of relatively new sociopolitical ideas, in particular the notion that everyone has the right to a continuously improving condition of life and that it is the responsibility of society (or the state) to ensure the attainment of that condition. Technical rationality then becomes merely the most appropriate means for achieving this new definition of the purpose of social life. Instances of the impact of ideas on practice, and of institutional change on ideas, are both readily available. The interaction of these forces across situations and over time should be a major topic for systematic study.

12. Convergence is accelerated and integration made tighter by the activities of increasing numbers of organizations that operate cross-

nationally. The impact of the cross-national organization is probably greatest in the case of those with some power to instruct or regulate, such as the multinational corporation, the International Air Transport Association, the International Postal Union, or the EEC. Considerable influence may also be exerted by organizations limited to the exchange of information and ideas, or to the stimulation of pilot projects, for example, the World Health Organization (WHO) or the Organization for Economic Cooperation and Development (OECD). It remains an open question whether these sources of directed and conscious policy produce more convergence than either technological imperatives or leading ideas.

13. Governments become increasingly preoccupied with problems of management, of running increasingly complex and elaborate systems related to the provision of services—and often even of goods—to vast populations. New entitlements are regularly added to those already enjoyed by citizens, thus generating new management burdens. The latest is the right to legal aid protected by "positive law." There seems to be no obvious cutoff point. Domestic politics become increasingly an elaborate technical debate about the relative efficiency of different management schemes and of different managers. In this particular respect, the prophecy about the end of ideology has been fulfilled.

14. Foreign relations also become increasingly—one might say almost predominantly—focused on issues concerning the management of the common public enterprise and its welfare consequences. Managing exchange rates, maintaining good trade balances, controlling the flow of migratory labor, setting the prices of agricultural goods, and preventing dumping become the chief preoccupations of most ministers of foreign affairs.

15. The convergence of the social systems and the increasing similarities of institutional forms, administrative practice, the patterning of interpersonal relations in daily life, and eventually of personal and social values satisfy one precondition for political integration that previously was largely lacking. What is attained, however, is no more than a necessary condition for such integration. It is not, in itself, a sufficient one.

Alliances seem to be possible no matter how great the gulf separating the social systems, even the levels of civilization, of those who join forces. Empires may bring under one administration the most diverse social orders. The spontaneous integration of sovereign and autonomous political units seems possible, however, only on the condition that the units have attained, to a high degree, common institutional patterns, cultural forms, and popular values.

Even under those circumstances, the resultant political unions may be fragile. But without meeting these conditions, they seem to have only slight hope of survival.

Settling on terminology can be reduced to a routine process to be quickly got on with, or it can be elaborated as a major intellectual enterprise in its own right. I incline toward the former approach. Nevertheless, some small set of terms must be defined, and some minimum clarification of how certain concepts are being used is indispensable. This will involve us in definitions of convergence and divergence and in exposition of some of the diverse forms each can take. I shall also raise issues and offer some guidance concerning a number of methodological questions: Which forms of change and stability should we study? With what level of social organizations should we concern ourselves? Over what span of time should we search for convergence?

Forms of Convergence

Convergence means moving from different positions toward some common point. To know that countries are alike tells us nothing about convergence. There must be movement over time toward some identified common point. The point may be fixed, as when 100 percent of school-age children enroll in primary school, or it may be moving, as when the proportion of the labor force in the tertiary or "service" sector has grown continuously in recent decades. Convergence need not, however, be expressed solely in quantitative terms. Constitutions, judicial systems, and administrative arrangements can all be either convergent or divergent. There is, moreover, more than one pattern of change over time that can lead to a point of convergence. Change may also stop short of actual convergence and still be of great significance if the units undergoing the change cross certain critical thresholds.

As the study of convergence is not a well-established field, there is likely to be more than the usual amount of ambiguity concerning relevant concepts and methods. Clarifying these issues and developing some degree of consensus and standardization is therefore a fundamental task at this stage of the field's development.

Simple Convergence

Convergence is most dramatically and unambiguously illustrated by birth and fertility rates. Zero population growth is not quite a fixed point in the same way as is 100 percent school enrollment. One cannot enroll more than 100 percent of an age group, but one can fall below zero growth by having a declining population.[1] Leaving aside this complication, however, it seems that the industrial nations are all converging on a condition of zero population growth by bringing the reproduction rate down to one, meaning that on the average each woman replaces herself with a single daughter. In the poorest countries, the average number of live daughters born to each woman is three or more; in the economically more advanced Third World countries it is down to 2.5, and in the wealthier nations it is at 1.2 or less. As poorer nations increase their per capita income the rate goes progressively down. And for those over the US$1,000 per capita threshold, the passage of time brings more and more countries to the point of stability in population growth.

Death rates have responded in similar ways. Such convergence is very notable in the upper half of Figure 2.1 with regard to overall death rates. The pattern is also strikingly illustrated in Figure 2.2. In 1955 the gap between the nations with the highest and lowest rates was 200 deaths per 1,000 among children aged five to fourteen. By 1975 the gap was cut in half, as all the other nations converged on the U.S. and Danish standard of fifty or fewer deaths per 1,000 children. Whether this number represents a floor below which nations will not go is hard to judge. In this case there is an absolute limit, a floor below which no population could go, represented by zero deaths per 1,000 children.

Convergence from Different Directions

Movement toward a common point does not necessarily mean movement in the same direction. Yet neglecting this obvious fact has created great confusion. If a certain divorce rate is typical of industrial countries, then some nations, as they develop, may experience rising divorce rates and some falling rates, both as part of the same condition of industrializing. In this case, the actual movement is in opposite directions, yet the outcome will be a true convergence.

In Western Europe the preferred age at marriage has traditionally been much later than in Eastern Europe, and in both sets of European countries men and women getting married have, on the average, been much older than the brides and grooms in most Asian countries. Since 1900 young people in Western Europe have been getting married at an earlier age than before, whereas in Eastern Europe and Asia they have been getting married at an increasingly later age than before. In Asia the change evidently has come about because the previous pattern of early arranged marriage seems incompatible with the conditions of modern life. In Western Europe the greater freedom of young people from financial dependence on their parents and the spread of the ideology of personal autonomy evidently combine to facilitate the establishment of a formal sexual union at earlier ages. Whatever the causes, the two sets of societies, although moving in opposite

FIGURE 2.1   Overall death rates

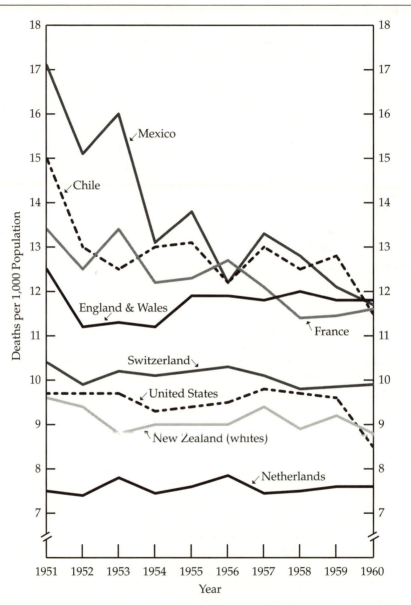

Source: Office of Population Research, Princeton University, and Population Association of America, Inc., *Population Index*, Vol. 28, No. 1 (1962), back cover.

FIGURE 2.2   Death rates at ages 5–14, annually per 100,000, selected countries, 1955–1975

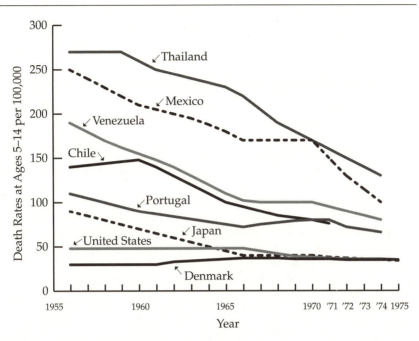

Source: Magda C. McHale and John McHale, *Children in the World* (Washington, DC: Population Reference Bureau, 1979), 34.

directions—one toward earlier marriage, the other toward later marriage—are converging. Whether or not these diverse cultures, still far apart in their preferences for a suitable marriage age, will actually meet, and if so, at what point, remains a moot question. It seems likely, however, that as more nations industrialize and modernize, the worldwide pattern will be for the modal age of marriage to be twenty-three to twenty-five for men and twenty to twenty-two for women.

Thresholds Versus Absolute Differences

Even when we have reliable numbers and clear-cut differences, we should avoid purely mechanical interpretations of the statistics we may come upon. A gap of twenty to thirty percentage points separating two countries may have quite different meanings depending on where the countries lie on some overall scale. There may be thresholds that are more important than absolute differences. Take the case of a girl being allowed outside the home

unchaperoned. That mere fact may be critical for a whole series of other social involvements, such as her ability to enter the labor market. The social
distance between being locked into the home or being free to go out at all
may therefore be much more important than the seemingly greater distance
between being free to go out alone and being free to have a lover.

Such sociocultural thresholds have their analogues in the fiscal, economic, and organizational realms. For example, thresholds evidently exist
with regard to the effectiveness of school systems. Once an essentially modern school system is in place and certain basic standards for facilities,
books, and teacher training are achieved, further investment to increase the
expenditure per pupil seems not to produce any significant improvements
in the academic performance of students taking standardized tests. Some of
the leading countries of Europe vary considerably in the investment per
pupil made by their respective school systems. However, in this set of countries there is virtually no correlation between expenditures per pupil and
the test scores of the students so benefited. So long as students are reasonably well matched as to social background and the selectivity of their national school systems, those on whom more is spent perform no better than
those from countries that spend less per pupil. Evidently, by the time they
have reached their present point of development all the industrial nations
are doing the essential things, and their students are performing near their
ceiling. Additional investment therefore produces little visible return.[2]

In less developed countries the situation is evidently quite different. There
the quality of facilities, the availability of books, and the qualifications of
teachers are so low that increases in expenditures bring definite improvements in pupil performance. Consequently these countries, subject to limits
on their means, have an incentive to continue to increase the expenditure per
pupil. Meanwhile, as policymakers in the more advanced countries become
increasingly aware of the low marginal utility of further investment, they will
resist raising per-pupil expenditures. These forces acting together should in
time yield convergence near the level of some general threshold that provides
optimal academic performance in relation to the amount expended per pupil.

Thresholds may of course be important not only in opening up a wide
range of possibilities, but also in narrowing future options. Thus a nation
may move rapidly from high to low death rates for children five to fourteen
years of age, but as the U.S. and Danish trends illustrated in Figure 2.2 suggest, once the rate is down to fifty per 1,000, further reduction is very difficult to achieve.

Qualitative Indicators of Change

Given our definition of convergence, the most appropriate indicators of
change would seem to be time series that permit objective measurement of

some major societal characteristic. Obvious examples would be demographic statistics of every kind, for realms such as occupations, health, education, social security, crime, and the like. Thus we are able to say that crude birth rates seem to converge toward seventeen or eighteen per 1,000, and death rates toward eight or nine per 1,000. By contrast, suicide rates show little sign of convergence but rather remain highly differentiated.

Unfortunately, many important indicators that could be expressed in statistical terms may simply not have been measured in ways permitting numerical representation. For example, in most of the advanced industrial countries of Europe there is evident a considerable movement toward direct participation by citizens in the control of the institutions, such as schools and health care centers, that provide them with services. In principle such increased participation might be measured, for example, by counts of the number of citizens who take part and the frequency with which they engage in different kinds of participatory acts. But because such statistics have evidently not been collected, we must accept more qualitative and imprecise characterizations, which should nevertheless not be neglected.

Curiously enough, some indicators that least lend themselves to detailed numerical expression give the most unambiguous evidence of convergence. This is especially true for constitutional and legislative provisions and for the creation of administrative and related institutions. Thus it can be shown that the national constitutions of most nations are convergent in progressively incorporating guarantees by the state to provide its citizens with access to education and health care, as part of an expanding list of additional entitlements.[3]

A similar pattern may be traced in the history of legislation creating national programs to ensure that individuals receive certain basic welfare benefits. Five such basic programs have been widely introduced: family allowances; unemployment insurance; sickness and maternity benefits; pension programs for invalidism, old age, and survivors; and insurance against occupational hazards. Germany is credited with having adopted the first program of this type in 1883, to provide sickness and maternity benefits. Tracing the spread of these five programs in nine representative advanced countries of the West, Heidenheimer and his colleagues found that by 1965 all the countries had converged in adopting the entire set of programs, with the exception of the United States, which, at least technically speaking, had not yet adopted a truly national program of family allowances.[4]

Another example of convergence that is clear-cut even though the measures are all basically qualitative comes to us from the field of administration. Economic development is systematically associated with the progressive addition of certain institutions and structures responsible for the formulation and conduct of national policy. This has been clearly demonstrated for the field of education in Latin America. First come ministries of education; later national educational planning agencies are created; and much later graduate faculties appear in the schools of education. The sequence seems relatively invariant, and nations converge on having the full panoply of such institutions as they enter the status of relatively advanced developing countries.[5]

Divergent Paths to Convergence

The ultimate adoption of the five basic elements of modern welfare programs previously described illustrates another important point, which is that the paths to a point of convergence need not be common or uniform; indeed, they may be quite diverse, even unique. Although Germany was the first of nine countries to adopt three of these programs as early as 1883, it was in only sixth place in creating a national program of unemployment insurance and seventh in adopting a national family allowance scheme. But by 1960 this did not matter, since by then, as we know, all nine of the nations under study had converged in adopting the complete set of five measures.

Most modern nations reduced their birth rates after, and presumably in response to, a decline in their death rates. But some nations controlled their population growth by following a different sequence, bringing birth rates down before the advantages of modern sanitation and medicine became effective in bringing death rates down. In much of France, for example, fertility declined before industrialization and urbanization, and simultaneous with rather than subsequent to the decline in mortality.[6] Over time, however, these differences sorted themselves out, and by 1975 French birth, death, and total fertility rates were very much in line with those of the other industrialized countries.[7]

Divergent movement that may seem the deviant case at one point may in fact define the norm around which other units will converge later on. Thus the French began to have small families in the late eighteenth century, long before such families became the general norm in industrial Europe. The forces that produced this deviation in France were probably distinctive. If our theoretical assumptions are to be sustained, however, we shall be obliged to show that the later appearance of these patterns elsewhere followed a fixed sequence and stemmed from common causes.

The path to the complete enrollment of all children in primary school, and eventually in secondary school, reveals a similar phenomenon, with different countries following somewhat different paths to arrive at the same ultimate destination. Thus the United States committed itself to widespread primary schooling from the earliest days of its development and achieved nearly universal schooling well before Great Britain.[8] In more recent times middle-income countries have also shown considerable variation in the paths they are following on the way to universal education up to the secondary level. Most gave marked priority to bringing primary enrollments to high levels before substantially expanding secondary schooling. Others, such as Iran, Jordan, and Egypt, raised enrollments in the two levels more in tandem. Still others, such as Jamaica, had quite high secondary enrollments relative to their primary school attendance. If the experience of the more industrialized may be assumed to foreshadow the future of the developing countries, however, these different paths will in time converge on near universal secondary schooling.

Parallel Change

If a point is fixed, then there is no ambiguity as to whether nations are converging on it. If the point is moving, however, then the relative rate of gain by each national unit becomes terribly important. Not long ago the proportion of the labor force in the tertiary—or service—sector stood around 40 percent in the United States and 20 percent in the USSR, a high degree of differentiation for two states that were so extensively industrialized. Now, if the rate of increase on its base were 10 percent per decade in the USSR and only 5 percent in the United States, they clearly would be converging. However, if the proportion of the labor force in the tertiary sector was increasing at 5 percent in each decade in *both* societies, then would it be correct to say that they were converging?

Probably the most salient example is provided by the endlessly discussed problem of the "gap" in wealth separating the less developed and the more industrialized countries. The total product in each set grew at approximately the same rate of just less than 5 percent from 1950 to 1964. Under these circumstances the poor could not close the gap separating them from the rich. Indeed, in absolute terms the gap increased. Some might therefore prefer to call such development *parallel* rather than *convergent* movement. This might seem especially appropriate terminology where it is difficult to specify either a fixed *form* or a fixed *point* toward which movement occurs.[9] For example, suppose that a rise in the proportion of people engaged in industrial work, or obtaining a secondary-level education, leads to greater autonomy and freedom of movement for young women. In Turkey this might mean being allowed to attend a local movie accompanied only by a girl friend or having some say in the selection of her spouse, whereas in England or the United States it might mean being free to put on a backpack and roam over Europe or to sleep with whichever young man takes her fancy. In this example both the systems are changing. Movement in both is in the same direction, in the sense that both are becoming more liberal. But if they preserve their relative distance, even though both are moving, can we sensibly say they are becoming more alike?

Given the very different points at which many of the countries we study started out and the distinctiveness of the social forms they may earlier have developed, a considerable part of the change we observe is likely to be of this parallel kind rather than of the sort that produces true convergence on a common standard. From 1950 almost all of the advanced industrial countries spent an increasing proportion of their gross national product (GNP) on social welfare. This was no less true for nations like Sweden, which were already heavily committed to such programs, than it was for those like Spain, which had lagged far behind. By 1970 all had more or less tripled the proportion of GNP they were devoting to welfare programs. Under these circumstances, they clearly would neither converge nor diverge. On the contrary, by 1972 each was higher on the scale, but each country had pretty well maintained its relative standing as leader or laggard. The pattern depicted in Figure 2.3 therefore well illustrates the process of nonconvergent parallel change.

Forms of Divergence

Although parallel change, by definition, fails to qualify as an instance of convergence, it does not contradict the key assumption of the theory of convergence. That theory assumes that insofar as they face comparable situations of action and are subject to comparable pressures of daily life, nations and individuals will respond in broadly comparable ways. Insofar as we can establish that the groups changing in parallel fashion had earlier been confronted by comparable conditions and pressures, to that degree we have gathered support for the theory underlying our analysis of convergence.

Our scheme must, however, allow for divergence as well as convergence. One should keep in mind that every instance of divergence does not automatically count as a challenge to the theory underlying the expectation of convergence. Nevertheless, we are under obligation to search for instances of divergence as assiduously as we seek examples of convergence. The instances of divergence that we find should not be accepted as the unquestioned "natural order" of things. Divergence needs to be understood and explained just as much as convergence. Before we attempt that task, however, we need to identify the variety of patterns and modes in which divergence presents itself.

Simple Divergence

Divergence means movement away from a given point, common or not, to new points farther apart than was the case in the original condition. Divergence may involve a few nations moving a great deal or many moving only slightly. On a summary scale of divergence this may seem to average out to the same amount of change; but the social significance of the two outcomes may be quite different.

FIGURE 2.3   Social welfare expenditures as a percentage of GNP, selected countries, 1950–1972

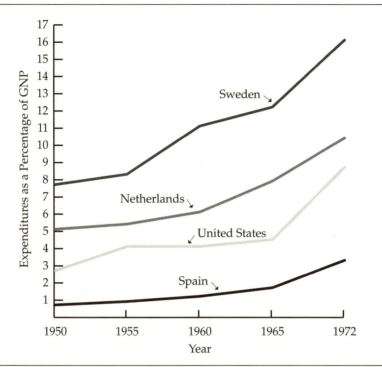

Source: Walter W. Rostow, *The World Economy: History and Prospect* (Austin: University of Texas Press, 1978), 360.

Divergence is most dramatically illustrated in the realm of production and the generation of physical wealth. Only a century ago, according to Gale Johnson (1973), the agriculture of the now industrial countries was little different from that of the Indian subcontinent then and today.[10] Grain yields were similar, and the sources of power were much the same. But by 1970 the differences were so great as to be often called amazing. For example, the amount of horsepower per worker available in the United States was forty-six, in Japan it was one, and in India, 0.008. French yields per hectare in 1880—expressed as a ratio—were 3.5, compared to one in India; by 1965 the ratio had increased to 20 to 1. In the case of industrial production, the rate at which the now advanced areas outstripped the less developed areas was even more marked.

Differences of this sort, which are combined in expressions of general wealth, produced ever widening contrasts. Living standards in Western Europe were twice those of countries outside its orbit in 1850; they rose to 10 to 1 by 1900 and were higher than 20 to 1 by about 1975, at least if one compared the richest and poorest countries.[11] Various forces are expected to widen the gap further, that is, to increase the divergence. According to one widely quoted estimate, the gap in income per capita separating less developed from developed countries, which stood at US$1,341 in 1965, will probably increase to $4,126 by the year 2000.[12]

Divergence is equally prevalent where it cannot be so graphically represented, as in the divergence of institutional patterns. A set of countries may all move to new points, or all adopt new forms of organization, yet not be any closer to one another than they were in the original case. Systems of legal regulation and administrative procedures within bureaucracies seem to follow this pattern. It seems inappropriate to call such movement parallel. Neither is it divergent in the same sense as in national wealth. Some standard term to express the idea would be welcome.

Shifts in the form of government illustrate the phenomenon well. Over time some one-party states changed by adopting a multiparty system of government. In the same period some multiparty governments were overthrown and became military dictatorships. Of ninety governments followed from 1950 to 1975, twenty-two democracies retained their form over the entire period, as did five one-party nations. All the remainder changed their form at least once, some repeatedly, switching from one system of government to another. Together they produced over 200 transitions from one of five forms of government to another. But at the end of all that movement the world of governments was more rather than less diverse. In 1950 the set of ninety countries was mainly made up of colonies and multiparty governments. By 1975 the colonies were virtually all gone, but the original set of ninety was now even more diverse, divided more or less equally between multiparty, single-party, and military governments. Table 2.1 tells the story as reflected in the original and final years, omitting mention of all the intervening switches.

Convergence and Cross-Overs

Convergence toward a common point is not a guarantee that once two or more systems come to be alike they will continue to be alike. Two converging lines may meet and fuse, but they may also cross and then start to diverge. This phenomenon is illustrated by the pattern of population growth rates for developed and less developed countries previously mentioned. From 1900 onward their growth rates seemed to be converging. As public health measures reduced the high death rates in the less developed countries their overall population growth rate moved up from its traditional low of one-third of 1 percent to come close to the 1 percent rate characteristic of Europe and other more developed countries. But the rate failed to level off at that point. With birth rates continuing high and more infants surviving, because they too benefited from improvements in public health, the growth

Table 2.1   Changes in the form of government of ninety countries, comparing 1975 and 1950

		1975			
		No Party (N = 2)	*Military* (N = 26)	*One Party* (N = 23)	*Multiparty* (N = 39)
1950	No Party (N = 2)	1 (50%)	1 (50%)	–	–
	Military (N = 3)	–	1 (33%)	–	2 (67%)
	One Party (N = 8)	–	1 (12%)	6 (76%)	1 (12%)
	Multiparty (N = 39)	–	9 (23%)	2 (5%)	28 (72%)
	Colony (N = 38)	1 (3%)	14 (37%)	15 (39%)	8 (21%)

Source: Michael T. Hannan and Glenn R. Carroll, "Dynamics of Formal Political Structure." Unpublished National Science Foundation Grant Technical Report No. 72, Department of Sociology, Stanford University, 1979, Table 1.

rate of less developed countries moved not merely up to but actually much above the previous rates for the more advanced countries. Meanwhile, growth rates in the more advanced countries fell as they began to achieve reproductive stability. What had seemed to be a convergent movement therefore proved to be only a meeting at a crossroads, from which point a rapid new divergence began.

The cross-over pattern may also be observed within sets of nations from the same region of the world sharing the same broad culture. In 1890 the countries of Europe differed considerably in their relative emphasis on providing secondary as against primary schooling. In each successive decade thereafter European countries came to be more alike in this respect, so that by 1930 they had all pretty much converged on a common pattern such that there were fifty-five to seventy secondary school students per 1,000 primary school students. But the convergence was followed by a new divergence. Each country adopted a different policy for distributing its resources among the two levels of schooling, so that by 1960 the ratios had again diverged dramatically, as may be seen in Figure 2.4.

Convergence Masking Diversity

Statistical indicators are by definition summaries of many single, discrete phenomena. Moreover, those statistics may be composites, summaries of several different indicators. Such summary indicators may come to be more alike as countries move along the continuum of development, and that fact

FIGURE 2.4   Ratio of students at secondary level to students at primary level, 1890–1960

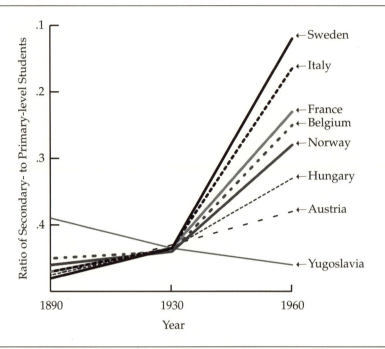

Year

Source: From B. R. Mitchell, *European Historical Statistics, 1750–1970* (New York: Columbia University Press, 1975), 749–771.

may be the result of common responses to significant imperatives and may reflect important shared experience. But the seemingly shared experience indicated by some convergent summary indicators may mask an actual divergence in the component elements making up the summary indicator.

In the period after World War II all the leading nations of the West allocated a larger and larger proportion of their resources to education. Between 1955 and 1975 the percentage of GNP devoted to public expenditures for education generally doubled, and the nations involved came closer to each other, clustering around a median standard of about 6 percent. However, underneath this common, and even slightly convergent, tendency to spend more money for education, there was a marked divergence in how the extra money was apportioned among the three levels of education. In the United States, for example, the additional resources were poured disproportionately into colleges and universities. From having had less than 20 percent of all funds in 1960, the colleges advanced to having 33 percent by 1975. This made possible a great increase in the number of openings, and the proportion of the eligible age group in college rose from 32 percent to an unprecedented 54 percent. In sharp contrast, Switzerland shifted resources mainly to its secondary schools. Its universities actually got a slightly smaller proportion of the now larger educational pie, and its university-level education continued to enroll only 7 to 8 percent of the eligible age group. Other nations in the set followed still different patterns. Sweden, for example, decreased the relative share of secondary schools, and France sharply increased the allocation to that level. All the countries were spending a larger share of GNP for education, and because GNP was rising all were spending much more in absolute terms, but this additional expenditure was being allocated in a relatively distinctive way in each of the different nations.[13]

Similarly, between 1950 and 1971 the United States, Great Britain, and Sweden all experienced approximately a doubling of the proportions of the population receiving relief payments, but the social groups receiving those benefits had a quite different character in each country. Of all welfare recipients in the United States, 60 percent were one-parent families with children; in Britain and Sweden the figure was only 16 to 24 percent. Yet, curiously enough, one-parent families in the United States are not much more common, at 11 percent of all families, than they are in Sweden at 10 percent and Britain at 9 percent.

Comparable contrasts are evident in other realms. The United States evidently is strong on free public services for the young but puts fewer resources into the elderly relative to Germany and France. They in turn pay less attention to protecting the environment. Thus summary indicators of expenditure, both absolute and proportional, may give a spurious impression of convergence and resultant similarity, thus masking actual variety and even divergence at the level of more specific actual policy applications.[14]

Convergence may also mask diversity when institutional change is at issue. The pattern is well illustrated in recent changes in the citizen's access to legal aid, especially in the case of the poor. Mauro Cappelletti and his colleagues see this as "a pervasive international phenomenon . . . an accelerating movement to make the legal system accessible to all citizens irrespective of income."[15] This movement has been markedly stronger in some countries than in others, however. For example, as of 1974 the Italian system was still based on nineteenth-century principles preserved in a law dating from the Fascist era, and the French and German systems were much less modernized than the Swedish and Canadian. Moreover, in implementing the "right to counsel," different countries have adopted markedly different approaches as to financing, as to whether the client has the right to choose his own counsel or must use a public law office, as to whether only some or all types of litigation are covered, and so on. Indeed, there seem to be so many marked and deepseated national differences in the provision of legal services that in many ways the Western nations now have less in common than they did in the nineteenth century, when the right to counsel was not widely recognized and the access of the poor to legal aid everywhere rested on charity.

Units, Levels, and Time

Assuming that we can reliably identify change patterns as convergent, parallel, or divergent, we must decide where to look for evidence of these processes. We must settle on the units we consider, the dimensions of those units of special relevance to us, and, most critical, the span of time over which change is assessed.

Scope of Coverage: The Sociopolitical Units

There are constant references to a process of change in "industrial societies." What is encompassed in that category? Different criteria will yield different sets of countries. Some criteria, if narrow enough, will by definition make our problem redundant—the definition itself assuring that all the countries studied will already be alike. Some restrictions—say, limiting oneself to Europe—are of more political interest because of the greater probability that, in that case, sociocultural convergence might lead to political integration. But such a restriction may limit the general social science significance of our inquiry, as one of the most interesting tasks is to ascertain how far non-European and somewhat less industrialized societies may be converging on some European model.

Whatever the subset considered, nation-states seem the most appropriate sociopolitical units of analysis. Every aspect of the sociocultural system is represented in nation-states, and nations, whatever their size, are the units used in reporting most social data. But from many points of view, the nation-state is a very arbitrarily selected unit, as different regions and administrative divisions within a nation may have very different socioeconomic characteristics.

If convergent change can only reasonably be expected in settings that are under the same major influence, then one should perhaps focus on subnational units, especially those selected more precisely on the basis of theoretically relevant characteristics. Thus, if industrialization is taken to be the defining characteristic of our units, it may be more appropriate to make comparisons in which Monterey stands for Mexico, Catalonia for Spain, and the North for Italy. There are some crucial theoretical objections to this approach and numerous practical ones, the most outstanding being that data are more likely to be available on most dimensions for an entire country rather than for its subunits. Nevertheless, the problem is amenable to a solution. Ansley Coale and his colleagues at the Office of Population Research at Princeton University have drawn together demographic data on

700 provinces of Europe back to 1890.[16] This permits a much more precise analysis that carries a minimal risk that national averages will disguise important variations between different parts of the same nation.

A different principle of aggregation is by region, with the region defined geographically, culturally, or politically. There may be convergence between regions without a matching convergence within each region. Thus after 1900 the age at marriage in countries in Asia and Africa on the one hand and Europe on the other came, on the average, to be closer despite the fact that *within* the set of Western countries the dispersion in the proportion of males married before age twenty-five became greater. Alternatively, the nations in any region may come closer together but in that very process draw their region away from others, thus increasing divergence on a worldwide basis. This pattern is illustrated by the relative equalization of per capita wealth within the set of industrialized countries, a form of convergence simultaneous with that group's collectively pulling ever farther ahead of the less developed countries. Regional treaties, pacts, trading alliances, and the like may contribute markedly to the process of convergence within regions, which pulls them still farther from other regions. Thus the regulations of the European Economic Community have strongly shaped institutional patterns, administrative procedures, working rules, and even products, greatly increasing the convergence of the societies in Europe participating in the community. At the same time, the dominance of communist parties of the Soviet type and the impact of the Council for Mutual Economic Assistance (Comecon) produced analogous effects within Eastern Europe. The divergence of institutional patterns has gone so far that there is serious question as to how feasible it would be effectively to reunite the two parts of Germany without great strain.

Geographical regions may be defined fairly unambiguously. But if we decide to limit our search for convergence to a set of countries grouped on the basis of a criterion such as industrialization, the bases for inclusion become quite problematic. A rough rule of thumb for identifying an industrialized country is that it have at least 25 percent of the labor force in the secondary sector and less than 25 percent in the primary sector. As of 1950 that rule would presumably have brought in most of Europe, North America, and Australia, perhaps New Zealand, and possibly Japan. A number of Latin American countries were on the periphery of the central cluster and would perhaps have been included as well.

If we excluded Japan and the Latin countries we might have difficulty deciding whether any observed convergence after 1950 represented mainly a "strain toward consistency" in European culture or was rather the product of independent economic, political, and social forces. Moreover, on some dimensions there is a ceiling that most of the advanced countries reached long ago, leaving no room for further convergence. That situation obviously exists when 100 percent of the eligible age group is in primary school, and there seems to be some force that restricts the proportion of the labor force in industry to a maximum of about 45 percent. Because there is no room left for further convergence on such dimensions, we must either go far back in the history of the now developed countries or study the more recent experience of the less advanced.

Applying the convergence model to the experience of nations so far apart in economic development, and culturally so diverse, obviously raises a number of special issues that one does not confront when one limits oneself to more homogeneous sets such as the industrialized nations or the nations of Europe. Yet the prospect of showing convergence across so great a gap presents an obvious challenge that is difficult to resist. And whether appropriate or not, the model is almost sure to be applied by some. Rather than attempt to block the model's application, therefore, it seems more appropriate to confront the adjustments this application requires and to attempt to learn from it as much as we can about the process of large-scale social change in modern times.

Simon Kuznets noted that despite divergence in per capita product and in the structure of economic growth, "in some aspects of economic and social structure the penetration of elements of modern economic growth brings about a *measurable* convergence between the LDCs [less developed countries] and developed countries." He lists the following as examples and illustrations of this convergence:

> . . . the shift from colonial status to political independence and national sovereignty . . . an instance of convergence with respect to the formal character of political structure.
>
> . . . movement toward what might be called modern ideology . . . the belief in the capacity of modern technology and society to reach high levels of material output per capita and expect that these material attainments can and should be pursued.
>
> . . . rises, limited as they are, in the shares of the I sector (industry and mining) within the LDCs . . . a modicum of modern technology within the boundaries of a less developed country represents a significant movement *toward* developed status.
>
> . . . increasing involvement of less developed regions in the network of international trade must have raised their foreign trade proportions and brought them closer in this respect to the developed countries.
>
> . . . comparison of death rates, and perhaps even morbidity between the 1920s and the 1960s would show marked convergence.
>
> . . . literacy would also show convergence; and so would proportions of population receiving primary education.[17]

There are some obvious additions various people would make to Kuznets's list. In the category of popular culture, some would emphasize the replacement of traditional skills by standardized production of "inauthentic" goods. In the realm of primary relations, some would emphasize the shift to the nuclear family, the erosion of community controls, and the spread of individualism and anomie. Others would stress the diffusion of rapid communication, especially of the mass media.

Kuznets's account says little of divergence, except to note the economic facts already mentioned. But here again there is much room for elaboration. As characteristics of the less developed countries that draw them apart from the more industrialized, we may note: the political features of one-party rule, the regularity of military intervention and of military government, and the peculiar U-shaped distribution on measures of political stability, with high frequency of both rapid turnover and long-term rule being most common; the tenacity of traditional forms of social organization and the intensity of loyalty to clan, tribe, and other local foci of allegiance; the persistence of traditional ideas, myths, and beliefs; and the clinging to traditional foods.

The prospect of extending this list at great length raises a fundamental issue, indeed a set of related issues. Can one judge the extent of convergence merely by elaborating a list of discrete movements? Is it not essential to have some scheme for weighting changes so as to distinguish the critical from the incidental or even trivial? And however we weight the individual changes, is there any meaningful way of combining them in an index or other summary measure so we can express quantitatively the direction and speed of movement?

Some changes occur only under very specific conditions, and those conditions may be experienced by only a limited sector of the population. Thus work in industry stimulates modern attitudes and values, which causes industrial workers in the less developed countries to resemble more closely industrial workers in the advanced countries. These two groups may be convergent, but can we speak of their *societies* as converging if only a small minority in the LDCs have the industrial experience that stimulates modernity in attitudes?

Can we sort out convergence on ends or goals and convergence on means? The Soviet Union may for some time have been converging on the model of the advanced, technologically sophisticated, science-based, consumerist industrial society epitomized by the United States or West Germany, but it was following a quite distinctive path to its presumably convergent goal. Is there a similar pattern evident in the less developed countries? Are they more convergent in the discernible end product, in the path to it, or in neither?

Foci of Change

The total society is too large and complex an entity to serve as the basis for most analyses of convergent and divergent tendencies. We must therefore specify which subsystems, and indeed which specific institutions and customs, are of interest. As we move from one such subsystem to another, we are likely to encounter different patterns of change proceeding at different rates. I noted in Chapter 1 the different rates of convergence in modes of production, institutional forms, social relationships, popular attitudes, and systems of economic and political control, and many more examples were provided in this chapter.

Change patterns may also vary within the same subsystem, indeed even within segments of a single institutional complex. In the round of daily living new types of clothing may diffuse very rapidly—witness the near-universal diffusion of blue jeans—whereas food habits change more slowly. Nations may quickly converge on a common standard and pattern of primary education, move more slowly in changing secondary schooling, and cling tenaciously to distinctive university-level systems. In the realm of the family, we find great erosion of parental authority but little reduction in visits to parents; sharp reductions in the size of family, but little change in the proportion of people who reach age fifty never having been married.

Such variation points our attention to what is perhaps the most critical problem in selecting the areas in which we explore convergence and divergence. The numerous realms of social life and the large number of lines along which each is organized provide us, potentially, with hundreds, even thousands, of dimensions we might examine for evidence of convergence. Given that fact, we must acknowledge that any single instance of alleged convergence may simply represent the workings of chance, a number that has been arbitrarily plucked out of a larger set of numbers and that therefore lacks real statistical significance. Our analysis will be much more mature, our findings more reliable, and our conclusions more compelling if we insist on multiple measures for each realm of social life. We can also have increased confidence in the instances of convergence we find if we are led to them by a theory rather than by merely coming upon them.

In an effort to meet these standards in a study of family change, I identified three forms in which family change might express itself—demographic, structural, and dynamic. In each of these realms I sought to identify up to ten discrete attributes of family systems that theoretical interest or scholarly tradition had identified as important.[18] For example, the demographic realm included reproduction rates, age at marriage, and the rate of divorce. The structural realm included patterns of residence, of descent, of inheritance, and so on. Maintaining these distinctions ensured that we would avoid unwarranted global generalizations about convergence in worldwide family patterns on the basis of a few scattered bits of evidence, and it held out the prospect that we could specify with some degree of precision exactly which aspects of family life were convergent in greater or lesser degree. How well I succeeded in these objectives may be judged by reading

Chapter 7, which presents in detail the results of this particular explanation of convergence in family patterns.

The Time Span

The span of time over which change is studied will greatly influence not only the character of our investigations but also the conclusions we may be able to draw. We may get quite a different impression if we start our investigation in the period before extensive industrialization, say 1850, or if we focus on the decades after 1950.

Consider, for example, runaway growth in population, commonly taken to be one of the most terrible afflictions of the less developed countries. Indeed, their rates of population growth are expected to be approximately double those in the more advanced nations for the period 1950 to 2000. But this differential advantage of the more industrialized is evident only back to about 1920. Curiously enough, during the nineteenth century the more "advanced" countries were experiencing much higher rates of growth than the less developed countries. Because of their high death rates, the latter then grew at only 0.3 percent per year, whereas the European rate was three times higher, at 1.0 percent.[19] It was Europe, therefore, that in the nineteenth century experienced a runaway population growth whose pressure could only be relieved by migration, explosive urban growth, and the devastation of mechanized war.

Focusing on the period from 1890 to 1930, we would be obliged to conclude that the eight countries in Figure 2.4 were converging on a standard ratio of secondary to primary school enrollments, but looking at the pattern after 1930 we see the opposite—a marked pattern of divergence.

Short spans, say of a decade or less, are likely to be particularly misleading. They frequently reflect historically fleeting sentiments, or short-term adjustments to special conditions, such as war or depression, but they are often interpreted in sweeping terms as representing dramatic shifts in long-term direction. For example, we should be cautious about assuming that the industrial countries are experiencing a basic shift away from legally confirmed marriages to more consensual unions.

Even more fundamental is the task of coordinating chronological and social time. The structural theory of convergence assigns no special significance to the mere passage of time. It assumes that change over time in one element of social structure comes about in response to prior change in some other influential feature of society, such as its level of industrialization or the degree to which it is urbanized. It follows that on measures of some dependent variables, societies should converge only to the extent that they have previously converged on the independent variable conceived as the cause of change.

The inference one must draw from this is that the common time series that shows where many countries stand at different periods is not the most suitable instrument for testing the structural theory of convergence. It would be much more appropriate to compare countries not by calendar time but by developmental time. We should not ask whether the reproduction rates in Japan and the United States came closer after 1900, but rather whether the rates came closer as the GNP per capita of Japan approached that of the United States, whatever the years involved. Although the ordinary passage of time does happen to reflect the narrowing of the income gap between Japan and the United States, the sheer passage of the years is nevertheless an imperfect and imprecise indicator of the presumed causal factor.

Of course the structural model and the objective facts of convergence need not coincide. The sheer passage of time may be associated with convergence even in the absence of prior convergence in major structural features of society like industrialization. To the degree that this happens, it strengthens the case for other models purporting to explain convergence, such as the diffusion model and the dependency model.

Given that the analysis of convergence is not an established field and that we wish to learn how better to think about and to study the phenomenon, there is reason to be rather open-ended about both the criteria for including countries and the span of time considered. This also leaves us free to use a wider range of the limited data available. So while striving to concentrate on the more industrialized countries in the most recent period, we should feel free to introduce examples from among the less advanced but still industrial countries and from the more distant past.

*   *   *

Clearly, in the study of convergence in modern social systems we face a great work—great in the demands it makes on us, but also great in the promise that we may yet discover and come to understand some of the basic laws of social change.

Part Two

COMPARING NATION-STATES

three

WERE THE SOVIET UNION AND THE UNITED STATES CONVERGING?

The Soviet Union no longer exists. However, through its long history there was a continuous debate among statesmen and within the scholarly community as to the probable long-term development and the ultimate fate of its unique socioeconomic and political system. One school of thought, which might be termed the pessimist and realist position, stressed the relative coherence of a set of characteristics that included the one-party dictatorship, the rigid Leninist ideology, the total state domination of the economy, a mobilized and regimented population subjected to regular acts of terror from its own government, and intense suspicion and implacable hostility toward the "bourgeois" democratic capitalist West, especially as epitomized in its leading representative, the United States. A second school, which might be termed the skeptical and pragmatic, acknowledged the terrible legacy of Stalinist totalitarianism but emphasized more the potential for change in the system stimulated by the processes of industrialization, urbanization, popular education, and the ever increasing reliance on science and technology. Whatever their differences, both of these schools were poles apart from a third group of analysts whose belief may be character-

Reprinted with permission from Alex Inkeles, "Russia and the United States: A Problem in Comparative Sociology," in *Pitirim A. Sorokin in Review,* ed. Philip J. Allen (Durham, NC: Duke University Press, 1963), 225–246.

ized as optimist and idealist. They claimed that the Soviet Union and the leading exemplar of capitalist democracy had much in common, and with the passage of time would come to be ever more alike. In short, they made the case for the convergence of the two systems. One vigorous proponent of the idealist position was the famous Russian-American sociologist Pitirim Sorokin, who developed his views in *Russia and the United States*.[1] An assessment of his theory and the evidence he adduced provides an opportunity to explore what may have been similar development trends in Soviet Russia and the United States, while also serving to caution us against a too facile and uncritical disposition to press the case for convergence.

Professor Sorokin's *Russia and the United States* grew out of a series of lectures he gave during the early years of World War II. His chief aim was to assess the chances that the wartime allies would continue to enjoy peaceful, or even cordial, relations in the postwar period. Nevertheless, one of the assumptions with which Sorokin approached his task of prediction was that "sociocultural similarities conduce toward peaceful relations between communities of men" (p. 162). In order to estimate the future course of U.S.-Soviet relations, therefore, he was led to examine the extent of sociocultural similarity between the two countries. Indeed, he acknowledged that the possibility of reconciling the American way of life and its system of values with those of Soviet Communism posed a problem "so important that it cannot either be dodged or passed by" (p. 177).

Professor Sorokin felt that it was a "fallacy" to argue that "there is an irreconcilable conflict between the Soviet and American way of life" (p. 209). Feeling as he did, he understandably sought mainly evidence of sociocultural similarity or congeniality between the social structure of the United States and that of the Soviet Union. His illustrations include instances of technological progress, economic growth, and the development of music and the arts. In the past hundred years these two countries, he argued, have become the "chief bearers of the torch of sociocultural creativeness." "Far from being polar antitheses," he concluded, "the two nations reveal a series of most striking similarities geopolitically, psychologically, culturally, and socially" (p. 161).

Some Features of Social Structure
in the United States and the Soviet Union

In response to Sorokin's analysis I have drawn up a series of brief statements comparing five of the major institutional realms of Soviet and American society: political structure, economy, social classes, family, and school. In those instances in which Sorokin made relevant comments, particularly with regard to the polity and the economy, I have reported his assessment. A separate concluding section presents a fuller assessment of Sorokin's contribution and its implications for students of comparative social structure.

Political Structure

Our era is characterized by the predominance of the centralized national state over the autonomy of the region and the diffuse power of the local community, both of which progressively lost their significance in the eighteenth and nineteenth centuries. Any comparison of the Soviet and American systems must therefore begin with a discussion of the nature of the state and its relation to the rest of the society. The contrasts here are understandably the most obvious, but they are nonetheless basic.

Despite Marx's emphasis on the primacy of economics, that is, of the mode of production and productive relations, in determining the character of the social order, the distinctive contribution of Lenin and Stalin was to reverse the formula and to demonstrate the possibility of determining the economic system through control of the political power. This is the basic meaning of Stalin's affirmation that the Soviet revolution was made "from above," from those "commanding heights" of which Lenin spoke so often. The Soviet state did not spring full grown from the head of Marx; indeed its development was never dreamed of by him, and if he had conceived it he would almost certainly have labeled it a bastard—no child of his. Credit for the conception must go to Lenin, but even he did no more than suggest its outlines and provide it the breath of life. The actual forging of the system was the work of a man initially as obscure and demeaned among the Bolshevik lords of creation as was Hephaestus among the Greek gods. While others busied themselves with oratory and stood on the front lines of the battle, Stalin quietly went about the unromantic work of fashioning an apparatus of control that in time carried him to the highest seat of power.

Almost from its very inception the Soviet Union knew only a one-party system in which all political power was concentrated.[2] Indeed, with the exception of a very few years this system functioned as a one-man dictatorship. In any event no one will quarrel with the characterization if we say that it was a self-perpetuating oligarchy. The Communist party never was a mass movement, certainly not in the sense that the trade unions or the Youth League were. For a long time it numbered its members in the millions, yet these represented only between 2 and 4 percent of the population. Although size was therefore not an absolute barrier to the adoption of democratic procedures, at no time was there effective *democratic* control of the leadership. On the contrary, the rank and file of the membership served mainly as the agent of those whom they nominally elected and controlled. Within the government, party members served as a kind of special extragovernmental bureaucracy for enforcing the party's decisions and checking on their application. Among the people, the party members served as a source of exhortation and inspiration in the effort to mobilize the masses behind the party's program. Soviet leaders placed great store on the *sem-*

blance of legitimacy. They feared the label of "adventurers" in politics, which would be applicable to them by Leninist standards if they acted without the consent and support of the working masses who presumably define each historic moment for appropriate revolutionary action. Hence the solemn play that was periodically acted out, of citizens voting for the Supreme Soviet and party members electing delegates to congresses of the Communist party. In all elections there was only one slate, which was officially designated, and for which one could only vote yes or no. In elections to the Supreme Soviet one was expected as a show of loyalty to disdain the available secret polling booth and to cast one's ballot openly and proudly for the officially sponsored candidates.

At every point this system was polar to that in those societies generally acknowledged to have democratic political systems. To qualify for inclusion in this group a country must have at least two political parties that are actually independent and autonomous. The concept of a loyal opposition must be accepted by the party in power, and the latter may not deny the opposition the reasonable opportunity to continue to work for its platform and the prospect of holding office in the future. This requires, as a minimum, that the group out of power has the freedom to hold political meetings and to propagandize for its program, to maintain an independent press and other organs of communication, and to criticize the policies of the government on all matters, including the most fundamental.

In no respect were these conditions met in the Soviet Union. The legislatures of all the democratic regimes of the world are in more or less continuous session, engage in protracted debate, and produce legislation that clearly reflects compromises among diverse interests and aspirations. Soviet legislative bodies, including the congresses of the Communist party, met infrequently or even rarely, concluded all their momentous business in a matter of days, heard almost no discussion, let alone debate, and produced legislation that, virtually without any alteration, represented the precise wishes of the leaders who convened the legislative session to give approval to policies already selected.

Even within the Communist party itself the maintaining of a free minority was not possible, since such groups were labeled as impermissible factions intending to destroy the "monolithic unity" of the party. There was a nominal rule that public organizations such as the trade unions were allowed to publish newspapers, but control of such papers was in fact in the hands of the ruling Communist party. Exercise of the rights of free speech and press were explicitly limited in the constitution to those forms that were in accord with the interests of the proletariat, and these in turn were of course defined by the Communist party.[3]

A democratic system assumes the general recognition and firm institutionalization of definite limits on the powers of all governments, including the central government. The United States has no doubt gone much further in implementing this principle than the more centralized government of France and, indeed, exceeds England in this respect. Nevertheless, in all democratic systems such principles as the inviolability of the judiciary, the rights of the local community, the rights of security of person and of property, and the autonomy of family and home reflect the general recognition and legal implementation of definite limits on the power of government. By contrast, we may note, in Sorokin's words, that "an almost unlimited and centralized regimentation of government is the heart of the Soviet system."[4] While endorsing Sorokin's general characterization of the Soviet system in this respect, I yet cannot accept his reservation that this was not distinctive to the Soviet Union, nor his assertion that such regimentation developed there mainly in response to the emergency of revolution and war. On the contrary, total political control represented a *typical* feature of the conception of government in the Soviet Union. This is not to deny that as the regime became stabilized or normalized, actions exceeding constitutional, legal, and moral and popular value limits decreased in frequency and extremity. That there was less need for repression after Stalin's death does not mean that in principle the Soviet leaders accepted the idea of legitimate limits on the freedom of action of the central authorities, or that they would hesitate to take drastic action should the situation require it, as they did on the international front in Hungary.

Even if we acknowledge the profound differences in formal structure and in the regular practice of politics in the United States and the USSR, is it not correct that the direction of change in the two political systems was such as to make them ever more alike? C. Wright Mills, for example, argued that effective power in the United States has drifted into the hands of a self-perpetuating elite that cuts across government, industry, and the military and that actually makes all of the important decisions affecting the fate of this country.[5] Numerous Sovietologists argued that the progressively entrenched vested interests of Soviet industrial management and military leaders severely limited the freedom of action of the Soviet political rulers. Does this suggest that each system was moving away from its polarized position toward some common middle ground? Perhaps, but the evidence on either side is far from compelling. If Mills were correct, it hardly seems likely that programs such as the Marshall Plan or the U.S. aid program in India and Pakistan could have been launched. As for the Soviet Union, if the leadership were increasingly forced to compromise the exercise of power to accommodate major social groups, then an autonomous and powerful army would hardly have permitted the demotion of Marshal Zhukov or the demobilization of the Soviet ground forces. A politically effective managerial elite would have demanded a larger role in shaping the decentralization of Soviet industry, and an even slightly effective political

opposition would hardly have allowed, even in defeat, the exile of its leaders in the persons of Molotov, Kaganovich, and Bulganin.

The differences in the formal structure and the informally accepted rules
of the game in Soviet and American politics had profound consequences in
the capacity of each system to act, and especially to act on itself, in order to
effect adaptive change. The essence of the democratic system is that it permits the embodiment of diverse groups and their interests in competing political organizations and programs. The democratic process then becomes
the slow, protracted, often inchoate development of compromise and adjustment between these interests in the gradual evolution of new programs
and policies. This feature of democratic systems was almost entirely absent
in Soviet society. This is not to say that the leaders had no need to reckon
with any group. On the contrary, it is evident that Soviet leaders, especially
after the death of Stalin, weighed very carefully the effects of various actions on popular morale in general or on specific segments of the economy.
They were especially concerned with morale as manifested in willingness
and ability to work hard or otherwise effectively to perform functions of
importance to the state. This mode of influence, however, has little in common with the direct participation by workers, managers, farmers, or others
acting as interest groups in the process of public discussion and the exercise
of influence through votes, funds, or appeals for public support. It is very
different indeed from direct action in strikes or nonviolent defiance of law,
as in the fight for civil rights in the southern United States.

One consequence of the suppression of such struggles is that there was
always a clear and precisely identifiable national purpose in the Soviet
Union, one defined by the only group with the right and the power to determine it. In the United States, by contrast, it is almost impossible to state a
clear and commonly accepted national purpose, except perhaps the principle of giving everyone a break sooner or later. This means that the Soviet
system was characterized by almost unlimited freedom of action, by exceptional capacity for adjustment of its internal organization to take account
of changes in either its externally defined situation or the internal structure
of the society. Since these changes could be made without full consultation,
and certainly without effective opposition by the various interest groups in
the society, the freedom of the Soviet leaders to adjust to changed circumstances, to adapt to developments arising from technological advances, or
to reorganize more effectively to meet changed goals was virtually unprecedented in modern society. It certainly gave the Soviet system, for good or ill,
an enormous advantage in competition with the governments of democratic societies, which must always consider the vital interests of major
strata of the society as a matter of principle, and in fact are often unable to
act at all effectively because of the resistance of entrenched local, parochial,
class, and related interest groups. On the other hand, for the Soviet Union

this meant that mistaken policies, which either crushed whole communities or wasted vast resources, were not subject to the checks and balances characteristic of democratic systems. The results could be, and often were, massive disasters for the nation.

Economy

It is one of those typical anomalies of history that the feature of the Soviet and American societies that in both Marxist theory and popular thinking most distinguish them was in fact far from being the most reliable indicator of the nature of the two systems. Sorokin argued that in the United States the role of the modern corporation and that of government intervention in economic life had transformed the "classic capitalist system," while in the Soviet Union the principles of mass ownership had in fact not been fully implemented. We may agree with his judgment that "in neither country do the real owners—the Russian people and the hundreds and thousands of shareholders in the United States—manage what they theoretically own" (p. 202). He may even have been right in saying that "American capitalism and Russian Communism are now little more than the ghosts of their former selves" (p. 179). Nevertheless, it is not very likely than anyone would mistake the one system for the other.

Both the Soviet Union and the United States qualified as exponents and embodiments of modern industrialism, with its glorification of mechanization and its fostering of large-scale production, rapid transportation, and vast urban complexes. Production as an end in itself, the preoccupation with the making of things, especially things that make other things, came in both countries to dominate the value system to a degree probably without precedent in history. Despite this similarity, the two systems remained profoundly different. Corporate and state ownership are very different forms which produce profoundly different consequences. Not the least of these is the fact that the big corporation, however much it may escape the control of its stockholders, may still be regulated by the state, whereas in the government-owned establishment the interest of state and economic enterprise are fused. Among the many consequences of this fusion is the vital fact that the freedom to strike is generally denied the employees of state enterprises, which in the Soviet Union meant that it was denied to everyone.

The outstanding characteristic of Soviet economic life was its uniform pattern. This contrasts sharply with the mixed nature of the U.S. economy, which involves government controls in some areas but not others. Large corporations predominate in some sectors while others, such as trade or newer industrial realms like electronics, tend to be dominated by smaller firms. It is rather striking to note in this connection that Sorokin said almost nothing of the role of planning. Planning was after all a distinctive feature of the Soviet economy; indeed, some would argue that it was the chief distinction. By contrast, in the United States planning is almost completely absent, at least in the sense of a centralized, coordinated program backed by the power of the state. This contrast was certainly less sharp when viewed from the wartime perspective from which Sorokin wrote, but it was certainly evident even then. In any event, after the war the U.S. economy returned to its more characteristic low level of control, whereas planning persisted in undiminished strength in the Soviet Union. The postwar decentralization of industrial administration under Khrushchev was not accompanied by any decrease in the importance of the centrally determined plans that the locally administered industries were obliged to follow.

Not only was the role of government in economic life profoundly different in the two systems, but so also was the part played by the mass of citizens. In their status as shareholders, Americans may be denied essential control over management, but they exercise profound, indeed almost absolute, control over industry in their role as consumers. By marked contrast, the consumer had almost no significance in the Soviet industrial scene. Economic planning for preeminence in heavy industry, government allocation of materials, and the administration of prices contributed to a chronic shortage of consumers' goods and to the high prices and poor quality of what was available. The situation of consumers was bettered and continued to improve in the post-Stalin era, but they still played a markedly different role in the structure of the Soviet economy from that they occupied in the United States.

One sector of the Soviet economy did somewhat approximate the economic pattern appropriate to a mixed economy, namely, agriculture. The State Farm, which was run on the same principles as a factory, came to be of increasing importance after World War II, especially in the newly opened steppe regions. Nevertheless, the collective farm remained the overwhelmingly predominant form of agricultural productive organization in the Soviet Union. Like the factory, the collective farm was subject to centralized planning and allocation of resources, and the greater part of its crop was purchased at fixed prices. Yet the collective farm was unlike the factory in that it ran on a modified profit-sharing basis. A part of its crop was sold in an open and only lightly regulated market. In addition the peasants had their own private economy alongside that of the collective, raising food on family plots not only for their own consumption but also for sale in the peasant market. We can by no means accept Sorokin's version of the common misconception that the peasant collective farm was "merely a modernized form of an old national institution—the peasant 'mir' and 'obschina,' or a variety of workers' productive cooperative society known to all countries and greatly developed in pre-revolutionary Russia" (pp. 203–204).[6] But we must acknowledge the collective farm as the structural feature of the Soviet society that at least in some degree approximated the principle of mixed economy that characterizes the United States and the democratic countries of Europe.

The similarities and differences in the nature of the two economic systems generated characteristic similarities and differences in the responses of the typical occupational groups working within each. This presents an interesting realm for sociological investigation, which Sorokin rather notably neglected. To a degree, both management and labor in the United States and the Soviet Union worked in a similar institutional setting. In both countries people worked in large-scale units functioning bureaucratically under centralized but distant centers of control. Each unit was expected to maximize the effective exploitation of the resources placed at its command.

A comparison of Soviet industrial managers with their counterparts in U.S. industry, therefore, revealed a striking number of similarities in their response to their situation. David Granick called to our attention the conflicts of line and staff units, the conflict between loyalty to one's shop as against that to the plant or the economy at large, the low level of worker participation in programs to encourage innovation, and the circumventing of bureaucratic rules and regulations promulgated at the top and meant to be executed at the local level.[7]

In addition, the researches of the Harvard Project[8] revealed that workers and other occupational strata in the Soviet Union responded to their life situation in ways comparable to the response of the corresponding groups in the United States and other industrial countries. For example, in both the Soviet Union and the United States the proportion enjoying job satisfaction was very high among professional and managerial personnel, and fell steadily as one descended the occupational ladder. In both countries the upper white-collar group felt the most important qualities of a job to be its intrinsic interest and the opportunities for self-expression it offers, whereas those lower in the occupational scale gave more emphasis to pay and security.

Whether such similarities are significant or merely curious and unimportant is debatable. Certainly such parallels should not be allowed to obscure persistent bases of structural differentiation. When discussing their occupational problems, American managers place labor relations and selling their product in a competitive market at the very forefront of their concern, whereas neither problem was ever mentioned spontaneously by Soviet managers. This difference in emphasis arose, of course, from the structural differences in the two economies. Under a system of planning, allocation of material, and high production goals, the Soviet manager's primary problems were to secure the materials to attain output targets. Since trade unions were defined as adjuncts of the Communist party in the task of mobilizing the workers and had no power to strike, labor relations hardly loomed as a major problem to the Soviet manager. This meant, equally, that the significance of the trade union to the worker in both countries was also profoundly different. Soviet workers were not particularly conscious of their trade unions. They did not look upon them as distinctively "their own" organization, and they certainly did not think of them as a militant force acting to advance the workers' interests. On each of these dimensions we should be obliged to place the American worker at the opposite pole. Differences of this order cannot be freely put aside for the sake of easy generalizations that suggest that the two systems had become so much alike that their similarities overshadowed the remaining contrasts.

Social Classes

In my examination of the economic system of the Soviet Union and the United States in the preceding section I stressed that certain similarities should not obscure the basic differences. In assessing the structure of stratification in the two societies I must reverse the emphasis and urge that certain differences between the two systems not be allowed to obscure the basic similarities.

True, the American "big capitalist" still exists, even though he exerts much less influence on the American scene. We must grant too that there was no equivalent in the Soviet Union of the independent small businessman, a socially important if not numerous element in the American class structure. Soviet peasants formed the largest class in that nation, and although there are some parallels between their situation and that of agricultural labor on large American ranches, estates, and farms, there is no very precise equivalent in the United States. Yet in important respects the Soviet class structure was like that of the United States. As industrial countries, both had the familiar strata of administrative-professional elites; white-collar; skilled, ordinary, and unskilled worker; and lower-level service personnel and farm labor in approximately that rank order of prestige and standing in the community. In both societies class position was predominantly determined by one's occupational position rather than on the basis of inherited characteristics, and one's occupational standing in turn rested largely on educational attainment or technical training. Both countries, therefore, qualify as open class societies characterized by substantial upward mobility. Under these conditions consciousness of class and interclass hostility tend to be modest and mild, and the sense of opportunity for the capable and willing is strong. Manners are informal, relations between classes easy and natural, and the feeling of equality pervasive. These easy relations are greatly facilitated in the United States by the absence of a history of traditional legally enforced class distinctions. The equivalent force in Russian history was the sharp break in the class pattern introduced in the early period of the Soviet Revolution.

Comparable structures encourage comparable responses. Soviet citizens talked about their class structure in much the same way as Americans do about theirs—beginning with the high frequency of initial denials that there were any classes at all in their country. There are of course distinctive attributes. The role of the political elite was much wider and their domination of the status scene infinitely more marked and pervasive in the Soviet Union. But equalitarianism was deeply rooted in the values of both sets of people and was institutionalized in both social structures. Indeed, there is probably no realm of social structure in which an American set down on the Soviet scene would have felt more at home. Considering this fact it is rather striking that Sorokin said almost nothing systematic about social stratification, classes, social mobility, and the like, since his thesis of increasing similarity of the U.S. and Soviet social structure receives considerable support in this area.

Family and Character Formation

One feature of the United States and the Soviet Union certainly exhibited in common is considerable confusion about the role of the family in modern society. The United States of course has never had a national family policy. In the earlier years of the republic such an idea was unthinkable, and in any event unnecessary. By the time it became apparent to all that a policy was essential, no one could propose any that was meaningful and could be implemented. Everyone is, however, piously agreed that the family is the very keystone of society and must be aided in every way.

Initially the situation was quite different in the Soviet Union. Engels's writings had made it clear that the family was expected to wither away under communism. After a number of rather foolish assaults on that doughty institution, it was the policy itself that withered away. In time in the Soviet Union, as in the United States before it, the family came to be defined as a pillar on which society rests. The family was called upon to shape the future by bringing up well-mannered, conscientious, courteous citizens who would not litter the streets, would work hard, and would strive to succeed in life.

In both the Soviet Union and the United States it proved very difficult, however, to ascertain just what one was supposed to do to bring about the beneficial results everyone expected from the family. The ineffectual pamphleteering by the Soviet Academy of Pedagogical Sciences and the women's magazines bears a striking resemblance to the message disseminated by the U.S. Children's Bureau and similar agencies in the U.S. Department of Health, Education, and Welfare. It cannot be said of either country that the government knew how to bring about the results it desired. In both cases it is evident that the government did not wish to become too directly

involved in internal family affairs. Consequently in both countries there
was much wailing and wringing of hands about juvenile delinquency and
the less serious but more widespread failings of youth: disrespect for parents and general disregard for authority; shirking work, and other forms of
irresponsibility, especially as regards money and property; emotional instability, volatility, and often explosive destructiveness. Since the character of
youth is laid down in the internal relations of the family, and these are relatively inaccessible to the respective governments, effective countermeasures
are not easily come by short of accepting full-time public responsibility for
the rearing of children—something no one is willing to attempt.

To an important degree each society had nothing but itself to blame, because in each the family was responding to forces emanating from the
larger society. Both systems stressed the future rather than the past and ac-
claimed youth as the hope of the future. American and Soviet society valued both daring and initiative, which leads to the encouragement of aggres-
sive self-assertion in the young and in turn often encourages disdain for
authority. In the Soviet Union, as in the United States, the obvious reason
for success as well as the validation of it lay in amassing prestige and income, with which in turn one amassed consumption goods, which again
fostered self-aggrandizement and a basic hedonism. Emphasis on the essential dignity of *every* person, and on the more radical belief in basic human
equality, weakens respect for hierarchical, formally constituted authority.

The virtual disappearance of the extended family and the progressive de-
personalization of the work setting in the modern office and in industry
have encouraged people to concentrate their search for emotional satisfactions on the few members of the nuclear family unit, and particularly on
the children. Modern parents manifest deep fear of loss of the child's love—
an interesting reversal of the classic training pattern in which emphasis was
laid on the *child's* fear of the loss of parental love. Parents are therefore led
to overindulge their children, which again contributes to producing in the
young an exaggerated sense of their importance and the expectation that
they be served and cared for without limit and without contributing their
own efforts. The result is often a person who secures rewards by effective
use of his personality and by the manipulation of others rather than by effort and mastery over nature and materials.

These tendencies in the larger society are, perhaps theoretically,
amenable to change. In most cases, however, they are part and parcel of the
basic social structure of most modern, advanced, and "progressive" nations. In many ways both the United States and the USSR depended on
these qualities, which are functional to the system. How often are we told
how important to the U.S. economy it is that people so strongly want
things and so deeply wish to accumulate them without end? Although a
passion for consumption goods could not be so easily satisfied in the Soviet

economy, the system also depended heavily on the strength of the desire for increased earnings felt by manual, white-collar, and professional workers.

If the family cannot be relied on to inculcate in the young certain values important to society, the society must seek to exert influence through other segments of the social structure that play a role in character formation and in shaping values. This was more readily accomplished in the Soviet Union. The greater and more intimate control over education exercised there by the central authorities (rather than by local school boards subject to parental influence) gave the government great leverage in using the primary school to indoctrinate children in the virtues of obedience, the values of group participation, the importance of cooperation, and a sense of obligation to the community. The more authoritarian structure of the school aided the regime's self-conscious effort to inculcate these ideas. Youth movements organized by the Communist party—the Pioneers enrolled children from age ten to fourteen, and the Komsomol took them from there—provided an additional source of training in social service and cooperative action. They also served to inculcate the values of self-sacrifice, submission to group discipline, respect for authority, and orderliness. They tried to teach the children the pleasure of sharing work and production rather than leisure and consumption.[9]

The United States lacks comparable extra- or non-familial socializing agencies of this type, at least on a scale that would influence a large proportion of the youth and do so with an effectiveness greater than that of the Boy Scouts. This is thought by some to be one of the most serious deficiencies in the contemporary American social structure.

Education and Schooling

Until the Soviet regime came on the scene no other large country rivaled the United States in the extent to which the society as a whole had accepted and implemented the principle of universal free education, and not only at the elementary but also at the secondary and to some degree even at the university level. Although the "struggle" against illiteracy, as it was called in the USSR, was there waged more dramatically, and with greater propaganda effect, the underlying forces impelling this development were broadly similar in the two societies. The dominant political ideology in both countries stressed the widespread and active participation of the citizen in the process of government and in the management of public affairs. In the United States this tradition can be traced back to Jeffersonian, and certainly Jacksonian, democracy, and in Russia it had its roots in the Zemstvo schools of the mid–nineteenth century, to which Sorokin called our attention.[10] The Bolsheviks revived this tradition and vastly extended the principle of mass action. Such participation, however, theoretically required an educated and informed citizenry. Education for all was the indispensable precondition for the attainment of that state in which every cook would help to run the government and every worker at the bench would take his turn at record keeping and administration.

Lenin's hopes for mass participation in government were not to be realized, but the impetus to widespread education was preserved because literacy was deemed a necessary qualification for effective participation in the more complex labor processes of modern industry and for the growing ranks of white-collar employees who serviced it. The same need was felt in the United States. Perhaps a more important consideration, however, lies in the fact that both systems stressed the right of the individual to secure full personal development of his faculties and to win a position in society commensurate with his native talents—goals that could be attained only by individuals with access to educational opportunities.

Neither the Soviet Union nor the United States quite fulfilled the goal of giving everyone all the education he or she is capable of absorbing. The United States, at a point where in terms of gross national product it was roughly twice as rich as the Soviet Union, did much better in the proportion of young people it provided a college education, but even at that point as many as one-third of the qualified high school graduates did not go on to college. More difficult to evaluate, but probably more important than the failure to meet the quantitative demands for higher education, are the changes in the conception of educational goals and the methods of their implementation.

Over the years Soviet education came progressively to be subordinated to training for vocational purposes, even at the higher levels, with less and less emphasis placed on general education as a means for personal rather than occupational or professional development. In the process an approach to curriculum and classroom atmosphere that had originally stressed freedom, initiative, and creativity was transformed to emphasize authority, obedience, and rote learning. On the American scene the popularization of education led to a general decline of standards and values and, at the college level, to the demeaning of education through replacement of the liberally educated man by the image of the college man as playboy.

Certainly, at their best both the Soviet and American educational systems had to be rated as quite impressive. The Soviet Union did a remarkable job in training a steady and large supply of teachers, doctors, engineers, technicians, and scientists needed by the nation, and the good students of the better American colleges can certainly qualify as people of broad culture and learning. At the average level and below, however, the Soviet educational system was a glorified trade school, and the American college was often a never-never land in which the youth passed time in a prolongation of adolescence, acting out their own impulses and living out their parents' fantasies of the good life before accepting adult responsibilities.

These differences are not merely happenstance, or cultural "accidents." They reflect important differences in the social structures in which the respective educational systems were embedded. The objectives of education in the Soviet Union were determined by the central political authorities, and the emphasis on technical and scientific training reflected both the primacy they assigned to production and economic development and the fear and hostility they felt toward free and full exploitation of philosophical, literary, and humanistic ideas. In the United States the local community has relatively complete autonomy over elementary and high school education. At the college level the importance of private money in both the support of educational institutions and the payment for the students' educational expenses permits the colleges to be relatively free of central control and dictation of the content of their curricula. This, along with the absence of any clear and compelling national purpose in education to which most would adhere, fosters the extraordinary diversity and complexity of the American educational system. It also permits the degradation of education encountered in many schools, and in parts of almost all American college student bodies.

Problems in Comparative Structural Analysis

No doubt Soviet and American social structure displayed some important, often striking, similarities, and in some respects they may have followed parallel paths in the course of their development. In addition to those developed by Sorokin, I have pointed to several others in the comparison of the two systems in the preceding section. Both nations qualified as large-scale societies, composed of populations of diverse ethnic origins, sharing a diffuse secular culture. The United States and the Soviet Union were outstanding in their devotion to the maximization of industrial production through large-scale organization, the exploitation of science, and reliance on widespread popular education. In both countries physical and social mobility was taken for granted in an open class system that stressed equality, challenged tradition, and encouraged individual and collective progress.

This list of similarities could be expanded to great length. The same is unfortunately true of the list of differences. Dictatorship, or at least one-party oligarchy, as against a multiparty democratic political system; state control and planning, as opposed to corporate management and the dominance of the market; controlled communication and governmental dictation in art, compared to free expression and private pursuit of the arts. Here again the list could be expanded to greater length.

We are therefore faced with the same difficulty that sooner or later confronts all efforts at the systematic comparative analysis of social structure, namely, that of combining or weighting similarities and differences to yield one composite judgment. Unfortunately, sociology does not provide any equivalent for such measures as gross national product, or per capita income, or rate of growth of industrial output, which permit us to combine diverse economic factors into one common and standard measure. There is no unified scale or metric with which we can reduce the similarities and differences in social structure, leaving us with a single score for the comparison of the Soviet Union and the United States.

Sorokin stressed the fact of change. However wide apart their starting points, he said, the two systems are "now little more than the ghosts of their former selves" (p. 179). Indeed, he argued that "economically and politically the two nations have been steadily converging toward a similar type of social organization and economy" (p. 208). There are many who would challenge this assertion, especially as regards the political structure and the economic organization of the two countries. Yet even if the two nations were moving closer together, the fact of convergence could be much less important than the nature of the differences that persisted. How can we then assess the relative significance of one or another similarity or difference between two social systems? Although he did not explicitly state them to be such, Sorokin implicitly suggested two relevant tests or standards of judgment. One is a test in action, the other a judgment based on values.

The test in action is provided by the pattern of relations between the United States and the Soviet Union after World War II. In the first edition of *Russia and the United States,* published in 1944, Sorokin at a number of points asserted quite vigorously a prediction about U.S.-Soviet relations in the postwar period. Since the two nations were not separated by deep-seated value conflicts and were socioculturally "congenial," this was "bound to perpetuate [the] noble record of peace between the two nations, regardless of the personal whims of their rulers." Sorokin went even further to declare: "If and when these rulers become unwise and begin to commit one blunder after another, there may conceivably be some temporary differences and quarrels between the countries. But even these conflicts are bound to be minor and can hardly lead to an armed conflict" (p. 162). At a later point he commented that the same forces making for similarity and congeniality of the two systems "presage still closer cooperation in the future—a welcome destiny, beneficial to both peoples and to the rest of mankind" (p. 209).

We need not labor the point that the development of the "cold war" relations after World War II, an unceasing arms race with indescribable powers of mass destruction, and actual armed conflict in Korea, all lead to the conclusion that Sorokin's prediction of cordial relations was hardly borne out by subsequent events. In the second edition of *Russia and the United States,*[11] which appeared in 1950, Sorokin acknowledged these facts and sought to explain why they were so, when "there was every apparent reason for the post-war continuation of American-Russian friendly relationships, and no apparent reason at all for the 'cold-war'." The cold war nevertheless suddenly replaced the previous cooperation of the two countries (p. 165).

In considering this change, Professor Sorokin argued that the popular explanation in terms of ideological, social, and economic differences was not adequate, because there were so many historic examples of cordial relations and alliances between the United States and other countries that were even more profoundly different from it than the Soviet Union. It is clear that Sorokin here shifted the basis of his argument. In the first edition he did not restrict himself to saying that differences did not preclude understanding. Rather, he mainly emphasized the similarities and asserted that the two nations were "steadily converging toward a similar type of social organization and economy."[12] Furthermore, he argued that it was above all these "similarities" and the "congeniality" of the two sociocultural systems that made for such good prospects for cordial relations. We must conclude, therefore, either that the theory is inadequate and that similarity in social structure does not make for a greater probability of cordial relations, or that Sorokin was incorrect in his assessment of the degree of congeniality between Soviet and American social structure. It is, of course, possible that he was incorrect on both counts.

The test of values provides quite a different basis for dealing with the fact that social science provides no single standard scale on which any two nations may be placed, but rather always confronts us with a list of discrete similarities and differences. Clearly, the mere number of similarities and differences, however important, is unlikely to be decisive. The critical question will be the *weight* each of us assigns to one or another factor according to his own scheme of values. On this score Sorokin made his position quite explicit in the second edition. While acknowledging some important differences between the United States and the Soviet Union, he judged them to be unimportant relative to certain other overriding common values such as survival. In the face of this common interest he ruled that all other "seemingly conflicting values . . . are so insignificant that their 'incompatibility' amounts to no more than the 'incompatibility' of the advertisements for this or that brand of cigarettes, each claiming superiority over all others."[13]

We do not deny Professor Sorokin the right to his perspective, but we need not automatically accept it for ourselves. Sorokin chose to judge the Soviet Union and the United States from a great distance, an Olympian height. Yet if we get sufficiently distant from the immediate and the concrete, any two contemporary large-scale systems will seem basically alike, just as any two men, no matter how different in character and action, are alike as "men." No doubt there were similarities in the two societies as great industrial nations. Without question we can in each and for both point to flaws, defects, failures, denials of liberty, denigration of values, and the like. When we have completed such a tabulation, however, there remain certain stubborn facts with which we must reckon. Probably the most important are the differences in the freedom of political activity, the share people have in deciding their future, the opportunities for free expression of the spirit in art and religion, which in the United States are at a level that compares favorably with most periods in history, but which in the Soviet Union remained at a point very near the bottom in the experience of Western European society.

It is very difficult to believe that in the judgment of history the differences in the political structure of the Soviet Union and the United States, and in their role in the period following World War II, will be seen as inconsequential. It may be true, as Sorokin asserted, that in both societies "germs" of the "disease" represented by the disintegration of what he called the sensate Western culture were equally abundant and active. Although the germ may be the same, and the illness equally advanced, this hardly makes the organism infected the same. Many features of the Soviet system violated the most profound principles of the liberal political tradition painstakingly built up in European culture over several hundred years. With regard to these differences we cannot agree with Professor Sorokin that "any sane person pays no attention to such incompatibilities."[14]

four

MODERNIZATION IN INDIA AND OTHER DEVELOPING COUNTRIES

Considering that this presentation is addressed to the faculty and students of the Administrative Staff College of India, one must immediately face the question, "Isn't this exercise essentially carrying coals to Newcastle?" Can someone from the United States tell such an audience anything novel or useful about Indian development and the economic and social issues it raises when its members live so intimately in the midst of it, are daily surrounded by Indian life experience, exposed constantly to the Indian mass media, and engaged continuously in the contacts and exchanges of Indian governmental life?

Two considerations help to legitimate my mission. First, I bring a comparative perspective. My entire professional life has been and still is devoted to comparing the problems of development in different countries around the world. When one is immersed in the life of a single country, touched by the events of daily life and influenced by the political, social, and communal assumptions, and even prejudices, that are typical of that country, it is very easy to lose perspective. Looking at only one case, especially if that case is as close to one as one's very own country, it is difficult to judge effectively and

Reprinted with permission from Alex Inkeles, "Modernization in India and Other Developing Countries," in *C. C. Desai Memorial Lectures*, 1975–1989 (Hyderabad: Administrative Staff College of India, 1989), 141–162.

objectively whether that country is progressing satisfactorily or not, and whether the development process is going fast enough, or is going too slow. One can, of course, judge that by some *absolute* standards. But most development issues are *relative* rather than absolute. Therefore, it is a great help to be able to compare one's progress and one's failings with those of other nations that might be thought comparable.

One comparison many are inclined to make involves China, where I have recently been engaged in supervising scholarly exchanges and in addition have spent four months traveling through many cities lecturing on subjects such as modernization. That has made me particularly sensitive on my return to India—this being my fifth or sixth visit—to the exciting possibilities for comparison and contrast between Indian and Chinese development. Relations between India and China are not the most comfortable, although they have been improving, and the two countries have a history of tension. Nevertheless, China is a very interesting and challenging basis for comparison because it too is an extremely large country with a rapidly growing population, and one with a long history of struggle for independence. China is much less multiethnic and multicommunal than is India, but it too has a multitribal population, especially on its perimeters. More critical, China has been trying to find its own distinctive path to development, just as India has, albeit by following a quite different model, especially in the political realm.

The experience of China is, of course, not the only relevant one. One also might ask about the countries of South America. There is much to be learned by comparing the development of Brazil with that of India. One can also look in other parts of Asia. For example, there is a meaningful comparison that can be made with development in Korea, a country much smaller, and in some ways less complex, but presenting a challenge to the Indian model of development.

The second consideration that I hope will legitimize my taking up today's theme with you is that I am an outsider who has no vested interest in urging India to take one or another course of development. I am mainly a scholar, a student of events, not a man of action. I am not engaged in politics, and do not practice as a consultant. I do not advise parties or governments, not even my own, on what course of development to pursue. Of course I know from experience that there is no such thing as a comment or observation about a country that does not have some political overtones for at least some listeners. And so the question arises, "Can one approach this problem in a completely neutral and nonpartisan way?" All I can assure you of is that I shall try. But mainly I hold open the possibility that something of value may be drawn from the experience of development in other nations, experience that India might want to use in reconsidering, as it is currently reconsidering, the path of development it has followed up to now and its future plans as well. To make such comparisons is not the same as giving advice. For people to learn from experience, they themselves must draw the conclusions from the information made available to them; in other words, they must advise themselves.

Thinking About Modernity

Modernity, which is the theme of my discussion, is many things. As a matter of fact, you might say it involves hundreds of things, and anyone who would struggle with the problem, either from the point of view of scholarship or from that of someone responsible for national development, very quickly discovers that. Nevertheless, while modernity is made up of many things, they are many things that are interrelated. They constitute, if you like, a *syndrome,* and it is the *set* of these elements that basically expresses what it means to be modern.

In reviewing what we mean by modernity I propose to talk about three different aspects of the modernization process: First, there is the theme of the modernization of *society as a whole.* Second is something I believe to be of special interest to the Administrative Staff College: the issue of what makes an *organization* modern. Third comes the area in which I have done my most extensive work, the question of what is a modern person and of how can we make an *individual* more modern.

Some Important Distinctions

However, before taking up each of these three levels of analysis, I should like to emphasize the basic distinction between the *outcomes* one wishes to achieve and the *paths* leading to those outcomes. There is a big difference between what we mean by a modern society, organization, or individual, which we think of as a goal toward which one is moving, and the *paths* that may or may not lead to that end condition. For example, there is a big difference between the historical paths that the West used to become modern and those that may be available today. The modernizing experience of the United States and Europe took place in a world situation very, very different from that which faces India, China, or Brazil today. But even among the contemporary efforts of nations to become more modern, there are many different models. In the economic realm, for example, nations must choose from among the communist, the socialist, the capitalist, and the mixed-economy models. They have the alternative of pursuing modernization under an authoritarian or autocratic form of government, as did Russia and China, or of attempting, as India has, the much more difficult task of moving towards modernity under conditions of political democracy.

One other general point on which one must be very clear, something that is often forgotten, especially by people of the West, is that no one is born modern. No country was created entirely modern. Neither is it in an *individual's* genes to be modern. Becoming modern is a learning process; it is a developmental process. Moreover—as I believe my research on the individual level shows most clearly—*everyone* has the *potential* to achieve more modernity. In addition, I want to stress that modernity is not a Western secret. The Western experience deserves to be studied very carefully, I believe. But modernity is not a uniquely Western quality. Modernity is a *general human quality*, as you will see from my description of it, a quality that people, regardless of their religion, regardless of their cultural tradition, may find meaningful and useful.

It is also important to recognize, however, that modernity and the development that goes with it cannot be counted on to come about as a completely spontaneous process. It does not just happen. It comes about because of the existence of policies of development that are either successful or unsuccessful, or if you like, correct or incorrect, or if you wish, productive or unproductive. Some of the paths that many presumed to lead to development have proved to be dead ends. Other paths have proved consistently to lead to progress and prosperity. Obviously it is critically important to discover, if we can, which is which.

Finally, and very important in India, one cannot talk about modernity without talking about values and cultural traditions. Every country starts on the path of modernization from a different historical point and in a given physical, economic, and political condition. Moreover, as they move from those starting points most nations become concerned, even preoccupied, with the potential threat that their prospective progress may pose to the preservation of certain traditional values that people wish to retain. It is the most challenging and interesting problem to decide how to combine or mix the elements of the traditional and the modern, preserving that which you wish to have from the past while you select that which you desire to take from the present. To policymakers and people alike this is one of the most fundamental challenges that exist in the contemporary era.

Having made these distinctions, which are important in discussing any of the three entities, I turn to the task of clarifying what it means, in turn, to be a modern society, organization, and individual.

Modernity at the Societal Level

Examining the societal level, I will suggest five main themes that, for me, represent what it means for a nation to be modern. But first there is one very important fact about most modern countries, namely their wealth, which must be discussed. We should differentiate between wealth and modernity. Most modern countries are well-to-do, but to be wealthy is not necessarily to be modern. To become well off may be one of the reasons *for* modernizing, but it is not the same as *to be* modern.

Most of the countries considered by general agreement to be modern are also relatively affluent. One simple way of expressing that is to note that they have a high GNP per capita. India, as is painfully well known, is by world standards a relatively poor country. Indeed, it is a very poor country. This fact is something it is easy to forget if one lives in the more urbanized, economically more successful and affluent parts of India. In the middle of Hyderabad, for example, with its high-rise apartments and its banks, shops, and dense automobile traffic, it is a little hard to keep in mind that one is in the midst of a country in which, according to the World Bank, the actual per capita income around 1986 was about $300 U.S. dollars a year.[1] This, incidentally, was almost exactly the same as the per capita income in China. By contrast, in the typical industrialized countries of the world the per capita income was approximately $13,000. The social distance between $300 and $13,000 is obviously very, very great. The income of the typical citizen of these advanced countries is more than forty times the Indian. Even making allowances for distortions introduced by the use of foreign exchange rates to arrive at these estimates, and making further adjustments to assess the true standard of living of the population, the differences remain imposing indeed.

One can see from this how steep is the road that faces a country like India that hopes to achieve for its people many of the qualities of life that are now so widely available in the more industrialized countries. It is interesting in this connection to ask what has been the ability of other countries, which may be relevant comparisons, to come at least somewhere close to goals of this kind. In Brazil around 1986 the per capita income was $1,800, which was about six times that of India, although in many respects Brazil might be thought of as a country broadly comparable in stage of development. Looking to Asia as perhaps providing more relevant comparisons, we find that Korea's per capita income was $2,400, which is a great deal better than in India, even though Korea was far from being the brightest star in the constellation of Asian nations.

Behind the income figures, of course, lie other, perhaps more fundamental facts, such as economic growth rates. Again I focus mainly on growth per capita because that best reflects the opportunity that the people have for improving their standard of living. India's rate of growth looks satisfactory if it is compared with that of the now developed countries in the earlier stages of their development in the late nineteenth and early twentieth centuries. But the countries in the world that are now advancing most rapidly are advancing at a higher rate of economic growth than we saw historically. Consequently, in order to make the kind of rapid progress that many nations hope for, they must have a contemporary rate of economic growth more rapid than the historical.

Quite a few developing countries have met that expectation, but it appears that India has not. According to the World Bank, the rate of economic growth per capita in India for the period of 1965–1986 was 1.8 percent per year. By contrast, in China it had been 5.1 percent per year, in Korea, 6.7 percent per year, and in Brazil, 4.3 percent per year. I would suggest that it is in these differences in the growth rate that we can find the reason why India is now so far behind these other developing countries. If you go back thirty-five or forty years, they were in about the same condition that India was in, but since their rate of growth was more rapid, they were able to achieve a higher per capita income by the time they came down to the mid-1980s.

Five Qualities of a Modern Nation

Why India's growth has not been greater, and what might enable it to grow more rapidly in the future, assuming one would want it to do so, requires a complex analysis. My contribution to this discussion must be limited to suggesting some of the qualities that define a nation as modern. I think of these both as the end-state or condition one wishes to achieve, and also as the qualities that can help a country to achieve the goal of developing rapidly. I leave it to you, however, in the light of some of your own experiences in India, to conclude how far these qualities are relevant to India's current and future development.

The themes I will consider are: emphasis on the generation, dissemination, and utilization of knowledge, especially as expressed through science and technology; combining the provision of social services to the population with emphasis on industrial development; stress on the health of the population; the distinctive lifestyles of the people in modern countries; and perhaps most important, some general guiding principles around which national life is organized in modern societies. Subthemes taken up under these general headings will be introduced to broaden the representation of features of a modern country that will be discussed, but even so the list of those matters I do discuss is inevitably selective and limited. For example, I will not discuss the important topic of population policy and the resultant demographic characteristics of nations that qualify as modern, in particular their ability to keep population growth at or near replacement levels and well below the level of growth of GNP, thus making possible an ever rising living standard.

The Role of Information, Science, and Technology

The first and most central characteristic of the modern society is that it tends, above everything else, to develop greatly its power to generate, disseminate, and utilize systematic knowledge. In particular, science and technology are highly valued, and indeed come to dominate most aspects of daily living.

There are many manifestations of the modern nation's emphasis on science and technology. One is the development of high technology in appropriate laboratories and industries. In this respect, India is in a much better condition than China, being far better supplied with high-level technical personnel and institutes capable of very advanced research. But we must distinguish what applies at the elite level and what is true of the "rank and file" of the population and of the common level of activity. I will cite some data later that indicate that in knowledge of science the typical Indian schoolboy and schoolgirl lag very far behind comparable students from advanced countries. Yet it is the opinion of most competent observers that a very important requirement for the growth of a country is to equip the typical young student with a fundamental grasp of the basic scientific principles of the kind tested by the International Association for the Evaluation of Educational Achievement, whose studies indicated, as we shall see, that India is not doing well in this regard.

Transportation and Communication.   Another reflection of proper attention to technology is the development of high-level intercommunication between all the elements of society. This applies not only to nation-spanning electronic communication of the most advanced kind, but also to the more prosaic communication that goes on for ordinary business purposes by telephone, and the kind of transport that goes by road and by air. I will not comment on the air transport situation in India because there is widespread awareness in the country of the difficulties Indian Airlines and Air India have been having in providing a level of service up to modern standards and equal to the expectations of the public.

I shall, however, allow myself an observation with regard to the roads. As I have gone around the world and talked about development I have often faced this query: "Mr. Inkeles, to modernize you propose many things, but if we could do only *one* thing, what should it be?" My answer, which may surprise you, has been: "If you can do only one thing, then build roads."

In my estimation, India has grossly underinvested in its road system. The virtues of a good road system are multidimensional. Roads link the most backward areas to the centers, so that influences can go from the center out to these areas. Roads encourage people to change their mode of production, to produce more because by road they can get their surplus to markets. Roads also stimulate the diversification of the products people produce because their markets desire variety. Moreover, poor roads generate substantial hidden costs, and often these are inequitably distributed and in unexamined ways. Thus anyone who operates trucks on roads of poor quality runs the risk of ruined tires and broken springs, while the goods carried may be similarly damaged. Running such costs is not only uneconomical; it is also inequitable to lay them thus on the farmer or trucker trying to get goods and people to and from the market or other destinations.

The Role of Education.   A reflection of the modern nation's concern for knowledge and information is found in its strong emphasis on education. This is an interesting and challenging aspect of the story of India's development.

India has been a land of very high hopes with regard to education. I know of no place where government and people have expressed more hope, or where there has been more government interest in and preoccupation, at least at a theoretical level, with the role of education within development. Moreover, India is a country outstanding in giving formal guarantees with regard to education, having written in its constitution its intention to give everyone a primary education. This was first written into the constitution in 1966. Yet, alas, India's approach to education, while characterized by high hopes and strong guarantees, has produced an unfortunately weak performance.

One way to judge the effort a nation is making in education is to ask what portion of the population is receiving education at given age levels. In a typical industrial country, about 95 to 97 percent of the eligible age groups are in school at the secondary level. In India, by contrast, of the age group that is eligible to go to secondary school, only 35 percent is actually attending. Of course the comparison with richer countries may seem inappropriate. Nevertheless, one cannot ignore the fact that these rates for India do not compare favorably with those for Sri Lanka at 65 percent or Korea at 94 percent.

Furthermore, India, compared to other countries, has not done as much for the education of its women as it might. For example, in most modern countries the proportion of women of high-school age who are attending secondary school is generally at least equal to that for the men. By contrast, in India the proportion of eligible women who are in secondary school is 24 percent compared to 35 percent of men. This makes India more like the typical less developed country than one might wish. Moreover, in many parts of India, as you know, the women are much further behind the men than these national averages would suggest. For example, in areas such as Rajasthan, as few as 10 percent of the women are achieving the secondary level.

The issue, incidentally, is not just a matter of whether one is rich or poor. Obviously, India can spend less per person in absolute terms because it is a poor country. What is critical in judging a country's modernity is the *ratio* of expenditure to income. One simple way of thinking about that is to examine the proportion that investment in education accounts for as a proportion of total outlays. India is spending 3 percent of its GNP for education. Countries that are advancing more rapidly are spending 6, 7, and 8 percent for education. It seems one must question whether or not India's strategies with respect to education are those most likely to stimulate development and the modernization of the country.

From these examples it is apparent how the comparative approach can help to formulate a series of questions that those setting policies for education might appropriately address, especially keeping in mind the need for national development. Perhaps most basic is the most global question: Compared to countries that have been or are now developing most rapidly, have we allocated a sufficient proportion of our GNP to education? Beyond that there are a series of more specific questions, all requiring difficult but important decisions. For example, whatever the total amount one spends for education, what proportion should be for schools in the rural areas as against those in the urban areas? How much should be spent for primary schooling as against the amount to be allocated for university-level education? And about the university level, one can ask: Given that we are an agricultural country, are we training enough people in genetics and plant breeding, or in veterinary medicine? Part of the reality of India, and incidentally the same thing is true in China, is that in both countries, each overwhelmingly agricultural, the proportion of university enrollees who are studying either agriculture or veterinary medicine is very, very modest indeed. Thus we see that in every realm a self-conscious approach needs to be taken to the question of national priorities appropriate to development seen in the context of comparative research and in the light of rational technical models.

Quality Control and Energy Policy.   A central element in the technological milieu of the more developed countries is an emphasis on quality control. Many comments by manufacturers and engineers indicate that this is an area in which India still has to make much progress.

One last feature of the technical climate of the more developed countries that deserves mention is their characteristic profile with regard to the use of energy. The more developed the country, of course, the higher the per capita consumption of energy. This is not necessarily commendable, but it is a fact, and it is sometimes used as an indicator of relative development. In line with this almost iron law of development, India's energy consumption has been rising as it develops economically. But there is another side to this picture, and that is energy *conservation*. The more modern countries are those that succeed in conserving energy so that the amount they need per capita, or per unit of output, can be reduced year by year. Again, we may perceive here an interesting interaction between what may seem the purely technical, on the one hand, and issues of social and developmental policy, on the other. Energy conservation does not seem to be at a high level in India. In the production of any given unit of electricity or other power for a plant, or in the making of any product, the amount of energy used in India still does not meet the standards set by nations at higher levels of development.

The Service Society

A second general characteristic of an advanced country is that it develops a combination of features that earn it the designation of an industry-cum-service society. As for the industrial element, in the typical advanced country 25 to 35 percent of the work force will be in industry. In India at the present time it is about 13 percent. So India has a lot of growth ahead of it with regard to that type of activity.

A closely related characteristic of the advanced nation, viewed in this perspective, is that it offers very elaborate programs of social welfare. The Indian Government has, from the beginning, committed itself to the idea of making social welfare a fundamental feature of its development. But the ability to carry out those programs, as indicated in the case of education already discussed, has been relatively limited.

Orientation to Public Health

Third among the general characteristics of the more developed countries is that they have a very strong orientation toward maintaining a high level of health in the population. This is manifested in many ways.

For one thing, they are very successful in reducing the level of infant mortality. This is generally expressed as the number who die in infancy of every 1,000 live births. In the more developed countries this rate had by 1986 got down to as low as ten; in India, it was about eighty-five, between an eightfold and ninefold difference. For India this was a big improvement over its 1965 rate of 151, but it still left it behind some appropriate comparisons among poorer countries, such as China at thirty-four and Sri Lanka at twenty-nine. Among the more intermediate countries, Brazil was backward in this category at sixty-five, which still put it well ahead of India, while Korea had achieved the impressive rate of twenty-five infant deaths per 1,000 live births.

National effectiveness in providing for the health of the population can also be measured by the figures on life expectancy at birth. In the industrialized countries as of 1986, seventy-three years was the average life expectancy at birth for males. In a progressive poor country, say Sri Lanka, it was sixty-eight, and in a middle-income country nevertheless backward for its category, such as Brazil, it was sixty-two. However, in India the comparable life expectancy was fifty-seven—a big improvement over the past but still suggesting the considerable distance the country has to go.

In good part such outcomes are connected to and depend on policies for control over pollution, improvements in sanitation and nutrition, immunization and inoculation, and a general rise in the level of personal consciousness in regard to safety. I do not have available data on the accident rates relative to the number of vehicles in India, but I suspect that the accident rate will prove to be relatively high per mile driven because the consciousness of safety, the awareness that people should develop a special discipline of the road, is something that still lies ahead for most of the people in India.

Lifestyle in Modern Nations

Fourth among the characteristics of the more modernized countries comes the lifestyle of the people, a topic that generally arouses a good deal of controversy in nations seeking to preserve their traditions against what has sometimes been called "the acids of modernity."

Mobility.   One of the notable characteristics of a modern country is that there is a great deal of personal mobility. Individuals change their jobs freely. In addition, their place of residence is flexible and freely chosen. They move around a great deal. They move within the city; they move from city to city; they move from one part of the country to another. In this respect, India and China are markedly contrasted. China approached the problem of development by freezing every person in his or her place, minimizing movement, partly because this fit the Communist regime's conception of central planning, and partly as a means of social and political control of the individual. India has instead acted in accordance with its commitment to being an open society. There are no restrictions in India on whether you leave your village or not. Neither are there restrictions on whether you go from one city to another.

It is important in this connection to stress again the distinction between being economically advanced as against being truly modern. The Soviet Union, for example, is generally placed among the more advanced countries economically, but for most of its history, almost up to its very end as a political entity, the Soviet Union did not permit its citizens the kind of freedom of movement found in India and in the typical modern country. That creates a great potential for Indian development that is lacking in China.

The mobile lifestyle in modern countries is also expressed in the extensive development of personal and public means of transportation. When I say public, however, I do not necessarily mean organized by government. In many places in the world the franchising of bus services so that there are monopolies of a single company or of a government agency has yielded very inadequate transportation for populations heavily dependent on public transport. Where these monopolies operate there are generally far too few buses, and those that run are often unsafe in the extreme. This condition arises either from lack of capital to replace the existing buses or because of lack of oversight by the city authorities. In any event, as one may observe in most cities in India, people spend inordinately long periods of time waiting at bus stations for buses that are very slow in coming, when they come at all, and that are incredibly overcrowded when they do arrive.

It seems appropriate, then, to ask whether or not in a society such as India there does not exist untapped entrepreneurial energy available in the population, so that the existing bus system could be significantly supplemented by allowing, under proper control, private individuals and groups to use cars, buses, and trucks to help transport the people? In fact, you already have in India a good example of what powerful effects such untapped entrepreneurial energy can produce once it is given freedom to operate. I have in mind the motorized rickshaw, which is a freely available form of transport in India, and by which a very large number of people are carried every day very economically and efficiently. But in between the public franchised bus system and this more individually organized personal-level system of transportation, India has not yet provided an intermediate arrangement.

In most of the advanced countries, a large part of their personal-level transportation is provided not by buses but rather is dealt with by use of the privately owned automobile. To reach such high levels of personal ownership of automobiles may seem to many people in poorer countries, and perhaps to some in this audience, to be a wonderful achievement. As someone who lives in such an environment, however, I can assure you it is not an unmixed blessing. The traffic problems that result are enormous. The pollution that can result is also very great. If I had my choice, I would favor more the fuller development of public transport on a much larger scale, and many Western countries are coming to think more seriously of that option.

Leisure Time Activity.   Leisure time activity, as an element in the lifestyle of citizens in the most modern countries, tends to be highly commercialized, with paid activity replacing spontaneous family or community based entertainment. This is most obvious in the case of media such as the movies and television, but it is manifest in other realms, such as travel, now so thoroughly packaged in the form of mass tourism.

Few elements of the modernization process have received such intense criticism, from both Western intellectuals and leaders of less developed countries, than this sort of commercialized entertainment. I share their grief over the loss of many rich and rewarding elements of popular and folk culture, and their distress about the inanities and even excrescences that our movie and television screens too often offer as entertainment. Yet there is one aspect of the spread of mass tourism as it begins to emerge in some developing countries such as India that I, at least, am heartened to perceive.

The phenomenon I have in mind is to be seen every day at historic sites and monuments all over India, places like the Fort in Hyderabad, for example, or the tombs in Delhi. What I have been struck and impressed by on my current visit is the contrast between what I saw at those sites on my earliest visits to India and what one sees today. In the 1960s if you saw someone else at those sites it was almost always a foreigner, someone from outside India. But today when one goes to an important monument in India one sees an overwhelming preponderance of people from India itself. The Indian people are clearly engaging on a significant scale in domestic tourism. In the process it seems they are getting to know and appreciate their national history and their communal heritage through personal contact with its physical embodiment in historical monuments to a vastly greater degree than had previously been the case. In turn, this new tendency in the populace presents a challenge to those responsible for the nation's further development. One wonders, would India not be well advised to invest in, to support and improve the facilities that make possible such tourism?

Organized tourism is an effective and economical way to facilitate travel as people seek to learn more about their country. It is an important form of recreation, and one of the more commendable and creative ways to draw off the ever larger share of income the expenditure of which is discretionary. However, for such a program to succeed requires adequate facilities, and in my estimation, India has not paid sufficient attention to this aspect of its potential development. For an important example of a nation that has done a great deal to take advantage of the potential for tourism inherent in its natural and historical treasures it might be appropriate to turn to Greece. Any visitor there cannot fail but be enormously impressed with the intensity of the development of the tourism industry. All the important sites are well described and highly accessible, and people have available a great variety of ways of getting to places, ranging from personal transport to elaborate group tours of great complexity. On arrival at the important sites individuals find many levels and types of accommodation available, extensive guide services, and so on. It is a highly developed and highly productive industry, and it has played a significant role in facilitating economic development and modernization of the infrastructure of facilities in Greece. It would certainly seem to offer India a major field for fuller future development.

Some General Operating Principles

All the features of a modern nation that I have so far mentioned involve specific institutions or structural features of society. They are generally physical in nature or can otherwise be readily identified. There are, however, other elements of the modern, which take the form of less obvious general operating principles, and these may be more important than any concrete forms or structures.

The Principle of Rationality.   First there is what may be called the principle of rationality in managing and guiding societal development. It requires that one bring to bear on the solution of social problems the best minds, the best reasoning, and the best technical capacity that can possibly be introduced. In many ways, India is committed to such an approach, since its civil service at the highest levels includes a considerable number of highly trained and technically very competent individuals. But India is also a democracy, a country in which political forces very often come in conflict with principles of sheer technical rationality.

Let us use the example of making an important decision, such as whether to buy some complex and expensive electrical generators or a fleet of airplanes from either country A or country B. In such matters it is feasible to arrive at a decision on purely technical grounds, but in a democratic society the purely technical decisions are likely to be heavily influenced by political considerations. Lest I be misunderstood, permit me to make clear, and to stress, that I am not in favor of eliminating politics from the making of decisions in matters of public policy, because democracy cannot be democracy without politics. But some balance must be found between these forces, so that the role of rationality and technical competence is maximized in the decision process, and the role of political interference is minimized, brought to bear fully only in those situations where its role is essential to the preservation of a democratic system.

Striving for Efficiency.   Striving to maximize efficiency is an operating principal characteristic of modern societies. One of the great preoccupations in the operation of any firm, and in the making of any product, involves the question, "Are we an efficient producer?" Nations, of course, are not firms, but like firms they must allocate scarce resources to achieve the most efficient utilization of those resources consonant with their national goals. My impression is that sensitivity to this issue in India has not been great. Other considerations seem to predominate. For example, judgments about the initial location of industry, or about the continuation of enterprises that are highly unprofitable, evidently are not ultimately justified by efficiency considerations. Of course, other appropriate social goals are also pursued through industrial location policy, such as stimulating employment in, or otherwise improving conditions in, backward or disadvantaged areas. Even within the limits of such considerations, however, there are location decisions that are more and less rational from the viewpoint of economic efficiency.

In this same vein, it is widely noted that for a great many products made in India the cost per unit produced is much higher than it need be, often to a degree great enough to put Indian production far out of line with world prices for comparable products. Where that is the case, of course, one is cutting oneself off from the prospect of having available resources that could be reinvested or used to make other products or to supply social services. I am told, for example, that the cost of making steel in India is the highest in the world market. We know, of course, that India is not one of those countries that insists on producing steel solely as a matter of national pride even though the country lacks the basic elements for making steel, such as coal and iron ore. In the area around Jamshedpur in Bihar, the country has very ample supplies of these resources. It is then a very interesting question as to why it is so expensive to make steel in India, especially given the fact that labor costs in India are much lower than in competing steel mills in many other countries. I do not have the answer. However, it might be interesting to explore the role that a lack of efficiency might be playing in driving up the cost of producing steel in India. Equally interesting would be an exploration of the causes of such lack of efficiency as might be established.

Seeking Innovative Flexibility.   Modern countries tend to be highly innovative and flexible. They move relatively readily from one process to another, from one type of production and form of organization to another. In addition, it is the mark of a modern system that it stresses a continuous process of self-analysis. It is self-reflective and self-correcting. India is properly reputed to have the advantage of a relatively innovative business class and a comparably imaginative science and engineering community. In addition, some elements in the civil service are broad in vision. Therefore, if India is not developing rapidly one must assume that other characteristics of the society and polity are slowing down progress. As an open society with virtually complete freedom of discussion, India would seem to be in a good position, given the will, to undertake a fundamental reexamination of the structures and principles that have been guiding its development policy over the past four decades.

Modernity in Organizations and Institutions

All the features that I mentioned as defining a country as modern basically apply to defining the modern organization. The treatment of organizations, therefore, requires much less time and detailed treatment.

A modern organization tries as much as possible to rationalize its activity. It avoids duplication, develops clear lines of responsibility, and systematically measures its cost effectiveness. A modern organization keeps open channels of communication, from top to bottom, and bottom to top, so that suggestions can come up from the lower levels as freely as orders come down from the top. In addition, it maintains a good network of lateral communication, so that people are in touch with each other at the same level within the organization while observing and maintaining contact with those in relevant outside organizations. A modern organization has an unauthoritarian style of leadership, one that manifests a great deal of flexibility and imaginativeness. The reward system in a modern organization treats the contribution made by individuals or units to the goals of the organization as the key factor in determining their reward. Those who contribute more are rewarded more. A modern organization is not rigid, but rather is ready to move from one place and situation to another. It has what I call "self-monitoring" and "self-testing" propensities. I mean by that, being preoccupied with issues like quality control, paying a lot of attention to one's internal effectiveness, checking and testing whether the organization is efficiently productive or not, and changing one's procedures according to indications from those tests.

To test the relevance and utility of this model of the modern organization, I propose an intellectual exercise. In this exercise you are invited to think about an organization you are connected with or otherwise know well, and to ask yourself how far that unit would satisfy the requirements I proposed for judging the modernity of an organization. You might think of it as a simple test with, let us say, ten elements, and the possibility of scoring each item from one to ten. Then any organization could be evaluated with the test, so that if it were completely modern it would get 100, and if it were completely unmodern it would get only a score of ten. People might well wish to start with the organization they work in, since they know it best. Gaining experience, they might then begin to rate other organizations they are familiar with. I rather doubt that this game will replace Monopoly, but it might nevertheless be a very interesting parlor game to introduce in some circles of specialists in administration. Of course, for more serious purposes of systematic evaluation it would be important to develop a more objective and systematic way of making this kind of judgment. In any event, it seems reasonable to suggest that each institution in a society should be examined according to the sort of criteria I have outlined. Such examination could, furthermore, be a major component in the process of assessing progress toward the general goal of modernization undertaken by each organization and by the society as a whole.

On What Makes an Individual Modern

In a research program stretching from 1964 down to the present time I have been studying the qualities of the person that mark an individual as modern, and seeking to discover the conditions that seem to give individuals those attributes. In the first stage of our research we compiled what seemed appropriate traits of the modern person by studying the social and psychological literature. On this basis we identified a set of personal characteristics, mostly in the form of values or attitudes, but also in the form of behavior, which had been widely identified as characteristic of individuals thought to be modern in their approach to daily life. We gave special weight to those attitudes and behaviors that we felt would best suit a person for life and work in a society and organization that had the characteristics we considered modern as described earlier. This list was augmented and refined by preliminary testing in a number of countries. We eventually developed a test that could be used, and has been used, in India and many other places, to assess whether any given person should be placed relatively high or low on the scale of modernity.

The scale is very much like a test that you could apply to an institution, as described earlier, but it was used with individuals rather than with organizations. Each person who completes our questionnaire can be given a score, with the lowest being zero and the highest 100. To get a score of 100 a person would have answered every question, and have acted in every situation, in accord with our definition of the modern individual. Initially we studied 1,000 men serving as ordinary workers in industry and agriculture in each of six developing countries, including India, as reported in my book *Becoming Modern*.[2] Subsequently, we added other countries and, having initially studied only men, later brought women and schoolchildren into our samples. The latest data came from Bulgaria in 1989, where a representative national sample of men and women between the ages of eighteen and thirty-five was studied.

With striking regularity we found that the different characteristics we measured held together in a consistent way even as we moved from country to country, and from group to group within a country. In other words, they constituted a syndrome, the kind of tight cluster of characteristics that, as noted at the outset, is the hallmark of modern society and organization. An individual who was strong on one of the modern characteristics was generally strong on the others. A person who placed in the middle of the scale on one of these characteristics was generally in the middle on the others, and the person who was low on one of these characteristics was generally low on many of the others. Certainly we did not find a perfect correlation, but the general pattern was unmistakable.

Ten Characteristics of the Modern Person

The modern person places a high value on education, for himself, for his nation, but above all, for his children. Of two people, both economically deprived, one will make sure that his child goes to school, the other will take the child out and put him to work. From our point of view, the one who keeps his child in school is taking a more modern course of action.

Second, modern persons tend to have a high opinion of science and technology. That does not necessarily mean that those in our samples had actual knowledge or understanding of science and technology. Keep in mind that we initially studied people of limited education, and in any event we did not ask questions about chemistry and physics. However, we did test people on attitudes, and there we found that the more modern individuals believed that their country should invest heavily in science and technology because that would bring significant returns in the form of improvements in the quality of life.

Third, we found such people to be very much interested in or oriented toward the information world. The more modern person tended to seek out the news and to be especially interested in international affairs rather than caring exclusively about domestic matters. Moreover, they were particularly interested in questions of economic management, the ways in which a country was progressing or was not progressing in its productive efforts.

The fourth defining characteristic of more modern individuals was their approach to citizenship or, if you like, toward political participation. We found that the typical modern person is more active in politics, he or she is more likely to join a political party, and is more likely to vote and to take an interest in politics. They are also more likely to join voluntary associations including, in the economic field, consumer or producer cooperatives or other organizations of that kind.

We found the fifth characteristic of more modern persons to be that they were relatively ambitious and tended to have aspirations to advance themselves economically. They were the kind of person who says, "I am not satisfied to stay at this standard of living. I wish to improve my condition." This is of course a very widespread orientation, although it is surprising how many persons have come to accept their condition and to cease striving to improve it.

A stress on individual responsibility was the sixth element in the syndrome of individual modernity. If you said, "We have a problem in life, how should it be solved?" this kind of person was unlikely to give a passive response, such as, "I must leave it in the hands of God," or "What will happen will happen." Neither was the more modern person likely to say, "Well, the government must help me." Instead he or she tended to say, "If I have a problem, I must work on it; I must seek a solution; I must see by myself or with the help of my friends, whether we can solve the problem."

Seventh, we found more modern people much more oriented toward planning their lives. They did not take the attitude that life will move along as it comes. Rather, for them the future was more fully elaborated in their consciousness, and these images of a desired future were used as guides to action in the present.

The eighth characteristic of these individuals was that they were very much oriented toward change. They did not insist on keeping everything the way it is. For example, we asked them questions to see if they were interested in—basically open to—new experiences. We had a hard time in some places finding the appropriate way to ask this question so that it was really meaningful. We were concerned that people would find it easy to claim they were ready for new experience, but when the moment for action came they would actually prove more timid or conservative than they cared to admit. We tried many different ways to find the right approach. At one point we went to distant villages and asked, "Supposing we get a helicopter here tomorrow, and we offer to take you for a ride, would you like to go?" Some people disappeared immediately and hid in their homes for fear that this might happen. Others said, "No thank you, I don't think I'd like to go!" But some said, "Well, yes, I might consider going."

Alas, we had no helicopter that we could bring in to test their interest, and we grant this situation might have been an extreme test of openness to new experiences. But this example should serve to illustrate the basic idea. We were searching out the people who accepted new ways of doing things, including new approaches to family planning. We were also testing for readiness to use objects of a different kind from those customarily used before. Examples would be: using more modern medicines, in addition to herbal medicines; being interested in meeting new people from a different background; or being interested in visiting new and distant places that individuals had not been to or seen before.

The ninth characteristic of the more modern person we found to be what we called "a sense of personal efficacy," meaning by that the opposite of being fatalistic. More modern individuals would not accept the idea that everything has already been decided; rather, they tended to feel that by organizing themselves, by organizing their community and the people around them, they could overcome their life's problems. For example, in an area that was very arid and that had no history of irrigation, we might ask, "Do you think it might be possible for the government, or for your community, or for you, to find a way to bring water to the area?" The more efficacious would typically say, "It is going to be very difficult, but I think we could do that, we could improve the water supply; give us some suggestions, give us some help in achieving this." The less efficacious would more likely shrug their shoulders and say that nothing could be done, because it was nature's way or God's will or human folly that stood in the way.

The tenth characteristic of the modern individual distinguished them by the special character of their approach to authority, and here we found a very interesting picture. The more modern person is open and flexible about authority, respectful of it but not *submissive* to it. We consider this a very important distinction. The more modern individuals were not always fighting authority; they recognized the importance to society of having effective public authority in place. Nevertheless, they were not inclined to be abject, always to bow toward authority without any independent thoughts of their own. They were prepared to put authority to the test and say, "You must show that you deserve to be followed because you can demonstrate that you are more capable, more competent, more knowledgeable. But if you don't show such qualities of leadership, then we don't necessarily have to follow automatically just because you are *the* authority." In addition, when modern individuals were asked to see themselves in supervisory positions, they showed themselves more willing to grant autonomy to others. They would give those under them more freedom to act on their own responsibility. For example, in family matters they expressed readiness to give their children more individual freedom to decide things for themselves.

Finally, there is a general characteristic we found in the more modern person, one that perhaps sums up the whole syndrome. Modern individuals, like modern organizations, tend to be self-directing and self-correcting; that is to say, they are autonomous but are continuously learning from experience.

As I have already noted, we were working not merely with a hypothetical model of the modern person. Our research in six developing countries had demonstrated that in the real world the qualities we had identified as the hallmarks of the modern individual held together to form a definite syndrome in ordinary people. Our scale gave us the means to distinguish effectively between those more and less modern in attitude, values, and behavior. Moreover, this syndrome of individual modernity proved to be basically the same in all the countries we studied initially—Argentina and Chile, Nigeria and Israel, East Pakistan (now Bangladesh) and India. Some observers objected, however, that the syndrome might not be universal because all the countries we studied initially were basically capitalist or free-market nations, including India—even granting that it has a large socialist component in its economy. We believed, on the contrary, that in a communist country as well, all the values we identified with individual modernity would hold together to form a syndrome much as they had in the other nations studied.

To meet this challenge it was necessary to apply the scale in a communist country, something that could not readily be done given the closed character of those societies. However, it has now been possible to apply the scale on a limited basis in Communist China, and as already mentioned, we also obtained a national sample in Communist Bulgaria. I think the results are unambiguous. The syndrome of characteristics that define and identify the modern individual holds together almost exactly the same way in Communist China and Bulgaria as it did in the other countries we studied. In other words, the syndrome we call individual modernity seems to be a general human characteristic. It does not apply to only one particular national culture or setting. It is not a Western versus Eastern conception. It is something that is plain human—manifesting itself as part of the ordinary common human world in much the same way in all places.

Social Factors Associated with Individual Modernity

No doubt, given the nature of their professional responsibility, my audience at the Administrative Staff College will be especially eager to know how the Indian population compares with other relevant national groups in possessing the qualities we have identified as modern. Two items of information are available, each of different character but both substantial enough to warrant serious attention. Both give one cause for serious reflection.

Science Knowledge Among Schoolchildren.   The first source of evidence comes from the studies of the International Association for the Evaluation of Educational Achievement, to which I alluded earlier. In their project, which I shall refer to as IEA, that association gave the same basic tests of scholastic achievement, adjusted to local conditions, in many countries all over the world.[3] The schoolchildren tested were carefully selected to be at comparable grade levels across countries. In addition, serious efforts were made to ensure that the subjects tested had indeed been presented in the classrooms of the children who took the tests, and had been assigned comparable importance in their respective curricula. The IEA administered tests on a number of subjects, but I will focus only on science knowledge, since I have already made the case for this type of knowledge as a particularly important indicator of the modern nation.[4]

The IEA test was designed to ascertain how well the children knew the fundamentals, the principles, of science. The test was given to schoolchildren in three different population groups, to those at age ten, at age fourteen, and then to students in the last year of secondary school. It was arranged so that the maximum score possible for the ten- and fourteen-year-old groups would be forty. That score would have been earned by a student who answered every question correctly.

A large number of the advanced countries were studied with this test. Although the averages earned by the children from those countries showed some interesting differences, basically they scored about the same way. In these advanced countries the children tested at age ten generally earned seventeen points. By age fourteen the children had been in school longer and had had the opportunity to learn more science, so, as you might expect, they had improved their performance and were typically getting twenty-two points. Let us keep this performance of children in the more advanced countries in mind as a kind of standard while we turn to children in the less developed nations.

In the first wave of this research, only four developing countries participated, but India was one of them, along with Chile, Iran, and Thailand.[5] Each of the less developed countries had a somewhat different profile, but basically they fell into the same range, a range much lower than that for the more developed countries. We present the scores for India only. The typical ten-year-old child who took the test in India earned a score of eight and a half—approximately half the number of points gained by an average child of the same age in the more advanced countries, one at the same grade level and with the same "opportunity to learn." At age fourteen, the average score in the more advanced countries, as you may remember, was twenty-two. In India, there was no improvement in the score shown by the four-teen-year-old children. It still remained at around eight or eight and a half points. Clearly, if one wished, as I am sure you do, that children should grow up with basic science knowledge, then these results suggest that India has a very substantial problem in assuring that the schooling it offers to its children will produce significant results.

It is important to note that India did not stand alone in this regard. The other less developed countries in the study also had comparably low scores. Such seemingly consistent disadvantaged performance on the part of the less developed countries inevitably invites the suspicion that these tests were in some way especially organized to reflect the curriculum of European or advanced country schools. But there is considerable evidence to indicate that the IEA designed its tests in consultation with representatives from the less developed countries. In addition, there is good general agreement among science educators as to what is basic in science, and the tests clearly focused on such material. Moreover, one could not claim a specifically Western bias in the tests, because Japanese children, certainly not Western, performed very well indeed. Moreover, in a later wave of the study, at least one relatively less developed country, Korea, showed that being from a less affluent country did not prevent children from getting high scores on this type of test.

It appears, therefore, that the main explanation for the results observed is not that the tests were somehow influenced by irrelevant Western standards or were somehow biased against the children from less developed countries. Rather, the outcome seems to have been the consequence of one of two other factors. It seems likely that the teachers in India were not sufficiently trained, and otherwise well equipped, to help the children learn science well. It may also be that there is something in the general environment that encourages children in some countries to absorb science knowledge in the course of their daily living outside of the school, whereas the general atmosphere in other countries fails to stimulate such absorption. In any event, these results suggest that on one important indicator of modernization India's performance was far below what the leaders of the nation would presumably like it to be, and certainly below where it needs to be if India is to move more rapidly forward toward developing a fully modern society.

The Individual Modernity Scale.   The second measure of comparative performance that I would like to mention comes from my own research on individual modernity. And here, the results are on the whole more encouraging.

As many of you are aware, one popular way to explain the slow pace of economic development and societal modernization in certain countries is to say that the problem lies in the culture of the nation, and in particular in the attitudes and values of the population, whose passivity, or fatalism, or conservatism is thought to inhibit the effectiveness of national development programs. This kind of thinking is often applied to India. My comparative research on individual modernity in six developing countries cannot completely resolve this issue, because we were not able to collect truly representative national samples. We did, however, study groups comparable in education and work experience across countries. These more limited samples yielded data that can help us to develop a more balanced impression of the facts concerning the attitudes and values of Indian workers and cultivators as they relate to issues of modernity.

As already noted, we found that the syndrome of qualities that identified the modern person had the same content and cohered as a syndrome in the same way in India as in the other countries we studied. Moreover, we found that the same factors that made a man modern elsewhere also made a man more modern in India. India was in no way unique in this respect.

In the first place, people in India became more modern the longer they stayed in school. Education was the most powerful factor in making people modern in India, as it was elsewhere. Every additional year people stayed in school earned them higher scores on the modernity scale. More schooling meant more inculcation of those qualities and characteristics that define individual modernity. More schooling meant that individuals would become more interested in information, more efficacious, and so on.

Second, and much less obvious, we found that the longer people worked in a modern type of productive enterprise, the more modern they became. Our contrast was between two types of factories, those we classified as more modern and those we classified as more traditional. We also contrasted those working in industry with those engaged in traditional agriculture. In general any industrial experience seemed to contribute significantly to making a man more modern. But if he was employed in a modern factory—let's say in the Mercedes-Benz truck factory in India, which was one of those we studied—then he advanced noticeably further on the modernity scale year by year. These findings led us to propose a formula. We argued that the factory is like a school. It seems to act as a special learning environment. By going to work in a modern industrial establishment people acquire new and important values that lead to their own personal development and, we believe, ultimately contribute to national development.

The third most important factor in making people modern was contact with the mass media. Reading a newspaper, listening to the radio, and watching television are all very important forces in changing basic attitudes and values, and in a relatively open and democratic society such as India the direction in which people change is toward becoming more modern.

I am sure that beyond knowing that the forces that make men modern worked in India much as they do elsewhere, you are eager to have the answer to a related but perhaps even more important and interesting question, namely, "How well did Indians, as compared to those from other countries, score on the general scale of individual modernity?" In this question we are, in effect, facing an issue similar to that raised by the science tests taken by the schoolchildren, although, as you will see, the outcome in this case is different.

Up to this point I have data for India that applied only to men, and only to those between the ages of eighteen and thirty-five employed as ordinary workers in industry and agriculture, as studied in my earlier investigation of individual modernity. To test the effect that one's culture, as against one's material advantages, might play in determining individual modernity we regrouped the samples from the six countries so that each national sample was matched to have the same average level of schooling, and likewise matched to be alike in average exposure to radio and television. We also took account of whether the matched samples lived in a city, because there are many modernizing influences in urban life that are lacking in rural areas. As a result of such careful matching we came to the point of comparing sets of men from six different countries who were as much alike in their life experience and circumstances as could be, except for the fact of their differing national origins. Since we had matched them on all the other factors, all that remained to distinguish them was their national, ethnic, cultural characteristics.

Of the countries we studied, the people of what was then East Pakistan, now Bangladesh, scored very much lower than did those from the other five countries. I offer no explanation for that outcome, but rather invite you to speculate on it. With higher scores than the Bangladeshi there was a middle category that included Chile and Nigeria. They were very closely spaced. Our Indian sample was part of this middle category, although it was slightly ahead of Chile and Nigeria. I must say that having worked in Chile for a year, I was surprised by the evidence linking its people so closely to the Nigerians and Indians in their average level of individual modernity. My expectation had been that the Chileans would score higher. In retrospect, I think that I was influenced in my presumption by the fact that, on average, the people in our sample in Chile had received more education than those sampled in India. But when we adjusted for that difference by the matching procedure, the people of India actually scored ahead of the Chileans. However, both these countries were well behind two others in our study. The Argentinean and Israeli samples scored significantly higher, even though in their case we had also applied all of the same statistical controls to make the samples as alike as possible in terms of the experiences that contribute to helping people get higher scores on the modernity scale.

As I have already indicated, I do not believe there is a modernity gene that is differently distributed in populations such as those of India or Israel or Argentina. When you get differences of the kind we observed after matching the people compared on education, occupation, and residence, those differences must be a reflection of some other *social factor* such as religion, some distinctive feature of the cultures compared, or some other special properties of the environment in which the individuals live. At the present time we are not in a position to eliminate any of these factors. At this point, however, I am inclined to give greatest weight to the influence of the general milieu.

In both Argentina and Israel the ordinary worker and farmer lived in a country that was relatively much more modernized than was true for the workers and farmers in the other countries we studied.[6] This was in part expressed in the facts about the per capita income of the various countries involved, but it extended beyond that to a number and variety of features of the respective nations as social environments. As nations, both Israel and Argentina were more modern on many dimensions. I assume that some of the incidental influences that come from living in an enriched environment became available to the workers and farmers in those countries. In popular parlance, "something rubbed off on them." We thus close the circle. Individuals who are modern will help their nations to become modern. But nations that have worked to modernize themselves in ways, and to degrees, that go beyond what is likely to come spontaneously from rising income will provide their citizens with an enriched environment that speeds up the process of individual modernization.

five

THE GENERALIST MEETS THE CHINA SPECIALIST

Of the many lines of cleavage that divide the scholars who study human behavior and its expression in cultural forms and social structures one of the most pervasive and profound is that which separates the generalist from those we may, for the sake of symmetry, call the particularist.

Both generalists and particularists, of course, assume behavior to be meaningful, and both seek to understand it and to explain it to themselves, to their colleagues, and sometimes to a wider audience. Beyond these common commitments, however, their premises and modes of operation put them on widely divergent paths. Generalists seek that which is common to the human experience and to understand phenomena across the variable spans of time and space, in diverse contexts, with different actors on the stage. Particularists feel that one can never escape the determinacy of time and place, that even if there are some things that are common across wide ranges of human behavior, these elements will always be manifested in combinations that are distinctive and even unique. For them, efforts to generalize are not only doomed to failure but also likely to be a snare and a delusion, keeping us from seeing things as they really are.

Generalists have theories, they delineate patterns, and they postulate regular sequences; they work with variables and dimensions abstracted from the concrete situation; they generate hypotheses meant for testing; when-

Reprinted with permission from Alex Inkeles, "The Generalist and the China Specialists" and "Holding Firm While Bending with the Wind," *American Asian Review*, Vol. 9, No. 3 (Fall 1991), Institute of Asian Studies, St. John's University, New York.

ever possible they seek to measure phenomena, often selected by sampling from some defined universe, and they see what they seek as the true as against the false. By contrast, for particularists theory is generally suspect, suggesting a kind of Procrustean bed to fit the shape of which complex reality will be artificially stretched and cut; scholarship in sources, or by direct observation and participation, are to them superior to denatured indices, variables, and the like; measurement is generally seen as infeasible, or inappropriate, and in any event as inferior to intuition, sensitivity, perceptiveness, artfulness, and the critical sense. For the particularist patterns are inherent in the phenomenon, emergent from it and distinctive to it, and cannot be imposed from without; sequences are complex, variable, and generally not truly repetitive; the appropriate model for the scholar is art, not science, the goal not certain truth but a variable interpretation resting on deep knowledge.

Orthogonal to the axis at whose poles stand the generalist and the particularist we may locate the comparativist. Comparativists are like generalists in that they use categories for description and analysis that they assume are general in their applicability. Social classes, income groups, elites and intellectuals, peasants and tradesmen, influence peddlers and go-betweens, capitalists and renters, heads of households and single-parent families are examples of social actors they may look for in many diverse times and places. Similarly, comparativists may work with a standard set of institutions and structures such as "the structure of authority," "the prestige hierarchy," the levirate and the nuclear family, or a "feudal" pattern of agricultural production. Alternatively, they may focus on processes that they assume to have wide applicability such as intergenerational mobility, class warfare, or adult socialization.

All generalists will to some degree also be comparativists, but by no means do all comparativists believe in or try to formulate general propositions. Comparativists are just as likely to stress differences as similarities. This renders their statements less objectionable to the particularist, who may indeed find their categories, suitably adapted, quite useful for his or her purpose. Just as often, however, the particularists will feel at odds with comparativists because they find that being pressed to use the standard concepts of the latter distorts the distinctive reality of the cultural forms and social organizations that they seek to describe and understand.

One does not run much risk of contradiction in asserting that studies of China have been and continue to be overwhelmingly dominated by particularists. Indeed, it may be argued that China studies are the epitome of the particularist mode of social and cultural research. Being by inclination and through long practice a confirmed comparativist and an aspiring generalist, I enter the territory of China specialists with some trepidation, concerned that I may be perceived as a quite alien presence or even as an enemy who has somehow insinuated himself inside the gates of a hallowed sanctuary. My justification for the incursion is that I was invited in by the chief gate-keeper of a scholarly conference of experts on China and, indeed, was specifically charged to examine the interaction—perhaps one might more frankly call it the confrontation—of the generalist and the China specialist.[1]

A much more important justification for undertaking this assignment, however, inheres in the massive presence of China itself. Since China accounts for one-fifth of all humankind, the utility of most categories for comparative social analysis and the validity of a major part of all social generalizations must surely be in question if they cannot be shown to apply to the Chinese case or be otherwise useful in studying China. And on the other side, the importance of China in itself and to the rest of mankind makes it imperative that any model with potential for increasing our understanding of that society and the process of change within it be brought to bear as fully as possible.

Given the obvious importance of the task, what would seem to be called for is less a confrontation than a collaboration between those with specialized knowledge about China and those comparativists who can be enlisted in the joint venture. However, given the formidable energies required for the mastery of Chinese, and the special nature of the relevant sources and the difficulties of becoming effective in their use, it seems likely that more will be accomplished by infusing the study of China with comparativist and generalist perspectives than by attempting to retrain any number of comparativists in the skills and competencies of the China expert. However the labor may be divided, I see three sets of questions to which the proposed collaborative venture must address itself: differences between Chinese culture and Leninism-Maoism; identifying processes of systemic change in China; and likely future courses for China.

Disentangling Chinese Culture and Leninism-Maoism

How can we best characterize the sociopolitical system that emerged in China after the revolution and the Communist seizure of power, especially as it stood in the last stages of Mao's dominance of Chinese society? Was it, for example, basically only a variant of the familiar model of the Communist totalitarian state whose main lines were delineated by Lenin and later elaborated by Stalin? Alternatively, was China's postrevolutionary development essentially one form of the widespread process of nation building characteristic of less developed countries in the postcolonial era? What elements of that system can convincingly be explained as consistent with and indeed as expressions of persistent and deep-lying tendencies in Chinese culture?

These questions, at least as formulated here, raise issues that in their nature do not permit mobilizing quantitative evidence, and for other reasons as well should not be expected to yield answers that can be shown to be unequivocally true or false. Nevertheless, the answers to them are fundamental to an assessment of the relative utility of particularist and generalist approaches for an understanding of the history of modern China.

It is obvious that a strong case can be made for the parallels between Mao's role in Communist China and the traditional system of authority as embodied in the emperor. The ruler is relatively absolute, subject to evidence of a mandate from some higher source; his activity is not limited to the realm of mundane administration but in good part, indeed predominantly, his message, life, and person must be the expression and advancement of a moral code to guide social organization and personal conduct; he defines the distinctiveness and even the uniqueness of the Chinese way of life, suitably reinterpreted, and affirms its superiority over all other systems in the remaining outside world of the barbarian; great works are expected of him, involving vast mobilizations of the population, often at incredible sacrifice of life.

These parallels could, of course, be much augmented and elaborated. For example, at a lower level of authority similarities may be adduced between the local role of the literati bureaucratic rulers and the cadres of the Communist system. Elaborate systems for close control of the population repeatedly operating in Chinese history may be called up as evidence. The striking weakness of formal legal institutions and procedures, indeed of the rule of law itself, may be evoked. Attention must surely be paid to deeply ingrained preferences to allocate resources, and to conduct business generally, on the basis of clan, family, and other particularistic identities and associations. Every expert on China can add significant elements of special interest to the list.

This line of analysis, when fully elaborated, could provide the basis for explaining much of the history of Communist China by fitting it to a model of cultural continuity. The model can be, and indeed often is, challenged from within the specialist community, the argument being that the perceived analogies and parallels are overdrawn, imprecise, and historically inappropriate. As a comparativist seeking to rise above this domestic quarrel I would urge a different mode of confrontation, one that pits the cultural continuity model against the developmental and Leninist system models. In my view the developments in Communist China are best understood as a variant of a general process of elite-directed forced national development characteristic of a substantial number of the great populations that were relative "latecomers" to the process of forging the modern industrial national state. From this point of view the starting point for the analysis of China should not be October 1949, nor indeed the creation of the Republic in 1911, but rather the point at which the first treaty ports were established and Chinese intellectuals began to grapple with the challenge to their traditional society and culture posed by the West, in particular by Western technology and the power it conferred on those who commanded it.

In this perspective China loses its uniqueness, indeed even a good deal of its distinctiveness, and one sees the parallels between its situation and that of Japan, Turkey, India, Iran, and most notably, the late years of Tsarist Russia and the early and middle period of development in the Soviet Union. In all these countries new elites, generally organized as a single dominant party, took on the task of forging new forms of state authority suited to the task of building a modern nation; the powers of the central state were greatly enhanced, resting on expanded and effective tax collection and new bureaucracies, more specialized, disciplined, efficient, and usually less corrupt. These elites shaped, enunciated, disseminated, and sought to inculcate in the population new ideologies of national community and national purpose, seeking to spread their influence through programs of nationwide propaganda for adults and mass schooling for children. They formulated plans and pushed the implementation of programs to build national power, generally on a base of increasing industrial capacity used particularly to enhance the capability of their respective military forces. Power, prestige, and financial rewards were reallocated, and new classes emerged as key actors in the social and political process. This list of the shared elements in the common drive to build modern nation-states in countries that their new elites perceived to be backward and undeveloped may be readily expanded.

Mention of the Soviet Union calls attention to the specific path toward modern national development that China followed after 1949, namely the Leninist-Stalinist model. Certainly Mao made his own distinctive contribution in the application of this model and its adaptation to Chinese conditions in the historical time in which he operated. Among his innovations were the campaigns of momentous and terrible consequence, such as "the Great Leap Forward" and the Cultural Revolution. Other products of his imagination were certain distinctive institutions and social arrangements such as the virtually total elimination of labor mobility even in the industrial sector by assigning workers on the writ of the central planners and then tying them permanently to their work units through a totality of dependencies and controls.

Giving full acknowledgment to whatever was Mao's distinctive contribution does not, in my view, profoundly alter a basic fact, to wit: the overwhelming majority of the economic, social, and political forms developed in Communist China were either directly borrowed from Soviet practice or could readily be derived from the canon of Leninist-Stalinist doctrine. As a rough rule of thumb, I would put the proportions of such derivative elements at some eight of every ten major institutional forms and standard practices that might serve to constitute the composite we knew as Communist China under Mao.

I am of course aware that what I am offering here are rather sweeping assertions that are minimally illustrated and not in the least documented. We are, rather, engaged in writing a new research agenda for social research on China. I submit that few tasks could be more engaging or intellectually challenging than that of disentangling and weighing the relative contribution to the formation of Maoist China of the three forces here delineated: the demands of nation building in the context of the twentieth-century world system; the models established by Leninist-Stalinist doctrine and practice concerning the development of Communist societies; and, finally, the influence of traditional Chinese institutions, values, and culture patterns.

Identifying Processes of Systematic Change in China

Can we identify significant social processes, especially processes of systematic change, in China that match, mirror, or duplicate those that have elsewhere been delineated as characteristic of large-scale complex social systems in the modern era? In other words, are generalizations about the direction of social change widely observed in many of the world's great nations from the mid-nineteenth through the twentieth century applicable to the Chinese experience?

In contrast to the first set of questions, those grouped under this rubric permit the formulation of precise hypotheses that can be cast in such terms as to be unambiguously falsifiable on the basis of statistical data. This is particularly true of a general theoretical orientation referred to as modernization theory. Broadly conceived, this perspective argues that to achieve national power and advance national development in the modern era nations are moved to adopt a fairly standard set of main institutional forms, which are themselves linked in a complex web of interrelations. Key elements in this process, variably given primacy by different theorists, are the familiar complex of industrialization; urbanization; widespread literacy and general education for the population at large; heavy reliance on technological advances and their underlying scientific base; dense communication networks and associated systems of mass communication; elaborate systems of transportation, especially those based on motor power; ever growing importance of government, particularly central government, in all spheres of life, but especially economic; and stimulation of various forms of popular participation in the political process. The list may of course be considerably expanded. Alternatively, one may attempt to reduce its complexity by condensing the whole process into a single succinct principle, such as: the application of self-reflective rational analysis to guide the attainment of explicit social objectives supplemented by appropriate technical means to achieve the solution of social problems.

Of course no one can deny that China, especially under Mao, departed in many ways from the model sketched. Nevertheless, it must be recognized

that in a number of respects China in the modern era, including China under Mao, did gradually introduce, albeit in limited ways, many of the elements that collectively constitute the institutional syndrome identified as
modern. The process by which it did so and the vicissitudes of that process
pose, in themselves, a fascinating challenge to the comparativist and generalist. That is not, however, my concern here. Rather I prefer to move to another level of the modernization theory.

At this level we ask whether those elements of the modern institutional
complex now introduced into China carry more or less the same consequences there as they do elsewhere in reshaping communal, and more particularly individual, behavior in response to the influence of new institutional
pressures? The answer to this question, furthermore, has a weak and a strong
form. In the weak form a "Yes" is qualified in various ways, as for example
by stating that the outcome depends on such factors as the compatibility with
the original culture of the new ways of thinking and acting, or that it depends
on the larger socioeconomic context, especially as concerns the differentiation of socialism from capitalism and of democracy from autocracy. The
strong form of the proposition argues that the transformative power of modern institutions is so great that the response of people to them will be very
much alike regardless of a population's cultural starting point or the larger
socioeconomic context in which they are located.

I am an adherent of modernization theory, and indeed incline towards
the strong version. My commitment rests, in good part, on my experience
in testing this theory fairly explicitly on developments in the Soviet Union
under Stalin. Concerning that ideologically and politically closely related,
but culturally very distinct, society I argued that preoccupation with the
distinct features of Soviet totalitarianism had caused observers to lose
awareness of an equally basic fact, namely, that "the substratum on which
the distinctive Soviet features are built is after all a large-scale industrial order that shares many features in common with the large-scale industrial order in other national states of Europe and indeed Asia." I went on to argue
the consequences of creating that institutional substratum, saying:

> Perhaps the most important general conclusion that emerges from our study is
> that in large measure the response of Soviet citizens to their social system is to
> an extraordinary degree comparable to the response of citizens in *other* large-
> scale industrial societies. . . . Thus we have observed that the *patterning* of val-
> ues about the occupational structure, of opportunities for mobility, of the eval-
> uation of education, of ideas about child rearing, of communications behavior
> and many other realms of experience is broadly similar in the Soviet Union
> and other large-scale industrial societies.[2]

Of course what proved true of the Soviet Union need not be true of Communist China, and among the many reasons for saying that is the fact that
China, while certainly large-scale, is still very far from counting as an indus-

trial society. Nevertheless, a significant part of its population has been drawn into industrial production and into associated activities in modern transportation and distribution. A substantial number of additional individuals know the experience of living in relatively modernized cities. Even the predominant rural population has been exposed to some form of large-scale organization in the form of the brigade and the commune, which for a period incorporated virtually the entire agricultural population. Literacy and schooling have been vastly expanded, exposure to the mass media has become very widespread, and everyone was to some degree exposed to the nationwide propaganda efforts mounted by the government and the Communist party during the numerous mobilization campaigns organized over the years. On this basis—while allowing for the fact that China is indeed in the earliest stages of industrialization and institutional modernization, and that the population is highly differentiated in the degree to which it has been exposed to modern influences—I offer a set of predictions, or perhaps better, hypotheses, as to what we will find when we can systematically test how far the Chinese population has conformed its values, attitudes, and behavior to the standards common to similar strata in other modern large-scale societies. In approaching these estimates two major caveats should be kept in mind.

First, note that my predictions are limited to comparable strata elsewhere, and are not meant necessarily to apply to the entire Chinese population. Thus we may have confidence in estimating the way in which industrial workers will view patrilocal residence for newly married couples, while being quite uncertain how farmers would view the same arrangement. Indeed, in most cases we predict only the *structure* of attitudes, that is, their patterned distribution across some stratified dimension such as level of education.

Second, it should be recognized that my estimates do not refer to absolute levels of opinion, attitude, and behavior but rather indicate trends or directions. This is especially critical because the number of years over which the Chinese population has been exposed to truly modern influences is limited, and the absolute amount of change may therefore be quite modest even though the trend line is quite strong.

The Family

Changes in family patterns are among the best understood theoretically and among the most fully documented processes accompanying modernization. The shifts in question tend to be ubiquitous in urban areas for all segments of the population, but rural populations are also commonly found to be responsive to the influences of education, mass media exposure, and the employment of women outside the home or the family farm fields.

The following predictions may therefore be made for the Chinese urban population: Commitment to the nuclear family at the expense of the extended kin ties should have increased substantially; choice of a marriage mate should have progressively moved out of the hands of the parents or the extended family, with arranged marriages being replaced by individual choice and mutual agreement of the couple concerned; increasingly couples should have met at school, at age-stratified social events, or at the place of work; the age gap separating husband and wife should have narrowed; the nature of the marriage ceremony should come increasingly to conform to the wishes of the couple, and should have moved in the direction of general standards set by the mass media, probably witnessing the infusion of elements from marriage rituals in the West; neolocal residence should become the most preferred mode for setting up a household after marriage and, subject to the limits set by the shortage of housing, should be a major and rapidly increasing share of all the actual arrangements made. Although I am less confident about predicting the fate of the bride-price and the dowry, I would anticipate that the former would lose significance and the latter might hold its strength and even increase in importance in response to rising wealth in the population. It is of course common knowledge but still of comparative interest that overwhelmingly women will work both before marriage and after. The first child should arrive later after marriage than in earlier times, and the spacing of children should be concentrated in the early years of marriage rather than being spread over the total span of the fertile years.

Some of these predicted changes, if they occur, will have resulted from direct intervention by government, but even then government policy may have acted mainly to reinforce spontaneous tendencies. Evidence with regard to some of these issues is already available in the work of Martin Whyte,[3] and more is being collected by him, but this realm should continue to be a fertile field for comparative research and the testing of social science generalizations.

Stratification

A surprising but nevertheless most firmly established social science generalization is that there is a relatively invariant rank ordering of the prestige of occupations across virtually all large-scale societies. First discovered by Inkeles and Rossi in the 1950s, this fact has since been widely documented by Treiman and others.[4] The Chinese revolution, of course, sought systematically and determinedly to change radically the usual pattern in the social standing of occupations, variously stressing either turning it on its head or eliminating the hierarchical effects by leveling—at least within the portions of the population whose "good" original class background gave them legitimate status within the new society.

My prediction is that this particular revolutionary effort can only have succeeded very imperfectly and temporarily, if at all, and that in broad outline the prestige ranking of occupations in China will be found now, and increasingly in the future, to be highly correlated with the hierarchy found in other nations. Some evidence with regard to this conclusion is already available, but it remains a subject with rich potential for further testing.

Similarly, with regard to income distribution, official ideology and apparent practice after the revolution seemed to orient Chinese society toward virtual elimination of differences in earnings and standard of living, at least within the urban as against the rural population. Experience in other countries, however, suggests that there are minimum degrees of income inequality that no society that is well differentiated in terms of occupation and power has escaped. There is good reason to argue that in fact China has stayed within familiar limits in this respect, and to predict that in the future it will move even further in fitting into the range commonly observed in large-scale complex societies.

Attitudinal Modernization

In my research on individual modernity I established the fact that in six developing countries diverse in culture and political organization the same set of attitudes, values, and behaviors cohered to form a psychosocial syndrome. Moreover, the forces that generated that syndrome—such as education, occupation, mass media exposure, and urban residence—were the same in all the countries and in each were comparable in the power of their influence.[5] In presenting the evidence that individual modernity was a *general* phenomenon, and that one could also generalize about its antecedents or causes, I repeatedly encountered a challenge concerning Communist China. Surely in China, the argument ran, the elements that made up the syndrome of modernity would be different, if indeed there would be any such syndrome at all manifested by the people of that Communist, egalitarian, and in so many ways distinctively anti-Western and even antimodern country.

While acknowledging that there might be some modest differences in the composition of the modernity syndrome, as indeed there were in other countries, I argued that the basic structure of attitudes and values that defined modernity elsewhere should also be manifested in Chinese individuals even when they lived under Communism. Moreover, I suggested that the same forces that had been identified elsewhere as working to make men modern should have the same effect in Communist China.[6]

Some preliminary evidence just recently presented to me by scholars from mainland China strongly indicates that the syndrome of modern attitudes and behaviors is in fact basically the same in China as we found it to be elsewhere. Moreover, the evidence indicates that the life experiences that stimulate the development of individual modernity in other countries also do so in China, and do so with relative and absolute power remarkably similar to that manifested in the other populations I tested.

Demographics

Few activities in the social sciences have developed the precision that demography has, and fewer still have generated so large an array of putative generalizations. The best known, and perhaps the most important of these is the theory of the demographic transition, providing a model of the general movement from a relatively stable condition of high mortality and high fertility in traditional undeveloped societies, through a transition period during the early stages of economic development yielding falling mortality with continuing high fertility, followed by a new equilibrium of low mortality and low fertility as higher levels of economic development and societal modernization are achieved. Many features of Chinese population growth and location have, of course, been powerfully influenced by vigorous government interventions, including Mao's initial infatuation with the presumed benefits of a huge population and the more recent "one-child family" policy. The long-standing restrictions on movement from the countryside to the cities have also undoubtedly played a special role. Nevertheless, it would seem to be a challenge of the highest order systematically to test the degree of China's conformity to and departure from the general demographic experience of nations in the course of their modern development.

These four examples of opportunities for testing social science generalizations against the Chinese case must suffice to suggest the possibilities, which are of course much larger. My examples are not only limited in number but also reflect my interests and biases as a sociologist who leans heavily toward psychological analysis and subscribes to many propositions of what is sometimes called modernization theory. Nevertheless, I hold the conviction that pursuing the applicability of such generalizations, both in sociology and in other fields of social science, would deepen our understanding not only of China but of the rest of the world as well. In urging this course, I do not mean to suggest that every extant generalization could be expected to fit the Chinese case. Our generalizations are not always that general. Indeed, a great many are limited to certain historical times, to specific contexts, and to particular types of social system. If they do not fit China we certainly need to know that, and must try to understand why. But if they do fit, then of course their relevance for one in five of all the world's population must perforce greatly increase their claim to general applicability.

Looking to the Future

Can we identify a set of adjustments China is likely to be obliged to consider if it continues committed to the general path of development on which it is launched? Here we seek not so much to test developments already clearly under way but rather to anticipate future activity under certain assumptions.

The analysis we follow here is based partly on the modernization model already described, partly on more general structural-functional theory, and partly on convergence theory. Functionalism specifies general needs of society to which some structured response must be developed. Modernization theory points to certain distinct structures as the more likely means of meeting certain functional needs, nominating them on the basis of their established compatibility with other features of large-scale, and particularly of industrial, societies. Convergence theory assumes, as does modernization theory, that common pressures drive modern nations to common solutions, but it also allows for the influence of diffusion, the borrowing and copying of social forms from those nations with unusual power or prestige that serve as models to be imitated by the latecomers.

The peculiar relevance of these models lies in the fact that for a long period of time, especially under Mao's influence, China sought to follow a unique path in specifying national needs, recasting the commonly identified functions of institutions or creating entirely new forms to meet uniquely defined social functions. The inutility of some of these special arrangements, such as the communal pattern of agricultural production, has now been fully recognized and that institution almost totally disbanded. But in the process a host of the functions that such an all-encompassing institution previously sought to meet are, at least initially, left unmet. The needs, however, persist. New institutional forms must now be developed to meet those needs. Moreover, the introduction of new forms of social and economic activity, such as expanded private trade, each in turn brings other challenges to which some response is required.

There are effective and ineffective alternatives, but the repertoire of appropriate responses is limited. The challenge to policy is correctly to identify needs and to adopt effective programs or structures to meet them. The challenge to scholarship is to anticipate the needs, to identify the range of meaningful alternative solutions for meeting them, to clarify the social consequences of adopting different alternatives, and to track the extent and quality of the performance of government and of social institutions in meeting the functional imperatives that societies confront.

Among the demands of a modern system China may be increasingly expected to meet, and among the structures it has either not developed or so far developed in only very limited ways, are the following:

1. A system of law in all its forms, most obviously of commercial law, but equally of other forms of civil law and of criminal law.

China has operated as a society almost totally without a formal legal system as such is commonly understood in other nations, including even many less developed countries. Along with the law, of course, must go the training of a legal profession, the creation of an appropriate court system, and above all, the inculcation in persons of power and authority of an awareness of the rule of law and commitment to follow it.

2. Relative freedom of labor and residential mobility.

China's approach to labor assignment is unmatched in any contemporary society. The nearest model, admittedly inexact, is that of a feudal manorial system or possibly of serf factory labor as practiced in pre-emancipation Tsarist Russia. No modern industrial order can efficiently operate under those conditions. China will be obliged to end the system of assignment of labor to work units, of fixing those assigned permanently to their units, and of having such units be obligated, and actually to serve, as total providers of housing, foods, and other basic services. In time, some comparable adjustment will be necessary with regard to the denial of rural residents' right to move, especially to move to urban areas.

3. Reevaluation of the importance of science and technology, and especially of R&D efforts, in the development of society.

This will require not only change in perception and values but also a large program of investment in training appropriate staffs, building productive R&D institutions, and, most difficult, linking them effectively to production entities and their needs.

Closely related will be the demand for higher education of all kinds. China cannot hope long to sustain its progress with so small a percentage of each eligible age cohort in college and university training. It must rapidly increase to at least 5 percent, and within decades to at least 10 to 15 percent, so enrolled.

4. A public system of social welfare.

The need for such a system will be driven in part by demographics, as the Chinese population ages, but also by changes in other institutional arrangements such as the dissolution of the communes and the anticipated change in the economic contract linking workers to their units.

5. Development of an adequate system of transportation and communication.

New patterns of economic activity, increased emphasis on internal and external trade, and the increased levels of interaction that are needed to operate a complex economy and polity will require great elaboration of the system of roads and other transportation networks, and especially of telephonic and other electronic communications channels.

6. Adaptation of the political system to permit organized interest articulation and increased popular participation in decisionmaking of a kind more meaningful to the participants.

7. Last, but certainly not least, China must find some way to restructure its economy, in particular its industrial production and service sectors, on more rational productive bases. This is a problem it shares with all the other so-called socialist countries, most notably with the Soviet Union in its phase of perestroika.

All this, and one might add more, certainly proposes a profound program of change for China's people and leaders, and it delineates a heavy agenda for the China specialists seeking to describe and understand the change process. One must hope that both communities are equal to their respective tasks.

Holding Firm While Bending with the Wind

My effort to bring the perspective of a comparativist and a generalist to the study of Communist China led Thomas Metzger to raise three issues. First, he asked how our analysis might be reshaped if we considered not only the mainland but also took the Republic of China (ROC) into account. Second, he requested that I take a stand on the role of culture in the modernization process. And third, again stressing the influence of cultural diversity, he questioned whether the convergence of modern social systems on some more or less common model may not be much more limited than my analysis seems to suggest it will be. These are all major challenges.

The Challenge of Taiwan

There should be no objection to bringing Taiwan into the analysis. To do so highlights the issue of success and failure in achieving the qualities that define a developed and modernized society and helps us to understand the possibilities and the limits on variant approaches for achieving the goal. But to introduce the case of the ROC, or indeed of any other national entity, in no way changes the basic model, and in no significant degree does it alter the specification of what is required to qualify as a modern society.

Dr. Metzger stresses the attainment of three pluralisms: economic, intellectual, and political. This approach is attractive for its parsimony, although it is perhaps too far a "stripped-down" model. In my analysis I stressed the rule of law, especially commercial and civil; full recognition of the importance of science and technology as an instrument for development; elaboration of technically advanced systems of transportation and communication; and individual freedom of movement, both occupational and geographic. A complete model would of course include many more elements, but the elaboration of the model is not appropriate or relevant here. What is of interest is a comparison of the degree to which the requirements for development and modernity were met in the two societies, that of the mainland and of Taiwan.

Operating in this mode we may note that the Communist party and the Kuomintang were both quite successful in creating a system of effective governance and public order in their respective territories, in both cases by creating a single-party monopoly over the exercise of political decisionmaking and the application of force. The modernization model predicts that with development in other realms, especially in education and production, the political systems of both the mainland and the ROC would experience strain as social change generated pressures for greater popular participation in governance, pressure for what Metzger calls political pluralism. The structure of the system established in Communist China provides no mechanism for accommodating such pressures, and the only alternative that the leaders are able to see is the sort of repression manifested in Tiananmen Square. By contrast, the Taiwanese government had been structured so that it did not face the same rigidity in responding to changed circumstance. Through the suspension of the long-standing rule of martial law, it had available a mechanism that could legitimate movement toward a multiparty system without the necessity—almost everywhere assumed in Eastern Europe—for extreme structural change and the immediate and total expulsion of the former political leadership.

Providing the population with a steadily rising standard of living, especially in the flow of material goods and services, and a continuously improved quality of life generally, is a universally acknowledged requirement for qualification as a fully developed and modernized society. It is of course in this respect that Taiwan has totally and overwhelmingly outstripped the mainland, with the former only decades away from qualifying as an economically advanced nation while the latter remains mired in the lower ranks of the world's poor nations. This outcome on the mainland followed from the Communists' imposition of a system of public ownership of all the means of production, central planning carried out mainly by economically illiterate politicians, systematic invasion of the production process by irrelevant political considerations, ignoring and even suppressing technical competence and scientific research and development, striving to build a self-sustaining economy as totally as possible cut off from the world economy, discouraging and even condemning private initiative, imposing extreme equalization of reward and a deadening uniformity of consumption patterns—the list could go on and on.

After stumbling badly at the start, and for a short period seemingly committed to a state-centric and even quasi-socialist development model, the authorities on Taiwan early on changed course and adopted a series of measures that were in most respects the opposite of those taken on the mainland. In the interest of development an atmosphere conducive to the conduct of business was created, laws were promulgated protecting property and providing a suitable climate for production and trade to flourish, integration into the world economy through trade was established as a target and facilitated by various forms of government action, the business class was accorded honor and respect, and so on. The whole complex of attitudes and behaviors was summed up in the first sentence of a recent editorial in the *Free China Review,* which stated: "The business of Taiwan is business." A comparable editorial in an equivalent journal from the mainland would likely still begin with the statement: "The business of China is building Communism."

Much the same sort of contrast would be found if one pursued the analysis across a longer list of the institutions and practices that make for development and modernization such as the rule of law, the support of science and technology and the related investment in higher education, the elaboration of advanced means of transportation and communication, and many other dimensions. Certainly there are realms in which the mainland has performed well, especially given the level of its resources. Among these one might cite the system for delivering medical care to the population, and of managing infectious diseases and related issues of sanitation, in a manner that yielded impressive improvement in general health and in longevity. Overall, however, the mainland remains a very poor and generally backward nation, while Taiwan comes rapidly closer and closer to having most if not all of the attributes of the advanced industrial countries of Europe and North America.

The Role of Culture

What role can culture have played in this outcome? Obviously it depends on what one included in the concept of culture. If we have in mind only the more narrowly conceived political culture of the dominant elites, then clearly the political culture of the Leninist-Stalinist Communist movement would be more or less sufficient to explain the differences observed. But clearly Dr. Metzger had in mind a broader conception of culture, one that encompasses basic attitudes and fundamental values, and deep-lying cognitive, affective, and conative patterns. Metzger urged that we give particular attention to the conceptualization and institutionalization of sacred-moral values and how they relate to judgments about the performance of the political center and to the person's economic performance. It is his view that in Chinese culture fulfilling the demands of the sacred requires of each ego high productive economic performance, while of the polity it requires totally moral performance. Translated into concrete action this orientation, Dr. Metzger tells us, produces industriousness and frugality at the individual level, and a tendency toward utopianism at the level of expectations about state and governmental action.

I think few if any will quarrel with the assertion that industriousness and frugality are notable characteristics of the Chinese people. Certainly they have manifested this quality on Taiwan and in other settings in which they are concentrated and are organized in politically distinctive communities, as in Hong Kong and Singapore; in countries such as Malaysia, where they are the dominant minority community; and in the numerous other places of the world where they are smaller minorities. Whether the manifestation of these qualities depends on some conception of the sacred or is rooted in other metacultural sources is beyond my competence to judge.

What Other Models Contribute

Cultural values cannot claim to be sovereign, taking precedence over all other considerations. The expression of cultural dispositions is limited by social-structural factors. Thus we may well ask why it is that the Chinese people do not seem so obviously industrious in mainland China, a question that must rise to the mind of anyone who has seen how the workers in most industrial plants in Communist China stand gossiping and smoking in convivial clusters around their idle machines. Rather than serving to establish the power of culture to shape social behavior this experience would seem more to support the proposition that social institutions have the power to mute the expression of even deep-seated cultural propensities.

This still leaves open the question of whether in Chinese culture the assumed link between the sacred and the performance of a political center induces an easy slide into utopianism. Clearly one might use this model in part to explain Mao's rhetoric and his occasional success in mobilizing the Chinese people in a frenzied outpouring of seemingly deeply felt devotional ardor. However, taking the comparativist perspective sensitizes us to the fact that similar manifestations have been characteristic of other totalitarian systems, focused on the persons of men such as Stalin and Hitler. This in turn suggests that Mao's style of ruling may have had less to do with Chinese culture and more to do with the model of totalitarianism.

To offer this perspective is not to challenge the impressive documentation that Dr. Metzger offers in his scholarly writings that there is a deep strain in Chinese philosophy and in the writings of Chinese intellectuals, both on the mainland and in Taiwan, to demand of the state and government that in its own actions and in its influence on mundane society it must achieve the highest possible state of purely moral action. Again the comparativist perspective suggests that it may be prudent not to assume too readily that such continuity in the written tradition produced by the generators and bearers of the high culture is necessarily matched by comparable sentiments, values, and expectations held by the majority of the population. How close the connection between the high culture and the living philosophy of the more average person may have been in the past is generally not knowable. But in the present era of the sample survey of opinion and attitude it has become possible to map quite precisely and in detail the working moral philosophy of the average man and woman. Such studies could readily be undertaken today on Taiwan, in Singapore, and, for the next few years at least, in Hong Kong. There is some hope that such studies may also be possible on the mainland in the not-too-distant future. We may then be able to test Dr. Metzger's assumption about the distinctiveness of the linkage that Chinese culture established between the sacred and the performance of the political center. Until that evidence is in hand I prefer to assume that certain political ideologies and governmental systems may be imposed by force on diverse populations with no necessary congruence between the deep-seated cultural propensities of the population and the operating principles of the political elites that have imposed themselves on those populations.

It will be apparent by this point that I am not prepared to concede unlimited power to historical culture as a force inhibiting the process of convergence across national boundaries. In any event, I think it is not useful to put the problem in such general terms. The challenge to research and theory in the study of convergence is to specify which aspects of social organization and of popular values and behavior are most likely to change, in which direction, and under the impact of which forces. I have elsewhere gone on record as believing that religions and legal systems are likely to be most resistant to the forces that make for convergence, whereas demographic patterns are likely to be highly convergent in societies at similar levels of development.[7] In addition, many popular attitudes toward work, leisure, savings, and interpersonal relations are likely to become increasingly congruent. So will many institutional arrangements, as in education, in social welfare programs, and in marriage and divorce. Thus the predictions I made about the future of marriage and the family in China were based on experience in studying related convergent phenomena in numerous other countries.[8] The reasonableness of these predictions could be settled today by doing the appropriate research on Taiwan. As applied to the mainland, however, only with the passage of time, further development of Chinese modernization, and the opportunity to study these developments at first hand in a more open atmosphere will it be possible to test the soundness of these predictions and the validity of the theory that underlies them.

Part Three

FOCUS ON INSTITUTIONS: SCHOOL AND FAMILY

six

CONVERGENCE AND DIVERGENCE IN EDUCATIONAL SYSTEMS

In the early 1960s when the senior author of this chapter was engaged in research on modernization in six developing countries, he spent a year in Chile, which at that time had a per capita income of about US$550, approximately one-seventh that of the United States at the time. Since his host institution was the Pedagogical Faculty of the University of Chile, occupying many buildings on a large and well-settled site with great numbers of students, he had no cause to be surprised that virtually every definitive feature of the system of education he had known in the United States had its analogue in Chile. But Chile was a nation whose history of independence was almost as long as that of the United States, and it had had almost 150 years to build its institutions. He assumed that the situation would be more distinctive when, in the same year, he joined the fieldwork teams of his project in India and Nigeria. These countries had won their independence only in 1947 and 1960, respectively, and thus had had less time to develop their national institutional structures. But the situation there proved to repeat the experience in Chile. Even in the relatively remote and isolated villages to which the fieldwork took him, he invariably found a building or

Reprinted with permission from Alex Inkeles and Larry Sirowy, "Convergent and Divergent Trends in National Educational Systems," in *Social Forces*, Vol. 62, No. 2 (December 1983), 303–337.

structure defined and locally recognized as a "school" and someone defined and recognized as the "teacher." These teachers, moreover, could identify the special aspects of their education that qualified them for teaching; called attention to their formal certification by the state authority; identified and described the "curriculum" that they followed; and could elaborate at length on the special problems they and the school had in relating to the local community and to the public education authorities.

This experience was the beginning of a realization of how extensive and pervasive has been the diffusion throughout the world of a relatively standard set of concepts, institutions, and practices that embody in remarkably consistent ways the main features of the modern educational system. We perhaps take for granted this sort of standardization and systematization in activities dominated by obvious technical imperatives, as in the structure and operation of a railroad system or an airline. But that such consistency should apply as well in a realm that would seem to permit endless diversity seemed much more notable. It became a by no means obvious fact of social existence, but rather one whose status as fact it seemed essential to assess and whose explanation, if it proved indeed to be a fact, one was compelled to pursue.

The task of measuring and otherwise assessing the origins and development of the modern school and its dispersion across the globe, and as well, the task of explaining both the similarities and differences in contemporary national systems of education, became the focus of the work of a small research group at the Hoover Institution and the sociology department of Stanford University in 1979. This report describes that investigation, including its guiding ideas and some preliminary and mainly illustrative findings.

The general theory guiding this investigation, including important distinctions between different forms and measures of convergence, has been described elsewhere (see Chapters 1 and 2). A succinct summary of our position, however, will surely be appreciated here. First with regard to the meaning of convergence, we have taken the position that:

> Convergence means moving from different positions toward some common point. To know that countries are alike tells us nothing about convergence. There must be movement over time toward some identified common point. The point may be fixed, as when 100 percent of school-age children enroll in primary school, or it may be moving, as when the proportion of the labor force in the tertiary or "service" sector has grown continuously in recent decades. Convergence need not, however, be expressed solely in quantitative terms. Constitutions, judicial systems, and administrative arrangements can all be either convergent or divergent. There is, moreover, more than one pattern of change over time that can lead to a point of convergence. Change may also stop short of actual convergence and still be of great significance if the units undergoing the change cross certain critical thresholds.[1]

One central feature of research on convergence must, therefore, be predominantly empirical. The work must seek to establish whether various institutions, social arrangements, attitudes, and values previously more diverse are becoming more nearly alike.

Insofar as such movement toward common institutional forms, orientations, values, and behaviors is actually found, we face the challenge of explaining the observed tendencies. We also face the challenge of specifying which elements of social organization will be more convergent and which less, and of explaining those instances in which our expectations for convergence and divergence may be contradicted by our observation. Such specification and explanation is the task of theory. Therefore we pause, briefly, to note the main relevant theories that shape expectations in work on convergence.

Similarities may develop in the social organization of societies at similar levels of economic development because there are "imperatives" built into the socio-technical systems they adopt which drive them to similar responses to common problems. This model therefore places great emphasis on the level of economic development of nations to account for movement toward common forms of social organization. Alternatively, convergence may result from simple borrowing, so that a model of the diffusion of innovation becomes appropriate. Where such borrowing occurs levels of development may be less relevant than integration in networks of influence through which ideas and social forms are diffused. Economic development may of course set limits on the capacity of a nation to institute systems available to be copied, and propensities to copy may enable nations to install convergent patterns more rapidly than one would have predicted from knowledge of their level of economic development.

When fully elaborated, the theory should specify which systems and subsystems are expected to be more or less convergent, and why. We note in this connection that we expect socioeconomic systems at the national level, such as "communism" or "capitalism," to be largely immune to convergent tendencies, and among major subsystems of national societies we expect legal systems to be more resistant to convergence than family and kinship systems. Within such subsystems one may also specify institutional forms that may be more likely to converge than others. Thus in the realm of education we expect primary school education to be more convergent than the arrangement for tertiary-level education.

As to measurement, the study of convergence poses a number of special problems, but it may also be stated quite simply. The essential requirement is an estimate of a number or a "quality" manifested by some set of social units at two or more points in time. The units will then be judged convergent if at successive later points in time they are, as a set, less far apart or dispersed than they were at earlier points in time.[2] Assume, for example, that we were considering the proportion of children aged six to ten attending school in three nations. If in 1900 the proportions were 50, 70, and 90 percent, but by 1980 they had changed to 90, 95, and 97 percent, then the nations would clearly have converged on a more common standard. If instead we were measuring attendance at universities, and the numbers had changed from 3, 5, and 7 percent to 20, 40, and 60 percent, then the countries would obviously have diverged even farther from a common standard than at the beginning of the period under observation. The changes one observes should of course be judged not by the unaided eye but rather by some objective measure.

In this report we rely mainly on the coefficient of variation, or c.v. The c.v. is the ratio of the standard deviation to the mean, and we feel that using it is preferable to using the standard deviation alone because it adjusts to shifts in the absolute size of the mean, which is very common when changes over time are measured in such things as, for example, expenditures per pupil, where the mean grows ever larger.[3] By this measure, then, nations have converged if they are less dispersed around whatever is their shared, or average standard, at time 2 as compared to what was true at time 1. When absolute convergence on a single point has occurred, the c.v. will be zero, since, whatever the mean, the standard deviation will be zero. Such absolute convergence is rare, but in some instances we do approximate it. More commonly one experiences only partial movement toward absolute convergence, as when the c.v. comes down by five-year intervals, for example, from 0.43 to 0.34, and then continues down to 0.33, 0.29, coming finally to 0.26, as it did for the female share of tertiary enrollments around the world at five-year intervals from 1955 to 1975.

Our approach to measurement is not limited to intrinsically numerical measures. Qualitative changes can also be assessed by this means if the quality measured can be assigned a number, as present or absent. Thus we can quite meaningfully ask whether the proportion of countries having specialized schools for the deaf showed a convergent trend between 1900 and 1980.

Where we have data for long historical periods, we refer to whatever span we could measure. For many dimensions, however, we are limited to data for the period roughly from 1950 to 1980. Wherever possible, we have in these cases measured convergence at five-year intervals, although to save time and space the main body of this chapter gives the c.v. only for the beginning and end of the longer period.

Our results are usually reported here for all available countries in the world, but we also regularly apply the convergence measure separately to subsets such as the wealthier, industrialized nations and the poorer, developing countries. These subsets are referred to as "Rich" and "Poor" throughout the remainder of this chapter.[4]

The Dimensions of Educational Change

If we assume that all the nations of the world are converging on a more-or-less common model of a national educational system, we need to specify the major dimensions of the model so that change may be assessed as bringing any given national system of education closer to or farther from the standard model. The task is complicated by the fact that we deal here with a moving rather than a completely stationary target. Even in the most advanced countries the educational system is still changing, in some instances not just in magnitudes but even in structure. Nevertheless, it seems not unreasonable to argue that the evolutionary process is sufficiently advanced so that a fundamentally stable structure exists, the main elements of which can be well delineated and whose parts are articulated in relatively enduring patterns.

Any scheme for describing a socio-technical system as large and as complex as a national school system will require distinctions that are somewhat arbitrary. Yet some set of distinctions is indispensable in order to manage complexity. We have found it convenient to divide the main dimensions (they may also be thought of as variables) characteristic of modern school systems into six sets: the ideational and legal; the structural; the demographic; the administrative and financial; the dynamic; and the curricular. Of these, all but the last will be dealt with in this report.

Ideational and Legal Dimensions

In the ideational and legal we include ideas about the nature and purpose of education. Especially indicative are the degree to which constitutions and basic legislation treat education as a right and an obligation, assert the primacy of the interest of state and society in the education of subjects and citizens, and specify the main outlines of and responsibility for mounting, supporting, and administering the public educational system.

We feel that the evidence is striking that all nations have or are converging on a common model in this realm. In that common model, society, and more particularly the state, declares the interest of the community in the education of the child; affirms that education up to continuously expanding limits is both a right and an obligation; and places on state, community, and parents the obligation not to hinder, and indeed to facilitate, the education of the children.

Beyond these basic convergent ideational and legal dimensions, innumerable other particulars of educational systems have been structured by a ubiquitous process of legalization. As John Meyer summed up the situation:

> Laws and state regulations define, compel, and classify pupils; specify days, hours, and years of attendance; and define much of the impact of education in

later life by occupational credentialing rules. They credential teachers, and specify their relevant properties. They lay out the required curricula, and sometimes even define the proper materials. They define and periodize the conjunction of pupils, teachers, and curricula: they also specify in detail the physical space in which this conjunction is to occur. . . . And the entire assembly of elements—pupils, teachers, curricula, and space—is approved by the state.[5]

While the source and degree of legalization and its consequent standards may vary, the legalization of educational order is an important element of the common model. Our reconstruction of the histories of the educational systems of sixteen European countries provides much illustrative data on these dimensions. The initial steps taken to establish public responsibility for elementary schooling show that by the end of the nineteenth century all had converged toward establishing it.[6] Though the pace and form of institutionalizing elementary schooling as a public concern varied between among countries, all did so regardless of the diversity of prior patterns of responsibility involving religious or voluntary bodies.

Compulsory education is another element in the standard model of the modern educational system. By the end of the first decades of the twentieth century the sixteen countries comprising our historical sample had converged by instituting compulsory education.[7] Ramirez and Boli reviewed the introduction of compulsory primary education worldwide and found remarkable homogeneity.[8] Nearly all nations had instituted some form of compulsion by 1976. Those that had not, planned to. More interesting, perhaps, is their observation that instituting compulsory education has become increasingly automatic, following more and more closely on the heels of political independence. Nations appear to be converging to the extent that they incorporate provisions for compulsory education even though the particular constellation of forces promoting and opposing it (religious bodies, entrepreneurs, labor, teachers, and the state) varies greatly from one nation to another.

The introduction of compulsion is but one of the general stages of state involvement in education. It tends to be followed by increasing specification of other requirements.[9] Later stages of the process involve the continuing formalization of schooling and the extension of the period of compulsory schooling. The United Nations Educational, Scientific, and Cultural Organization (UNESCO) reports widespread similarity in the global distributions of the ages at which compulsory education commences (six years is the model) and of the duration of compulsory education, though the latter is less narrowly defined.[10] Williamson and Fleming tested convergence theory as applied to the duration of compulsory education in ten industrialized countries.[11] They found empirical support for a pattern of convergence. In 1900 the mean duration was 6.1 years and the c.v. was 0.40, and in 1969 the mean had risen to 8.7 years and the c.v. had declined dramatically to 0.07. Our replication of this exercise for the year 1980 showed that the mean duration had risen further to 9.1 years, but the c.v. had slightly increased to 0.10.[12] We interpret these results as supportive of the argument that there is a decided movement toward a common model involving an expanded period within which education is a duty. At the same time, these findings illustrate a problem we sometimes encounter in studying patterns of change, namely, that the pace and especially the direction of movement are not always consistent. Clear convergent trends are occasionally followed by periods of new *divergence*. Only future observations will determine whether the behavior of the coefficients of variation reflect a temporary fluctuation departing from the central trend, or instead point to a new divergent pattern.

The Structural Dimension

Under the structural dimension, the category we intend most fully to elaborate, we include the main features of the organization of the educational system as a whole, and of individual units within the system, much as one might approach the firm or the factory as a unit of organization within an economic and productive system.

Because the university has existed at least since the twelfth century in more or less recognizable form, we fall easily into the error of assuming that the primary and secondary systems have a comparably hoary pedigree. Nothing could be further from the truth. The elementary school in a shape recognizably comparable with its modern form dates from only the eighteenth century. Assigning a precise date at which a modern observer could recognize the existence of what we call secondary schools is more difficult, since their defining functions, such as university preparation and extending elementary education, evolved over many centuries. Formal institutions performing the former function could certainly be identified by the seventeenth century. Moreover, the systematic articulation of these three levels of education is a still more recent development, with the clear division of school levels, a precise delineation of their special role in the larger system, and the specification of well-defined paths leading from one level to the other, all being features largely developed only in the late nineteenth century.

Before this system was in place there was no standard path for progression through stages of educational preparation leading to the university. People prepared for entrance to the university by various and generally individually developed paths, such as study with a parent, with a tutor, or on one's own; at a seminary or monastery; by preparatory courses in the vicinity of the university and perhaps under the tutelage of part of its staff, and so on. Often these alternative arrangements coexisted with the developing secondary system well into the nineteenth century. The implementation of school-leaving certificates and examinations, as initiated in Prussia, for example, around 1810, delegitimated alternative paths and standardized the route to the university through duly authorized secondary schools.

Indeed, some of the structural features of school organization most taken for granted have relatively recent origins. The very idea of the "class" itself, the school cycle (i.e., one level of difficulty per year), and the grouping of children in a given class by age are all features standardized and diffused only in the sixteenth and seventeenth centuries.[13]

Well into the nineteenth and in some cases the twentieth century, elementary schools were not connected to the secondary system and thus were not truly primary schools. Elementary schools through the eighteenth and nineteenth centuries were reserved for children from lower social origins. Such children entered the system for only a few years of training, and their only opportunity for further education was in the training schools for primary school teachers. Pressures from the popular masses for access to further education were largely met by extending the elementary course, that is, by establishing upper cycles of elementary education rather than by allowing movement from the elementary into the more elite secondary schools, which often had their own special lower grades. As late as 1910 Arthur Perry classified Germany, France, England, Austria, and Sweden as possessing discontinuous schooling systems; in other words, they had not formally adopted a school ladder with clear-cut steps leading steadily upward.[14] Such discontinuous systems prepared the future secondary student through preparatory schools attached to the gymnasium or lycée, or through a private system of tutors. Not until around 1920, in both France and Germany, were common primary schools widely established and the curricula of primary and secondary schools linked.[15] By contrast, we expect our studies of the contemporary period to show that virtually all nations have moved, and moved rapidly, to a relatively standard pattern of multitiered education, with each school level precisely delineated as to function and form; with thoroughly defined paths leading from one level to the next; and with increasing degrees of formal articulation of the steps in the system.

Such articulation of the levels of education depends heavily on the development of other standard patterns and procedures both *within* and *across* the different school levels. Among these are the setting of technical standards for teaching competence, and the training and certification of teaching personnel in special ways designed to ensure attainment of those standards; the development of formal curricula to guide the content and sequence of instruction, generally applied to large regions or nationwide; and the utilization of formal methods, including standardized tests, for evaluating successful completion of elements of the curriculum and of steps and stages on the educational ladder.

When tutors worked in the home, or groups of families combined resources to support a teacher, the teacher's competence was judged informally, perhaps by recommendation of some respected figure, but certainly not by formal certification either by a government agency or a training institution. Specialized training institutions for elementary teachers began to be created by approximately 1735 in the German states. Often these early normal schools were controlled by religious bodies, and as a consequence, professional and academic competence was usually of less importance than the candidate's character and religious orthodoxy. The professional training and certification of primary school teachers, and even more the requirement of higher education, were to be developments of the future.

Today, virtually without exception, teachers must meet formal criteria, generally set by the state. These are usually met by pursuing study at special institutions such as normal schools or by pursuing specified courses at other types of institutions deemed competent to offer the appropriate instruction. Certification and licensing have become well-nigh universal as a means of specifying competences to teach to different ages, in different types of school, on different subjects, and so on. This is true for both primary and secondary school teachers.[16]

The development of formal curricula to guide the course of instruction, often enforced on a regional and in some cases a countrywide basis, has become nearly universal. This contrasts markedly with the pattern followed by the individual tutor or the small community school of premodern times. There each instructor developed his or her own conception of what should be learned, in what sequence subjects should be studied, on which books the lessons would be based, and so on. Despite the near universality of the *principle* of the standard curriculum, there is of course still a good deal of variability in how the principle is applied, especially as concerns the degree of standardization among territorial administrative units.

Within the classrooms of the same school, within schools of the same region, and within regions of the same country, more-or-less uniform curricula may be insisted on. Thus, in the fifteen countries studied by Friesen and associates,[17] the degree of centralization in the control of the curriculum varied considerably. Only seven of the fifteen had a nationwide standard curriculum, as in France. Features of the political structure, such as federalism, and peculiarities of history, rather than the stage of economic development, seem to be the prime explanation for the degree of national centralization in curricular matters.[18] But centralized or not, in poor countries as in the rich, the *principle* of the curriculum to guide instruction has become virtually universally accepted and widely followed.

The standard curriculum and the integration of the steps of the educational ladder both further stimulate the general adoption of formal tests, a feature of the modern school system that has, as well, its own independent justification. The measurement of progress by regular and formal testing has become another of the virtually universal features of modern schooling. The periodic "test" to measure progress, and the calendrical "report card," although varying in form, are essentially ubiquitous. Other kinds of testing, conducted on a formal and regionwide basis, though not quite universal, are also widespread. There are tests for judging readiness to enter kindergarten, and at the other end of the scale, tests to certify the presumed readiness for practice of lawyers, doctors, psychologists, and a host of other professionals and paraprofessionals.

Further evidence on the structural differentiation of national education systems is provided by Adams and Farrell.[19] They found remarkable regularity in the order or sequence in which a wide array of educational institutions and structures were adopted by Latin American and Asian nations. Furthermore, the degree to which nations have differentiated structures was found to be highly related to a nation's level of economic development.

The comparative study of national systems of higher education initiated by Burton Clark provides a rich source for testing the extent of convergence in those systems, especially in the well-documented cases of Europe.[20] Those sources permit one to assess the degree to which the organizations making up higher educational systems are moving in common to adopt certain practices and forms. Among the potential sources of further convergence in higher education are the general movement toward the use of the department instead of the chair as an organizational form for most disciplines; toward a multiple-tier structure, meaning greater vertical differentiation based on distinctions between undergraduate and graduate education; and toward a multiple-sector structure, meaning greater institutional differentiation based on an expanding division of academic labor.

So, while retaining many distinctive patterns derived historically, national systems of higher education will nevertheless come to have many more features derived from a common model followed in most countries.

The Demographic Dimension

In the category of the demographic we include all the measures that treat the number and characteristics of schools, teachers, and especially students. Typical measures under this heading are those describing the proportion of the appropriate age cohorts attending different levels of schooling; the ratios of students in different types of schools, such as general secondary versus vocational secondary schools; attrition rates; grade repetition rates; proportions continuing schooling at the transition point between one level and the next; and teacher-pupil ratios.

The most frequently examined aspects of demographics are the ratios of the eligible age groups enrolled at the respective levels of the school system.

These include the ratio for the preschool and the primary, secondary, and tertiary levels. Although the absolute proportion of any age group attending school may be influenced by the economic resources available, with any given amount of money a country can decide to put more into primary schools and less into secondary, or reverse the emphasis, or spend equally on the two levels. The question we address is whether nations are converging in the extent to which they provide education to those in the relevant age cohort at each level.

From descriptive analyses of primary enrollment ratios for the period 1955 to 1979 we know that countries steadily converged on complete coverage. The coefficients of variation observed at five-year intervals across this period regularly declined, moving from 0.44 in 1955 to 0.21 in 1979 for the world as a whole, with comparable patterns for the Rich and Poor subsets of nations as well.[21] There are obvious ceiling effects here, since in time 100 percent of the age cohort comes to attend primary school, and no further growth is possible. Nevertheless, this must be counted as an important instance of convergence, since there clearly is no natural "law" that would require that all children attend primary school, thus pushing all countries up against the "ceiling."

Even more dramatic is the convergence that has occurred in the secondary enrollment ratios, especially since at this level of schooling ceiling effects have been much less operative. In 1955 the mean secondary ratio for the world was 22.1 percent with a c.v. of 0.91, whereas by 1979 the mean ratio had risen to 55.9 percent and the c.v. had steadily declined to 0.51.[22] The trends in other groupings of countries were comparable, and even more marked among the Rich nations. Thus with both the primary and secondary enrollment ratios we find strong support for a convergent pattern of change.

Perhaps more interesting is whether convergence is occurring in the enrollment ratios at the preschool and tertiary levels, where, clearly, the influence of any ceiling effect is still truly minimal. Table 6.1 shows the movement of these ratios over time. For both preschool and tertiary levels we observe definite indications of movement toward more common patterns. The percentage of the eligible age group enrolled at each school level approximately doubled or even tripled over the respective observation periods, but the dispersion within the set of countries was reduced as more and more countries came to have similar ratios in attendance.

It might be objected that the proportion of the relevant age groups attending any school level is too obviously determined by the level of a country's resources to be a strict test of convergence. But that argument cannot be made against use of the ratios of enrollment in different types of school such as secondary vocational versus academic. The same is true of rates for the repetition of grades. They provide an important test of convergent tendencies, independent of the level of economic development.

Table 6.1   Average percentage of students enrolled at preschool and tertiary levels

	Year				
	1960	*1965*	*1970*	*1975*	*1979*
Preschool[a]					
Worldwide					
mean %	na	9.6	11.7	16.8	na
N		73	73	73	
c.v.		1.37	1.29	1.10	
In rich countries					
mean %	na	14.6	17.8	25.3	na
N		46	46	46	
c.v.		0.98	0.91	0.73	
In poor countries					
mean %	na	1.2	1.3	2.3	na
N		27	27	27	
c.v.		1.57	1.33	1.09	
Tertiary[b]					
Worldwide					
mean %	5.4	8.1	10.2	14.1	17.9
N	80	80	80	76	48
c.v.	0.96	0.92	0.85	0.74	0.54
In rich countries					
mean %	8.5	12.7	15.3	21.0	22.4
N	40	40	40	38	31
c.v.	0.62	0.58	0.58	0.44	0.33
In poor countries					
mean %	2.3	3.5	5.0	7.4	9.8
N	38	38	38	37	17
c.v.	1.16	1.08	0.85	0.82	0.75

N = number of countries used in calculating the mean; c.v. = coefficient of variation; na = not available.

[a]The preschool ratio is the proportion of the age group aged 0–4 enrolled in public and private kindergartens, nursery schools, and infant schools attached to schools at higher levels. Only a constant set of nations that were independent in 1965 were included in the analysis.

[b]The tertiary ratio is the proportion of the cohort aged 20–24 enrolled in all institutions of higher education. Nations included in the analysis were those that were independent in 1960. Results from an analysis of a constant number of cases are comparable.

Sources: Data are from UNESCO, *Statistical Yearbook,* various years.

Repetition rates presumably reflect the degree of selectivity in a system. We may reasonably expect considerable variation in national preferences regarding such selectivity, which would yield divergence, or at least sustain diversity rather than convergence. To the extent that this selectivity standard was culturally entrenched, the repetition rate patterns would be quite resistant to change. Bray illustrates this sort of persistence of cultural tradition by pointing out that the relatively high repetition rates characteristic of France, Belgium, and Portugal are also visible in their former colonies, whereas the former colonies of countries with low repetition rates tend to have the lower rates characteristic of their former colonial rulers' home country.[23] This cultural legacy, once it is embedded, appears to be quite resistant to change. At the same time, there are cost factors that are felt everywhere, and those should stimulate school officials to minimize repeating grades. In addition, widespread pressures to democratize access to education could act to reduce repetition rates. What then is the actual outcome?

Using data provided by UNESCO on the percentage of those enrolled in grade one who are repeaters, we assessed the trend across the period 1965–1979. We found, in this case, that the characteristic pattern is one of divergence rather than convergence. In 1965 the mean proportion repeating in the world was 19.2 percent ($N = 37$) with a corresponding c.v. of 0.52, and by 1979 the mean had steadily declined to 12.0 percent but the c.v. had consistently increased across time to reach 0.77 ($N = 25$). The pattern was comparable with the Rich and Poor sets of nations, although the mean proportion actually repeating in the Poor set was considerably higher at each observation point.[24]

Stimulated by this clear instance of divergence we further explored the demographic realm by examining two additional measures: pupils-to-teacher ratios, and the comprehensiveness of secondary schools.

Ratios of the number of pupils per teacher indicate average national class sizes. Class sizes may reflect distinct national preferences for particular instructional styles. For example, larger classes tend to require something like the lecture method, whereas the smaller classes lend themselves to more individual instruction. On the other hand, factors affecting the supply of teachers may be critical. Among more advanced societies, where enrollments have virtually ceased to grow, the teacher training system is well established, and abundant resources are available to absorb the major cost of schooling, which is teacher remuneration. Therefore, we might very well expect pupils-to-teacher ratios to decline and stabilize at some "rational" minimum.

We are fortunate in having data on pupils-to-teacher ratios for European nations covering a long time span. We find that the ratios sharply declined over the course of the past century and also showed a strong convergent trend. The average European class size was 60.4 students per teacher in

1860, with a c.v. of 0.41. Over the next one hundred years the average class size declined to 27.7 and the c.v. to 0.22. This trend was equally evident among both Western and Eastern European nations. Interestingly, the postwar divergence of Western and Eastern Europe in terms of political-economic systems has not been reflected in any divergence in their pupils-to-teacher ratios.[25]

However, turning to worldwide data and to a shorter contemporary period, we found a different pattern. Class size showed continuous declines, but there was no clear evidence of convergence. For the world in 1955 the average pupils-to-teacher ratio at the primary level was 33.3, with a corresponding c.v. of 0.28 ($N = 77$). By 1979 the average had dropped to 27.6 pupils per teacher, but the c.v. had slightly risen to 0.35, although its path of change was irregular between these time points. This pattern of change also applied to the sets of Rich and Poor countries, although for the latter the mean was naturally considerably larger.[26] These figures show that although a general downward movement of average national class sizes is quite evident, a corresponding pattern of convergence is not occurring worldwide in the contemporary period as clearly as it did in the past century of the European experience. Whether the European experience of convergence will prove unique, or instead foreshadows what is likely to happen later in other regions and worldwide, can only be judged after the passage of a longer span of time.

Last under the category of demographics, we offer a brief look into the degree of comprehensiveness of secondary schools. We perceive, as have others, such as Levin,[27] a movement toward comprehensiveness in the secondary school. The primary quantitative indicator of comprehensiveness is the proportion of secondary pupils enrolled in vocational as opposed to general academic programs. The larger this proportion is, the lower the comprehensiveness of the secondary school system is considered to be. Comprehensiveness in the secondary school can also be reflected in more qualitative features, for example, policies of selection, rules of interprogram transfer, and rights or opportunities for access to higher education. Comprehensiveness is therefore a multidimensional feature of the secondary school.

Looking to the quantitative trends, we find that everywhere except in the Eastern European countries there is moderate movement to increase the role of the comprehensive secondary school. In 1955, exclusive of Eastern Europe, the world had a mean proportion of students enrolled in vocational programs of 23.7 percent with a c.v. of 0.61 ($N = 58$). By 1975 the average had declined to 17.5 percent, although the c.v. had moved upward to end at 0.77 ($N = 49$). In brief, the trend was moderately *divergent*. The trends over the five observation points (1955–1975) for the Rich and Poor sets of nations were quite similar, although the proportion enrolled in vocational programs was smaller and declined more dramatically for the Poor group of nations.[28] Clearly, considerable variability persists in this indicator of comprehensiveness, even though most nations now have a somewhat lower proportion of students in vocational programs. The major exceptions to this trend was in the nations of the Eastern European communist bloc. The proportions of secondary school pupils they kept in vocational forms continued to be in the 50 to 60 percent range throughout the twenty-year period from 1955 to 1975. This represents an important instance where the type of political-economic system rather than the level of economic advancement evidently was the decisive factor in generating a divergent pattern.

Looking at the qualitative indicators, however, one gets a rather different impression. Those indicators suggest that comprehensiveness is rapidly gaining in popularity and that most nations are converging on the model of more comprehensive secondary schooling. This comes about without being reflected in the numbers just described, because many nations preserve the outward form of the vocational school while transforming its character. As a result, many students are on the official lists as enrolled for vocational education when in fact their program and status are less and less distinguishable from those of students in nonvocational schools. For example, the age at which the choice of a strictly vocational track must be entered is postponed until later and later in the student's career; students are less locked into their track, being more free to switch over to the nonvocational school at many points; and the graduate of vocational school, rather than finding his or her program terminal, is permitted to go on to advanced, that is, tertiary-level, education. Such trends have been noted and documented in many advanced countries, including Denmark, Sweden, Yugoslavia, and Japan.[29]

Administrative and Financial Dimensions

An increasingly complex administrative and financial structure is another feature associated with the modern school system. Here we consider the governance of the individual school, its relationship to some community, and its integration into some larger system of education at local, regional, and national levels. The levels at which decisionmaking and control are located and the character of the participants regularly involved are of special interest as patterns of governance in school systems. The financing of these structures is also of interest. We include in this realm the forms of fund-raising, the balance between public and private contributions to education, the distribution of responsibility for fund-raising across the levels of public authorities, and the expenditure on education relative to other public goods.

Certain elements and characteristics of educational administration and governance have become nearly universal. These include the presence of a national ministry, department, or office of education; a national, regional, and/or state level substructure charged with actually administering and co-ordinating the individual schools; a system of inspection; and a specialized position within each school, such as that of a principal or schoolmaster, whose occupant is charged with school management.

Knowing only the contemporary situation, we might be lulled into taking these features for granted. Certainly one is tempted to do so on discovering that Adams and Farrell's 1967 study of seventy-seven developing nations, mostly those not long independent, found that 99 percent had already established a ministry of education, and 95 percent had an inspectorate. Thus it appears completely natural in the *modern* world for the government to get into education and to create a ministry of education more or less simultaneously. But the record of history reveals quite a different picture. Our review of the educational histories of many European nations revealed numerous instances of a long lapse between the entrance of public authorities into the arena of schooling and the establishment of a ministry of education or its equivalent. England and Prussia are but two examples. In England, public authorities entered the arena of schooling by founding a national system of grants in 1833, but not until 1870 was a government inspection made mandatory, and only in 1899 was the Board of Education established. In Prussia, public responsibility for schooling was ushered in with the General School Regulations of 1763, but the creation of a department of education was delayed until 1817. Newer nations that more recently inaugurated their public educational systems, in contrast, tend to adopt such institutions as if they were automatically part of any modern educational system.

Although these features are now global, there remains substantial variation in national systems of educational administration and governance. They differ greatly in the scope and nature of the participation in the administrative process that they permit or require of members of the community. They also differ considerably in the degree to which their schools are controlled from a central authority or are the responsibility of the local communities in which the educational establishments are situated. A few examples will demonstrate the variability.

Inspectors are widely used by governments and other authorities to ensure conformity to standards and curriculum. Thus Friesen and colleagues[30] found that all fourteen of the nations they studied had a system of inspection.[31] Nevertheless, among these fourteen nations six distinct arrangements were represented, expressing a combination of local, state, and/or national control of the inspectors. The arrangements ranged from "local only," as in the United States, to "national only," as in Israel. Four nations did not possess local governing boards at all. The remaining ten possessed either local school boards or local school advisory committees.

National variations in the representation of groups on administrative bodies, and in the participation of groups in educational decisionmaking, are extensive. Considering the representation and power of teachers on public bodies affecting education, Passow and associates found considerable differences in the eighteen nations they studied.[32] They developed a summary score based on five areas of decisionmaking, with a maximum possible score of 4.0. England ranked highest among the set of more advanced nations with a score of 2.1, and Belgium ranked lowest with a score of 0.8. Among the few developing nations examined in this project a comparable range was found, with Chile ranking highest (score 2.0) and Iran lowest (score 0.6). Given this outcome, it seems appropriate to conclude that this dimension is not a simple function of economic development. They also examined the occupational and social position of those regularly participating in the decisionmaking process for designing the primary school curriculum. Again there was significant variation. Though ministry officials participated to some degree nearly everywhere, the eighteen nations differed a great deal on whether such groups as church officials, political groups, professors of education, or the teacher-training faculty regularly participated.

We have presented evidence of a considerable movement toward a common set of basic administrative structures and positions, but we also find great variation in national administrative arrangements and patterns of governance in education. While we acknowledge variation, we are led by the convergence perspective to ask: Are these variations diminishing? In other words, are nations reforming structures and patterns of administration and finance so as to lessen the differences stemming from their diverse political systems and historical traditions? Both our review of the literature and our preliminary research findings suggest that the answer is yes. In this context, alas, we cannot *prove* the point, but it should help to illustrate it by calling attention to the convergence that has been occurring in the control of public mass schooling.

In the control of the schools it is clear that nations differ considerably in how they divide administrative labor and authority among the different levels of government. Some distribute authority and responsibility largely to upper levels of government and are in that sense more centralized. France, Belgium, Italy, and Sweden fall in this category. Others distribute authority and responsibility largely to lower levels of government. Among those more decentralized are Canada, the United States, and Switzerland.[33] Within this framework, convergence can result from two types of redistribution of authority. The first occurs where more centralized agencies delegate responsibility to regional or local levels, and the second occurs where more decentralized local units yield their authority to regional or central control. The evidence suggests past and continuing convergence in both types of movement.

Movement toward the delegation of authority to lower bodies by more centralized systems is documented by several studies. An investigation by

UNESCO concluded that in systems dominated by the central government there is a tendency to increase the importance of local and regional organs of educational administration.[34] This administrative reform is accomplished by empowering regional offices to make decisions in local matters on the basis of existing policies of the ministry. Central governments are also delegating authority and responsibility for certain matters, or for certain levels of schooling such as the primary, to local communities. Some of the nations within which these reforms were observed are Australia, the countries of Eastern Europe, New Zealand, and Thailand.

Coombs and Merritt[35] and Beattie[36] report that central authorities, at least among more advanced societies, are moving to strengthen local involvement in and control of the schools. They note an expansion, starting in the 1960s, of parental participation in the management and control of schools within the more centralized systems of France, Italy, and Sweden.

At the other end of this U-shaped distribution we find a corresponding tendency on the part of more decentralized systems to go in the opposite direction by expanding the control and responsibility for education at the higher levels of government. The United States provides one important example of this tendency, and the available cross-national data suggest that the tendency is widespread. Ramirez and Boli report that national political control (or centralization) over primary and also secondary education tended to increase around the world in the period from 1955 to 1965.[37] Given that many countries had already established high levels of national political control, their evidence suggests that convergence is occurring through the redistribution of responsibility, this time upward, within more decentralized systems. Of course if centralized systems are decentralizing, and decentralized systems are moving to greater centralization, the ultimate outcome is likely to be convergence on some middle ground.

Closely related to the responsibility of public authorities for educational administration is their responsibility for educational financing. Everywhere this financial burden has grown as a result of several important characteristics of schooling in the modern world. Not only has the proportion of children in schools gone up, but also an ever larger proportion of them are now in public schools and hence must be carried by the public budget.[38] Public authorities, relying on a limited tax base, nevertheless become responsible for the schooling costs of ever more children as public education spreads and, in addition, must rely on ever more expensive labor. Second, there has been a steady move to eliminate supplemental sources of funds, such as fees paid by parents. This source of revenue, formerly available to school authorities, is now largely gone as a result of the widespread introduction of free schooling for the full span of compulsory education.[39] Finally, the public financial burden has grown as the number of years that people spend in school increases, especially because this extends the period of free schooling into the more costly secondary levels.

Given these facts, we might well expect the typical proportion of the gross national product represented by the public expenditure on education to be an ever increasing number. And so it is. This proportion actually doubled between 1955 and 1979. Worldwide the mean proportion in 1955 was 2.2 percent ($N = 42$) with a c.v. of 0.47, while in 1979 the mean had risen to 4.8 percent ($N = 31$) and the c.v. was 0.44. This is an example where the world trend was not convergent, but convergence was discernible among a subset of Rich nations in which the mean rose from 2.7 to 6.0 percent over the period of 1955 to 1979 and the c.v. declined from 0.40 to 0.27.[40] This situation was created by the fact that the early laggers in proportional spending (for example, Italy, Switzerland, Australia) closed the gap between themselves and the early leaders (for example, Canada and Japan). Nevertheless, any conclusions must remain tentative because these measures do not include expenditures for privately run schools except insofar as they are publicly supported.

Even if the proportion of national product expended for education is identical in two nations, they may still differ dramatically in the mode of fund-raising (or the source of funds), and in the distribution of financial responsibility among levels of government. Nations especially differ as to whether the funds for financing education are derived exclusively from general receipts or from special education taxes in addition to general receipts. Among those that levy special taxes, furthermore, they vary in whether the taxes are national, state, or local.[41]

Nations also vary in the degree to which their systems of educational finance are centralized, that is, the degree to which the share of educational funds contributed by local levels of government is small or large relative to the contributions by the regional (or state) level and especially by the central government.[42] For example, the proportion of all public (as contrasted with private) expenditure on education provided by the central or federal, as against local, government in 1965 was 81 percent in Italy, 69 percent in Sweden, 64 percent in Colombia, 36 percent in Japan, and 12 percent in Canada.[43] Such extreme national differences in the distribution of financing responsibility are usually attributed to the structure of the political system as being either federal or unitary. In addition, it is generally assumed that poorer nations, lacking resources at local levels, and nations under strong pressures to achieve equality in education, use centralized control of expenditure to compensate for regional differences in wealth and thus achieve their national policy objectives.[44]

Our concern is to see whether these differences are becoming less marked, and whether nations may be moving toward a more nearly common standard. A number of observations suggest that they are.

Edding's conclusions are representative of those arising from research on this topic. Observing changes in the distribution of educational expenditure by levels of government for a considerable number of countries, and for pe-

riods of up to eighty years in some cases, he described the dominant pattern
of change as follows:

> A number of highly developed countries, therefore, seem to be moving toward
> a compromise. Some having had, in general, a highly centralized system of fi-
> nance, are tending to recognize the exceptional needs of education by delegat-
> ing to lower levels of government some responsibility in this field. Other coun-
> tries, which have in the past had a strong dominance of the lower levels of
> government in the finance of education, have given, in recent times, more influ-
> ence to the central finance of education.[45]

Edding thus points to a pattern similar to that we noted as applying to
the convergent movement of the administrative system, as centralized and
decentralized systems move toward each other and thus seem likely to
reach some future common ground.

Interpersonal and Institutional Dynamics

Our category of dynamics encompasses mainly measures of attitude and
value and patterns of interpersonal relations between and among teachers,
pupils, administrators, and parents as actors in the formal educational enterprise.

Among the issues of interest are the treatment of pupils by teachers, especially as they may respond to the pupil's social class or ethnic origins; the
conception of and approach to "order" in the classroom and the school, including approaches conceived as more or less "democratic" and "authoritarian"; rules concerning forms of address and signs of respect as well as
those involving dress codes; the education of women and the acceptance of
coeducation, that is, of mixing of the sexes in school and classroom and of
equality in the choice of subject by the sexes. Other forms of inequality organized around regional, ethnic, and religious differences will be considered in this context. We also include here parental conceptions of education
and their involvement in the child's education.

Unfortunately, we cannot hope to find strictly comparable data across
nations and time on many of these dynamic aspects of education because
they are not measured in government statistics and there are very few research studies that deal systematically with these issues in a cross-national
perspective. Those few that do, moreover, have mostly not been repeated
over time, and hence are not well suited to our purpose.

Although attitude, value, and interpersonal relations patterns will be difficult to document, we expect to be able to show numerous instances of
convergence in these realms as well. Three related topics concerning which
we expect to find evidence of convergence are teacher attitudes, classroom
dynamics, and instructional styles. Specific teacher attitudes and opinions

worth pursuing are those that deal with: qualities a teacher believes he or she should foster in a child; methods to improve the teacher-child relationship; and the perceived major problems of teaching. The Organization for Comparative Social Research (OCSR) survey of teachers in seven advanced nations provides a benchmark for further observations on precisely these teacher attitudes.[46] We are inclined to assume that these nations are converging in the desire of their teachers to foster self-development in their pupils rather than qualities such as deference and obedience.

Classroom dynamics, in particular patterns of relationships between teacher and pupil, have also received very limited comparative study. Pupils' rights and the degree to which the teacher stands in loco parentis are two aspects worth pursuing because we believe them to have important implications for the issues of order in the school and classroom. The United States, Germany, and England were characterized with regard to those issues for the period around 1910 by Monroe,[47] providing us with a benchmark. Though it was then clear that marked similarities had already developed, many striking differences were still evident. For example, the pupil's obligation for proper deportment and the extraschool scope of the teacher's authority varied greatly among the three nations. We wonder, then, whether the process of homogenization has continued, and spread to other advanced societies, or whether such differences have persisted.

The instruction styles employed in the classroom have likewise not been extensively studied cross-nationally. This topic includes the style for delivering lessons and the teacher's and pupil's conception of the pupil's role as learner. These together do much to shape interpersonal dynamics at the classroom level. It is generally believed that instructional styles vary between the industrialized and the developing countries, with the former utilizing individuation as the guiding principle and the latter employing more traditional rote methods and "whole-class" techniques.[48] But we do not have data measuring these tendencies over time as a basis for assessing convergent and divergent tendencies.

We consider the participation of women in education, and especially in coeducation, one of the most important aspects of equality in education. We are confident that a worldwide movement toward coeducation has occurred, and continues to occur, despite substantial differences in the policies with which different countries began their national education systems.[49] For the end of the nineteenth century Lange[50] reported considerable variation among leading nations of the world in the percentage of elementary schools operating on a coeducational basis. The United States was the most progressive with an estimated 98 percent of the schools coeducational, followed, in order, by Austria (88 percent), Switzerland (85 percent), Germany (Prussia) (73 percent), England (68 percent), France (24 percent), and Italy (18 percent). This great diversity reflected religious and other cultural differences. Despite the fact that most of those religious differences persisted, by the late 1960s all but France had come to be located within the set having 80–100 percent of its schools in the coeducational category. And even France had reached 57 percent.[51] Here we have a striking instance of convergence that future research should be able to confirm and document.

A distinct although closely related issue concerns the proportionate representation of women in education. Data collected by UNESCO from the 1950s to the 1980s showed that, especially among the richer, more industrialized countries, the female shares of both primary and secondary enrollments were very near the ceiling of approximately 50 percent, with very little variation across nations.[52] In fact, the female shares at the primary level, at least among the more industrialized nations, had already come up to the ceiling by the early 1930s.[53] Female shares at the secondary level, however, were considerably more heterogeneous around the early 1930s, reflecting differences that had persisted from the 1880s.[54] Thus convergence toward sexual parity in school participation has characterized advanced societies over almost the whole of this century, coming first at the primary level and then the secondary.

The movement toward sexual parity in participation in higher education is a more recent phenomenon. Women first gained formal rights for systematic entrance to the universities of European countries within a surprisingly short time span, with most countries first granting access on an equal basis during the period of 1870 to 1900. Switzerland led the movement in 1867, with Germany one of the last to adopt the common policy, acting only after 1890. Within the world today there is almost universal agreement on the legal right of women to have access to higher education. Except for some Arab states, worldwide convergence on this issue is virtually absolute.

Nevertheless, the consequences of this policy for actual female participation rates have been quite variable historically. To answer the question of whether nations are converging in the proportion of women enrolled at the level of higher education, we may start with data compiled by Hans for seventeen nations that allow us to go back in time to the early 1930s.[55] At that time the mean female share was 23.3 percent and the c.v. 0.38. By 1955 the mean proportion of female participation in higher education for the same seventeen more industrialized countries was 25.9 percent, and had steadily increased to 38.8 percent by 1975. Concurrently the coefficients of variation steadily declined at five-year intervals from 0.28 to 0.14.[56] If, despite a break in continuity, we are permitted to consider these two sets of figures as though they represented one long continuous time series, then that series provides striking empirical support for a pattern of convergence. These trends should be further documented and the inquiry extended to assess convergence in the curricula of female and male institutions, and in patterns of subject matter specialization by sex in higher education.[57]

Equality of access to higher education may, quite obviously, also be evaluated from the standpoint of social class origins. The Organization for Economic Cooperation and Development (OECD) developed crude figures describing the chances of access to higher education for a child from a working-class background relative to those of a child from a professional or managerial-class background for two periods, one around 1960 and the other for a decade later, around 1970.[58] Concentrating on the eleven countries that provided data at both times, we find the following: In 1960 the average estimated ratio of chances to enter higher education was 36:1, with a range of 8:1 (United States) to 83:1 (France); by 1970 the ratio was down to 14:1, with a range of 2:1 in the United Kingdom to 28:1 in Luxembourg. Accompanying the improved chances of access for a child of working-class background was a declining coefficient of variation. In 1960 is was 0.84, whereas by 1970 it was down to 0.71. This is therefore another incidence of apparent convergent movement.[59]

Finally, under the category of dynamics, we may briefly note conceptions of education held by parents and parents' involvement in the child's education. We believe that it will be possible eventually to show convergent tendencies in parental conceptions of the goals and purposes of education, with general movement from a primary focus on education as mainly of instrumental value to an increasing emphasis on education either for the fuller development of the person or "for its own sake." A few preliminary surveys exist (for example, Hastings and Hastings)[60] and will provide data for cross-sectional evaluation as well as a basis for future longitudinal comparisons.

Conclusions

In the light of the evidence we have presented it is clear that the tendency for national educational systems to converge on common structures and practices is pervasive and deep. It is manifested at all levels of the educational system and affects virtually every major aspect of that system. Not all of this movement, however, is true convergence, in which all the nations come to some single point with very little variation around their central tendency. There are also many instances of parallel change, in which the nations move together toward some new standard, but remain as dispersed around this new norm as they were around the old. Moreover, the record also shows some movement contrary to our expectation, in instances in which educational systems diverge rather than converge with the passage of time. The pattern revealed by the evidence examined in this chapter is summarized in Table 6.2.

Documenting the extent and penetration of convergent tendencies, as we have done, does not of course explain the observed tendencies. Rather it es-

Table 6.2 Testing for convergence in educational systems

Educational Dimension	Pattern of Change[a]	Comment
Ideational and Legal		
Public responsibility	C	
Provision for compulsory education	C	
Duration of compulsory schooling	C	Renewed divergence among more advanced countries?
Structural		
"School" forms	C	
Articulated ladder structure	C	
Preparation and certification of teachers	C	Variability in professional and academic training
Principle of standard curriculum	C	Variability in central control and standardization
Formal tests	C	Universally used; variability in type and function
Organization of higher education	V	Except for a few structures, distinctive forms persist
Demographic		
Enrollment ratios	C	Most characteristic of primary and secondary levels
Repetition rates	D	
Students-to-teacher ratios	M	Europe converges historically; recent data: no convergence
Secondary school comprehensiveness	M	Divergence in vocational shares; convergence on principle indicated by qualitative changes
Administrative-Financial		
Ministry of education	C	Variability in role
Inspectorate	C	Variability in level of government responsible
Local governing boards	V	Some do not have; others vary in type
Teacher power and participation	V	
Participants in decisionmaking	V	
Administrative responsibility by level of government	c	Slow movement to a middle ground

Free public schooling	C	Strongest convergence among most advanced
Public expenditure/GNP	c	Special taxes vs. general receipts
Mode of fund-raising	V	
Financing centralization	c	Slow convergence toward a middle ground
Interpersonal and Institutional Dynamics		
Teacher attitudes	V	
Classroom dynamics	V	
Instructional style	V	
Coeducation	C	Strongest at primary and tertiary levels
Female schooling participation	C	Convergence on sexual parity moving up ladder over time
Social origins and access to higher education	c	Slight convergent movement among more advanced but much variability persists
Parental conceptions of education	V	

[a]Key to entries:

C = A well-documented and marked convergent tendency has been observed in the adoption of a policy or structure, or in the level of a dimension.

c = A slower, more moderate convergent tendency has been observed.

D = A divergent tendency has been observed.

M = Results are mixed. Different patterns of change obtain when different samples are examined or different indicators of the same dimension are observed.

V = The dimension has not been examined with longitudinal data, but existing studies suggest considerable variability.

tablishes a fact that, now established, invites an explanation. And it seems unlikely that the explanation can be simple if it is to match the complexity of the patterns we have observed. Convergence in education is in fact a response to pressures from other elements of the social system, most notably pressures arising from the requirements of operating a large-scale, complex, technologically based economy and society. The operation of such forces undoubtedly accounts for the fact that we so often observe a strong correlation between the adoption of new educational forms and practices on the one hand and national levels of economic development on the other. But while economic development remains differentiated, it should lead to the persistence of differences, even if in the form of parallel change rather than actual convergence. For definite convergence to occur, therefore, one must posit the operation of other forces as well.

The operation of ceiling effects provides one obvious mechanism whereby educational systems may converge even when wealth continues to differentiate. Short of a strict ceiling, marginal returns from economic progress may become so small that, once over a given threshold, all national systems come to be pretty much alike on certain dimensions of their educational systems. Diffusion surely must also play a major role as international standards come to be widely accepted, especially those set by the world's leaders or those advocated and encouraged by international agencies such as the OECD, UNESCO, the International Monetary Fund, and the World Bank. The propensity to imitate the leaders, the moral force of international organization, and the persuasive efforts of experts and technical consultants all can act to move countries to a common standard internationally even when their economic development would not require, and indeed must often strain to support, the educational programs favored by the international elite. It is this set of forces, we believe, that accounts for the frequent reduction of differences in the educational forms characterizing the more and the less economically advanced sets of countries.

Working against these pressures to converge are a number of forces that act to maintain differences, and even to stimulate distinctive and even divergent forms of educational structure and practice. Differences in level of economic development, already mentioned, are among the most important of these. Such differences distinctively shape the needs of the societies, and also set marked limits on what they can afford to undertake by way of providing educational services. Political systems are another force for differentiation, leading, for example, to the special status of the communist bloc countries as the chief protagonists of vocational secondary schools. Historical traditions, especially when expressed in long-established national forms of governmental structure, are another force generating obstacles to convergence. Thus the centralized control of education is much more marked in societies such as France than it is in countries that have a federal structure, and the latter also tend to be characterized by greater regional variation in expenditures on education.

Of course differences in economic capacity, in the political system such as between capitalism, socialism, and communism, and in historical experience and tradition can be, and as we have seen often are, overridden by the pressures to adopt similar educational structures and practices, pressures driven by a dynamism of their own. To sort out which of these drives are most compelling for which aspects of the education system, and to delineate the reasons for this variation, is the task that stands ahead for us.

seven

MODERNIZATION AND FAMILY PATTERNS

The theory of societal convergence assumes that on a number of major dimensions the industrial societies of the world are developing common forms of social organization. In this view differences in institutions, in values, in modes of living, and in the ways individuals relate to each other all become increasingly less marked as societies become more industrialized and urbanized and their populations more highly educated and increasingly subject to the influence of the media of mass communication. An exception is generally made for political systems and modes of economic control, so that nations are not assumed to move increasingly toward either dictatorship or democracy, capitalism or socialism, as they develop industrially. But the family definitely falls within the scope of the theory, and the adherents of this view believe that they have discovered a worldwide movement toward what William Goode calls "the conjugal system," that is, a family system that places relatively little stress on the extended kin network, focusing instead mainly on the nuclear family. This modern syndrome also assumes that young people will have considerable say about the choice of their mates; that they will be more likely to set up their own households in a pattern of neolocal residence; that families will be relatively small; and that the system for reckoning descent will be bilineal, that is, will emphasize both the male and the female line.[1]

Reprinted with permission from Alex Inkeles, "Modernization and Family Patterns: A Test of Convergence Theory," *Conspectus of History*, Vol. 1, No. 6, ed. Dwight W. Hoover and John T.A. Koumoulides (Muncie, IN: Department of History, Ball State University, 1980), 31–62.

Convergence and the Family

The expectation that social patterns have been converging, including those related to the family and kinship, rests on a number of assumptions. Central among these is the belief that certain standardized social arrangements have the capacity to shape individual attitudes, values, and behavior in relatively standard ways, even when those arrangements are introduced into quite different cultural contexts. Thus it has been demonstrated that in developing countries men exposed to the conditions of employment in modern factories develop a much stronger sense of personal efficacy than do individuals from the same culture whose living is made in the pursuit of traditional agriculture. Farmers enrolled in certain types of cooperative movement also develop more efficacy than those not brought into the movement. Following this model we may conclude that individuals from different countries who face increasingly common conditions, such as industrial employment and urban living, should respond in similar ways, as, for example, in reducing the number of children they have. It is assumed, in effect, that there is an imperative or logic intrinsic in certain socioeconomic conditions. As those conditions become more prevalent, so should the common or standard human response to them.

Other reasons are also adduced to support the expectation of convergence. World system theory assumes that the modern world is dominated by certain "core" states or societies, notably the United States, and perhaps also the Soviet Union. Patterns adopted in these core states are believed by some to be imposed on the peripheral societies by various means, subtle and less so. Whether the patterns are indeed "imposed" or instead eagerly sought out by those who borrow them, the spread of mass media and the prominence of the core societies in shaping the content of mass communication worldwide are assumed to help ensure the diffusion of common expectations and patterns of behavior. Multinational corporations of global reach are also thought to make a contribution both in creating and diffusing such common patterns.

Critics of the convergence theory challenge both the theory's assumptions and its purported empirical findings. They are more impressed by evidence of the persistence of distinctive traditional family arrangements, and they note the emergence of new variant forms quite different from the standard conjugal model.[2] To think of the family as so passive, so responsive in structure and content to the shaping of a variable economic system, runs counter to the assumption that the family is but one characteristic manifestation of a pattern of culture and that it expresses the distinctiveness and even the uniqueness of such cultures. It would follow from this that societies that had attained the same level of wealth, and even of technological sophistication, would continue to have different family patterns because those societies carried different historically given cultures. In this view family patterns are assumed to be decidedly persistent, and such change as they may undergo is expected to be greatly constrained by tradition and to express the distinctive cultural tendencies of the group undergoing the change.

So long as the discussion continues at this rather general level, both the convergence theory and its opposition must strike one as quite plausible. Moreover, if one is satisfied by the citation of merely *illustrative* evidence, either position may seem to have been proved correct. We need to state the contrasting theories more precisely and to be specific as to which of the many dimensions of family and kinship patterns are relevant to a test of the two theories. Being thus systematic we may achieve a more adequate assessment of the general power of the convergence theory. And by distinguishing precisely which dimensions of family life do and do not respond to the socioeconomic pressures of modernization, we are likely to stimulate advances in the sociological theory of the family.

In making my contribution to the continuing discussion, I decided to examine the facts with regard to three broadly defined aspects of family and kinship patterns. The *demographic* realm was to encompass evidence that expresses family events as numbers and ratios, most notably in the form of marriage and birth rates. The *structural* realm was to encompass the formal rules governing family and kinship arrangements, such as those affecting the choice of marriage partner, residence, descent, and inheritance. The third set I thought of as covering *family dynamics,* that is, the less formal and less rule-bound, but vital, patterns of interpersonal relations. Under this heading I intended to study, for example, the extent to which spouses share household tasks or the young show respect for elders. Clearly, many specific elements of the complex we think of as the family or kinship system could be classified as falling under more than one of these rubrics. Nevertheless, this rough division proved quite serviceable.

Under each rubric I planned to identify approximately ten issues, themes, patterns, and the like that scholars working in the field had noted to be of substantial interest and importance. These issues were then to be restated in such form as to permit an objective test of whether or not this specific element of family and kinship organization or behavior seemed to converge on some common ground. To make that judgment it was necessary to have some measurement standards. A few comments on methodological issues are therefore called for at this point.

We cannot claim there has been convergence merely because we find two or more societies to have the same birth rate or to follow identical rules about where a newly married couple shall reside. To establish convergence we must show that the respective societies came to this common point after starting from initially differentiated positions. And though it is gratifying to be able to find any empirical regularity in human affairs, we cannot be satisfied merely to give evidence of convergence. Our objective is to explain and predict the outcome on the basis of a causal theory. Insofar as convergence theory asserts, for example, that it is industrialization and urbanization that cause birth rates to fall and nations to converge on a pattern of zero population growth, we should be able to demonstrate the connection. Ideally, the demonstration should be not only cross-sectional but also longitudinal. That is, we should not only show that those nations on higher steps of the ladder of industrialization and urbanization have lower birth rates: We should also demonstrate that *within individual countries,* as they moved historically from a less to a more industrialized and urban condition, they also shifted to lower birth rates and eventually to zero population growth.

At the same time, we should not fall into the error of denying that nations are converging on a common form or rate merely because the direction in which some are changing is nominally opposite to the direction of change in others. Suppose, for example, that nations were converging on a common norm with regard to the age at marriage, such that the model bracket for women was to be the age of twenty-two. Countries in which earlier marriage had prevailed would, if they were to move to that level, manifest a *rising* average, whereas countries in which a later marriage age had been common would show a *falling* average. Thus, to converge, these countries would have to move in nominally opposite directions.

Movement toward an ostensible common norm does not in itself assure ever reaching it. And reaching a common point is no assurance of maintaining it. The slopes of the lines on a chart that bring two nations together may equally drive them past their crossing point into a new pattern of *divergence.* Indeed, our model must allow for the probability that nations that previously had similar family patterns may respond to new similar conditions in sufficiently different ways now to constitute evidence of divergence, rather than of convergence.

We may of course observe patterns of change that are neither convergent nor divergent. Change can be parallel, with the direction and the rate of change over time being the same for two units that, in consequence, maintain their distance even though each is changing markedly. If two nations that were manifesting such parallel change on some family characteristic, such as age at marriage, had in the preceding periods also been experiencing comparable rates of industrialization and urbanization, we would have increased confidence in our assumption that it was the latter that caused the former. But, alas, the evidence could not serve as an instance of convergence.

On first approaching the study of family change in modern times, I was confident about what I would discover. I had expected to find on every hand clear evidence that the organizational features and behavioral patterns of family life were moving toward a common norm in response to the ubiquitous pressures of modernization. Given that many countries would start at widely separate points, I was prepared to find that actual convergence had been achieved in only a few instances, but the general tendency in that direction I assumed would be unmistakable. In the meantime, those features that were not actually convergent I anticipated would at least manifest strong evidence of parallel change. Finally, I expected to find that it would be only the exceptional dimension of family relations that would continue uninfluenced by the forces of change initiated in the occupational, residential, and educational realms.

If I had been able to complete my master plan I should by now have had up to thirty "tests" of the correctness of my assumption—ten under each of the three main rubrics described earlier. The pace of scholarship being less amenable to precise programming than one might wish, however, I decided to present the result far short of the original goal. Incomplete as it is, the analysis so far carried out justifies some tentative conclusions.

There certainly is considerable evidence of convergence precisely along the lines predicted by our theory. But instances of convergence, while not being the exception, are certainly not the invariant rule. On the contrary, I frequently found family and kin patterns continuing to be remarkably stable in the face of great variation in their surrounding socioeconomic conditions. My sample of tests of the convergence theory as applied to the family is so far too small and insufficiently random for me to hazard a guess as to whether more than half will support the convergence hypothesis. In purely probabilistic terms, as well as in actual experience, any social science theory that is confirmed in 50 percent of the tests to which it is submitted has achieved an unusually high degree of support, since by chance alone only some 5 percent of all tests would be expected to offer even modest confirmation of any hypothesis.[3]

Nevertheless, there will certainly be enough instances of contrary evidence to constitute a formidable challenge to the universality of the convergence hypothesis. To account for these different patterns one must supplement the theory of convergence with other explanatory models, several of which I have introduced in the main body of this chapter.

Demographic Indicators

If patterns of human action in family-related matters are converging in industrialized and industrializing societies, we should be able to observe the tendency most clearly by looking at demographic indicators. The theory that calls for measures such as those of fertility to respond to the pressures of modernization is one of the most thoroughly elaborated and vigorously asserted. In addition, demographic indicators are expressed numerically, have fairly unambiguous meaning, have been relatively standardized by governments, and can be obtained for rather long spans of time. This therefore seems an appropriate point at which to initiate our exploration.

On Declining Fertility

Greater national development expressed especially in increased industrialization, urbanization, and wealth brings declining birth rates. This process may be observed in cross-sectional analysis, in which we look at all countries on the scale from richest to poorest, and is equally evident in longitudinal analysis, in which we observe the same country over time. Declines in birth rates seem to follow at a fairly constant pace upon changes in national development, particularly in urbanization, industrialization, education, and female labor force participation. The evidence is notably unambiguous and suggests a powerful process of relatively universal applicability. The most developed countries seem about to converge on a pattern of zero population growth.

As we go up the ladder from the poorer to the richer countries the birth rate falls steadily from a high of almost forty-five per 1,000 in those with per capita incomes under US$100 to seventeen in those with incomes of $1,000 and above. The gross reproduction rate is a much more meaningful figure, but it is available for only a few countries. Accepting that limitation, we note the same pattern. In the poorest countries the average number of live daughters born to each woman is three or more, in the more advantaged of the developing countries it has fallen to 2.5, and in the nations with over $1,000 per capita income it is down to 1.2, which means that as a group they are approaching zero population growth.[4]

What is true as we move across countries arranged by wealth is also true as we move across time within particular countries. Inevitably, over very long spans of time there are fluctuations produced by wars, depressions, and other massive social forces. The long-term movement, however, is unmistakable. Thus in the United States a cohort of 1,000 women born between 1835 and 1839 produced 5,395 children, but each successive cohort produced fewer children so that the last group on record as having completed its productive cycle, namely, those born in the 1920–1924 period, produced only 2,701 children, or half as many as the cohort born less than a century earlier.[5]

Although there is no guarantee that the future of the more developed countries foreshadows that of the now less advanced, the recent evidence of their fertility over time indicates that they too are experiencing a decline in population growth year by year. At all levels of economic development there was a decline in the gross reproduction rate between 1960 and 1970. Taking a representative count at each income level, we find that in the $100 category Bangladesh experienced a decline from a rate of 3.5 to 3.1; from among nations having $100 to $200 per capita, in Turkey the rate declined from 2.9 to 2.6; within the set of more industrialized but still less developed countries, having incomes between $375 and $1,000, Brazil experienced a decline from 2.6 to 2.5; and the U.S. rate fell from 1.8 to 1.4. Among the other most developed countries a few had actually achieved a stable reproduction rate by 1960, notably Japan and Romania, and by 1970 they had been joined by the Federal Republic of Germany, Finland, and Greece, with Sweden and Luxembourg just on the verge of crossing that magic line.[6]

In the reproduction of population we evidently have a clear-cut case of convergence on a standard of stable reproduction and consequent zero population growth. The most advanced countries began to reach this position around 1960. Intracountry analysis shows the movement in this direction to have been steady over a span of a hundred years in response to the combined impact of industrialization, urbanization, education, and female employment outside the home.[7] Cross-sectional analysis shows that each step up the economic ladder brings the less developed countries progressively closer to the norm in the more developed, giving reason to believe that in time they too, one by one, will reach the same plateau. So marked have these tendencies been in the decade since 1968 that two leading analysts of these trends concluded: "Population decline has become the dominant trend in both underdeveloped and developed nations."[8]

Age at Marriage

The exceptionally late age at marriage of men in Ireland is often noted. That fact is commonly explained as being a result of the system by which parents kept their sons waiting to inherit the family farm and hence unable to marry, because only by having access to his parents' land could a son hope to support a family.

This tale immediately suggests a model to explain whether people marry late or early. It assumes that individuals would prefer to enjoy the rewards of marriage as soon as possible, but that the couples are restrained by objective factors, most notably by the lack of the means to support themselves. Presumably, to the degree that individuals come into such means of self-support earlier, or can otherwise escape restraints and controls imposed by others, they will marry earlier.

Exactly what constitutes constraint, and what are resources, and how one gets them are complex matters, difficult to measure precisely. But it might reasonably be argued that one consequence of urbanization and industrialization is to reduce dependency on an older generation that is holding on to land. Instead, one substitutes for land numerous possibilities for earning that are relatively independent of the good will or formal assistance or parents. Consequently, with urbanization and industrialization, and in particular with the creation of great impersonal labor markets, marriage should be contracted earlier. Professor Goode read the limited evidence available as of the early 1960s as indicating precisely this outcome, stating: "In the West age at marriage has been dropping for men, and to a lesser extent for women."[9]

A rather different perspective leads to the prediction that the age at marriage should *increase* rather than decrease in response to urbanization and industrialization. Rural communities tend to marry young women off quite early, partially as a precaution against the loss of virginity, partly to increase the prospects that there will be more children, valued as they are for farm labor. Ansley Coale notes that countries in which the custom of arranged marriage, and especially of child marriage, has disappeared, have inevitably experienced a sharp increase in the average age at marriage.

As a measure of "nuptuality" Coale uses an index having a value of 1.00 if all women aged fifteen to fifty are married, with lower values as the number of younger unmarried persons increases. A later average age at marriage, leaving more of those under twenty or twenty-four unmarried, has the effect of lowering the index. Europe, given its long-standing pattern of late marriage combined with a high rate of celibacy, has in modern times yielded an index of nuptuality generally around .5. By contrast, in many parts of Africa and Asia it was generally at .75 and sometimes went as high as .90. Under the circumstances, there would seem to be considerable room for convergence. One form it could take would be for the widely separated Asian and European patterns to come closer together. Another would be for countries within any region, such as Europe, to become more alike. For example, there could be a reduction in the contrast separating countries in which women married late, such as Sweden or Holland, and countries in which women married early, such as France or Spain.

Coale notes a number of countries that in modern times experienced sharp reductions on his index of nuptuality. Korea's index was at .91 in 1935, but by 1966 had fallen to .75. Hong Kong, Taiwan, Singapore, and the Asiatic provinces of Russia also experienced substantial declines, meaning that people were increasingly mature by the time they married.

On the other side of the world, most European countries, according to Coale, were experiencing a rising index, meaning that marriage was coming earlier. In France and the Netherlands, the increase in the index began no later than the mid–nineteenth century. Elsewhere in Europe the rise began only in the 1930s, but was speeded up in the 1940s. Thus Coale's more extensive data seem to support Goode's conclusion that the age at marriage has been falling in European societies.

The basic data from Coale's research, which covers 700 provinces of Europe, certainly seem to suggest a convergent movement involving a later average age at marriage in Asia and Africa and an earlier average in Europe and the areas reflecting its cultural influence. My own independent check of Coale's thesis seems to support his assumption at least in part. Since the turn of the century Western Europe moved quite unmistakably toward earlier marriage in thirteen of the fifteen countries I studied. In 1900 in the average European country, 88 percent of the men were still unmarried by age twenty-four, but by 1970 the figure was down to 76 percent. For women the change was from 72 percent to 52 percent. The situation in Eastern Europe, and more so in Asia and Africa, is harder to document for lack of comparable data. But insofar as countries in those areas have been changing, they are mainly moving toward later marriage for both men and women. Hence we seem here to have an example of convergence, albeit one that is coming about slowly and that still leaves great gaps between and even within regions.[10]

The impression that Europe is tending toward earlier marriage seems contradicted by the fact that in the United States the median age at first marriage rose by one full year for both men and women between 1965 and 1977. But we must be careful not to be swept up into concluding that any one decade is a sure indicator of long-term trends. There are many social currents that can, in any given decade, move personal preferences as to what is the "right" marriage age sharply up or down without basically altering the long-term pattern. From 1890 on, as the United States became more industrialized and urbanized and its population better educated, the median age at marriage fell gradually, decade by decade.[11] Thus for men it went down from 26.1 years in 1890 to 24.3 in 1930, and reached its lowest level of 22.5 years by 1955. After that it started moving upward, reaching twenty-four by 1977, which put it back at the 1930 level.[12]

Given this pattern, it seems imprudent to draw any conclusion about long-term shifts. Rather, what one can say is that Americans seem to have a characteristic preference for men to marry around age twenty-five, and despite some fluctuation according to the era, this preference has remained remarkably stable over time. Such stability of the preferred marriage age in other societies has been thoroughly documented elsewhere by Hajnal. In Bavaria, for example, the preference for men to marry around twenty-seven and women around twenty-five seems to have held steady from 1721 down to 1896.[13]

Of course the past can be swept away, and we could be entering a new era with regard to popular images as to the proper age for men and women to marry, with a marked drift toward later ages. But the evidence for an alleged general European drift toward postponement and late marriage is far from consistent.

Jan Trost looked at the crude marriage rate for fifteen countries of Europe plus Canada and Japan to test his impression that in the 1960s and early 1970s the marriage rate was elsewhere going down just as he had observed it to do in Sweden and Denmark.[14] To his surprise he found no consistent trend or pattern—some countries showed a steady state, others went up or down, but most did not seem to converge on any standard. Indeed, any proponent of convergence theory must take considerable pause from the fact that in two such industrialized, urbanized, and culturally similar countries as Sweden and the United States, young people enter marriage at such different ages. As of 1970 almost half of the young American women were married by age twenty, whereas in Sweden only 15 percent had at that point in their lives so committed themselves. In brief, the proportion married by age twenty in the United States was more than three times that in Sweden.[15] Hence even if we were to argue that the age at which people enter marriage is somewhat responsive to independent earning opportunities, we would be obliged to acknowledge that it is much more influenced by national cultural norms. These norms may change in parallel ways in several countries.[16] Nevertheless they show much less propensity to converge on a common standard similar to the fertility rate on which the world's industrial countries are so rapidly converging.[17]

In summary, the data on the age at marriage present us with a complex picture. Interpretation is rendered even more problematic by the extensive variation of the indicators used by different investigators and the historical period on which they base their judgments. And, as we have seen, short-term changes, that is, changes over any one decade, can be treacherous in their ability to mislead us as to the long-term patterns actually maintained over periods as long as 100 and even 200 years. The following conclusions may, however, be tentatively offered as a reasonable approximation of the true picture:

The most fundamental fact about the age at marriage is its variation from one culture area of the world to another. We know that for a period of at least 200 years the West European pattern has involved late, the East European much earlier, and the Asian markedly earlier marriage. As of 1900, characteristic proportions of men still single at age twenty-four were: Norway, 86 percent; Bosnia, 63 percent; and India 35 percent.[18]

Even within nominally more homogeneous culture areas, nations have typically manifested quite diverse cultural preferences about the right age for marriage. In France in 1900 only 58 percent of women were still single by age twenty-four, whereas in neighboring Switzerland 78 percent were still unmarried. Such intraregional contrasts have persisted to this day. Indeed, between 1900 and 1970 they have become more marked, providing an example of divergence.[19]

Individual nations seem to manifest a characteristic preference for a particular age for marriage, maintaining that norm over very long periods despite marked changes in the population's place of residence, occupation, and education. We illustrated this point earlier for the United States and Bavaria, but numerous other examples are available.

Despite the long-term stability characteristic of most nations, some countries have experienced dramatic change in the typical age at marriage. This has been most marked in Asia, and within Asia in those countries that have been modernizing most rapidly. Thus in Japan the proportion of women who had their first marriage between the ages of fifteen and nineteen fell dramatically from 1920 on, starting around 18 percent, then only 4.3 percent in 1940, and finally a mere 2 percent by 1955.[20] What came about spontaneously in Japan, largely in response to urbanization and industrialization, came to much of Communist China through a concerted political effort that evidently has brought the typical age at marriage to what, for China, is the remarkably late norm of twenty-five.

Since the age at marriage has been getting earlier in Western Europe and later in Eastern Europe, Asia, and Africa, the combined effect of these changes in different regions of the world must be recognized as an instance of convergence.

However, certain facts, such as that the regions of the world start from such diverse positions, that family change is generally slow, that many nations still have not been caught up in the modernization process, and that others preserve their cultural norm relatively intact despite modernization, mean that the extant patterns are still highly differentiated. We will be a long time awaiting a worldwide standard, if one should in fact be in the offing.

Percent Ever Married

The pattern of Western civilization seems to call for nine of ten people to have been married before reaching the age of fifty. These figures are derived from census statistics, and so they reflect official definitions of "marriage," which usually mean a formal and legal certification of cohabitation. Many will have lived as conjugal couples without benefit of formal sanction, so that the official statistics about the percentage "ever married" are surely underestimates of the true proportion.[21]

Two great forces, which probably strengthen each other, seem to be operating here. First, we can assume the existence of some rather deep-seated human need for establishing and maintaining relatively enduring conjugal relations. But we must also allow for the interest of society in encouraging such relationships as a means for regulating sexual expression, ensuring the next generation, and arranging for the orderly placement of individuals in each society's kinship and social support system.

Entire culture areas, and individual societies within culture areas, do vary in the strength with which they manifest the general tendency to get everyone married. The strength of the drive evidently increases as one moves from West to East. Asian countries seem to have a particular aversion to leaving people unmarried. At the turn of the century in most Asian countries no more than 1 percent of the women up to age fifty were left unmarried, and the East European standard was not far different at about 3 percent. In sharp contrast, the countries of Western Europe were, in the same period, typically leaving 15 percent of the women unmarried. These figures of course apply only the percentage "ever married" by late adulthood. Death and divorce would have left many more without a spouse as they approach the age of fifty.

Variation within the same culture area is dramatically illustrated by the well-known case of Ireland. As of 1950 only 67 percent of men under fifty had ever married. As late as 1970 the proportion of single men at age fifty in Ireland was two and a half to three times the proportion in the typical country of Western Europe.[22]

Since in Western culture we openly practice neither polygamy nor polyandry, the proportion ever married tends to be roughly the same for men and women. There is certainly no iron law ensuring this outcome. Powerful objective facts can produce anomalies, as in frontier colonies settled by men without women. Thus in Australia in 1900, 90 percent of the women had found men, but among the too-numerous men only 76 percent had ever succeeded in marrying.[23] Such conditions, however, are both unusual and transitory. In general, in the European experience, the proportion of men and women who go into old age unmarried is quite close, as it is in Asia and Africa as well.

The propensity of the citizens of any country to form relatively enduring contractual sexual unions is remarkably stable for each country and region, despite dramatic shifts in the occupations, residence, and education of the population. In 1900 Denmark was an overwhelmingly rural country. Of men between the ages of forty-five and forty-nine, 9 percent were unmarried. By 1974 Denmark had become predominantly urban and industrial. Of men between the ages of forty-five and forty-nine the proportion unmarried was still 9 percent. Between 1920 and 1975 Japan underwent a profound transformation, bringing it from the status of a newcomer to development to the condition of being one the world's leading industrial and commercial powers. Of men forty-five to forty-nine, the unmarried comprised 2 percent in 1920, and still 2 percent in 1975. These are not isolated cases selected to beguile the reader. They represent the common experience of dozens of countries in Western and Eastern Europe and Asia.

Although these instances of continuity are striking, it would be misleading to suggest that the propensity to marry is an invariant pattern, frozen into place in each culture and society. There have been some fairly sharp declines in spinsterhood and bachelorhood in Europe over the seventy-five-year period since 1900. For example, by 1970 or so, the percentage of women "never married" by age fifty had declined from the 1900 level as follows: In Iceland from 29 to 10 percent; in Sweden, from 19 to 7 percent; in Portugal, from 20 to 12 percent. Indeed, in sixteen countries of Europe, outside the East, the median came down from 15 percent to almost 11 percent.[24]

However, countries in Eastern Europe that in 1900 had left very few women unmarried had not markedly changed that pattern by 1970, and the nations of Asia continued their cultural tradition of seeing to the eventual marriage of virtually every woman well before she was fifty years old.[25] If there is any convergence on this measure, therefore, it is coming mainly from the tendency of north-central European culture bearers to allow fewer men and women to get to age fifty without having been married at least once.

In sum, our explorations of the proportions ever married revealed a pattern different from that presented by either fertility or the age at marriage of younger people. In the case of fertility we were most impressed by the strong and steady convergence on a pattern of stable reproduction. In studying the age at marriage, we were most struck by the exceptional stability of the distinctive age at marriage preferred by each nation and maintained by it in the face of great transformations in other aspects of social life. Looking at the data on the percentage ever married, however, we find most notable the propensity of individual desire and social pressure to combine in assuring that virtually everyone has been married before reaching the age of fifty. In brief, fertility is convergent, age at marriage is a relatively stable national characteristic, and being ever married seems more a pan-human need.

Although there are variable culture norms that make spinsterhood and bachelorhood more or less acceptable in one or another society, this differentiation seems minor compared to the forces that seem so inexorably to push people into relatively long-term sexual commitments. And that fact is of course only partially captured by official statistics of registered marriages. One effect of modernization may be to induce individuals to take more trouble to formalize and register their marital unions, and pressure from governments may accelerate the process. In that case, some of the nations that show unusually large numbers of people still unmarried by age fifty may come into line with the overwhelming majority. This may then be taken to be an instance of convergence. That trend may, however, be offset by the tendency of many young people in some of the most advanced countries, such as Sweden, to avoid registration of their conjugal relations even after the arrival of children. Whether formally registered or not, these seem to be fairly stable and relatively enduring relationships. Even when they are broken they seem to lead shortly, as do most formal divorces, to the subsequent establishment of a new conjugal relationship. These facts strengthen our impression that the prime factor in explaining the ubiquitous high proportion "ever married" is a deep-seated human need for a stable, intimate, sexual union, a need that asserts itself with more or less equal force in all places at all times.

Demographics Summarized

Of the three measures of the demographic characteristics of the family we examined, only one showed a clear-cut pattern of change converging on a common norm. Fertility is everywhere declining in response to economic development, and the advanced nations converge at a net reproduction rate which brings zero population growth into sight.

The age at marriage, however, showed no clear-cut and regular response to the social and economic changes experienced in Western nations since the mid–nineteenth century. The most outstanding fact about the age at marriage is that it seems to reflect distinctive cultural norms that are relatively invariant over long periods. Within the same broad cultural spectrum, countries that are also equally industrialized and urbanized nevertheless manifest markedly different preferences as to the age most suitable for marriage. However, there is evidence of substantial change toward later marriage in the more rapidly modernizing countries of Asia. Combined with a slower movement toward later marriage in Western Europe, this trend does seem to constitute an instance of convergence.

Still a third pattern was presented by the data on the proportion ever married among those who had reached the age beyond which a first marriage was rather unlikely to occur. Among those who reach the age of forty-nine, approximately 90 percent of men and women have ventured into marriage at least once. In this case we seem to encounter a pan-human constant, a percentage varying very little across the set of industrialized nations and within each of them over time.

There are, of course, more than three demographic indicators reflecting family patterns. I did not select these three to illustrate the three patterns that emerged. They seemed appropriate to investigate, and I pursued them because they had been salient to leading investigators in the field. Whether the same proportions would hold if we extended our indicators to number six or ten, only further investigation will reveal.

Family Structures

In turning to the structural features of the family we gain some advantages that are not available in examining demographic patterns or internal family dynamics. Information about the structural features of the family can be obtained for periods much farther back in history than even the most complete demographic series will allow us to reach, and the facts are available for many societies that kept no population records. Comparing and contrasting the internal dynamics of family relations requires that we have intimate personal accounts, or we must be able to conduct personal interviews, and what we conclude depends a great deal on subtle and personal interpretation. By contrast, the structure of family and kinship, based as it is on rules and formal, even explicitly contractual, understandings, permits relatively precise and unambiguous classification. We can ascertain readily, and generally precisely, whether descent is patrilineal or matrilineal, whether residence is neolocal, whether property passes by primogeniture, whether marriages are arranged, and whether dowry is or is not paid and, if paid, in what form.

One of the most fundamental propositions of the comparative sociology of the family is that the technico-economic level of a society in substantial degree shapes the forms of family and kin organization. In hunting-and-gathering societies people move about in small, loosely coupled bands, and the strongest bond is within the conjugal family, with extended kinship ties more weakly elaborated and maintained. Under conditions of settled agriculture there is a shift in emphasis, with the extended kin ties becoming much stronger, indeed generally dominating the conjugal family. With the later development of industrialization, family patterns shift again.[26] As phrased by William Goode in what has come to be the classic formulation: "Wherever the economic system expands through industrialization, . . . extended kin ties weaken, lineage patterns dissolve, and a trend toward some form of the conjugal system begins to appear—that is, the nuclear family becomes a more independent kinship unit."[27]

The same mode of analysis has also been applied to explain the emergence and persistence of distinctive family forms, such as the female-headed household that attracts so much attention in discussions of welfare policy in the United States. Actually, female-headed families emerge in many other societies when certain conditions are met, for example, where there is considerable surplus labor population, payment is individual rather than familial, and there are jobs available that can readily be reconciled with continuing child care.[28] These conditions are not time bound. They may therefore explain the appearance of substantial numbers of female-headed households in eighteenth-century England, on Puerto Rican sugar plantations, and in the densest urban ghettos of New York.

While the processes of industrialization, urbanization, and modernization have not totally eliminated variant family forms such as the female-headed household, they have drastically reduced variability even in relatively homogeneous culture areas such as the European continent. In seventeenth- and eighteenth-century Europe, despite popular images to the contrary, the small conjugal family was already widespread, but it existed alongside a wide assortment of different family forms that expressed distinctive cultures and reflected the adaptation of the family to diverse geographical, economic, and political conditions. Such distinctive family forms are now either totally eliminated or appear only as curious anomalies. The stem family, once widespread in Austria, France, and Germany, is no longer to be found there; married brothers do not now keep their families together in the same house, as they frequently did in France and Italy; one must look into remote corners of Eastern Europe to find the rare example of the huge and complex households that once were so prevalent there; and early teenage marriage, once a major, indeed the predominant, mode in parts of Russia, is now seldom encountered, having been replaced by much later marriage.[29] Instead of this rich variety, European families today are virtually uniformly of the conjugal type; households are small, generally close to the median number of four persons; marriage generally comes in the mid-twenties; and older people predominantly live apart from their children in their own residences.

The experience of Europe therefore seems to argue for convergence in family structure. But some of these changes began well before industrialism. Thus in France it is clear that as early as the seventeenth century, the immediate family was already becoming more important relative to the interests of the wider kinship group.[30] Doubts are then raised as to whether this convergence was really a general response to changing patterns of economic activity rather than being a shift specifically internal to European culture.

Inevitably people look to Japan as the critical test case, since there we have a non-European society that experienced rapid and extensive industrialization and urbanization in modern times. It will perhaps be no surprise that different people read the evidence on Japan as leading to different conclusions. I am personally more persuaded by those who argue that the rapid change in Japanese economic life has launched a powerful long-term trend toward the nucleation of the family.

Frequently cited, and admittedly substantial, evidence supporting the claim that the Japanese family system persists in its traditional forms comes from both census reports and opinion research. The single most impressive fact is that the percentage of all households that qualified as being "nuclear" rose by only eight points, from 55 to 63 percent, between 1920 and 1970, a period over which the level of industrialization and urbanization increased greatly. Even Tsuneo Yamane, who believes strongly that the Japanese family is becoming nuclear, is obliged to acknowledge that: "The rate of change seems slow when contrasted with rates of such phenomena as economic growth. . . . "[31] The percentage of nuclear households may, moreover, mislead us, since any older parental couple can usually live with only one of their mature children, thus leaving all their other offspring in the condition of having one-generation households. It is therefore more appropriate to check on the proportion of the elderly who live with their children. As late as 1973 in Japan 75 percent of those over sixty-five were living with their married or unmarried adult children. For their part, the children of these elders, at least those born before the end of World War II, seem overwhelmingly to accept the appropriateness of having their elderly parents live with them.

To counter these striking facts, those who believe that the Japanese family is nevertheless going the way of nucleation note that in each successive generation born after World War II, the preference for neolocal residence becomes stronger. We meet here again a familiar dilemma. Reading the current situation alone we can easily conclude that family structures resist change and that the traditional forms persist with remarkable tenacity. When we look at evidence of change over time, however, we may discern a long-term trend that, if continued, will inevitably erode the dominance of the old forms. It certainly is impressive that in 1971 half of Japan's young people in their twenties still said that they wanted their elderly parents to reside with them. But the figure was undoubtedly much higher in 1950, and it seems very likely to be much lower in 1980. Indeed, we can document a number of instances in which attitudes once considered fundamental to the structure of the Japanese family system underwent profound change during the limited twenty-year span from 1953 to 1973.[32] Tsuneo Yamane seems correct in asserting that the trend in the structure of the Japanese family is "from patrilineal to bilineal descent, from patrilocal to neolocal residence, from patriarchal to equalitarian relationships, and from continuity to self-liquidation."[33]

Within European culture there is still a good deal of variation in the proportion of older people who live with their grown children. Jan Turowski reports that in Poland around 67 percent of the old who have children live with them in one household. He put the comparable rates at 42 percent for the United Kingdom and only 20 percent in Denmark. In the Polish case urban-rural differences were substantial, with 76 percent of the peasants but only 57 percent of the nonagricultural population following the custom of living with children.[34] Similar forces evidently were operating in Japan, where the extreme limits on the size of urban houses and apartments is adduced to explain, in part, the increasing reluctance to share a common household with one's children.[35]

The Polish and Japanese examples suggest a common response to a common experience, namely, modern urban living. But urbanism cannot explain the differences between Britain and Denmark that Turowski noted. Neither is the rate of urban growth in the United States sufficient to explain why living with married children, already at an extremely low level, was further reduced by almost half between 1940 and 1970. By 1970, of the total who were sixty-five and over, no more than 6.5 percent of men and 16 percent of women lived with their grown children.[36] The key to this process is the attitude about maintaining one's independence and maximizing one's freedom of movement, by minimizing both one's dependence on others and their dependence on oneself. A whole series of forces built into the pattern of urban industrial life moves individuals to maximize their independence in this regard. Only one-third of American parents believe that their children have an obligation to their parents for all the latter have done for them, and the overwhelming majority consider it best to maintain a household separate from that of their children.[37] Even in Japan, where not more than 15 percent of the elderly maintained their own household in the 1970s, the intention to live alone was expressed by more than one-third of those approaching old age. Another third, while indicating an intention to live with children, stressed that they did not want to be financially dependent on them.[38]

Even when family structures are preserved, the actual patterns of human relations within them may be so transformed as to change profoundly the significance one might otherwise attach to the apparent persistence of tradition. Consider, for example, the dowry, which persists in Greece to a degree many find surprising considering the relative modernization of the country. In the past the requirement that a young woman bring a dowry to her marriage made her totally dependent on her parents and obliged her to accept their choice for her marriage partner. But today young women go to work in factories, offices, and shops to earn their own dowry. Having earned the dowry themselves, they also now exercise the prerogative of selecting their husbands to suit themselves rather than their parents. The form persists, but its significance as an indicator of the young woman's dependence and lack of autonomy is quite different.

Similar changes in the meaning of patrilocal residence occur even as the form is preserved. In the traditional Japanese family the elderly parents living with their mature children were the dominant authorities in all matters. Today they must learn to cooperate in a joint household and adjust to the rhythm, style, and needs of the young people. Moreover, the young wife, once looked on as either a subordinate new daughter or even more burdened by the dominance of the older female household head, can now claim to be treated more and more according to the rules applying to an ordinary "in-law."[39]

Industrialization and modernization evidently bring about a good deal of convergent change in the structure of family arrangements. Although the changes are partly a matter of sentiment or ideology, the key fact bringing about these structural changes is the shift to industrial employment, which makes young people much less economically dependent on elders. The shift to urban residence also adds both opportunities for independence and constraints militating against maintaining large households. Young people achieve much greater autonomy in selecting a spouse; the residence for a young couple is much likelier to be in a physically separate household; the household budgets of the new and the old families come likewise to be separately maintained; and an emphasis on bilateral relations replaces the more common emphasis on either the paternal or the maternal side. The increased independence and autonomy of the young is synchronous with a decline in both the scope and the strength of the authority of parents and elders. Moreover, many of the traditional patterns that seem to persist unchanged are in fact transformed in actual practice.

These examples call attention to the importance of considering the dynamics of interpersonal relations as they express tendencies toward divergence and convergence in the family under conditions of modernization.

Family Dynamics

Some seven to ten themes regularly emerge in discussions of family dynamics under modern conditions. Since family relations are complexly intertwined, the boundaries separating one dimension from another are necessarily overlapping and perhaps even arbitrary. Nevertheless, we can see the situation more clearly if we keep the issues discrete. It facilitates testing our ideas against such facts as are available and makes it more likely that we will recognize realms in which change is resistant or actually moves in directions opposite to the general trend.

Importance of the Family to the Individual

Few popular ideas are more widespread than the belief that the importance of the family in human affairs has been weakening, that the family as an institution is under great strain, that family relations have become brittle, that families are not really important to people anymore, that the home is now no more than a place to hang your hat or is perhaps useful only as a springboard for jumping off to somewhere and something else.

Some of these observations may be correct, depending on what is meant by the words used. Rising divorce rates, for example, can be effective support for the argument that family relations have become more brittle. But taking into account most appropriate indicators of what is important to people, one cannot make a convincing case that in modern society the family has suffered a substantial decline in its human importance relative to the other institutions and relations in which individuals invest their emotions, their loyalties, and their time. Indeed, the main thrust of change may well be in just the opposite direction, at least so far as concerns one's immediate family. As Edward Shorter put it, in *The Making of the Modern Family* (1975), there is "a drift towards domesticity all over Western society."

Rather than suffering a decline, the family either remains, or becomes, one of the most important social objects or institutions—often the most important—to most individuals. As a focus of personal loyalty, solidarity, and commitment in the modern world the family seems equal to or greater in importance than one's extended kinship network, clan, country, job, caste, or religious group.

Since to many this statement will surely seem to run counter to the most obvious of objective facts, it may help if I give some evidence in support of it. In Libya, Finland, and the United States people were presented with a list of institutions and groups and were asked to indicate for each whether their feeling toward it fell at the pole of absolute solidarity or was less intense. Among residents of five Finnish cities 85 percent described themselves as feeling absolute solidarity with their family. In several small cities of Pennsylvania the proportion was 94 percent, and in three cities of Libya the same.[40]

Clearly there is no basis here for arguing that economic development and modernization erode the *absolute* importance of the family, nor its *relative* importance, since in all three countries the family as a focus of solidarity far exceeded in importance all the competition. Thus in Finland the proportions expressing absolute solidarity with other representative foci of collective loyalty were: nation, 71 percent; ethnic group, 48 percent; and local community, 29 percent.[41] This suggests, if generalization from one country is permissible, that in modernization the family does not necessarily become "stronger," but allegiance to it becomes so outstanding because individual commitment to other objects of primal identification becomes relatively weaker.

The conclusions derived from this particular study are supported by others that approached the issue from different angles. Thus Ornauer and colleagues asked people from eleven advanced countries, "Do you hope that people will be more attached or less attached to their families than they are today?" The median proportion who wanted less attachment was a mere 6 percent. The economically more developed did not more often wish for less attachment. Indeed, India was the only country in the set in which a majority wanted to keep relatives more at a distance.[42]

Reporting for entire populations, as I am here, inevitably means glossing over differences in emphasis among those in different positions in the social hierarchy or in the life cycle. Thus 81 percent of all parents in the United States consider the family "a very important value," and it earns this rating above all other values, whereas among college youth only 68 percent so rate the family, placing it behind "self-fulfillment" and "education."[43] But it remains notable that more than two-thirds of American college youth in 1973 considered the family "a very important" value, so designating it more than twice as often as religion and more than three times as often as patriotism or money.

In sum, then, the family remains vitally important to people in the modern world. Indeed, for all but a few it is the association that they most value, the institution they most cherish, the focus of their most important hopes and aspirations, the relationship in which they are most intensely engaged and to which they are the most deeply committed. Modernization has not reduced the relative standing of this relationship in competition with others. Indeed, there is some basis for arguing that modernization has enhanced the importance individuals assign to the family precisely because it has weakened the strength of attachment to other foci of affiliation and allegiance. Whether there has been a decline over time in the absolute importance individuals assign to their family ties, we cannot say with assurance because we lack comparable measures going back in time.

It seems unlikely, however, that there has been much decline. For one thing, the absolute percentage currently affirming the importance of the family is so high that the figures cannot have been much higher earlier. For another, the cross-sectional data that permit us to look simultaneously at countries on different steps of the ladder of economic development reveal no pattern suggesting that individuals feel less solidarity with the family in the economically more advanced countries. We must echo the conclusion reached by Mary Jo Bane when she summed up her review of American families in the twentieth century by selecting a title indicating that the family is *"Here to Stay."*[44]

The Importance of Kin Ties

Many of the standard commentaries on the change in the family presumed to accompany urbanization and industrialization claim that there has been a marked decline in the frequency and importance of kinship ties. This view has been strongly challenged by others who find evidence of continued vigor in the frequency of contact between kin and the personal significance of such kinship ties in the industrial working class in England and the United States. After reviewing much of that evidence Goode concluded: "The extended kin network continues to function and to include a wide range of kin who share with one another, see one another frequently, and know each other."[45]

Goode's conclusion is echoed by others making independent assessments of the issue on the basis of rather different evidence. For example, an analyst of personal time budgets in twelve countries noted that even in such highly industrial countries as the United States and Germany, a person's best friend proved to be a relative in some 40 percent of the cases. That, and other evidence, led Annerose Schneider to assert: "There is no evidence for the assumption of many sociologists . . . that as a consequence of industrialization the relations which are based on ascribed memberships—such as interaction with relatives—diminish or disappear."[46]

Certainly there is no doubt that kinship networks "continue to function." But to show that something remains active does not in any way disprove the assertion that it has become diminished. In their defense of the family and of kinship ties in Western societies many commentators commit the error of assuming that by demonstrating that kin ties are still much in evidence they have disproved the claim that industrialization and urbanization weaken the extent, the diversity, and the intensity of kinship ties. We are fully prepared to agree that the fact that 49 percent of the people in Detroit see their relatives at least once a week proves that kinship networks are still alive. But that fact alone tells us nothing about changes over time, that is, about the possible decrease in such contacts. Twenty years earlier the figure may well have been 60 percent and forty years earlier 75 percent. We simply do not know, but it certainly seems as plausible to claim a decrease in such contacts as it is to claim that they continue undiminished.

Drawing firm conclusions regarding the continued vitality of kinship ties is further complicated by the probability that the experience of stability or change is likely different for different aspects of the relations with kin. For example, the number of visits to relatives may not have been much reduced because, as Goode suggests, people today face fewer difficulties of transportation and communication. But if ease of transportation and communication facilitate contacting one's relatives, it should also stimulate turning to them for advice about life's problems. On this issue we have some interesting and sober data.

American parents in a national sample were asked where they would turn for advice in case they had a problem in raising their children. Of twelve obvious sources of help presented to them, they were least likely to turn to their relatives. Indeed, 42 percent explicitly rejected their relatives, whereas only 17 percent named them as the source they would "most likely" turn to. By contrast, 49 percent said they would turn to teachers and 34 percent to school psychologists.[47] Although we have no comparable opinion poll for 1940, and certainly not for 1900, it is hard to believe that at the turn of the century so few parents would have considered relatives most appropriate and so many would have judged them least appropriate sources of good advice about raising children.

Lacking precise data over time for a single nation, we are forced to turn to the cross-sectional data permitting a comparison of countries at different levels of economic development. In my own six-nation modernization study we found that the feeling that one had an obligation to help a first cousin and a more distant relative was much stronger in the less developed countries. As is so often the case in these comparisons, however, the more developed countries were also those more European in culture. Therefore, we cannot tell whether the observed contrasts more reflected differences in level of development or differences in culture.

William Form's study of auto workers confronts us with a similar difficulty, since his set of four countries included three of European culture plus India.[48] In his study somewhat fewer auto workers in India, 45 percent to be exact, said that they would confide in relatives, as against about 54 percent in the three countries sharing a European culture. But the pattern in the three European countries hardly suggests any correlation between level of economic development and the readiness to confide in relatives. In the United States, Italy, and Argentina the proportion ready for such confidence was more or less exactly the same despite the fact that the countries represent three well-spaced rungs on the ladder of economic development. Whether the similarity in the pattern of the three more industrial countries reflects their having come closer together over time cannot be assessed from available data.

All in all, then, the cross-sectional analysis now available must be seen as ambiguous, or otherwise inconclusive, as it bears on the question of whether kinship ties are eroded in the course of modernization. If there are systematic changes, they must be assumed to be manifest in some realms and not in others. Thus it remains a very open question whether contact with kin, as in regular visiting, is much reduced in urban and industrial settings. At the same time there seems rather compelling reason to assume, and some evidence to argue, that the character of the interaction and the nature of the demand one can make on kin has changed considerably.

Relatives cannot be expected, in the same degree as in the past, to make material sacrifices to help one out, nor to mobilize themselves in support of one's aspirations or in defense of one's interest. Neither can they as effectively constrain one in the choice of profession, spouse, or other public role, in the interest of the family's "good name," which is another way of saying that kin, like parents, no longer have the same authority over the individual as before. As Shorter put it, today people see relatives "rather as friends, and come together with them for all the expressive, personality-oriented reasons. . . . "[49] Over a decade earlier, Goode made much the same point, saying "a qualitative change . . . has taken place [so] that, to a considerable extent, relatives are now assimilated to the status of 'ascriptive' friends." While affirming that change, Goode characterized it as "impossible to measure."[50] I am more sanguine about the possibility of measuring it, but readily admit that at the moment we can still bring forth very little detailed evidence to support our hypothesis.

Parental Authority and Youth Autonomy

The ambiguity and uncertainty about many areas of family change are replaced by firm conviction and general agreement over one issue, namely, the decline of absolute parental authority and the concomitant rise in the autonomy of youth that accompany and express the modernization process.

The transformation of the roles relating parents and children is strikingly illustrated in family relations in Japan, the nation that, among the "late developers," has made the most rapid, indeed dramatic, shift from agricultural traditionalism to industrial modernism. In traditional Japanese society the family was organized as a "house," a continuity through time.[51] Each generation, in its turn occupying "the house" and enjoying the use of its property, was considered to be merely acting in trust, with a legal and moral obligation to transmit the heritage intact. The individual was totally subordinated to the needs and interests of the house. The household head bore the ultimate responsibility for the collective and had great power to decide and to enforce his decision. The choice of occupation, marriage partner, even place of residence for the young was in his hands. The Confucian ethic obliged all the persons of lower rank in the household, and especially the children, to obey, show respect, and manifest a selfless piety. The father was expected, indeed was praised, for being a strict, exacting, even awesome teacher, guide, and disciplinarian.

As late as 1875 this was the *ideal* and, in the majority of homes, it was evidently the *actual* pattern of relations between father and children. After one hundred years of rapid social change—and especially after some forty years of highly accelerated economic growth, urbanization, and industrialization following World War II—the status and role of the Japanese father seems to have been totally transformed. Hiroshi Wagatsuma gives us the following striking details: When, in 1973, junior high school students in Tokyo were asked—on Father's day, no less—whether their fathers gave them any guidance about what the fathers wanted for their children's future, almost three-fourths said their fathers never discussed such matters![52] To add insult to injury, the vast majority of those who got such advice from fathers said that they would not follow it. A mere 3 percent were left who would accept father's guidance in life. Almost half of the adult population felt that the father's authority was weakening. Less than 18 percent of a sample of college students felt able to honor their father by still calling him "awe-inspiring," as he was commonly considered to be in the past, and even fewer saw him as "strict." Indeed, many people spoke of their father as "indulgent," and public commentators, less bound by ties of affection, were more blunt and called him weak and insignificant in comparison with his former social role.

Compared to the Japanese, the American family before industrialization was certainly less characterized by such strong authority in the male head of the household. Especially under frontier conditions, the older generations could not so readily exercise their influence, and young people could more easily strike out on their own. Still, the information we have on contemporary attitudes strongly suggests that in the United States as well, parental authority is much reduced and the autonomy of youth much increased. Thus a national sample of the parents of children between six and twelve years of age showed surprisingly little interest in turning to their own parents for advice when they had problems raising the children. Only 27 percent would turn in that direction, approximately the same proportion as those who would turn to friends and many fewer than the 49 percent who would turn to teachers. American parents may still predominantly believe in "strict, old-fashioned upbringing and discipline" as the best way to bring up children, but it is startling how little control they expect to have over the long term. In 1977 between two-thirds and three-fourths of the parents of young children affirmed that "children have no obligation to their parents regardless of what the parents have done for them."[53]

Striking as this response may be, it should not be assumed that the United States is outstanding for the limited relevance of parents as exemplars and as guides to the making of important life decisions. In Denmark, for example, young people consistently, and by wide margins, prefer their friends over their parent as guides to what books to read, what to do about personal problems, and even with regard to issues of morality and value.[54] Although the parents are by no means reduced to total irrelevance in these matters, they are very far from the virtually unquestionable authority of the traditional family. Indeed, they often are not even *primi inter pares*. Friends, the mass media, experts and professionals, and above all one's personal preferences come increasingly to be the prime determinants of the decisions young people make about the things that matter to them.

Convergent and Divergent Forces

We started with the question: "Do family forms and dynamics converge on a common pattern as nations become industrialized, urbanized, and modernized?" The answer is "Yes," but that response must be much qualified. Convergent change is evident in some realms and not in others. And even where we perceive clear-cut convergence, the path to it is not always straight but rather is often curvilinear.

If we are to have a powerful general theory of the family's responses to social change, the theory must account for the fact that people give up having children, but they do not give up having spouses. It should explain why young people in Japan have come to consider their aged parents as irrelevant as guides to life but still overwhelmingly continue to accept the obligation to have them live in the same household. It would have to explain why the proportion of the labor force made up of women converges at close to 40 percent in "European" countries, whereas in those same countries the proportions of married women who work continue to be markedly differentiated.

No such general theory now exists. It may well never be developed, because the diversity and complexity of the phenomena we confront seem to require the application of a combination of explanations. Yet we understand enough to say what some of the elements of such a complex scheme might be, and to suggest how their joint application might more effectively explain the already observed phenomena and better predict those that are as yet unobserved.

My basic aim is to describe and explain how one societal subsystem, that of the "family" and relations within it, responds to changes in the other elements of the social structure, such as shifts in the mode of production and distribution or in the residence of the population moving from rural to urban settings. The response of the family may be to continue unchanged, or to change in specified directions. Since I am interested in convergence, it makes a great deal of difference to me in which direction things move. I am therefore especially eager to know whether the change process makes more alike family patterns that previously were more differentiated according to the region, the culture, or the economic and political context in which they were embedded. In this approach I am assuming that the family is the "dependent" variable, responding to changes in other elements of the social system. I will not explore here any evidence that suggests how family patterns may limit or otherwise influence change in other features of a society.

The Forces that Induce Convergent Change

Among the major forces that are presumably impinging on individuals in ways that lead to the development of new institutional arrangements for the family, or that might be expected to change the individual acceptance of and performance in family roles, are the following:

- Technological changes, especially in the modes of production and distribution, within which larger framework we assign particular importance to the new forms of work or employment.
- Ecological changes, especially in where people live, within which frame we attach particular importance to the gathering of population in one or another ring of the great urban conglomerations.
- Changes in the laws, especially those specifying the rights and obligations of individuals in their family relations, and the rights and obligations of family and kin groups vis-à-vis the larger society.
- Changes in the expectations and norms with which society collectively confronts each individual, and each unit such as the family. We assign particular emphasis here to the spread of new conceptions of morality, autonomy, and self-fulfillment, diffused from centers of cultural influence, especially by new media of mass communication.

Changes in Power and Authority.   Cross-cutting these conventionally defined realms are certain themes or dimensions common to them all. Thus the changes observed may be categorized as shifts in the relative power that different individuals wield or in the extent of the resources they command. Such shifts in resources and power are evident in the increasing autonomy of women and in the decreasing authority of parents.

When the legal status of women is changed to extend their right to inheritance and property ownership, to vote, or to hold public office, or when women go to work outside the home and get money income in their own hands, they command more resources and gain in power in their relations with men, with relatives, and with the society at large. Such shifts in power—the potential that comes with command of resources and expresses itself in increased autonomy and independence—are ultimately reflected in the structure and content of familial relations. If a young woman cannot get a husband without a dowry, and the dowry can only be provided by her parents, she has little choice to but accept the man they select for her. When she has earned the dowry by her own free labor, she will have a substantial chance to say to which young man of *her* choice it will go. And when he realizes that his wife has the potential to bring in considerable earnings after marriage, the same young man may come to marry the young woman without any dowry at all.

Parental Authority.   The dowry is found in only a few countries in Europe. But in the decline of the authority of parents, and especially of the father, we have another example in the shift in the relative power of family members that seems strongly determined by a large set of forces that act in concert and seem to produce a comparable effect in all the industrial countries.

In the modern industrial occupational structure one does not inherit one's father's job, nor does one generally learn the most fundamental occupational skills from him. Moreover, the rapidity of technological change makes it apparent to the young that fathers are neither suitable models nor relevant instructors in the realm of work. Urban settings and their associated educational facilities and mass media provide the young with rich alternative sources of instruction. At the same time, the density and complexity of economic activity in these settings vastly increase a young person's options, making available the many different types of work that may be found in a large impersonal job market. Independently, the legal rights of parents come to be restricted. They are obliged by law to assure their children of an education and are not free to put them out to work before some specified age, such as sixteen, by which time the children are adult enough, if they desire, to go off on their own. Attitudes and values have meanwhile been shifting to emphasize the right of each person to discover his or her special talents and to seek work expressing them. Access to work comes to depend less on parents and more on an open market. Demographic processes generate a preponderance of young people, giving them extra social weight relative to the old. Finally, none of the great historical crises of recent times seem to require a return to the wisdom the old can bring—indeed historical developments seem increasingly to cast doubt on the soundness of the world that the elders have built and are passing on to the young. A decline of parental, especially paternal, authority seems then almost overdetermined.

Falling Birthrates.   Some might quarrel with the claim that parental authority is everywhere eroded by the forces of industrialism and modernism, but the evidence with regard to falling birth rates is completely objective and would seem to be quite unimpeachable. The decline in fertility provides us with one of the most clear-cut instances of a uniform and profound change resulting from the simultaneous impact of a number of basic social forces all working in the same direction.

Changes in the occupational structure, especially in the shift from country and farm to city, industry, and office act greatly to reduce the potential value of children as a source of needed labor. Some might still want them as security for their old age, but such children must seem a costly way to achieve that objective if they cannot earn when they are young. Increasingly, therefore, people either save or rely on government old-age pensions. Legal obligations are in the meantime changing, with the state acting as the protector of all children, insisting we send them to school rather than to work. Urban housing makes for limited space. Women are more educated and more often employed outside the home—they can perhaps manage two children, but a greater number quickly begins to become an obstacle to continued effective employment. All these forces induce people to limit the number of children they have.

Forces Resisting Convergence

Our anticipation that certain social forces unleashed in all industrial countries will produce parallel or convergent change in family relations must be tempered to allow for the operation of other forces that influence the family in a different way, preventing, muting, or distorting the shifts one would anticipate on the basis of changes in the occupational structure or in the level of female employment. Two sets of such countervailing forces may be identified. The first consists of cultural patterns, the second of basic human needs.

Culture Patterns.   Citing culture patterns as a source of resistance to changes in family relations may at first sight seem a redundancy. Family relations are themselves culture patterns. We might break out of this chain of circular reasoning if we could identify a hierarchy of cultural values in a given society. If that could be done unambiguously, then we would have a basis for explaining why some otherwise widespread changes in family relationships did not occur in certain societies even when the objective conditions for such changes were well met. We could then argue that the changes in family relations that were elsewhere produced by objective circumstances were not manifested in certain other countries because making that particular change would have forced the people to violate their higher-order values. Thus it might be argued that in some Oriental societies, such as China or Japan, respect, indeed veneration, for elders is so central an element of the value system as to prevent young people in those cultures from responding in the same way as did Europeans to forces that weaken the importance, authority, and claims of older people.

Unfortunately, we cannot produce a simple test of the soundness of this argument, because we do not have available an independently derived hierarchy of values for most cultures. Indeed, we often "discover" which values are dominant in a given society only by observing the very resistance to change that we are here trying to explain. Consequently, when we invoke higher-order cultural values to explain the cases in which an expected family change fails to occur, we generally do so on an ad hoc and post hoc basis. That is clearly not very satisfactory, and for the future we must strive to deal with the issue more systematically.

Basic Human Needs.   Basic human needs play a different role than do distinctive cultural values, but they too may act to limit the impact of objective conditions on family patterns. Since basic human needs must be assumed to be more or less the same in all human populations, they cannot be invoked to explain the deviation of any one country from a general pattern of change. They may, however, be invoked to explain why some family relations persist virtually everywhere despite massive changes in numerous closely related realms.

We may take as our first example the remarkable stability and generality of the statistic for the percentage of the population "ever married" among those who have reached the age of forty-five to fifty. Birthrates decline sharply, divorce rates fluctuate wildly, the number of women who never had a child declines markedly,[55] but through it all the proportion of the population that gets married remains remarkably stable around 90 percent and above in Europe and at even higher levels in Asia. Why should that be?

We cannot convincingly invoke pressure from *structural* changes to explain a *constant* in family relations. The same structural transformations that have profoundly influenced so many other aspects of family relations could equally plausibly explain the fact of a sharp decline in the proportion of people who never married—if such a decline had occurred. But it has not occurred. It seems that there are basic needs for sex, for companionship, for physical and psychological support, which cannot be as satisfactorily provided by other social arrangements as they can by having a conjugal or marital relationship. This is not to say that basic human needs *require* that people live as married couples. There are obviously many alternative ways of providing for the same basic needs. Sex needs, for example, might be met by casual liaisons, or by more enduring ones outside of the marriage mode. As the need for security in old age comes increasingly to be met by government welfare programs, people can and do give up having the large number of children they formerly saw as necessary to support them in later life. But not all substitutes are equally acceptable. Others may be fine in themselves but do not lend themselves to being combined, comfortably, with other needs-satisfying arrangements. Marriage may persist undiminished in frequency while so many other arrangements are dropped or basically changed because none of those others has the ability, which the institution of marriage has, to optimize satisfactions without too severely conflicting with the role demands made on individuals in a modern industrial society.

Husbands Helping Wives. Another striking example of the persistence of traditional patterns despite massive social change is the failure of men in even the most advanced industrial societies substantially to increase the amount of time they give to household chores even after their wives have entered gainful employment outside the household. Thus in the United States unmarried men, even those with children, spend about the same amount of time doing household chores before marriage as after, and the amount is nominal, less than half an hour per day.[56]

In a study of twelve countries it was found that, as a rule, about 95 percent of the women do household chores even when employed, whereas for employed men the median percentage participating in such tasks was only 47 percent.[57] The average time put in by the typical working woman with children was 244 minutes per day. Because so few men participated at all, average time on household chores for employed men with children was typically, a mere twenty-nine minutes per working day.[58] In other words, although both husband and wife work, the women spend almost ten times as many minutes per day in household chores. Moreover, socialist countries did not have a better record than the capitalist countries.[59] Typical of the tone of discouragement that pervades discussion of this issue is the following comment by two women sociologists comparing recent trends in socialist Poland and nonsocialist Finland: "The division of household responsibilities between husband and wife is relatively traditional in both countries; it is the wife who carries the main burden of housework whether she is gainfully employed or not." They went on to say that although there is a tendency for husbands of working wives to help with household chores and children, "In both Finland

and Poland patterns of family life are changing relatively slowly."[60] This echoes the multicountry time budget study that reported, "The amount of housework done by employed men is not basically affected by occupational status, marital status, or the presence of children."[61]

Evidently, women's employment has little or no power to influence how much help they get from their husbands in doing the chores that keep a household going. Being at work should make the women more equal to their husbands in arranging the division of household chores, since the husband cannot claim greater pressure on his time when his wife also works. Neither can he claim greater need for rest. Moreover, gainfully employed women command more resources, and their earnings give them potential independence and otherwise support their claims to equality of treatment. Such forces act to free women from the dowry, from the obligation to accept marriage partners they have not chosen for themselves, from the pressure to have more children than they wish, and from the necessity of continuing in marriages they can no longer tolerate. Yet these same forces seem powerless to induce men to offer their employed wives anything even remotely resembling an equal share of effort in performing essential household chores.

We should then perhaps not be too surprised to discover that there are realms of interpersonal relations in the family that seem successfully to resist those forces of social change that have transformed several other patterns of marital relations. But it is distressing that we find ourselves without a theory that can convincingly explain why the forces of change influence this particular marital relationship and not that. To refer to "human needs" is no help in explaining why married men do not give their employed wives more time to deal with household chores. Male dominance may be high in the hierarchy of cultural values in many countries, but it has not prevented women from achieving more nearly equal treatment in other realms such as in voting and in the control of property. A distinct possibility is that there is some little understood force that induces intimates to maintain a high degree of division of labor and task specialization, especially in the closest relationships, such as in marriage. This possibility and others await discovery and exploration as we extend and deepen our study of ways in which family patterns resist the pressures of modernization.

Conclusion

In investigating change and stability in the family, we have identified three modes. The elements of one set of institutional arrangements and of interpersonal relations patterns change in parallel fashion in different societies, and in some cases even converge on a single pattern for all the advanced industrial nations. On the basis of my explorations in progress, I would tentatively include in that set: residence patterns, choice of marriage partner, parental authority, fertility rates, and rates of female employment. All the elements of this set seem to respond in comparable ways to changes in other aspects of the social structure, and I feel rather confident that we can "make sense" of these responses. They may be understood as adjustments that individuals and institutions make to accommodate the larger forces of social change that go with mass production, urbanization, pervasive popular education, mass communication, and other features of industrial and "post-industrial" society.

But family relations are evidently too complex and subtle to respond uniformly even to a uniform set of influences. The same forces that produce parallel and even convergent change in some patterns of family relations seem relatively powerless to affect others that, on initial inspection, seemed equally likely candidates for change. An example is the proportion of married women who work, a figure that remains strikingly low in some countries despite substantial industrialization and urbanization. To deal with these resistances to change readily adopted in most other places, we are forced back to explanations in terms of distinctive cultural sensitivities and higher-order values. Unfortunately, such explanations are too often produced only after we come upon some exception to the rule, and we have trouble explaining why higher-order values inhibit some changes and not others.

Still other realms of family life present us with yet a third mode of change, the mode of relative constancy. Despite all the shifts, twists, and turns observed in some realms of family life, there are patterns that seem to remain strikingly constant across countries and over time. An outstanding example is the percentage ever married during the years before old age sets in. These constants suggest that certain basic human needs so much favor one institutional form over another that no amount of change in other features of social organization can succeed in driving them out. One such pattern may be that which links a man and a women in a long-term association through some arrangement similar to what we call "marriage." Another may be the "nuclear family," about whose universality there is much current debate.[62]

We may claim to have made considerable progress in understanding how the family varies in response to stability and change in other aspects of social structure and culture. We must also acknowledge that a great deal remains to be done. And as we master the explanation of the change and stability we have already identified, some new elements of both change and stability may be discovered. It seems highly likely that with the passage of time some of the pockets of resistance to uniform change will come more to follow the general pattern. And some of the "constants" may become more variable.

Even more than most foci of social research, the interaction of the family and society seems a particularly subtle and elusive phenomenon. Those who engage themselves with it operate under the condition that the great Rabbi Tarfon set for his pupils when he said, "It is not your part to finish the task; yet neither are you free to desist from it."[63]

Part Four

FOCUS ON PROCESS

eight

SOCIAL STRATIFICATION: NATIONAL COMPARISONS OF OCCUPATIONAL PRESTIGE

During the latter part of the nineteenth and the first half of the twentieth centuries the factory system of production was introduced, at least on a small scale, to most areas of the world. The factory has generally been accompanied by a relatively standard set of occupations, including the factory manager (sometimes also owner) and his administrative and clerical staff, engineering and lesser technical personnel, foremen, skilled, semiskilled, and unskilled workers. In the factory, authority and responsibility are allocated largely according to the degree of technical or administrative competence required for the job. In addition, the allocation of material and social rewards, the latter generally in the form of deference, is closely adjusted to levels of competence and degrees of authority and responsibility. The pattern of differentiation of authority is undoubtedly functionally necessary to the productive activity of the factory, and it may be that the associated pattern of reward differentiation is also functionally necessary.

Reprinted with permission from Alex Inkeles and Peter H. Rossi, "National Comparisons of Occupational Prestige," in *American Journal of Sociology*, Vol. 61, No. 4 (January 1956), 329–339.

There is, however, no clear-cut imperative arising from the structure of the factory as such that dictates how the incumbents of its typical statuses should be *evaluated* by the population at large. One possibility is that in popular esteem the typical occupations will stand relative to one another in a rank order strictly comparable to their standing in the formal hierarchy of competence, authority, and reward in the factory. It is also possible, however, that the popular evaluation of these occupations will be quite different. Indeed, where the factory system has been introduced into societies like those of Spain or Japan, with well-established values based on tradition and expressive of the culture, one might expect significant differences between an occupation's standing in the formal hierarchy of the industrial system and its position on the popular ranking scheme.

Thus the interaction of the two systems—the standardized modern occupation system and the individual national value pattern for rating occupations—presents an interesting and important problem in comparative sociology.

We may posit two extreme positions in this interaction, while granting that it might be difficult to find live exponents of either. The extreme "structuralist" would presumably insist that the modern industrial occupational system is a highly coherent system, relatively impervious to influence by traditional culture patterns. Indeed, she might go so far as to insist that the traditional ranking system would in time have to be subsumed under, or integrated into, the industrial system. Consequently, her argument would run, even such occupations as priest, judge, and provincial governor, not part of the modern occupational system and often given unusual deference, would come in time to have roughly the same standing relative to one another and to other occupations, no matter what their national cultural setting.

By contrast, an extreme "culturalist" might insist that within each country or culture the distinctive local value system would result in substantial—and, indeed, sometimes extreme—differences in the evaluation of particular jobs in the standardized modern occupational system. For example, he might assume that in the United States the company director would be rated unusually high because of Americans' awe of the independent businessman and large corporations, or that in the Soviet Union the standing of industrial workers would be much higher relative to managerial personnel than in Germany, with its emphasis on sharply differentiated status hierarchies. Furthermore, he might argue that the more traditional occupational roles assigned special importance in particular cultures would continue to maintain their distinctive positions in the different national hierarchies. Indeed, he might hold that the characteristic roles of the modern industrial system would come to be subsumed within the traditional rating system, each factory occupation being equated with some traditional occupation and then assigned a comparable rank.

A systematic test of these contrasting positions is not beyond the capacity of contemporary social research. A standard list of occupations—say thirty or forty in number—might be presented for evaluation to comparable samples from countries representing a range of culture types and degrees of industrialization. The list should contain both standard industrial occupations and the common, but differentially valued, traditional roles (e.g., priest, legislator, etc.).

Data are available which, though far from completely adequate, will carry us a long way beyond mere speculation on these matters. In the postwar years studies of occupational ratings have been conducted in and reported on five relatively industrialized countries: the United States, Great Britain, New Zealand, Japan, and Germany.[1] In addition, the authors have available previously unpublished data for a sixth country, the Soviet Union.

Since these six studies[2] were, on the whole, undertaken quite independently, our ideal research design is clearly far from being fulfilled. Nevertheless, the data do permit tentative and exploratory cross-national comparisons.

The Comparability of Research Designs

The elements of similarity and difference in the six studies may be quickly assessed from the following summary of their essential features:

Population Studied

United States: National sample of "adults" fourteen years of age and over; 2,920 respondents

Japan: Sample of males twenty to sixty-eight years of age in the six large cities of Japan; 899 respondents

Great Britain: Written questionnaires distributed through adult-education centers and other organizations; 1,056 returns (percentage returned unspecified)

U.S.S.R.: Sample of displaced persons, mostly in displaced-persons camps near Munich, Germany, and some former displaced persons now residing on eastern seaboard of United States; 2,100 written questionnaires

New Zealand: Sample collected mainly by interviews with inhabitants of towns of 2,000, and partly by mailed questionnaires (12 percent returns) sent out to towns of 4,000; 1,033 questionnaires and interviews used

Germany: 1,500 Schleswig-Holsteiners: vocational-school students, university students, and male adults (not otherwise specified); adult sample only used here

Overlap Among Occupations Studied

Each study involved a different number of occupations, ranging from eighty-eight in the case of the National Opinion Research Center American study to thirteen in the Soviet research.

In order to make comparisons between pairs of countries, each occupation studied in each research was matched, when possible, with an occupation in the data gathered in the other country. In many cases it was necessary to disregard the information about an occupation in one of the paired countries because no comparable occupation had been studied in the other. In other instances, in order to increase the number of occupations that could be compared for any given pair of countries, occupations were matched that were only very roughly comparable, for example, Buddhist priest and Christian minister, or collective farm chairman and farm owner and operator. In most cases, however, a direct correspondence characterizes the pairs of occupations that are being equated. The reader is invited to turn to Table 8.5 at the end of the chapter, in which the lists of occupations used from each of the researches are printed. The occupations listed on any row or line were matched. The number of pairs of similar or identical comparison is shown in Table 8.1.

Nature of Rating Task

United States: Respondents were asked: "Please pick out the statement that best gives your own *personal opinion* of the *general standing* that such a job has. Excellent standing, good standing, average standing, somewhat below average, poor standing."

Japan: Respondents were given a set of thirty cards and asked: "... Think of the general reputations they have with people, and sort them into five or more groups, from those which people think highly of to those which are not thought so well of."

Great Britain: Respondents were told: "We should like to know in what order, *as to their social standing,* you would grade the occupations in the list given to you. [Rate them] ... in terms of five main social classes ... ABCDE."

U.S.S.R.: Respondents were asked: "Taking everything into consideration, how desirable was it to have the job of (———) in the Soviet Union? Very desirable? Desirable? So-so? Undesirable? Very undesirable?"

New Zealand: Same as in Great Britain.

Germany: The source is unfortunately not very specific about the rating task assigned. The respondents were apparently asked to rank-order a list of thirty-eight occupations presented as one slate.

Table 8.1   Number of identical or similar occupations, rated by pairs of nations

	United States	Great Britain	U.S.S.R.	Japan	New Zealand	Germany
United States		24	10	25	24	20
Great Britain			7	14	30	12
U.S.S.R.				7	7	8
Japan					14	19
New Zealand						12
Total occupations studied	88	30	13	30	30	38

Computing Prestige Position

With the exception of the German study, each research presents a "prestige score" for each of the occupations studied. These scores, computed variously, represent in each case the "average" rating given to each of the occupations by the entire sample of raters used. The German study presented only the rank-order positions of the occupations.

One is not sure whether differences between nations are generated by the differences in the questionnaires or the differences in the nations themselves. However, similarities in the prestige hierarchies, particularly when they are striking, are somewhat strengthened by the same lack of comparability in research designs and in the occupations matched to one another. Similarities may be interpreted as showing the extent to which design and other differences are overcome by the comparability among the prestige hierarchies themselves.

The Comparability of Occupational Prestige Hierarchies

Since each study included some occupations used in another study, it is possible to compare the prestige hierarchies of occupations in pairs of countries by computing correlation coefficients for the scores (or ranks) of occupations. The fifteen correlation coefficients that result are presented in Table 8.2.[3] It will be seen immediately that the levels of correlation are considerably higher than the magnitude to be expected if there were only rough agreement on placement in the top and bottom halves of the prestige hierarchy. Indeed, twelve of the fifteen coefficients are above .9, and only one is below .8. The three coefficients below .9 all concern the Soviet ratings, which, it will be recalled, involve only a very small number of occupations, maximizing the chances for lower correlations arising from merely one or two "mismatches."

For most of the comparisons, furthermore, the findings go beyond establishing mere comparability of rank orders. With the exception of the correlations involving Germany, each coefficient represents the relationships be-

Table 8.2   Correlations between prestige scores (or ranks) given to comparable occupations, by pairs of nations

	U.S.S.R.	Japan	Great Britain	New Zealand	United States	Germany
U.S.S.R.		.74	.83	.83	.90	.90
Japan			.92	.91	.93	.93
Great Britain				.97	.94	.97
New Zealand					.97	.96
United States						.96
Average correlation	.84	.89	.93	.93	.94	.94

See Table 8.1 for numbers of occupations involved with each comparison. All coefficients are product-moment correlations, with the exception of those involving Germany, which are rank-order coefficients.

tween prestige *scores* given to the same occupations in two different nations. Hence there is a high relationship between the relative "distance" between occupations, as expressed in score differences, as well. In other words, if, of two occupations, one is given a much lower score than the other by the raters in one country, this difference in prestige scores and not merely crude rank order also obtains in another country.

It should also be noted that these high correlations were obtained by using samples of occupations that were not strictly identical from country to country, including very crude comparisons such as that already mentioned of collective farm chairman and a farm owner and operator. One may anticipate that if the occupations studied were more uniform, the similarities of prestige hierarchies from country to country would be even higher.

In other words, *despite the heterogeneity in research design, there exists among the six nations a marked degree of agreement on the relative prestige of matched occupations.* To this extent, therefore, it appears that the "structuralist" expectation is more nearly met than is the expectation based on the culturalist position.

Each of the six nations differs in the extent to which its prestige hierarchy resembles those of other nations. The average of the correlations for each nation, contained in the bottom row of Table 8.2, expresses these differences among nations quantitatively. Thus we may see that the American and German occupation prestige hierarchies are most similar to those of other nations, and the Soviet and Japanese hierarchies are most dissimilar. When we consider that the Soviet Union and Japan are, of the six, the more recently industrialized cultures, we may see there some small degree of evidence for the culturalist position.

Furthermore, if we examine the correlations among the three nations that have the closest cultural ties and that share a common historical background and language—Great Britain, the United States, and New

Zealand—we find these coefficients to be among the highest in Table 8.2. Again, the evidence to some extent supports the interpretation of a small "cultural" effect. However, the coefficients in question are not sufficiently distinguished in size from those involving Germany[4] and the three Anglo-Saxon nations to allow much weight to be given to the influence of the common Anglo-Saxon culture. In other words, whatever the national differences among the six, they do not greatly affect the general pattern of the prestige hierarchy.

National Patterns of Occupational Prestige

Although the relationships among the six occupational hierarchies are very high, they do not indicate one-to-one correspondences among the national ranks of occupations. Each nation shows some variation from every other, and the international discrepancies may perhaps throw further light on the relationships between social structure, culture, and occupational prestige.

One possibility is that unique aspects of the culture or social structure of a particular country determine distinctive appraisals of a certain type or types of occupation. National differences are thus to be interpreted in a unique fashion for each country.

A second possible explanation is that it is the type of occupation that engenders disagreement, some occupations being similarly rated everywhere and others yielding no consistent rating. To some extent these contrasting explanations are similar, respectively, to the culturalist and structuralist positions discussed earlier.

Here again the available data place marked limits on the possibility of a definitive answer, but it is nevertheless feasible for us to go some distance in exploring the problem. In order to obtain some means by which to assess the presence or absence of disagreement among nations, regression equations were computed to predict the prestige positions of the occupations in one country as against the prestige positions of the comparable occupations in each other country. Ten such equations were computed, interrelating the prestige hierarchies in the United States, Japan, Great Britain, New Zealand, and the Soviet Union but excluding Germany, since the published data on that country indicated only the rank order of occupations. Those occupations that lay more than one standard deviation of the estimate of the regression lines were arbitrarily characterized as occupations over which there was a disagreement between the two nations involved.

Applying this criterion, we have presented in Table 8.3 the discrepancies in ratings between all relevant pairs of nations. The columns show the occupations rated higher by a given country in relation to each of the other countries represented in the rows. Reading the table by rows, we find the occupations rated lower by one country than by others, not forgetting that each compari-

Table 8.3 Discrepancies in the rating of matched occupations, by pairs of nations

	Rated Higher in Japan	Rated Higher in U.S.	Rated Higher in Great Britain	Rated Higher in New Zealand	Rated Higher in U.S.S.R.
Rated lower in Japan		Minister, farmer, insurance agent, carpenter	Minister, farmer, insurance agent	Minister, farmer, insurance agent	Accountant
Rated lower in U.S.	Company director, labor leader, reporter (news), street sweeper, shoe shiner		Accountant, chef, street sweeper	Accountant, farmer, truck driver, street sweeper	Engineer, worker
Rated lower in Great Britain	Reporter (news), street sweeper	Civil servant, truck driver, minister, building contractor, electrician		Truck driver	Worker
Rated lower in New Zealand	Reporter (news), street sweeper	Civil servant, building contractor, bookkeeper, electrician, dock worker	Chef, bartender		Worker
Rated lower in U.S.S.R.	Factory manager, farmer	Scientist, farmer	Farmer	Farmer	

We consistently designate any cited occupation by the title closest and most familiar to Americans. For example, we used minister in preference to Buddhist priest, electrician rather than fitter (electrical). For the exact titles, see Table 8.5

son of a pair of countries involves a somewhat different set of occupations from the comparison of ratings for any other pair of countries. Only a few occupations, such as farmer, teacher, doctor, factory manager, and some form of industrial worker, were rated in all five countries and therefore appear in all the pairs of comparisons. Some occupations, such as judge, were rated in only two countries and therefore appear in only one paired comparison.[5]

Table 8.3 serves to highlight the special positions held by certain occupations in particular countries. For example, the Japanese Buddhist priest rates lower than a minister in each of the three available comparisons, and this undoubtedly reflects the cultural differences in structure and role between the Buddhist religion in Japan and the Judeo-Christian religion in the three Anglo-Saxon countries. Equally notable is the consistently lower position of farm manager as rated by displaced persons from the Soviet Union. Though the occupation of collective farm chairman is not strictly comparable to those with which it is matched, there can be no doubt that the displaced persons regard that occupation with a special ambivalence arising out of the position of agriculture in the Soviet economy from the 1930s onward.

Despite the clarity with which a particular occupation may stand out, it is difficult to find any definite *pattern* characterizing the disagreements expressed by any one country. Of course such a pattern, if it does exist, may be obscured in our data by the modest number of occupations rated by each country, as a result of which there are seldom more than one or two occupations of a given type in each of the comparisons. Thus, it would be hazardous to assume that since the Japanese rate the occupation newspaper reporter higher than do Americans, Britishers, or New Zealanders, they would also rate *occupations of this type* higher than the other countries. Nevertheless, it will be noticed that in the country with the largest number of comparisons, the instances of disagreement involve a wide variety of quite disparate occupations. Those rated higher in the United States, for example, range from building contractor to farmer and from scientist to dock worker and appear to have little in common. The same range and absence of a common denominator are shown by the occupations rated lower in the United States. Furthermore, the discrepancies do not consistently appear in all the relevant comparisons: Farm owner is out of line in only two out of four comparisons; as to truck driver, the two recorded disagreements go in opposite directions, that occupation being rated higher in comparison with Britain and lower in comparison with New Zealand.

International Comparability of Types of Occupation

If there is no clear-cut pattern of deviance by country, is there perhaps a tendency for certain types of occupation to be foci of disagreement? Perhaps if we classify occupations according to the features of social structure or cul-

Table 8.4   Discrepancies in prestige position according to type of occupation

Occupation Types[a]	Proportion of Discrepancies (percent)	Number of Comparisons
Professional	16	31
Industrial	24	29
Political	25	16
Traditional crafts	27	11
Clerical and commercial	32	37
Agricultural	50	16
Service	63	20

[a]Examples of occupations included in each type are as follows: *Professional:* doctor, minister, teacher, etc.; *industrial:* industrial worker, company director, factory manager, engineer; *political:* judge, civil servant, etc.; *traditional crafts:* bricklayer, carpenter, fisherman; *clerical and commercial:* accountant, bookkeeper, salesman, small entrepreneur, etc.; *agricultural:* farm owner and operator, farm hand; *service:* shoe shiner, barber, porter, streetcar conductor, etc.

ture to which they are most closely related, we may gain further insight into the interaction between culture, social structure, and occupational prestige hierarchies. To explore this question, we grouped all the occupations into seven basic types: industrial, clerical and commercial, professional, political, traditional crafts, agricultural, and service occupations.[6] In Table 8.4, we have indicated the number of international comparisons between pairs among the five countries, again excluding Germany, that could be made involving the occupations in each class of occupations. We have also indicated the proportions of those comparisons that yielded disagreements. Disagreements were recorded on the same basis as in the preceding table, that is, on the basis of predictions from regression equations.

Because our findings so far have so strongly supported the structuralist expectation concerning the influence of industrialization in producing uniformity, our initial expectation may well be that occupations closely allied to the industrial system will enjoy highly comparable standings from country to country, whereas occupations more remotely connected would be the focus of international discrepancies. Table 8.4 indicates, however, that industrial occupations are not outstanding in the degree of agreement about their social standing. Instead, the *lowest* proportion of disagreements is shown by the professions. In addition, other occupational types, such as the political occupations and the traditional crafts, which are not necessarily closely allied to the industrial system, manifested levels of disagreement as low as that enjoyed by the industrial occupations. Only the agricultural and service occupations yield a degree of disagreement that sets them apart from the other occupational groups.

Accounting for these discrepancies appears to require a combination of arguments. In the first place, some types of nonindustrial occupations are easily assimilated to the industrial system. The traditional crafts serve as the prime example here, since the skills involved in such occupations as bricklayer, carpenter, and plumber have a close resemblance to the skills of industrial workers. Indeed, some crafts have been partly incorporated into the industrial system, and, it may be argued, such occupations are easily placed within the hierarchy of industrial occupations and may tend to assume roughly the same position vis-à-vis industrial occupations. Likewise, some professions, such as engineering and applied scientific research, have a most immediate connection with the industrial system, and others, such as architecture, are easily equated with it.

However, closeness or assimilability to the industrial system will not suffice to explain the relatively stable position of other professions, such as doctor. Nor will it serve to explain the low proportion of disagreement concerning the political occupations. We must recognize that the nations being compared have certain structural and cultural features in common, in addition to the presence of industry. For example, they share certain needs, as for socialization, and their populations likely share some valued goals, such as for health and systematic knowledge, which ensure relatively comparable standing to doctors, teachers, and scientists. Furthermore, all the countries compared have in common the national state, with which is associated a relatively standardized occupational structure ranging from ministers of state to local bureaucrats. In addition, both the professions and the political occupations are highly "visible," and agreement as to their standing is probably facilitated by the relatively objective and easily perceived indexes of power, knowledge, and skill manifested by their incumbents.

The types of occupation that generate the greatest amount of disagreement are highly variant and unstandardized or difficult to assimilate to the industrial structure. Agriculture may be conducted, as in Japan, on relatively small holdings, on collective farms as in the U.S.S.R., or, as in the western plains of the United States, in "agricultural factories." Being a farmer means very different things in each of the five countries, quite unlike the standardized image of the machinist or the factory manager. It can be anticipated, however, that as agriculture tends to be similarly organized in different countries, agricultural occupations will achieve more uniform standing.

The "service" occupations—barber, shoe shiner, chef, street sweeper—show the greatest amount of variation. Many of them antedate the industrial system and are found in agrarian as well as industrial societies. They have no fixed position relative to the industrial order, nor are they similar to typical industrial occupations, as are many of the traditional crafts. They therefore appear to be most easily evaluated according to the traditional culture. Personal service in countries like Japan and Great Britain, in which a servant class was historically well developed and benefited from intimate association with an aristocratic upper class, may still be regarded as not so degrading as in the more democratic societies, such as the United States and

New Zealand. In fact, the greatest discrepancy to be found among all the comparisons involves the differences in prestige position accorded to chef in Great Britain as compared with either the United States or New Zealand, although in the case of the former the match was poor, since the comparable occupation was "restaurant cook." As these services come to be organized and mechanized—as in modern laundries or restaurants—they will become more thoroughly integrated into the larger economic order and may in time achieve more strictly comparable status from country to country.

All told, it would appear from this examination of international discrepancies that a great deal of weight must be given to the cross-national similarities in social structure that arise from the industrial system and from other common structural features, such as the national state. The greatest incidence of discrepancies occurs for occupations that are hardest to fit into either the one or the other structure. To this extent the structuralist position that we outlined earlier seems to be more heavily borne out in these data.

Summary and Conclusions

To sum up, our examination of occupational ratings in six modern industrialized countries reveals an extremely high level of agreement, going far beyond chance expectancy, as to the relative prestige of a wide range of specific occupations, despite the variety of sociocultural settings in which they are found. This strongly suggests that there is a relatively invariant hierarchy of prestige associated with the industrial system, even when it is placed in the context of larger social and cultural systems that are otherwise differentiated in important respects. In addition, the fact that the countries compared also have in common the national state and certain needs or values, such as interest in health, apparently also contributes to the observed regularity of the ratings, since both professional and political occupations are foci of agreement. Perhaps the most striking finding is the extent to which the different classes of occupation have been woven together into a single relatively unified occupational structure, more or less common to the six countries. At the same time, there is strong evidence that this relatively standardized occupational hierarchy does not apply without major exception to all occupations in all large-scale industrialized societies. In some instances, important disagreement may arise from the distinctive role of a single occupation in a particular country. In the majority of cases, however, the disagreement appears to involve certain classes of occupation, notably agricultural and service, about which there is only modest agreement. Disagreement probably reflects differences in the length and "maturity" of industrialization in various countries but also clearly results from differentiations in sociocultural systems that may well be relatively enduring.

Table 8.5 Occupations and scores/ranks

United States		Germany		Great Britain		New Zealand		Japan		U.S.S.R.	
Occupation	Score	Occupation	Rank	Occupation	Score	Occupation	Score	Occupation	Score	Occupation	Score
Physician	93	Doctor	2	Medical Officer	1.3	Medical Officer	1.4	Doctor	7.0	Doctor	75
State governor	93							Prefectural gov.	3.8		
College professor	89	Univ. professor	1					Univ. professor	4.6	Scientific worker	73
Scientist	89										
County judge	87							Local court judge	4.7		
Head of dept. in state government	87	High civil servant (Regierungsrat-höherer Beamter)	4	Civil servant	6.0	Civil servant	7.0	Section head of a government office	7.2		
Minister	87	Minister (Pfarrer)	6	Nonconformist minister	6.4	Nonconformist minister	5.9	Priest of a Buddhist temple	12.5		
Architect	86	(Elec. engineer)[a]	10					(Architect)	9.5		
Lawyer	86			Country solicitor	2.6	Country solicitor	3.8				
Member of board of directors of large corporation	86	Factory director (Fabrikdirektor)	5	Company director	1.6	Company director	3.6	Officer of large company	5.5	Factory manager	65
Civil engineer	84	Elec. engineer	10					(Architect)[b]	9.5	Engineer	73
Owner of factory that employs about 100 people	82							Owner of a small or medium sized factory	10.2		
Accountant for a large business	81			Chartered accountant	3.2	Chartered accountant	5.7	(Company office clerk)[c]	16.1	Bookkeeper	62
Captain in regular army	80	Major in armed forces	8							Officer in the armed services	58

(continues)

Table 8.5 (continued)

United States		Germany		Great Britain		New Zealand		Japan		U.S.S.R.	
Occupation	Score	Occupation	Rank	Occupation	Score	Occupation	Score	Occupation	Score	Occupation	Score
Building contractor	79			Jobbing master builder	11.4	Jobbing master builder	10.7				
Instructor in public schools (teacher)	78	Elem.-school (Volksschullehrer)	11	Elem.-school teacher	10.8	Elem.-school teacher	10.3	Elem.-school teacher	11.7	Teacher	55
Farm owner and operator	76	Farmer (Bauer-mittelgrosser Betrieb)	13	Farmer	7.3	Farmer	8.1	Small independent farmer	16.4	Chairman of collective farm	38
Official of inter-national labor union	75							Chairman of national labor federation	10.8		
Electrician	73			Fitter (elec.)	17.6	Fitter (elec.)	15.8				
Trained machinist	73	Skilled industrial worker (Industrie-facharbeiter)	24								
Reporter on daily newspaper	71			News reporter	11.8	News reporter	13.8	Newspaper reporter	11.2		
Bookkeeper	68	Bank teller (book-keeper in bank)	19	Routine clerk	16.1	Routine clerk	16.4	Company office clerk	16.1	(Bookkeeper)[a]	62
Insurance agent	68	Insurance agent	20	Insurance agent	14.6	Insurance agent	16.1	Insurance agent	20.2		
Traveling salesman for wholesale concern	68			Commercial traveler	12.0	Commercial traveler	14.1				
Policeman	67			Policeman	16.1	Policeman	15.5	Policeman	16.4		
Mail carrier	66	Postman	23								
Carpenter	65	Carpenter	18	Carpenter	18.6	Carpenter	17.0	Carpenter	20.2		

Corporal in regular army	60							
Noncommissioned officer	31							
Machine operator in factory	60				Latheman	21.1	Rank-and-file worker	48
Machine operator (Maschinen-schlosser-Geselle)	26	(Compositive of fitter, carpenter, bricklayer, tractor driver, coal hewer)[e]	20.5	(Compositive of fitter, carpenter, bricklayer, tractor driver, coal hewer)[e]	20.9			
Barber	59					Barber	20.5	
Clerk in a store (Verkäufer im Lebensmittel geschäft)	58	Shop assistant	20.2	Shop assistant	20.2	Department store clerk	19.8	
Store clerk	28							
Fisherman who owns own boat	58					Fisherman	22.0	
Streetcar motorman	58					Bus driver	20.9	
Conductor	33							
Restaurant cook	54	Chef	13.8	Chef	21.8			
Truck driver	54	Carter	25.8	Carrier[f]	20.2			Rank-and-file collective farmer	18
Farm hand	50	Agricultural laborer	25.5	Agricultural laborer	24.4			
Farm laborer (worker)	36							
Coal miner	49	Coal hewer	23.2	Coal hewer	24.7	Coal miner	23.7	
Restaurant waiter	48							
Waiter (Kellner)	30							
Dock worker	47	Dock laborer	27.0	Dock laborer	28.3			
Bartender	44	Barman	26.4	Barman	28.3			
Street sweeper	34	Road sweeper	28.9	Road sweeper	28.9	Road worker	24.8	
(Unskilled laborer)[g]	38							
Shoe shiner	33					Shoe shiner	26.9	
Bricklayer	27	Bricklayer	20.2	Bricklayer	19.3			
Clothing-store owner	12					Owner of a retail store	15.3	

(continues)

Table 8.5 (continued)

United States		Germany		Great Britain		New Zealand		Japan		U.S.S.R.	
Occupation	Score	Occupation	Rank	Occupation	Score	Occupation	Score	Occupation	Score	Occupation	Score
		Tailor	14					Tailor	17.7		
		Street peddler	35					Street-stall keeper	24.9		
				Business manager	6.0	Business manager	5.3				
				Works manager	6.4	Works manager	7.9				
				News agent and tobacconist	15.0	News agent and tobacconist	15.4				
				Tractor driver	23.0	Tractor driver	22.8				
				Railway porter	25.3	Railway porter	25.3				

[a]Used here only for comparison with Japan. For comparison with other countries, see row beginning "Civil engineer" under the "United States" column.

[b]Architect is the only occupation of a technical nature in Japan and was used here as a comparison only with the Soviet Union.

[c]Used here only for comparison with the Soviet Union. For comparison with other countries, see row beginning "Bookkeeper" under the "United States" column.

[d]Used here only for comparison with Japan. For comparison with other countries, see row beginning "Accountant for a large business" under the "United States" column.

[e]Used here only for comparison with the Soviet Union. For comparison with other countries, see individual occupations as they appear later in the table.

[f]As there was no comparable occupation with New Zealand, the occupation substituted was carrier.

[g]Used here only for comparison with Japan.

nine

COMMUNICATION: LINKING THE WHOLE HUMAN RACE

The nations and people of the world have become and continue to become interconnected and interdependent to a degree totally different from the level that prevailed through most of human history. We are all becoming part of a totally new type of global social structure. A single worldwide social system is emerging, one loosely organized and still continuously evolving, but with enough shape and form already developed to make the effort to delineate it meaningful and practical. Two of the main elements of that new system are greatly expanded world trade and the reorganization of production on a global basis. My focus here is on another element, *communication*—the transmission and exchange between and among individuals and institutions of information, ideas, techniques, art forms, tastes, values and sentiments. Of particular interest are those messages that cross national boundaries and thus contribute to the linkages that increasingly make the world a single social system.[1]

Reprinted with permission from Alex Inkeles, "Linking the Whole Human Race: The World as a Communication System," in *Business and the Contemporary World*, ed. H. L. Sawyer (New York: University Press of America, 1988), 133–174.

The Great Transformation

Throughout most of human history the vast majority of individuals could know of and have significant contact with only a relatively small circle of people, and generally those had to live physically in close proximity as members of the same band or as residents of the same village or similar primary community. Contacts with individuals outside this narrow circle were rare and limited, and mobility was so restricted as to ensure that these contacts would bring the outsider—say, an official or a trader—to the individual, and not the reverse. Modern methods of transportation and communication have totally transformed these historically dominant patterns. The ties linking individuals across national boundaries and over great distances that initially grew rapidly have recently begun to expand at rates that can only adequately be characterized as phenomenal.

Postal Services

The first great transformation in interpersonal communication both within and across national boundaries was effected by the development of national postal systems. For example, in the United Kingdom rising literacy and the stimulus of an expanding business community yielded a more than tenfold increase in mail within a thirty-year period, from a total of 82 million items in 1839 to 933 million by 1869. Steady growth over the next century brought the total amount of domestic mail in the United Kingdom to over 11 million items in 1983.[2] As national postal systems came to be linked through the Universal Postal Union, there was a comparable rapid rise in the exchange of mail across national borders. Thus by 1981 some 6.5 billion letters and postcards were sent across national borders, equal to about 4 percent of the volume of comparable domestic mail worldwide.[3] However, the importance of international relative to domestic mail has actually been decreasing in recent decades, at least in the case of the more developed countries, as newer technologies have come to provide vastly more rapid and often more reliable means for communicating across national boundaries.[4]

The Telephone

In contrast to the situation in the post offices, telephone exchanges are undergoing a much more rapid rate of increase in international traffic than in domestic, at least in the case of the more developed countries. In the period from 1966 to 1984 the median rate of increase in international calls for West Germany was about 15 percent, whereas the domestic increased at only 8 percent per year. In Japan, reporting only for the period from 1967 to 1979, international telephoning grew at a rate of over 20 percent per year, and the domestic only about 3 percent.[5]

In the 1950s telephone calls that crossed the boundaries of the United States increased in frequency at a rate of 7 percent per year, a rate sufficient to double the number of international calls every decade, but between 1966 and 1984 the median increase rose to 24 percent per year, which would double the number of such calls about every three years. Consequently, over the thirty-four-year period from 1950 to 1984 the number of such calls outgoing from the United States evidently increased an astounding 540 times.[6]

By 1984 the number of international phone calls originating in West Germany was more than 369 million, and in the United States, 419 million.[7] Assuming that incoming calls match the outgoing on a one-to-one basis, it is likely that by 1988 the number of international phone "conversations" in which U.S. residents participate will reach 1 billion.[8] In 1986 AT&T, which controlled all but a small part of the U.S. market for international telecommunications, grossed over US$6 billion in revenues from this one source alone, some half of which it then had to share with the national postal, telegraph, and telephone administrations with which it is linked overseas. It is another sign of the growing importance of cross-national communication that income from international calls rose at a rate more than double the increase in income from domestic services.[9]

Although it is by now a century-old mode of communication, the telephone continues to enhance its ability to cover great distances efficiently by continuous improvements in the technology developed to carry its messages over land and sea. Indeed the leaps are often staggering. The great advance of the early 1930s was the coaxial cable, which could carry twenty-four telephone channels. Currently a standard cable can carry 8,000 telephone channels simultaneously, but with the use of optical fibers it is anticipated that cables will be developed to carry 500,000 telephone calls or their equivalent in other services.[10]

As for crossing the seas, the current standard submarine cable can carry up to 4,200 voice channels. Because earlier cables had less capacity, the thirty-odd international underwater cables that had been laid up until 1980 were collectively capable of carrying only 17,000 circuits. Currently this capacity is being greatly increased by the laying of an optical fiber cable, expected to be operational in 1988, which will carry 40,000 voice circuits at the speed of light under the Atlantic Ocean. Under a new technical standard, of which practical testing began in 1986, such cables will allow the transmission of voice to be supplemented by video and data moving along the same channel.

Satellite Services

Meanwhile, satellites had been launched with many thousands of additional telephone circuits to carry messages across borders and over seas.

And here again the pace of technological advance was dazzling. As a result of these surges in technology and the associated cost reductions, satellites could claim, as of 1986, to be carrying half of all international telecommunications and two-thirds of the traffic specifically identified as international telephonic communication.[11]

By 1984 the number of commercial satellites in orbit had risen to 150, the greatest part of these having been launched in the previous five years. At the end of 1987 more than 100 communication satellites were in a queue awaiting the availability of launch vehicles, whose shortage was made acute by the delays forced on the industry by the space shuttle disaster in 1986. Indeed, it is estimated that over the next ten years some 200 commercial satellites must be orbited to replace worn-out equipment and to provide expanded services. To take advantage of this window of opportunity both the Soviet Union and China are offering to use their rockets on a commercial basis to launch satellites, although so far they have few takers. Greater success has been enjoyed by Arianspace, the commercial arm of the European Space Agency. Following their start-up in 1979, they enjoyed fourteen completed launchings by 1986, but they also experienced four failures. Then, after redesigning their rocket, they again achieved a completed launch in September 1987. How great the demand is may be judged from the fact that Arianspace reports having a backlog of orders from forty-six customers prepared to pay a total of US$25 billion for launchings through 1991, and that is only about one-third of the backlog of the launching business.[12]

Only a portion of these satellites are for truly international communication, in which the key actor is INTELSAT, the International Telecommunications Satellite Organization. INTELSAT is the product of international agreements and reports to the United Nations, but unlike most elements of that body it is an operating company designed to provide channels in space for international telecommunications on a commercial and nondiscriminatory basis. It achieves its purpose by maintaining communication satellites in geostationary orbit over the Earth's main oceans, of which technology its seer, Arthur C. Clarke, had predicted that "it will link together the whole human race, for better or worse, in a unity which no earlier age could have imagined."[13]

By a recent count INTELSAT sold its services to 170 countries, 109 of which were actual members of the organization. As of 1984 INTELSAT had fifteen satellites in orbit, collectively providing some 50,000 circuits, with the latest model INTELSAT VI, supposed to be launched in 1987, making a great leap up to 80,000 voice channels on a single satellite. INTELSAT's satellites are connected to some 300 Earth stations located in more than 130 different nations. These stations are in turn linked through a network of 1,600 Earth-level pathways, or more than 100 per satellite.

INTERSPUTNIK was designed to serve the Eastern bloc and some Soviet satrapies elsewhere, but it carries only about 1 percent of the world's space traffic because its members actually rely mainly on INTELSAT.[14] When this INTELSAT system is joined to the international cable network, and both in turn are linked to the various national systems for telecommunications, the result is effectively to link every one of the 600 million telephones on Earth with every other, anywhere on the globe. It is then no wonder that this incredible web has been dubbed "the largest integrated machine ever built."[15]

Press Services

Over the past century, first wire services, then radio, followed by television made immediate and real to billions of people certain events and personalities. In the case of the press, four great Western news agencies each day gather and disseminate a vast amount of news and features. For example, the U.S. agency United Press International (UPI) serves ninety-two countries in which it provides its services to over 2,200 newspapers plus thirty-six national news agencies; the French agency Agence France-Presse (AFP) is subscribed to by sixty-nine national news agencies and through other arrangements simultaneously gets its material into 152 countries.[16] These and other Western news services, if supplemented by Tass, the Soviet news agency, could put across the desk of a subscribing newspaper in Bombay or Buenos Aires a flow of some half million words a day. And if these sources seemed culturally too confining, editors could turn to reports from some forty news agencies from the less developed countries organized in the News Agencies Pool of Non-aligned Countries, or to Interpress, which is a UNESCO-sponsored Third World news service. Through their elaborate chain of wire and satellite connections these sets of international news agencies have the potential of focusing the attention of a large part of the literate world on a single event, issue, or personality.[17]

Radio and Television Services

Newspapers, of course, can reach only the literate. Radio overcomes that barrier. Even in the less developed world, at least outside the poorest countries, the great majority now can listen to the radio, and their stations have access to the same news services as does the press. Music, moreover, requires no translation and so the same popular song can be almost universally diffused by radio. And for those who have the greater means required, television adds the dimension of the visual, so that distant persons, places, and events may be simultaneously observed. By 1983 there were still twenty-five countries in Asia and Africa without television, but more than 100 nations, including the majority of the less developed, had television at least in their major urban areas. New countries were coming onstream rapidly, and all systems were expanding considerably.

For television the analogues of the international news agencies are VISNEWS and UPITN. The scale of their global reach is reflected in the fact that the second of these two organizations alone sends films, tapes, and programs by satellite to more than 200 stations in over seventy countries.[18] Wealth and technology inevitably influence a nation's chance to participate in this new method of diffusing communications. Thus, as of 1985 only nine low-income countries versus forty-five middle-income countries participated in satellite networks. Nevertheless, many Third World countries were a considerable presence in the business. India and Brazil were early possessors of national communication satellites, and Mexico expected to join the club in 1985. Moreover, some of the less developed countries have themselves become centers of diffusion to other nations. Indonesia, for example, uses its satellite to link and provide materials to countries in Southeast Asia, and ARABSAT serves some twenty-two members in the Middle East and North Africa.[19]

As the reach of these and related systems becomes wider and wider, more and more of the people who were previously outside the world network of communication linkages are drawn into it. Thus the Communist China that Chairman Mao so long kept tightly compartmentalized and almost hermetically sealed against the outside world now has television in all twenty-nine of its provinces and is building more than 7 million new sets each year. As a result, 80 percent or more of the households in the major cities have television sets. Countrywide, of course, the figure was much lower, at 20 percent of households, but even in areas with very few sets, the location of receivers in public places and the gathering of viewers in the homes of those who have sets brings the percentage of individuals who watch regularly up to 60 and even 80 percent, depending on the region.[20] Over millennia the millions of China could never know the face of their local governor, let alone that of their emperor, but for their contemporary descendants, seeing and hearing the face and voice not only of their own premier but also of an American or a North Korean president has become a familiar and even commonplace experience.

When they can be induced to act in concert all these media have the power to create a truly worldwide audience, one that can simultaneously focus the attention of vast audiences on the same actors in the same time and space. Elihu Katz has suggested that we call these "media events" and has nominated as examples of international and even global significance the coronation of the queen of England, the funeral of President Kennedy, some of the visits of the pope to sites outside Rome, and the Olympic Games.[21] We may surely add the 1987 Reagan-Gorbachev summit in Washington. Of these, the Olympic Games are clearly of most universal appeal, and this is reflected in the estimates that via all the media combined the Los Angeles

Olympic Games of 1984 garnered a total audience of 2.5 billion persons. That means that half of the human race was more or less simultaneously linked as observers of this greatest media event of all time, something not only physically impossible in earlier times, but unimaginable as well.

Business Communication

Within this worldwide audience there are of course many distinctive sub-groups and special interests. For example, the geophysical exploration industry has hundreds of thousands of detectors scattered over the Earth's surface and in its seas, and in a single year they will record one quadrillion (10^{15}) bits of geophysical data.[22] One of the most important and rapidly growing of the special interest communicators is the world of production, commerce, and finance, that is, the world of business. Thus, of 121 million telephone access lines available in the United States about 18 percent are devoted to business organizations, and if one adds the lines devoted to data transmission, then business commands about one in four of the available lines. Moreover, this proportion has been steadily rising. Indeed, business communication may be the most rapidly growing sector in both domestic and international telecommunications.

Data transmission represented about 15 percent of the world's telecommunications market in 1985, but near the end of the decade of the 1990s it is expected to account for as much as 40 percent.[23] Characteristic of this trend are the newly developing international Value Added Networks (VANs), largely used for business, which were expected to grow at a rate of 40 percent per year in 1987.[24] In recognition of the growing importance of such communication INTELSAT launched a special International Business Service (IBS) in 1983, configured as one of the newest integrated digital networks and specifically designed to serve the needs of the international business community. It has experienced phenomenal growth, expanding from a mere seven circuits at the end of 1984 to 161 full-time (64 kbps equivalent) circuits by the end of 1985.[25]

Although this rapid rise in the use of satellites reflects the general increase in the volume of business communication, a crucial element in the shift to satellites are the factors of cost and time. Thus a large corporation may in one day of business transactions accumulate a record equal to thirty megabits on a disk. To send the information from coast to coast by land-based facilities would require almost fourteen hours, whereas by satellite at 3.0 megabytes per second it would take only seven minutes.[26]

Such great savings in sheer time on the line would not mean so much, of course, if the seven minutes of satellite time were enormously expensive. But the main story has been one of extraordinary and continuous reductions in the cost of satellite channels as improvements have been made in each subsequently launched unit. Expressed in constant 1984 dollars, the cost of a single voice channel went from $57,000 on INTELSAT I in 1965 to a mere $370 on INTELSAT V-A/V-B in 1984.[27] This reduction was made possible by the fact that launching costs increased only modestly, whereas the number of circuits carried by each satellite increased enormously, going from 480 live channels in the first satellite sent aloft in 1965 to 30,000 on those launched in 1984, with a further rise to 80,000 planned for those to be launched in 1986 and 1987, an increase in capacity of 166 times in little more than twenty years.

Communications as Big Business

Just as business is a big communicator, so communications is big business. The investment made in the infrastructure for telecommunications alone currently accounts for one-tenth of the gross fixed-capital formation in the United States and Europe. When one adds the fixed-capital formation for other forms of communication, and then augments that with the current expenditures for communication *services,* it becomes evident that private, public, and commercial communication in all its aspects probably represents at least 15 and possibly 20 percent of any modern economy. Unfortunately, different sources and analysts may use different conventions in aggregating and disaggregating these vast expenditures. In addition, the pace of technological and related organizational change tends to blur what were once important contrasts, such as that between data transmission and data processing. Consequently, it is difficult to present a definitive picture of the details of worldwide expenditures on communication, but some of the most salient facts are suggestive of the magnitude of this operation.

In 1985 U.S. factories alone shipped an estimated US$52 billion of communications equipment. About 29 percent was spent for telephone and telegraph equipment, of which the United States generally absorbs about one-half of the total world production. The rest of the $52 billion went for broadcast, studio, communications, navigation, and other equipment. All this was largely independent of the market for computers and software, the separate worldwide sales of which were expected to reach $155 billion in 1987.[28] Revenue from the *services* provided by all this equipment must be distinguished from the cost of the physical infrastructure. Thus the operating revenues from telephone and telegraph services in the United States in 1985 amounted to $105 billion, which required the employment of some 950,000 persons.[29]

When we add to telecommunications radio and television, film, newspapers, and book and journal publishing, it becomes evident what a vast, complex, and costly enterprise is involved. A narrow definition of the communication industry, which I have been using, would show it to account for some $217 billion in the United States, or about 4.5 percent of the country's gross national product (GNP) in 1987, and a broad definition would credit it with well over 10 percent of the GNP.[30]

The printing and publishing industry exemplifies the magnitudes involved. In the United States alone the industry encompasses 53,000 establishments employing 1.3 million, and in 1986 they shipped products valued at almost $100 billion, of which about one-third was accounted for by purely commercial printing. This market was not solely domestic. Because English is so widespread and American textbooks and technical works are so much in demand, the United States in 1986 was able to export books valued at $610 million. Even Communist China, which carefully husbands its very scarce foreign exchange, paid out $20 million in 1986 to purchase books printed in the United States.[31]

As sources of information, books and the great libraries that have been their traditional repositories are increasingly in competition with information stored and retrieved electronically. From a modest beginning in the 1970s this industry has recently grown at about 40 percent each year, and by 1985 there were some 2,800 databases available on-line worldwide, with the United States having a commanding but declining lead. Although the greatest share of the activity involves business, finance, industry, and economics, there are vast databases serving law, science, and medicine.[32]

A significant proportion of personal income goes into purchasing objects and services for communication. To select but one small item, we may note that the worldwide market for records totaled US$12 billion in 1983, nearly one-third of it spent in the United States.[33] Beyond recordings, in 1987 the U.S. consumer spent some $83 billion of personal income on mass communication, somewhat over half of it on radio and television sets and services, some 30 percent of it on newspapers, books, magazines, and other print media, and a residue of about 15 percent for film, theaters, sports, and other admissions.[34]

Meanwhile, through these same media a different kind of communication, namely advertising, drew some US$114 billion from U.S. business establishments in 1987, and those expenditures have been rising at a rate of 11 to 12 percent per year. In recent years the U.S. expenditure for advertising has been about one-half of the world total. But the habit of advertising, stimulated in good part by efforts of the multinational corporations to advance their name and product, has been spreading rapidly throughout the world, often producing purely local elaborations and inventions of considerable ingenuity. So powerful is this tide of activity that it is predicted that by the time the twenty-first century arrives the global advertising bill will be some US$780 billion per year.[35]

The Content of Worldwide Communication

Channels of communication across national boundaries have no significance unless they can carry mutually intelligible messages. For that to happen there must be mutually comprehended symbol systems available. Of all human systems of communication, language, in particular the verbal or oral, is arguably the most ubiquitous. Some might press a claim for gesture as the most common, and it surely could claim second place. Sign language occupies a special niche, combining the elements of both verbal language and gesture, although it is of course used by only a very limited and particular population. In that it perhaps shares its position with a whole set of specialized media of communication that collectively may be designated professional-technical symbol systems.

This set includes the notation systems used in mathematics, music, and chemistry, on topographic and cartographic maps, and in electronic wiring diagrams. Rules of the game, as in chess, might well be thought of as falling in the same group, but I prefer to treat them as a transition to a third category, which I call the popular or mundane symbol systems. As the designation of this category suggests, these are the symbols used in the course of conducting the everyday business of living. Included in this category are the signs by which the prices of goods at given quantities are indicated. For those living in the more affluent world, road signs are a good example, the most obvious being the red light symbolizing "stop" and green "go," a distinction that in China survived unchanged despite the efforts of the Red Guards to reverse the order during the height of the Cultural Revolution. Religious symbols fall into this set, as for example in the special form of the cross that indicates the Russian Orthodox Church, or the lamb and fish representing Jesus in Christian iconography.

Logos to identify the nature of the business conducted in different locations may also be placed in this set. Thus a large pair of eyeglasses hung over the door of a shop will tell its story, just as a knife and fork will tell another, although perhaps less unambiguously. In its modern form the commercial logo comes to be distinctively identified with the products of the large multinational companies. Coca-Cola and Pepsi-Cola signs are perhaps the best known—they can be "read" or decoded correctly virtually anywhere in the world regardless of the local language. Political symbols may be thought of as similar to the commercial logo, or as more akin to the religious symbols and therefore as deserving treatment as a separate category. The Union Jack, the Stars and Stripes, and the Hammer and Sickle serve to represent this genre. In sports the signals by which the officials—designated as umpire or referee or the like—indicate whether there has been a score, a legitimate play, or a foul, and of what kind, make up yet another subset of common-man everyday symbols.

Symbols may be abstract, as I conceive the blinking red light to be, or they may be very concrete and pictorial, as in the painting of Christ's descent from the cross or a sculpture of the birth of the Buddha showing him emerging from his mother's rib cage. Any set of symbols may have a quite small and highly specialized vocabulary, as in the case of road signs, or it may be vast and indeed virtually unlimited, as in the case of the vocabulary of a modern language.[36] The symbols may be highly discrete and largely unrelated, as in the case of commercial logos, or they may be heavily dependent on context for meaning, as is the case for a letter in an alphabet, which generally has meaning only when linked with other letters in a word.

Similarly, the order in which symbols appear may be unimportant, or at least set minimal constraints on meaningful communication, or there may be hard-and-fast rules governing the order of the elements of a symbol system, as in the case of the syntax for most languages. Vocabulary and grammar also set limits to the ability of a symbol system to communicate the interrelations and sequencing of events so as to tell a story. An appropriate road sign may be able to tell you that there has been an accident in the road ahead of you, but it can communicate little or nothing of the circumstances surrounding the accident or of the sequence of events before and after the event. In sports, the right sequence of signs from the referee can tell you that there has been a foul, that team A was "offsides," that they are being given a five-yard penalty, and that play will resume on the forty-yard line. While thus being potentially coherent and informative, the official's repertoire is quite inadequate for describing the rich details of actual play, which the language of the sports announcer permits him to communicate.

The ability of individuals to understand each other's communications is no guarantee of good fellowship, especially if the signals being sent are hostile or threatening. If shared symbol systems were sufficient to create brotherhood, we would not have had the long history of civil wars that has characterized human experience since Cain slew Abel. Nevertheless, community and communication go together. Indeed, one way of defining a community is to assess the degree to which individuals share a common language and a set of other symbols that have more or less the same meaning for all. Even with communication in mutually intelligible symbol systems, understanding is always problematic and sympathetic understanding even more so, but without such communication there is virtually no hope of expanding the circle of those who in some degree can act together to achieve common and mutually rewarding social goals. Across ethnic and cultural divisions within nations, and across boundaries between and among nations, the degree to which symbol systems are shared is a key factor in shaping prospects for common action to advance welfare and to ensure peace.

Despite the obvious advantage that would accrue to humanity from having them, we are almost totally lacking in symbol systems that permit near-universal, to say nothing of truly universal, communication. There are, however, some developments that move us closer to that goal. The widespread diffusion of the physical channels of communication already described, although far from completely linking everyone on Earth into the same network, has gone very far in that direction and involves a process that will surely see such linkages established worldwide early in the next century.

The achievement of the goal of universal physical linkage is not very problematic. What is problematic is our ability to develop the means for mutually intelligible communication over the physical channels that will soon be established universally. Great investment in translation will of necessity be a major part of that process. It must begin within the internal structure of the machinery of communication itself. As we stand now, analogue systems of telephonic communication are in effect speaking a different language from that of digital systems, and, as many discover to their dismay, computers made by different manufacturers have a great deal of difficulty communicating with each other. With larger systems of telecommunications and data transmission, switching and interface problems are the central issues. One major step in achieving mutual intelligibility in the signals sent by different national telecommunications industries was achieved in the early 1980s through the adoption of a standard switching interface called X.25. Although the U.S. TELENET system took the lead, the complexity of such operations was reflected in the fact that it required sharing the initiative with Trans-Canada Telephone System, the French Post and Telegraph Organization, Nippon Telegraph and Telephone, and the United Kingdom Post Office.

Beyond the elimination of such barriers within the architecture of the technical components of our systems of communication, it will also be critical to develop languages and other symbol systems that permit mutually intelligible communication over the now more open physical channels without the costs and other limitations of translation. There are many ways in which this goal can be achieved. Organized sports, and particularly international competitions such as the Olympics, may play a special role in increasing our limited repertoire of universally comprehensible symbol systems. For the foreseeable future, however, translation will continue to be an indispensable aid to cross-national and cross-cultural communication.

Translation as a Path to Communication: The Printed Word

The inability to understand each other's languages is the greatest barrier to sharing the culture of other people. The solution is of course to attempt translation of the works of other cultures into one's own language. From ancient times, great works of philosophy, science, religion, and literature have been made available to wide segments of humankind by this means. Thus Roman civilization depended heavily on translations of the great works of Greek composition, as later Islam drew heavily on the contributions of both of these predecessors. In turn much of what medieval Europe knew of science came to it from Islamic sources. Of course, when few could read, and books had to be laboriously transcribed by hand, those who could be reached directly by these translations were very few in number, however important they were individually in the courts of great rulers or in the councils of major religious centers.

Books in Translation. With the spread of literacy and the aid of rapid mechanical printing, the prospects for wide sharing of the written work of other cultures are enormously expanded. The more recent growth has been notable. Thus for 1932 the INDEX TRANSLATIONUM noted only some 3,200 translated titles published in six countries, but by 1978 UNESCO found translations published in seventy-four countries and the number of titles translated showed an eighteenfold increase over the period. This reported increase may give too sanguine a picture, because the first listings in the INDEX may have been underreported. The more complete records for recent periods indicate that the number of titles being translated increased by about 25 percent in the decade from the 1960s to the early 1970s. This is a considerably more modest rate of increase than that manifested by many other forms of international communication, especially the electronic channels. Moreover, the latest reports available indicate that the number of translations may actually be declining. Nevertheless, the translation of over 53,000 titles reported for the latest available year, 1980, indicates a wide diffusion of this part of the world's cultural property.[37]

Unfortunately, as is often true in the realm of world communication, nations do not participate equally in the cross-national diffusion of literature. Germany, France, Spain, and the USSR are very active in translating books, each accounting for between 6,000 and 8,000 titles per year, according to the latest data available in 1985. Very small countries such as the Netherlands and Denmark translated some 2,000 or 3,000 books each year. By contrast, the less developed countries, in general, are not very active in book translation. Contributing to this situation are shortages of foreign currency, scarcity of paper, and limits on the size of the available local audience. In addition, ethnic and religious interests and sensitivities in many Third World countries, especially when combined with great powers of political censorship, also act to inhibit book translations. In any event, there are objective grounds for concluding that the slowdown and even decline in book translations may be disproportionately determined by the action of less developed countries, while the more advanced continue to surge ahead.[38]

The sources contributing to the translation flow are also not equal. Almost half of all the titles translated are literary works; the number in this one category equals the combined number in all others, such as books on social and political issues, those dealing with practical matters, and so on. Equally concentrated is the original language of the books. English is overwhelmingly a more important source than any other language. Thus, of some 53,000 titles translated around 1980, about 23,000, more than 40 percent, were books originally in English. French, German, and Russian contributed about 6,000 titles each, so that collectively they contributed less than English alone. With these four languages so dominant, all the rest of the 100 or so major languages in the world had to divide up the honor of contributing the remaining 20 percent of the titles.[39]

This process of translation has made it possible for some books to achieve extraordinarily wide geographic distribution. Probably the all-time record is held by the Bible. Since 1815 it has been made wholly available in close to 300 major languages, and the New Testament has been translated into over 600 languages. Portions of the Scriptures are available in an additional 1,500 less important languages, and there are 555 new translation projects underway. This means that these texts are available in a very large proportion of the estimated world total of living languages. Indeed, only some 4 percent of the world's population is left without having at least some part of the Bible available to it in its native language. Together the numerous editions of the Bible yielded some 2.5 billion copies between 1815 and 1975. Despite this enormous backup supply, the printings get larger each year, with 1987 output running at about 46 million complete Bibles and 67 million New Testament copies a year. These great numbers become much larger if one includes printings of portions and selections along with the entire Bible. On that basis the total printing goes to over 600 million items for 1986, and a total of almost 8 billion for the period 1947 through 1986.[40] The distribution of the Koran in translation has over time also been geographically great and numerically surely vast.

Works of politics compete in being widely distributed in great numbers. Copies of *The Communist Manifesto* have appeared in many dozens of languages in untold numbers. The writings of Lenin are perhaps the leading example of the worldwide distribution of political literature. His works have been translated into 222 languages, and in the early 1980s there were about 450 translations of his works each year, a number greater by far than those credited to any other author. These great distributions no doubt owe much to the special concern of different interest groups, religious, political, and other, but such considerations cannot explain the extraordinary diffusion of works of literature. It is thus heartening to find Tolstoy almost number one among all cited, with 1,063 translations in twenty-two countries in the decade 1961–1970. In a lighter vein stand the novels of Agatha Christie, whose eighty-seven books have been printed in over 300 million copies in more than 100 languages. Children too share in this experience of translation. Indeed, Walt Disney Productions holds the record for the decade 1961–1970, with 1,102 translations to its credit.[41] Clearly, very large and diverse audiences are being linked worldwide by a common interest and are sharing a common experience through their exposure to these written works.

Magazines and Newspapers

Of course books are not the only form of print entering into translation. Indeed, some magazines achieve an international distribution that puts them equal to or ahead of the giants of international publishing such as the Bible. Foremost among these is *The Reader's Digest*. In recent times each monthly issue has appeared in fifteen languages as well as in Braille, organized in some twenty-five national editions, with a total distribution of some 28 million copies per month.[42] In some regions of the world, notably in Asia, it is the largest circulation magazine regardless of type.[43]

Limitations set by low levels of literacy and widespread poverty mean that books in translation and world-circulation magazines can hope to reach only a small share of the world's population, so small as to merit for them the designation of elite communication. To reach the great masses of the literate population requires turning to the world's 60,000 newspapers, and especially to the 8,000 dailies, which together enjoy a circulation of some 500 million. Again these are unequally distributed, with about one-third in North America and another third in Europe—including the USSR—leaving all the rest of the world with the remaining third. That means that there are still a few countries, as in Africa, with no daily newspaper at all. Further, in most of the remaining countries on that continent the papers, generally weak in resources and poor in quality, can print only some twenty copies per 1,000 people as against the 200 to 300 per 1,000 people in the more developed countries. Still, worldwide the ratio for dailies is about 110 to 120 copies per 1,000 people. Dailies are of course supplemented by newspapers that come out less often, most commonly as weeklies. In some advanced countries these will outnumber the dailies by three or even five times. And though generally focused overwhelmingly on local affairs, they often carry national and international news as well.[44]

Making allowances for the age distribution of the population and for multiple use of the same copy, including its being read aloud, it is not unlikely that a billion people get at least some exposure to a newspaper each week. We may then wonder how this multitude, some one in five of the total of humanity and close to one in three of its adult population, may be linked by its newspaper exposure to the rest of the world living outside the boundaries of the individual nations in which they reside.

Few papers are wealthy enough to support their own foreign correspondents. To report what is happening in the world they must rely on international news services or agencies. According to a count published by UNESCO such agencies are together pouring out some 32 million words a day. Jonathan Fenby is not alone in calling this number "awesome," but he is in a better position than most to help us recognize some limits on these numbers not evident to all. He points out, for example, that the same 1,000-word story sent out by a single agency, say Reuters, through some twenty different subscriber services and regional desks belonging to that agency, will end up being counted as a 20,000-word output by the UNESCO method of tabulation.[45]

In actuality a much more controlled and limited flow of news results from the practice of the wire services to select and package material for different regions, say Latin America or Asia, along the known lines of interest in each part of the world. Consequently, the flow of foreign news to any given national agency will be both more limited and more comprehensible than is suggested by the huge totals described by UNESCO.

At the upper end of the scale, the Japanese agency Kyodo will each day receive some 600,000 words of foreign news, only some modest part coming from its own correspondents abroad, with the great majority coming from some fifty agencies to which Kyodo subscribes. This is still a formidable flow. At the other end of the scale, a poor country in Africa might subscribe to no more than three or four agencies, and if it received some 20,000 words from each, the total flow would at most be 80,000 words. These are, moreover, figures applying at the equivalent of the wholesale level, since national agencies like Kyodo further select and repackage the news in smaller batches sent out to the individual newspapers (and radio stations) that buy Kyodo's services and through which those papers and stations are linked to the outside world. After eliminating the duplication of stories on the same event from different agencies, selecting those of interest for Japan, and then cutting even those down to usable size, Kyodo sends out only some 12,000 words of foreign news daily to its subscriber newspapers.[46] Whatever the significance of these numbers, of course, they are less important than knowing the content of the messages they carry.

Newspaper Content. A study of the distribution of news sent out by five major agencies to Europe, Africa, and the Middle East in 1980 showed by far the most important focus to be international politics and relations, with about one-third of the news items dealing with that theme. Economics and domestic politics came next, each accounting for about 13 percent of the stories. Stories about sports ran a close third with about 12 percent of the items. After that the categories dropped off rapidly, with social life involved in only some 2 percent, and art, culture, and science together accounting for less than 2 percent of the stories.[47] Other studies indicate that approximately the same pattern has persisted for some time and applies to different news services.[48]

Inevitably, U.S. agencies such as the Associated Press carry more news about the United States, and European agencies, such as Reuters, carry more news about Europe, in a ratio of about two-to-one in favor of the home territory of the sending agency. The content of what goes out from the services also varies by the nature of the region receiving the material. Thus in some services to Latin America more than 20 percent of the stories would deal with sports, no doubt reflecting the South American infatuation with soccer competitions, whereas some Reuters services to the Middle East seemed to contain no sports news at all.[49]

After all the selection by the international services and subsequent screening by the national agencies, it is in the end the individual newspaper editor who decides what his or her readers will learn of world events through their newspaper. Editors may, of course, operate relatively freely, or they may be under tight control from owners, government officials, political party bosses, religious leaders, or other forms of censorship. Tightly controlled or not, editors and their papers will adapt the content they present to the character of the audience they are trying to reach. Thus in the United Kingdom the so-called "quality" newspapers such as *The Guardian* typically devote almost one-quarter of their space to external events, including sports abroad, whereas the more popular newspapers such as the *Daily Mirror* manage to give only one-tenth or less of their space to events abroad.[50] The pattern is similar in less developed countries. Thus in Brazil *O Estado de São Paulo,* generally considered to be the most distinguished and influential newspaper in the country, regularly devotes at least eight of its forty-eight or so pages to foreign news, whereas the more popular *O Globo,* about the same overall size, will give considerably less space to foreign affairs while using those pages for fuller coverage of sports events.[51]

As a rough rule of thumb we may expect a central city newspaper that is of the elite or so-called "prestige" variety to devote at least 15 percent, and more likely 25 or even 30 percent, of its news space to foreign news.[52] In the case of more popular central city newspapers as well as of the main paper in more provincial cities, the proportion of material reporting developments abroad will be from 10 to 20 percent. In both cases, of course, we must allow for exceptions in particular countries and specific newspapers.[53]

Within the limits of whatever foreign news the papers do carry, most editors evidently assume that their readers will be strongly interested in news from the region in which their country is located. Some 40 to 50 percent of the foreign news published in newspapers in the countries of Asia, Africa, Latin America, and even Europe was, in each case, focused on other countries in the respective region.[54] Nevertheless, this left room for the remaining half or more of the foreign news stories to convey information about people and events in parts of the world outside the region in question. A large part of that remainder inevitably focused on the United States, the USSR, and other world leaders whose actions impinge most powerfully on the condition of other nations. It is, however, easy to exaggerate the prominence of these main actors on the international scene in the news reports in typical papers around the world, an impression that some studies done in the 1960s strongly fostered.[55] The overwhelming weight of the evidence for more recent times leads to the surprising conclusion that in most newspapers, Third World countries are paid more attention than "First World" countries in the ratio of about two-to-one. Thus, in the newspapers of sixteen representative less developed countries studied in 1978, the Third World accounted for some 30 percent of the foreign news items, whereas the First World netted only 15 percent.[56] But this pattern is not limited to the press of the less developed nations. In Great Britain, for example, material about North America, meaning mainly the United States, made up 18 percent of the foreign news items in the 1970s, whereas the Third World areas combined captured 36 percent, again a two-to-one ratio.[57] The situation was much the same in a study of the four leading newspapers in the United States.[58]

It is of course important to know what is being communicated about foreign areas in whatever fraction of the newspaper is devoted to them. A rough division would assign 40 to 50 percent of the stories to the category of international relations, including military matters; economic issues will account for 15 to 20 percent; and the domestic affairs of the foreign countries for some 10 to 15 percent. It is apparent, then, that this division leaves little room for material on cultural development abroad or for descriptions of how people live their daily lives.[59] Here again there is variation depending on the country involved and whether or not the newspaper in question is part of the elite press or is oriented more to the mass public. Thus the breakdown for newspapers in the Arab world did not include a separate category for sports, and such stories were presumably incorporated in the 5 percent classified as human interest stories, whereas in Asian newspapers 12 percent of news about Third World countries dealt with sports events, an amount of attention twice that given to military affairs and equal to the space given to all other news about domestic affairs in the foreign countries.[60] In Great Britain the more popular newspapers stick to the current news events abroad, whereas the "quality" newspapers carry many feature stories about foreign regions and personalities. In *The Guardian* such features made up 13 percent of all foreign news, but in the mass circulation *Daily Mirror* such stories accounted for less than 1 percent.[61]

Communication by Radio

Wire services send their foreign news not only to newspapers but to radio and television stations as well. Reuters, for example, sends its material directly to more than 400 radio and television stations, many of which are abroad. In addition, the local radio stations worldwide can get news of foreign events by subscribing to their respective national news agencies, which in turn are linked to the international wire services.

Although radio does not escape the problem of linguistic specificity and the necessity of translation, it does escape the limitations set by low levels of literacy. In addition, the development of the mass-produced handheld transistor radio brings the cost down so low that all but the most destitute household may have one. Moreover, the low cost of the set and the ease of sharing it reduces the cost of each exposure to a level far below that of a single issue of a newspaper. Equally impressive is the ability of radio to overcome the obstacles of distance and other challenges to the distribution of newspapers in isolated places with difficult access. One can go to the remotest village in India or to the settlements on the greatest heights in Latin America and find peasants at work in their fields with a transistor radio hanging from a nearby branch or pole, thus potentially tying their owners almost instantly into events occurring anywhere in the world.

No nation is without its broadcasting station, and the larger countries of course have many stations to blanket their territory. Consequently, the less developed countries alone have more than 8,000 stations, broadcasting mostly on medium wave, and worldwide there are just over 30,000 stations, and these figures do not include China. With more than 50 million net receivers added to the supply each year, the world total reached a billion sets by 1976, and the 1987 total should have reached 1.6 billion sets. That would yield a ratio of close to one set for every three persons, or one for every two above the childhood years.[62]

If these receivers and stations were distributed uniformly worldwide, then by multiple use of the sets in families virtually everyone in the world capable of understanding the radio could be within listening range of one. Alas, the distribution is far from equal. The less developed world has only one-fifth of the broadcasting stations to serve some three-fourths of the world's population. When it comes to the sets themselves, the advanced countries are more or less saturated, generally having almost 800 sets per 1,000 people. In the United States there are almost two sets per person, and in most developed countries an average of one set per person. By contrast, the low-income countries were reported to enjoy but a fraction of that level, providing one set for approximately every ten persons in the population.[63]

It is probable, however, that these figures reported to and by UNESCO under-enumerate the availability of the small and inexpensive transistor radio. Moreover, growth in the number of sets available has been very great, with Africa, the poorest continent, increasing its supply of radios sevenfold in the fifteen years from 1960 to 1975,[64] and in the decade that followed, many of the African countries again doubled the number of radio receivers in the hands of their citizens.[65] Moreover, as ownership diffuses, it becomes physically easier for those who do not own a radio themselves to have the opportunity to hear one. Thus in Kenya a 1980 survey showed that only 35 percent of the rural people owned a radio, but almost double that number, 69 percent, claimed to listen to the radio.[66] Given these patterns, it seems likely that by the end of the twentieth century everyone will be brought within the range of a radio to which they can listen regularly. This would make radio the first truly universal channel of communication.

It apparently has not proved simple or easy to assess in detail just what goes out over the airwaves in different nations, but a study of ten representative countries in the less developed world indicated that typically about 40 percent of the broadcast time went to what the researchers considered to be "serious programs" as against "entertainment." They classified as "serious" those programs that gave news and commentary as well as materials on religion, school programs, and adult education.[67] Given that the proportion that was explicitly news, commentary, or description of matters foreign was likely only a modest part of this "serious" programming, one must reach the sobering conclusion that for the typical citizen in most developing countries the flow of international news and commentary via radio may occupy but a very few minutes each day. A review of the role of the news in the broadcast day in seven typical less developed countries found that in the worst case only 6 percent of broadcast time went to news, with the average at 20 percent—against an average of 40 percent for music. About 30 percent of the news items broadcast were international in nature, and 13 percent regional. Surprisingly, this gave foreign matters about the same weight as national news, the remainder being purely local.

Despite the oft-repeated claims that news agencies of the advanced countries dominate the selection of news in less developed countries, less than 20 percent of the radio news stories broadcast was taken from them.[68] Of course limits of time are not a sure indicator of the focus of individual attention, nor of the extent of the impact. Moreover, newscasts are not the only point of access through radio for things international. That flow may be supplemented on the "entertainment" portion of the broadcasting day by reports on international sports events and the transcription of foreign music.

Communication by Television

Compared to a single transistor radio a television set is quite expensive. It also makes stringent demands with regard to electricity, and it has a decidedly restricted range. All this largely limits it to urban centers and their environs, at least in the case of the developing countries. It too may not escape the necessity of translation when it uses language. Yet it has the towering advantage of making the enormous leap over the limits of verbal communication by entering into the realm of the visual, or pictorial. With that leap the possibility is attained of direct and universal communication without the need for translation.

The television camera brought the battlefield in Vietnam not only into the living rooms of the United States but into those of Europe as well. Shots of the police clubbing the blacks in Soweto, South Africa, or of the poor in the shanty towns of Santiago, Chile, tell a story that can be read equally easily by viewers in Athens, Greece, and in Athens, Georgia. Moreover, television's coverage of extranational material is not limited to the news. Through special features it can widely disseminate knowledge of the physical characteristics of foreign countries, their regions and their cities, and spread knowledge of how people abroad live, work, and recreate.

Because of its relatively high cost and its technical limitations, television, in contrast with radio, will be found for sure only in the high- and middle-income countries. As late as 1979, seventeen of forty-five low-income countries did not have television broadcasting. A later report for 1983, using a broader definition of geopolitical units that included dependent territories, found that forty-five of a total of 216 such entities did not have any television broadcasting.[69] In addition, in many of the middle-income countries only a few main cities had such broadcasting, again a contrast with the relatively blanket coverage of the radio stations. At the same time, however, television's growth has been phenomenal. The number of transmitters worldwide more than doubled between 1970 and 1980, and currently there are well more than 50,000 in operation. Their distribution is highly unequal, however, with less than a tenth of the transmitters located in the developing countries.[70] Technical considerations, plus the substantial barrier of higher costs, have kept both the number of receivers and the equality of their distribution at lower levels than is the case for the radio. Data from UNESCO (for 1983) report a worldwide distribution of 131 sets per 1,000 people, with the developed countries at 437 and the less developed at a mere twenty-six per 1,000. In the case of the less developed countries, that works out one set for every thirty-eight persons, so that even with the communal group watching that is common in those countries, a very large part of the population would be left outside the circle drawn around any set.[71]

Television Programming.   Cost and technical factors also play a distinctive role in shaping the broadcast content of television as contrasted with radio. For many countries, perhaps even for most, it proves much less expensive to purchase material from abroad for rebroadcast at home than to attempt local production. In addition to being less costly, the imported material, at least in most developed countries, is likely to be of higher technical quality than what can be produced domestically. For news that is to be read aloud by a "talking head" not supplemented by pictures, television stations can rely on the same wire services that supply the nation's newspapers. However, since the main advantage of television is the pictorial, TV producers seek, wherever possible, to have pictures accompany the voice presentation of the news. For this purpose all but a few must rely on an international agency such as VISNEWS, which provides videocassettes in a matter of days, and more or less instantaneous transmission of pictures by satellite to stations all around the world.[72]

Nevertheless, television news and information programs seem to be less dominated by foreign sources than some imagine. A worldwide study conducted in 1983 showed the largest foreign influence in television news and information programs to be in Asia, where 30 percent of such material came from outside the broadcasting country. The comparable figure for Latin America was 20 percent, for Africa, only 8 percent, and for Europe, 5 percent. The explanation, of course, lies not only in the cost of foreign services but also in the fact that people are more likely to be interested in local or national news than in what happens in faraway places.[73]

Similar pressures of cost and limits of technology influence television stations, especially in the less developed countries, to fill their subscribers' screens with non-news programs produced abroad and subsequently sold on the world market. In ten representative less developed countries studied by Katz and Wedell for the year 1973/74, the lowest proportion of imported programming was 30 percent in the case of the Nigerian Broadcasting Corporation, and the figure ranged up to 60 percent in Peru and 65 percent in Cyprus.[74] This yielded the seemingly anomalous situation that on the evening of July 15, 1975, viewers in Bangkok could choose between three American programs, *Manhunt, The FBI,* and *Get Christie Love.* Also widely—one might say ubiquitously—shown in this and other less developed country capitals were *Hawaii Five-O* and *Kojak.* Of course not all of the imported programs thus shown came from the United States. The United Kingdom contributed its share, as did France and Japan.[75]

All of this might well have been taken as positive evidence of the internationalization of communication. However, it could also be, and was, described as subverting local cultural traditions and as being a form of cultural imperialism.[76] In addition, it meant a drain on foreign currency reserves. Many nations, therefore, responded by trying to restrict the inflow of foreign programming while building up the supply of those locally produced. Thus, as part of its 1968 revolution, the new junta governing Peru called for increasing the proportion of locally produced material shown on television to 60 percent from their average at the time of less than 40 percent. That such efforts were only partially successful, however, was demonstrated in a large follow-up study for 1983. It showed 70 percent of prime-time broadcasting in Ecuador to be from foreign sources, 55 percent in Algeria, and 61 percent in Zimbabwe. Moreover, this deficiency, if such it be, was not limited to less developed countries. Prime time in Austria was

61 percent of foreign origin, and in New Zealand, 65 percent. Even the nominally "closed" socialist countries of Eastern Europe imported a fourth or more of their television fare, and of that part a surprisingly large proportion, close to 60 percent, came from nonsocialist countries. The United States, the source of so much of everyone else's imports, took only 2 percent of its broadcast material from abroad, against a general average of about one-third.[77]

By contrast, some less developed countries managed to reduce significantly the proportion of their television programming that they imported, and others were able to keep the waves of foreign material at a low level. Between 1973 and 1984 Brazil reduced its importing from 60 to 39 percent of all programs, and Venezuela from 50 to 33 percent.[78] India limited foreign material, even at prime time, to below 10 percent, Pakistan to 12 percent, and the Philippines, despite American influence, to 20 percent. The combination of a large internal market and ideological controls enabled the Soviet Union and China to produce all but 8 percent of their programming locally.

There is also some evidence of a fuller internationalization of the worldwide television programming market, reducing the overwhelming dominance of American exports. For example, cartoons made in Japan have begun to replace those from the United States, and Brazilian programs now go out to ninety nations. Mexican programs, especially their *telenovelas*, have become a major ingredient in the broadcasting of most Latin American countries, and Mexican broadcasting into the United States, targeting its Spanish-speaking population, gives it the fourth largest network audience in the country.[79]

Communicating Through Film

The moving picture considerably preceded television as a medium based on the visual. It played this role with regard to disseminating the news as well. For many years, from the 1930s through the 1950s, no movie program in the United States was complete without its introductory newsreel. As is the case with television, the film generally cannot rely on the visual alone, but must combine its presentation of pictures with language, either spoken or written, in the form of titles. Yet the film has certain distinctive advantages over television as a form of communication. Its large screen gives it greater interest and impact; its use of a special segregated setting focuses attention and increases concentration; and its ability to command more extended blocks of the viewers' time enables it to develop longer and more complex stories. All these contribute to making it a powerful medium of communication. Although its audience has been partly cut into and absorbed by television, the film continues to have enormous attraction, drawing a vast audience throughout the world.

The high cost of making moving pictures in the style of the elaborate Hollywood spectacle makes it important to bring each film to as large an audience as possible, which in most cases means having it widely disseminated beyond the country in which it is made. However, the technology of making films is such that, unlike something like a satellite, it cannot easily be monopolized by the wealthiest countries. Taking advantage of that fact, and understanding the possibilities of the low-budget movie, makes it possible for less developed countries to produce entertainment films on a large scale. Thus it comes as a great surprise to many that the U.S. production of feature films, numbering close to 400 in 1983, is far exceeded by that of India. India's production of over 700 films made it the world's leader, as it has been for many years by annually producing about one-fifth of the total world production. Hong Kong, Mexico, and Brazil are also significant producers, each having produced more than 100 films in 1983. As a result of such efforts, the less developed countries managed to produce more than half of the world total of 3,690 feature films made in 1983.[80] Moreover, many of the films made in the less developed countries are suitable for export, and some are extensively distributed beyond their respective national borders.

The widest foreign distribution, and almost certainly the greatest impact in spreading nonnative ideas and experiences is commanded by the smaller production of the United States, and to a lesser degree, that of the United Kingdom and France. Virtually all the countries reporting to UNESCO imported some films from the United States, and in seventy-four of the eighty-seven reporting nations films from the United States constituted 10 percent or more of their imports. Moreover, in many cases, such as Nigeria and Gibraltar, U.S. films were 80 percent or more of their imports. Nevertheless, the films produced by the studios of some of the less developed countries also enjoy very wide circulation. Indian films, for example, constituted 10 percent or more of the imported films in thirty-two of the eighty-seven countries, accounting for as much as 90 percent of the imports in the Maldives, 60 percent in Kuwait, and 50 percent in Somalia. The films produced in tiny Hong Kong managed to win 10 percent or more of the import market in Ghana, 60 percent in Thailand, and 45 percent in Brunei.[81] These figures suggest that the full-length movie is the leading instance, and perhaps the sole instance, in which the less developed countries play a truly major role, even if not the predominant one, in the worldwide exchange of communications material.

The Movie Audience.   Once made, a moving picture can be disseminated without the need for the complex technology required to disseminate television programs, but this may be offset by the fixed capital costs of maintaining the buildings to house the twenty to forty theater seats per 1,000 people that most countries provide. Of course there is always the alternative of converting other space, such as a gymnasium or meeting hall, for use as a theater, and films can be shown outdoors as well. In the latter case, however, the need for a power source is an obstacle, as it is likely to be even indoors in underdeveloped or remote regions. Some nations have attempted to meet this challenge by using self-contained mobile units. Cuba, for example, has more mobile units than fixed cinema locations and reports annual attendance at these mobile projector showings almost equal to that in regular theaters.[82]

UNESCO sources indicate that the rate of movie attendance per inhabitant in the more developed countries is less than eight times per year, whereas in the less developed countries it is less than three.[83] Of course excluding the smallest children from the count would raise those numbers. Moreover, when one multiplies the rates by population, the size of the resultant audience becomes quite substantial. Thus Korea's 300 cinemas show to 44 million per year, Mexico's 3,000 theaters to 300 million, and the 16,000 movie houses in the United States to more than a billion annually. Worldwide, the number of attendances is approximately 16 or 17 billion per year, a number that has been relatively stable for a decade.[84]

Large as some of these numbers sound, one should be aware that the total instances of exposure to the screened film each year are not great when compared with the frequency of radio listening or television watching, which are not only everyday affairs but which may also occupy many hours in a single day. Of course television vastly increases the audience for films by reproducing them on the tube, and VCRs have further widened their circulation. Nevertheless, the big screen continues to play a critical role. What the screened film lacks in frequency of contact, it may make up in strength of impact, since in surveys people often report that of all the media with which they have had contact, the films they have seen had the greatest effect. Certainly the film is a powerful medium for introducing people to the physical form of distant places and to the social arrangements and patterns of personal interaction in foreign cultures. It is precisely for this reason that governments and religious organizations are so often moved to censor films, to restrict their audiences to select groups, or to forbid their showing altogether. Films depicting sporting events, by contrast, tend to be considered ideologically neutral, and their distribution across national boundaries is relatively uninhibited.

Overcoming the Translation Barrier and Communicating Without Words

The obvious advantages to humankind of being able to communicate without the burden of always translating our mutually incomprehensible languages has led many to urge us toward the adoption or development of a universal language. The impulse to find such a language is strengthened by awareness of numerous languages that have achieved the status of lingua franca over wide geographic areas having many different local languages in use. Examples include Arabic for a long period after the eighth century in the Near East and Africa; Latin in medieval Europe; French throughout the Western world's diplomatic and aristocratic circles in the eighteenth and nineteenth centuries; Swahili in most of East Africa in the nineteenth and twentieth centuries. In each instance, however, the language widely used served special purposes or social strata—as in trade, diplomacy, or religion.

Today English, despite its extremely wide utilization, suffers from a similar limitation by being the language of science, preeminently, and to some extent of diplomacy and commerce. Despite its wide adoption, therefore, it is far from satisfying the criterion of a universally used language. Indeed, by the simple criterion of the number of different nations in which it serves more or less the entire population, Spanish may be argued to be more nearly universal than English. And neither English nor Spanish can claim to be understood by as many people as can understand Chinese, although this applies to its written form rather than to the spoken language with its mutually unintelligible dialects. In any event, neither Spanish nor Chinese seems destined to become a language known to all humankind. Meanwhile, Esperanto, constructed explicitly to give the world a language that would be understood by everyone, everywhere, seems unable to secure adoption in any but the narrowest circle of adherents to its great idea.

A Language of Gesture

Though we are unlikely to escape the necessity of translation to ensure worldwide communication as long as we remain in the realm of spoken language, there are forms that have great potential for the direct communication of meaning universally comprehended. These are the language of gesture, the pictorial, and sports. And of these three I believe the prospects for universalization of the language of sport are the greatest.

Some gestures do seem to be universally understood. Both a smile and a frown will be recognized as such everywhere. A sharp blow may be a universal communicator. One of the grimmest exemplifications of this truth was in the polyglot Mauthausen concentration camp where the rubber truncheon used by the guards was called *der Dolmetcher,* meaning "the interpreter: the one who made himself understood to everybody."[85] But the list of gestures that are unambiguous across cultures is actually quite limited. The same nod of the head can mean "yes" in one culture and "no" in another, as Europeans discover to their dismay when visiting India. And visitors to southern Italy, to name but one region of many that could be cited, quickly discover that even being familiar with or part of European

culture is alone not sufficient to ensure an understanding of the vast repertoire of highly expressive local gestures in use there.

It is challenging to confront the fact that in the period just after World
War I the silent films made in Hollywood constituted almost 90 percent of
those shown all over the world. Although they did use occasional written
titles, their communication depended predominantly on pantomime. Indeed, there have been geniuses in the language of gesture who have managed solely through that means to communicate to people of quite diverse
cultures rather complex ideas and sequences of action and meaning. Char-
lie Chaplin was the greatest of these, and he surely came close to developing a universal language of gesture. Marcel Marceau too has displayed a
similar capacity. However, such genius seems extremely rare, and its character always idiosyncratic. Thus there seems to be little prospect that, on
the basis of the genius of these men, we could construct and introduce into
use a generally understood language of gesture.

Looking to the various forms of sign language in use does not offer a solution either, because they are tied to existing national languages. The experience of working with national sign languages has certainly provided a basis for creating a universal and systematic version. Indeed, the World
Federation of the Deaf has developed and published such an international
sign language, called Gestuno. Whatever its value for the deaf, however,
such a language would seem to be considerably less advantageous for universal use than a constructed oral language, and it seems likely to fall short
of even the limited success Esperanto has enjoyed.

The Role of the Pictorial

Much of the pictorial also needs no translation. Culturally specific qualities
of painting, such as the Western use of perspective, or the Chinese convention of building a painting in linear vertical fashion, certainly require some
adjustment on the part of viewers coming from other cultures that follow
different conventions. Nevertheless, a nature scene in these styles, or in any
other basically representational tradition of painting, is highly accessible to
viewers from very diverse cultural backgrounds. The same will be true for a
still-life, or a portrait—that is, cultural boundaries will not prevent correct
identification of the objects portrayed. It is for this reason that paintings
such as those in the Lascaux caves speak to us so directly today regardless
of how many millennia separate us in time from their painters, and no matter how great the contrast in the conditions of our lives and those of the
original cave-dwelling artists.

Some forms of sculpture are closely related to the pictorial, and like Lascaux paintings can speak directly to people sharing no other language. Certainly this is true of the sculptural analogue of the still-life, that is, sculp-

tures that represent common animals or basic human relations, as in the case of the female with a baby at her breast. Nonrepresentational painting is not so immediately accessible, but the barriers to understanding seem to be more matters of level of education or modernization than of linguistic difference. The same transcendence of the limits of spoken language can be achieved by abstract sculpture. It is interesting to note in this connection that in 1987 a great collection of the sculptures of Henry Moore was put on permanent display in an outdoor museum in Hakone, Japan, and apparently communicated exceedingly well to the numerous Japanese who have been flocking to view the pieces.

The challenge to communication through the pictorial increases sharply, however, when we go beyond simple identification of objects, persons, and primal relationships and move to communicate more complex ideas and interrelated sequences of meaning. As ever larger numbers from different cultures lacking a common language come to interact more and more closely in new types of shared space such as highways, airports, elevators, hotels, and swimming pools, it becomes imperative that a language of signs be available that does not require translation for effective communication. Quite apart from the literacy issue, this becomes necessary as a consideration of efficiency. Often there simply is not enough space available to write out all the appropriate languages, and even if there were, the time required for people to locate their own language in a long list may be prohibitive under the given circumstances, as is the case of instructions meant for persons in fast-moving automobiles, or of those for turning on a fire alarm. To meet this challenge the world is increasingly developing universal signs. The smoking cigarette with a large red X across it comes gradually to be understood everywhere as meaning "No Smoking." An entire vocabulary of road signs to indicate no parking, no passing, left turn only, and so on has been devised and is being disseminated throughout the world.

Road signs use the pictorial to express quite simple ideas, but they are not well developed for communicating sequential and interrelated messages. The cartoon is better suited to such purposes. Its virtues for telling stories to those unable to follow a written language have been recognized for centuries. Thus when Christianity sought to impress on the minds of the uninitiated the events of the creation or to tell the stories of its saints and martyrs, it covered the walls of its monasteries and churches with cartoons. In the modern world the effectiveness of the cartoon is dramatically demonstrated in the impact that the more talented political cartoonists have made. The cartoon's universality was clearly demonstrated by Walt Disney, first with Mickey and Minnie Mouse, and then with a host of other characters. As they become increasingly complex, however, these efforts at universal communication through the cartoon come to depend increasingly on the verbal as a supplement to the underlying pictorial structure, and hence once again require the services of translators. Thus one of the most popular comic strips in *O Globo,* Brazil's largest newspaper, is the American "Beetle Bailey" renamed "Recruta Zero" with the translation substituting references to the Brazilian army for those originally applying uniquely to the U.S. Army.[86]

Music as Transnational Communication

Music has high potential as a universal language, although through most of human history its transportability has been limited, especially when it had to cross the great regional cultural divide that separated the musical traditions of the East and West. Modern cultural exchange programs bring Peking Opera and gamelan orchestras to the United States and Europe, but their audiences are very limited. A much more widespread diffusion is evidently granted to the corpus of the so-called "classical" music of the West, which can be heard continuously played in hundreds of coffee houses in the major cities of Japan. This is one of the few instances in which the balance of trade currently favors the West, and indeed it much favors Europe over the United States. Thus in 1985 Europe sent the United States some 14.3 million long-playing records of classical music, whereas U.S. exports to the European Community totaled only about 2.5 million recordings.[87]

The success of this genre, however, is dwarfed by the appeal of the music of mass culture, perhaps best exemplified by the worldwide popularity of the group that generated such a special fervor that it was given its own distinctive name—"Beetlemania." Since the Beetles communicated not only through musical scores but equally through the words of their English-language songs, the geographical spread of their popularity becomes even more impressive. More recently, comparable success in reaching into virtually all corners of the world seems to have been won by new popular idols. Madonna has the power to draw young fans from all over Japan to pack themselves 35,000 deep in Tokyo's Korakuen Stadium, part of an audience of some 2 million spectators before whom she will perform on a single tour covering three continents.[88] Michael Jackson's record "Thriller" followed up its 1983 sales of US$16 million by reaching an unprecedented $38 million in 1984, with a surprising 40 percent of those sales outside the United States. His 1987 recording of "Bad" was expected to achieve sales of 100 million copies worldwide, helping to make him not only a very big name but very big business as well.[89] In recognition of this sort of appeal a special program called *Music Box* is now broadcast by satellite specifically targeted at the youth of sixteen countries of Europe. Despite the many different languages these young people speak, the network is convinced that "our type of programming has a universal appeal which transcends national cultures."[90]

Sports as a Universal Language

Many sports are confined to a single country or its offshoots. Thus football, in the American version, is largely limited to the United States, and cricket to Great Britain and a few of its former colonies. Some other sports have become much more widely played and are followed by audiences across a considerable range of countries. Tennis is one of these, golf perhaps another. Ping-Pong would qualify, as certainly would volleyball, and soccer likely is the most widely diffused and probably enjoys the greatest mass following.

If any sport is to be played in more than one country, those who propose the engagement must confront an ineluctable fact. It is not possible for teams to play with each other unless they both know, accept, and follow the same rules. It is not sufficient to translate the rules followed by one set of players into the language of the other team. The rules must be identical. In another sense, therefore, the players must be able to speak the same language. This also applies to the referee, and not only with regard to his understanding of the rules, but equally as concerns the signals he will give to express his decisions. The same condition applies to the audiences. They must all know the same set of rules and understand their application in the same way. In a sense, then, once they have mastered the rules of the game, in whatever original language that was done, the spectators now, with this mastery of the rules, have come to share a common language. Whatever their native language, all of those watching the game can read it just as they could a story or a play, although the elements are pictorial and gestural rather than verbal. A game has a beginning, a middle, and an end; it unfolds in a given sequence; it involves an equivalent of vocabulary, syntax, and grammar; every element has meaning, as does the game and its performances as a whole.

Through the sports event, therefore, it becomes possible for vast audiences simultaneously to "read" the same game as it occurs, and thus in effect to share the same experience, without the necessity of translation from one language to another. There is, admittedly, a limitation on the sharing of experience, in that what is common is the ability to understand the story as it unfolds, but not to communicate it. If the several national audiences that easily followed every nuance of a game as they watched it were afterward obliged to tell each other what had gone on during the game, they would once more be thrown back on their individual national languages and be able to communicate, again, only through translation.

It is worth remembering, however, that notational systems have been and are still being developed that permit each play of a game to be described in sequence, so that ordinary language is not required to give a complete account of a game as it was played. Those used to describe chess games are perhaps the best known, but systems exist for soccer and football as well.

These are truly nonverbal universal languages. It may not be expected, however, that they will be much used by those who follow sports, even in the case of the most dedicated, and their use by mass audiences seems improbable in the extreme. For them, the meaning of sports events depends overwhelmingly on seeing them "live," as they happen. Their meaning also depends in good part on elements not intrinsically part of the play but rather part of the setting for the play—the size of the audience and the brilliance of the color scheme it creates, the flow of the crowd, the blare of the announcements, the ritual of the players coming on the field, the shaping of the first formations. These are the elements of communication mostly outside of ordinary language. They require us to approach major sports events as having a special character and requiring for their analysis the tools used to understand ceremony and ritual. But in this respect international sports events, which include the Wimbledon Tennis Championships and preeminently the Olympics, have a special status because their ritual cannot be local or parochial. It must speak to and be understood by people of all nations and cultures. And it has distinctive potential for uniting or dividing the world's inhabitants.

Summary and Conclusion

The remarkable recent expansion of the scope and speed of communication lends itself to hyperbole and, unfortunately, even to hype. It is therefore very appropriate for critics to dampen the overly enthusiastic by calling attention to the fact that the world is still far from being a global village, that most people still spend most of their lives in familiar and narrow circles communicating only with those close to them in physical and social space. The acknowledgment of this condition, however, does not contradict the fact that we have recently lived through and continue to experience a profound transformation in how, with whom, and about what we communicate. My own view is more in accord with that of Asa Briggs, who listed the "communications revolution" among the eight most important developments by which history will judge the twentieth century, characterizing it as "a basic technological revolution comparable to the Industrial Revolution and to earlier eras of radical change in human history that involved the mind as well as the body."[91]

I conclude by briefly sketching seven salient features of this new communications environment: its scope and immediacy; its unprecedented rapid rates of change; its marked technological breakthroughs and the associated dramatic reductions in costs; its particular pattern of persistent inequality; its generation of tighter linkages and greater interdependence; its fostering of an emergent world culture; and the fear and hostility that this development mobilizes.

In the past an entire island could disappear beneath the Pacific Ocean without anyone knowing of it, and a great city could be covered by ash with only its inhabitants and those in sight of the volcano as witnesses. Today, minutes after an earthquake shakes Tokyo we learn of it on our radios in New York and London, and almost immediately afterward can see the shaking buildings on our television sets. They place us visually, aurally, and almost tactilely in the midst of a battlefield in Vietnam, in the eye of a hurricane off Florida, and in the center of a race riot in South Africa as these events unfold. Virtually everyone has become an end point in an extraordinarily complex network that makes it possible for any person in the world to be linked to any other, and for all to be involved simultaneously in the same communication process. In addition to all our other attributes, characteristics, statuses, and roles, we all have a new identity as a part of a continuously changing but permanently present world audience.

The scope and immediacy of these connections has grown and continues to grow at exceptionally high, indeed often unprecedented, rates. Africa triples the number of television receivers in operation in one decade; Brazil does the same with its telephones; within a few years of their introduction VCRs are found in half the homes of some rich nations, and even a poor country like India reports 700,000 units already in place in 1987; Japan increases the number of calls placed to overseas destinations by some 21 percent per year; and the demand for satellite circuits doubles every three years.

The pace of these developments both is driven by and acts as stimulus to technological breakthroughs and the associated dramatic reductions in the cost of communicating any bit of information. In twenty years the power generated by a communications satellite increases by thirty-two times, and its circuits by sixty-two times, and the next unit on-line will in one stroke double these capacities. Even more remarkable, the per-bit cost incurred in storing information with the aid of programmable memory chips decreases by 1,000 times in ten years as a result of compressing 300,000 transistors onto a single chip. Such developments make it possible for a company that previously required thirteen hours to transmit its day's business record now to send it all out in a seven-minute burst. These, of course, are among the more dramatic advances, but they are approximated at many levels and in diverse forms of communication.

The speed of technological advance and the associated dramatic reductions in cost play a considerable role in shaping the distinctive pattern of inequality that characterizes the field of communications. On the one hand, the fact that high technology is fundamental to advances in communication tends to exclude the poor nations, and indeed a large number of the relatively advanced, from any significant role in shaping the course of future events. This condition is epitomized by the U.S. control of some 80 percent of the computer market, Japan's even greater dominance of the market for VCRs, and their almost total joint monopoly on the development of fiber-optical communication. On the other hand, bringing down the cost of transistors and chips means that we are very close to having a transistor radio in every household on Earth. Consequently, their governments permitting, the poorest individuals in the least developed countries can hear the same news at the same moment delivered by the same international wire services as are available to the richest citizen in the most advanced country.

As a result of such technological development we are more tightly linked, more interdependent, more vulnerable to the consequences of each other's actions. There is no way to erect barriers that can prevent a crash in the New York stock market from having almost instantaneous repercussions in all the other markets of the world and ultimately cascading its effects downward to damage the livelihood of a cacao farmer in Nigeria or the coffee grower in Colombia. Moreover, we are vulnerable not only to the actual actions of each other but also to the ghosts in our machines, so that the failure to interpret correctly the track of a flock of geese on the radar screen, or the action of one malfunctioning miracle chip, can trigger an alert, sending squadrons of atomic armed bombers aloft, and put us all within minutes of the possibility of total annihilation.

This general vulnerability is but one element of a much larger set of experiences and activities that our common linkage to the modern means of communication permits us to share. These shared experiences become elements in the emergence for the first time in human history of a truly universal world culture. We come increasingly to share the same movies, television programs, music, and sports events. Our clothing becomes more alike and our cooking and ways of eating more internationalized at every turn. Interpersonal relations and patterns of marriage, birth, and death become increasingly homogenized. Of course endless and profound differences persist from society to society as well as within the same nation or community. A single world culture is not a fact but rather is only an emergent of which only a few elements are firmly established. Nevertheless, the process is clearly well under way, and there is not much reason to believe that it can readily be reversed.[92]

Those more moved by an ecumenical spirit are not only comfortable with this trend, but they are also eager to promote it as the presumed precondition of a world of peace and plenty that they believe must be based on world citizenship and universal brotherhood. For others these trends are anathema, and they generate fear and revulsion at the prospect of a loss of distinctiveness, the erosion of ethnic and religious diversity, the abandonment of tradition, and the insidious diffusion of modernity. Ayatollah Khomeini's Islamic revolution in Iran is one manifestation of this reaction. But the expression of such fears is not limited to the less developed countries, nor is the tendency to express them in extreme language. Thus Helmut Schmidt, former chancellor of the Federal Republic of Germany, seriously argued that if commercial television programming via a Pan-European satellite were allowed to reach within the Federal Republic, such programming "could ultimately pose a greater peril for German society than any danger inherent in nuclear technology."[93]

Running counter to these tendencies to build Berlin Walls around local cultures are the recent moves of two nations that previously followed a policy of cultural isolation longer and more absolutely than any others in modern history. Communist China's official policy is now one of "openness to the world," and Gorbachev's slogan of glasnost carried a similar message. How far such policies will be implemented and how long they will be maintained are inherently uncertain. But their simultaneous and independent adoption, and in the case of China the policy's considerable implementation, is surely an important indicator of the direction in which the world will ultimately go.

ten

A CENTURY OF DUE PROCESS GUARANTEES WORLDWIDE

We here report the results of a content analysis focused on the due process rights or guarantees that were provided to citizens living under all the national constitutions extant in the world at twenty-year intervals during the period from 1870 to 1970. Our study had three objectives. First, we sought to test the assumption that the granting of procedural guarantees by national constitutions was, over time, both being expanded *within* countries and being diffused worldwide *across* all countries, thus providing additional examples of the tendency for institutional forms to diffuse around the world and consequently for nation-states to converge in their institutional structures and practices, tendencies already observed and documented in other realms such as the family, education, and retirement.[1] Second, we recognized the need to seek out patterns of differentiation as these might be manifested by subsets of countries viewed temporally, regionally, or culturally. And third, we hoped to explain the observed patterns by reference to appropriate political, economic, and sociocultural forces. In this chapter we address systematically mainly the first two objectives. With regard to the third objective we here make only a modest excursion, hinting

Reprinted with permission from Alex Inkeles and Jon C. Hooper, "A Century of Procedural Due Process Guarantees in Constitutions Worldwide: Testing the World Polity and Convergence Models," *Tocqueville Review,* Vol. 14, No. 2 (1993), 3–52.

at the economic and sociocultural antecedents and consequences of the constitutional granting of due process rights.

Before we present the results of our content analysis we should make clear what we understood due process to encompass and why we thought it important to measure, why we pursued the subject in constitutions, how we developed our sample of constitutions, and how we measured presence or absence of due process rights in the constitutions we sampled.

What Is Procedural Due Process and Why Is It Important?

Justice Felix Frankfurter declared that "the history of liberty has largely been the history of procedural safeguards."[2] A moment's reflection on the situation of anyone living in the United States should make it apparent that his statement is not mere hyperbole and not just a matter of history. Were it not for their due process rights Americans could be arrested in their homes without a warrant and could be sentenced to prison without a chance to defend themselves. In less extreme circumstances, but in situations nevertheless vital to the individual, they could, without their due process guarantees, be denied their social security benefits without a prior hearing; be suspended from school for a term on the mere whim of the principal; or be kept on in a mental hospital when no longer sick or dangerous but merely eccentric.[3]

There are many ways of classifying the rights of citizens and of communities as life in the modern world confronts them with the all-pervasive power of the state, and indeed of other massive organizations such as major business corporations, gigantic school districts, and vast hospital complexes. The scheme probably best known to sociologists and political scientists is that developed by T. H. Marshall, who stressed the distinction between civil, political, and social rights. This classification, although useful for the purpose of sequencing the extension of rights in Britain over time, was, as Marshall acknowledged, "dictated by history . . . more . . . than by logic."[4] Most important, Marshall's classification notably neglects a category that is central in the tradition of American legal analysis, whose lead we follow. That category is made up of the rights collectively called due process rights. Those rights, in turn, are conventionally divided into those that are "substantive" and those that are "procedural."

A vast number of legal scholars have labored at elaborating the distinction between substantive and procedural due process.[5] Unfortunately, the discussion has often had the effect of obscuring rather than clarifying the distinction, and Jerry Mashaw is not alone in asserting that "the attempt can never be wholly successful because the questions are functionally inseparable."[6] Nevertheless, in this study we coded only those rights we considered to be procedural, and so we must specify how we made the distinction.

We understand *substantive* rights to be conditions of the person, such as the right to live, to be free, or to be secure in one's possessions. At least in Western civilization the individual's basic right not to be deprived arbitrarily of these conditions by government has been affirmed in the fundamental law since the time of the Magna Carta. In more recent times some nations have considerably augmented the list of basic substantive rights affirmed either in their constitutions or in legislation. Notable among these additions, now often referred to as "positive rights," are the right to be educated, to be properly housed, to be free from hunger, and even to enjoy privacy. For example, the current constitution of Ireland guarantees to all citizens "the right to an adequate means of livelihood," and the Japanese constitution, along with the more common guarantees of freedom of religion and of assembly and association, goes on to guarantee even academic freedom.[7]

In general, *procedural* due process rights restrict or restrain the power of the state or of some other corporate body should it attempt to deny or fundamentally limit the ability of a person to enjoy his or her substantive rights. For this reason they are sometimes referred to as "negative rights."[8] Procedural guarantees come into play under two conditions. First, and least ambiguous, is the situation in which the state wishes to deprive a person, or a protected corporate entity, of a substantive right. Suppose, for example, that the state considered someone a danger to others and wished to lock him or her up, thereby denying the person's substantive right to be free. If the appropriate due process guaranties were in place, the state could take such action only if it followed certain procedures. For example, commitment to a mental institution would be permitted only on the basis of appropriate medical diagnosis by a competent medical authority; confinement could not be continued without regular treatment and periodic review of the person's condition; and if the person could not be proved any longer to be dangerous to self or others, then he or she would have to be released.[9] All such restrictions or prohibitions on the action of government in seeking to limit someone's liberty we treat as procedural due process guarantees, since they specify procedures the government must go through when it seeks to deprive a person of a substantive right.

Procedural due process rights may also come into play not only to *prevent* the government from acting but also to *oblige* it to take certain action in order to secure a citizen a substantive right that he or she has not been enjoying because the state has failed to provide the means necessary to its enjoyment. In other words, procedural due process rights may be exercised not only to *proscribe* but also to *prescribe* certain government action. For example, students with handicaps can use due process to oblige the several states of the United States to make their schools physically accessible to the handicapped through the addition of ramps, elevators, special drinking fountains, and even special showers.[10] Similarly, prisoners, relying on the constitutional guarantee of freedom from punishment that is cruel and unusual, have used the courts in the United States to oblige states to provide their prisoners with meaningful work and with activities of a recreational and educational nature.[11] From one perspective such a suit against the government might be understood to *proscribe* its behavior, that is, to prevent the state from inflicting inhumane punishment, but from another perspective such a suit can be seen as intended to *prescribe* the provision of services and conditions that are essential to the prisoner's rehabilitation.

In its most fundamental sense, then, procedural due process means the assurance that actions significantly affecting the interests of individuals or groups may not be taken by public or private authorities except by following specific procedures or rules that are set down and agreed to by law as appropriate to the circumstances. The earliest important restrictions of this kind were placed on the kings and other sovereign rulers, as in the case of the Magna Carta and its famous clause in which King John, in 1215, promised that "no freeman shall be taken, or imprisoned, or disseised, or outlawed, or exiled, or in any way destroyed . . . except by . . . the law of the land." That same document provided other essential procedural guarantees, as, for example, that the king would not "delay right or justice."[12] The language of the Magna Carta was echoed in the Constitution of Sweden of 1806, in which Article 16 declared, "The king . . . shall not deprive anyone or allow anyone to be deprived of life, honor, personal liberty or well-being without legal trial and sentence." Of course such restrictions were placed not only on monarchs but on democratic governments as well. The Fifth and Fourteenth Amendments of the U.S. Constitution are also often noted for their provision that neither the federal government nor any state "shall . . . deprive any person of life, liberty, or property, without due process of law. . . . "

Language comparable to that used in these classical sources was incorporated in another and more recent landmark document, and one of the widest applicability, namely, the Universal Declaration of Human Rights adopted by the General Assembly of the United Nations on December 10, 1984. Its key phrase is "equal protection of the law." It further specifically forbids "arbitrary arrest and detention" as well as arbitrary deprivation of property. In addition, it requires a "a fair and public hearing by an independent and impartial tribunal," and that trials be "public," with the accused having "all guarantees necessary for his defense." Here too we find the characteristic language that is the most common marker of concern with procedural due process. It comes in Article 29, Paragraph 2, which specifies that "in the exercise of his rights and freedoms, everyone shall be subject *only to such limitations as are determined by law.*"[13]

Although initially applied to action by the sovereign, and then by the state and its agents, procedural safeguards gradually came into play in an increasingly wide range of situations, extending from courts to administrative agencies such as housing authorities, licensing boards, and finally to employers in such matters as dismissal. Thus in Great Britain, where the principle of "natural justice" operates in ways very similar to due process in the United States, procedural guarantees were further extended to the private realm in the late nineteenth and early twentieth centuries, so that, for example, a trade union was obliged by the decision in *Labouchere v. Wharncliffe* to provide proper notice and a hearing before it could expel a member, and the same guarantee was made available to constrain the expulsion of a club member from his private club.[14] Succinct accounts of the extension of due process guarantees provided by the U.S. court system and under English administrative law have been provided by Mashaw and Schwartz, respectively.[15]

Apart from its general form as lawful procedure, the understanding of what due process encompasses has gradually evolved into a series of specific assurances against arbitrariness, precipitousness, capriciousness, and unreasonableness of action by public and other authorities involving civil as well as criminal actions. The idea is often summed up in the concept of "a fair hearing," which includes such specific protections as adequate notice, the right to question witnesses and to examine documents, to be represented by counsel, and particularly important, the right to have one's case judged by an impartial decisionmaker.

The desirability of being protected from arbitrary and capricious actions by officials and of being able to obtain a fair hearing in the face of intended or actual actions against one's person, property, and interests would seem so obvious as hardly to need discussion. But the historical fact is that the patent desirability of such protection was no insurance of its being provided to all persons. On the contrary, it took a long process of development, and often of struggle, to reach the point where procedural guarantees were acknowledged as basic rights of all persons and were progressively enshrined in documents such as the Universal Declaration of Human Rights. Moreover, historically the extension of such rights, even when granted by the powers, was generally severely restricted to certain classes of person. Thus the Magna Carta was mainly an agreement between the king and his barons, and its more sweeping and historically most important guarantees specified only "freemen" as protected from arbitrary action by the king. In the United States the Fifth Amendment certainly did not provide slaves with any procedural due process protections, and the Civil War and the Fourteenth Amendment were required to bring the American Negro under that umbrella, inadequate as its protection may have been in actual circumstance.[16]

Indeed progress in the struggle to win due process for the average citizen has historically been uncertain and uneven. Thus in the United States, from about 1880 to 1935 the Fourteenth Amendment was invoked mainly to prevent the several states from regulating various industries. For example, the Supreme Court, in *Lochner v. New York,* relied on the Fourteenth Amendment to strike down a New York State regulation designed to prevent bakeries from obliging workers to work more than sixty hours a week. In this period almost no cases before the Supreme Court relied on the amendment to limit government action *against individuals.* Those few pleas by individuals that got as far as the Supreme Court generally were given short shrift.[17] Thus as late as 1950, in *Bailey v. Richardson,* the Court held that a government agency had no obligation to give a hearing to one of its employees before dismissing him. It was only after 1970, through the precedent set by the case of *Goldberg v. Kelley,* that individuals in increasing numbers found that they could get the help of the U.S. courts in enforcing their procedural rights as protection against arbitrary action by government in all manner of civil and administrative matters.[18]

In Great Britain, over many decades starting in the late nineteenth century, the courts used the principle of natural justice to limit arbitrary action by government in fields such as housing and with regard to dismissal from office. This pattern was abruptly changed in 1948 when the House of Lords, in what is known as the Stevanage case, concluded that the protection of natural justice was extended only in those cases treated in a judicial setting and need not apply in those presented before an administrative board or tribunal.[19] This decision was a great setback for the average citizen, since increasingly individuals could not manage their lives without encounters with the state apparatus, and they had to turn to such boards and tribunals to get relief from arbitrary actions by officials who had denied them access to entitlements, privileges, and resources they thought of as their right by law. Thereafter it took almost two decades to restore the principle of natural justice to something like its former significance as a restraint on arbitrary action by government in Great Britain.

The extension of due process guarantees and their application to ever broader categories of persons may, then, be taken as a *critical index* of the development of human rights and of the progress of nations toward granting equal standing before the law and equality of treatment to all individuals subordinated to the power of the state. This transition, which is of course far from completed everywhere in the world, has been aptly described as movement from the status of "subject" to that of "citizen," with all citizens understood to lay claim to a bundle of rights and privileges as well as obligations.[20] Beyond the issue of who is included or excluded from the status of citizen, the sheer number of procedural rights specifically granted to the typical person, and the breadth of their application, may in turn also be taken as an important indicator of the growth of human freedom. By counting the frequency with which these procedural rights are granted we can assess increases and decreases in the ability of ordinary citizens actually to attain the substantive rights their citizenship nominally allots them.[21] Such progress, if it occurs, can be measured country by country and, more broadly, can be assessed for the global society as a whole.

Why Study Constitutions?

Assurances of due process are generally most fully elaborated in statute law, especially in administrative law, and in the decisions of courts interpreting those laws. Indeed, a cogent argument may be made that laws are far more important in ensuring due process than are constitutional guarantees. Those who take this position note that England, home of that fountainhead known as the Magna Carta, has no written constitution, yet it can be argued that its citizens are well assured of due process under law. Certainly this was the view of Albert Venn Dicey, who said of the Habeas Corpus Acts that although "they declare no principle and define no rights, they are for practical purposes worth a hundred constitutional articles guaranteeing individual liberty."[22] But others argue that the lack of a constitutional guarantee of due process leaves the British citizen much more exposed to grave risks to his rights. English judges may question witnesses, silence counsel, admit even stolen evidence, and give pointed personal evaluation of evidence to the jury. Conduct of this sort by an American judge, Graham Hughes affirms, "would often be found by an appellate court to constitute denial of the defendant's constitutional rights to counsel and due process." This "flaccid quality" of English judicial practices, Hughes tells us, "owes much to the deadening nature of a system which has no Bill of Rights."[23] Increasing recognition of this problem has led to the view, voiced by Lord Scarman, that "the United Kingdom must now adopt a written constitution . . . providing the citizen with greater constitutional protection against abuse of power."[24]

While emphasizing the importance of written constitutions, we certainly do not mean to deny that a fully adequate analysis of the diffusion of due process guarantees would require one to study not only constitutions, which may be only the tip of the iceberg, but administrative law and court decisions as well. There are, however, good, and even compelling, reasons for beginning an investigation of the worldwide diffusion of due process rights by looking at constitutions. First and foremost there is the fact that constitutions are generally defined as the supreme law of the land. This means that in most nations both the limits on and the expansion of procedural due process in law, in administration, and in the courts are likely to be considerably influenced by what the national constitution says. Yet we must acknowledge that in a substantial number of countries, especially in the contemporary era, governments have paid very little heed to the procedural guarantees written into their respective national constitutions. Is there then any justification for an inquiry into whether the constitutions of such nations do or do not specify that their citizens be protected by procedural due process rights? We think there is.

Constitutions have great symbolic significance. In the modern world, and especially in the case of new nations, a constitution is an important element in legitimating the status of a people and a territory as serious contenders for recognition as part of the community of nations. As William Andrews so aptly said: "A newly independent nation may have its birth registered through admission to the United Nations, but a Constitution is normally required as a baptismal certificate."[25] Furthermore, it may be argued that the legitimacy of a nation-state will be assessed not only by the mere presence of a constitution but also by its form and content. If, as some believe, there is a worldwide community standard for nations whereby their legitimacy is assessed, which is the view of the world polity theory discussed later, then might it not be that providing for procedural due process guarantees has become part of that standard? If so, we would expect new nations to include such guarantees in their constitutions as a way of responding to world-system pressures that specify at least an outward conformity to certain international standards.

Moreover, even if governments do not mean to observe the usual procedural guarantees, they may find that they have given a hostage to fortune by writing such provisions into their constitutions. Once written, constitutions have a tendency to become consecrated, often taking on great moral and symbolic significance. Thus even in absolutist and totalitarian nations such as the Soviet Union long was, citizens frequently referred to the Soviet constitution in making a plea for their right to lawful and humane treatment. All this makes it appropriate to assess the importance nations assign to procedural due process by studying changes in their constitutions alone, without necessary reference to actual administrative practice and judicial action.

In addition to these theoretical justifications for studying constitutions, there were also practical considerations for beginning our inquiry with these documents rather than with a study of legislation. To measure due process actions with any degree of precision in the laws, the administrative boards, and the courts of any number of nations would be a formidable task, and to do so over any length of time would be possible only by mounting a social science project so vast that it is almost inconceivable that it could be financed, given the funding levels typical for the social sciences. By contrast, constitutions have the advantage of being well-defined documents that are more or less readily accessible. Therefore, an attack on the diffusion issue based on them, though it does not eliminate all problems of definition and sampling, nevertheless recommends itself as a much more feasible enterprise without necessarily sacrificing meaning or significance.

The Standardization of Constitutional Forms

Since constitutions were the basic documentary source for the analysis presented here, it is in order to offer a brief discussion of the nature of such documents as it might influence our investigation.

Every one of our readers will surely know well at least one constitution, but most are likely to be unaware of the fact that all modern constitutions display a great degree of isomorphism, being very much alike in structure and form. Of course this does not mean that they are identical. On the contrary, many details are quite different from one constitution to another. Thus one-party states have constitutions quite different in certain major respects from those in multiparty states, and those with a unitary structure are governed by constitutions importantly different from those for federations. Nevertheless, it will become apparent to anyone who attempts a systematic analysis of constitutions that their structure and form are in general quite similar. Indeed, on the scale of comparison used in this study, the isomorphism of constitutions was to us quite striking.

At least two reasons may be adduced for this condition. First, the function of all constitutions, the task they are meant to perform, is basically the same everywhere. They are all formal documents constituting the highest law of the land "by which a society organizes a government for itself, defines and limits its powers, and prescribes the relations of its various organs *inter se* and with the citizen."[26] The second, and rather different, reason for the isomorphism of constitutions comes from the fact that when new constitutions are written their authors evidently do a great deal of copying from other constitutions. Indeed, compilations of constitutions have been made with the express purpose of facilitating their study and emulation during the process of writing a new constitution. Thus Charles Martin and William George thought of their compilation as enabling those writing new constitutions "to ascertain by comparison what are the fundamental principles of public law; what are the different modes of distribution of powers; what are the prescribed rules for exercising power; and in what ways powers are limited for the protection of life, liberty, and property—in a word, what is the modern, responsible, constitutional state."[27]

That these compilers were not just living in a world of fantasy is evident from the actual history of the writing of various constitutions. Delegates to the National Australian Convention that was called to write a constitution in 1891 were provided the texts of the basic law of Canada, Switzerland, the United States, and South Africa.[28] Looking to write its basic law, the Irish Provisional Government circulated the texts of some eighteen constitutions, including those of Poland and Estonia. And a collection advocating a new Philippine constitution provided the complete text of the constitutions of eight nations, including Japan and Mexico.[29] In particular, the

Constitution of the United States has had a considerable impact as a model, and, as Carl Friedrich noted, after each of the world wars "discussions of American institutions filled the records of constitutional debates."[30] This process of searching the world for relevant models for national constitutions continues to this day.[31]

However, not all nations had the same freedom to follow models of their own choosing. The so-called "Stalin Constitution" adopted by the USSR in 1936, for example, one expressly designed to be a significant ideological as well as a legal instrument,[32] served as a more or less obligatory model for the constitutions of most of the East European countries that came under Soviet domination after World War II.[33] The Constitution of the United States, apart from its general influence, played a much more direct role in shaping several constitutions after World War II, the case of Japan being perhaps the most notable. There, according to one account, "General MacArthur . . . authorized three American lawyers in the Army Judge Advocate General's Corps to draft a constitution within six days . . . on February 12 the Americans completed their draft, and, by February 22, the document had won the approval of the Emperor."[34] Although not a simple copy of the American, this May 1946 Japanese constitution shows, as may be imagined, obvious lines of influence emanating from the former.

The example of Japan is but one of numerous instances in which newly emergent nations sought assistance from outside experts in drafting their constitutions. So extensive was this activity as dozens of new nations were formed in the postcolonial period after World War II that writing constitutions came to be called a "cottage industry," and one specialist could claim alone to have worked with more than forty governments since 1966.[35] However, such claims of a homogenization process must be balanced against the many case studies that argue, as Miriam Kornblith did for the Venezuelan experience, that "Constitution making is a field where political struggle takes place—very often in a decisive fashion. Thus, the debates on the [Venezuelan] Constitutions reveal the values, intentions, and disagreements of the main actors and the achievements and failures of each process."[36] These contrasting views of the relation of constitutions to the particular social and political milieus in which they are embedded have serious implications for our analysis, raising issues to which we now turn.

Theoretical Orientations and Hypotheses

The research we report here was conceived as part of a larger program of investigations in world system analysis. World system analysis is a general orientation which assumes that it is productive to consider all the nations and all the world's population as participating in a single social system.[37] However, such a general orientation does not in itself provide specific predictions. In developing more systematic hypotheses we turned to two world system models that are closely related but are also differentiated in important ways that influence the expectations one derives from the two models. These two are the "world polity" model and "convergence theory."

The world polity model has been named and developed by John Meyer and his associates. First presented in 1979, the theory argues that, especially after 1945, the world developed a single "organizational and cultural milieu that penetrates all countries with common . . . demands." These common demands are held to shape national policy "*regardless* of the various structural characteristics" that otherwise differentiate nations from one another. Instead general norms or standards of what a nation should be like and what it should do develop and diffuse throughout the world, and again "this set of diffusion effects is *common to all countries* in the world independent of their variations on other structural characteristics." The theory was originally applied to explain the worldwide expansion of education, but it was explicitly asserted to apply to most, indeed all, realms of national development. Thus the world polity model asserts that "although countries vary in terms of wealth and economic structure, *all* nations pursue common national economic development goals."[38] After its initial formulation this theory was elaborated and applied in a number of investigations of different topics, but its basic assumption was not changed.[39]

Convergence theory as elaborated by Inkeles[40] shares with the world polity model the assumption that the world is witnessing "the convergence of social systems and . . . increasing similarities of institutional forms [and] administrative practice." Moreover, it too allows for a process of *diffusion* to bring about common national forms and practices, especially under the influence of international agencies such as the International Postal Union.

Beyond this point, however, Inkeles's convergence theory departs sharply from the assumptions of the Meyer model. In convergence theory the expectation that nations will adopt common administrative and judicial forms is explicitly made dependent on meeting certain specific conditions. For example, the expectation of convergence is limited to the advanced industrial societies of the world, and the theory argues that even then institutions will converge only insofar as nations face similar *internal* problems such as an aging population. Convergence theory also explicitly allows for the possibility that nations facing common problems will nevertheless yield different outcomes because of the influence of their having experienced a different historical development. Moreover, in sharp contrast with the universalistic thrust of the Meyer theory, the Inkeles approach argues that "the convergence process is highly differentiated, proceeding at variable rates in different realms of the sociocultural system." Specifically identified as likely to be more resistant to convergence were religion, law, and the politico-economic system.

Applied to our material on constitutional due process guarantees, these two theoretical schemes would yield some shared predictions, but they also generate some different, even sharply divergent, expectations. Acknowledging the influence of the cottage industry of constitution writing, both theories would predict that the number and the content of due process guarantees in national constitutions should become more alike over time. However, the world polity model would expect this to happen worldwide, especially after 1945, whereas the convergence theory would hold this expectation firmly only with regard to the industrially advanced nations, leaving it an open question whether the newer less developed countries would conform to any general model.

So far as concerns differences in the historical origins of nations, world polity theory would expect them to be overwhelmed by the pressures to conform to a world standard of what a proper constitution should be, but the convergence theory would hold open the possibility of substantial differentiation based on regional, cultural, and historical influences. Hence it would lead us to expect the world's constitutions to be differentiated into subsets on the basis of socioeconomic structure, religion, culture, or colonial history. According to this view the constitutions of Europe might be quite different from those of Latin America, and dominant powers might give a special cast to the constitutions of countries they dominated, as in the case of the United States vis-à-vis Latin America, or the USSR in Eastern Europe, or France and England in their far-flung former colonies. Another source of differentiation might be the philosophy of government and the approach to national development adopted by the leaders of nations, especially new nations whose constitution writing was to some degree done on a tabula rasa and undertaken largely at the initiative of new elites. Rather than passively accepting the models brought to them by the experts from the constitution-writing industry, these leaders may have had their own internally generated agendas that served to counter the homogenizing influence of the professional constitution writers. For example, Professor Blaustein reports that in over two years of trying he failed to persuade the new leaders of Zimbabwe, to whom he served as adviser, to include a version of the equal rights amendment in their new constitution. His explanation was that "it went against tribal cultures."[41] It may also have gone against the perceived power interests of the new rulers of that land.

The Codes in Our Investigation

Since we were working across many cultures and legal systems we obviously confronted a formidable challenge as to whether a concept so intimately linked to the Anglo-Saxon legal tradition could be meaningfully applied in so wide a variety of contexts and over so great a range of time as our study design involved. Examination of the relevant literature indicated that procedural rights were well understood in most legal systems, although these systems were evidently markedly differentiated in the degree to which procedures such as fair hearings, written charges, and confrontation of witnesses were specified by law or were otherwise guaranteed. In general, however, the language of procedural due process is immediately recognizable. As early as 1870, for example, Article 20 of the Paraguayan constitution stated: "No inhabitant of the Republic shall be punished without trial and conviction under laws in effect at the time of the offense. . . . Trial shall always be as provided in Article 11 [by jury]. No one shall be compelled to testify against himself, arrested without a written order of a competent authority, detained more than twenty-four hours without being informed of the charges against him." In Japan, by contrast, the formal legal concept of a fair hearing came into being only in the period after World War II on the basis of Article 31 of the constitution, which used the conventional language affirming that "no person shall be deprived of life or liberty, nor shall any other criminal penalty be imposed, except according to procedures established by law."

Guided by legal theory and history, we took an empiricist approach by reading through a number of constitutions to see what we might find there that we could identify as falling in the same realm as the procedures identified by the literature. We found that the most common pattern was for constitutions to make reference to some general requirement for procedures established by law, such as was the case for Magna Carta, the U.S. Constitution of 1791, the Japanese constitution of 1946, and the Universal Declaration of Human Rights. To cover these instances we created a specific code category which we labeled:

1. *the general clause.*

Apart from such a general clause, we found that the matters identifiable as due process issues dealt with in the constitutions fell into four groups. Two of these were intimately related to the realm conventionally thought of as involving due process, namely, matters concerning arrest and court or trial action. We therefore explicitly coded their mention in any constitution. Under *Arrest* we had a specific code for any mention of the following:

2. *the requirement of a warrant;*
3. *the specification of limits of time* after which formal charges must be made, or limiting the time an arrestee may be held;
4. *the documentation of arrest action,* generally including the requirement of written charges; and
5. *the requirement of 'habeas corpus.'*

For dealing with *Court Procedures,* specifically those involving a trial, we had separate codes for the mention of:

6. *the right to trial;*
7. *the timing of the trial;*
8. *the right to counsel;*
9. *the right to jury;* and
10. *the right to appeal.*

Other realms involving what are generally recognized as due process considerations focused on:

11. *the confiscation of property,* where hearings and documentation are at issue; and
12. *compensation,* not only in relation to loss of property but also because of other injuries or damages that state action might cause the citizen to suffer.

With our code for compensation we came to a borderline, the crossing of which took us outside the set of actions conventionally accepted as falling within the realm of due process. We decided nevertheless to extend the concept to cover one additional matter by taking account of:

13. *the right to petition,* and the supplemental
14. *right to have one's petition responded to* by the authorities to whom it is addressed.

In our decision to include the right to petition and hearings, we were influenced by the attention this matter was paid in the constitutions we examined, and on reflection we concluded that it could arguably be considered a general procedural matter akin to the more specific right to a hearing in trials and in administrative actions. We thought of the right to petition as *procedural* rather than *substantive* because, at least generally, no particular content is specified for the petitions in those constitutions that grant this particular right to be heard. As a rule, citizens can evidently petition with regard to any substantive issue. The petition is, in other words, a procedure whereby the petitioner increases the chances that he or she will actually enjoy some substantive right or privilege that has so far been denied him or her. In that way, it shares the general character of procedural rights, which prescribe the paths that must be followed in the *process* of either granting or denying substantive rights.[42]

Taken all together, then, we covered five realms—arrest, trial, property, compensation, and petition. Divisions within these realms, plus the general clause, made for a total of fourteen different procedures that could maximally be coded for any one constitution.

We feel that all of these fit the conventional conception of what qualifies as a procedural due process guarantee. Some might find our definition too broad.[43] But since we were careful to differentiate each realm and its subordinate procedures, our method permits imposing stricter definitions and different combinations in the effort to assess whether, how far, and in what form constitutional due process guarantees may have been diffusing worldwide. Others might find that our codes took too narrow a view of due process, noting, for example, that we did not provide a separate category for the right to cross-examine witnesses at one's trial or to be advised of the explicit grounds for a court decision against one. The main reason for these omissions was practical, that is, our initial review of a sample of constitutions indicated that their mention was not frequent enough to justify a separate code category. We also rest our case on the argument that the standings of countries, at least in *relative* terms, would not be likely to differ significantly when each nation had only fourteen chances to score rather than sixteen or eighteen.

Study Design and Sampling

Having decided what we would look for in the constitutions, we had to settle on which constitutions to examine, a choice influenced by the fact that, as in any research, we operated with resource constraints. Since we were interested in establishing a pattern of long-term stability or change, we hoped to cover a period of at least 100 years. But given that the average year over that span of time would present us with some seventy-five extant national constitutions, we faced the prospect of coding some 7,500 documents. Moreover, our initial search for sources indicated that it often took a great deal of effort to locate some constitutions, quite apart from the time required to code those we could locate. We recognized, then, that it was going to be totally beyond our resources to achieve the maximum goal of coding *all* constitutions extant in *all* of the past 100 years, and we had to settle on some more limited target. After some experience in locating and coding constitutions, it was apparent that the maximum our personnel resources could encompass would be about 500 documents, and we had to decide how that number might be most meaningfully distributed geographically and over time.

Our alternatives were to sample nations or years or both. One possibility would have been to follow only one small subset of countries, but to do so year by year, over the 100-year span. But then we would have been representing mainly Europe and the Americas, which produced the first constitutions, and thus would have failed to satisfy our aspiration to develop a picture of the *worldwide* distribution of due process rights.

Another approach would have been to take half of the available constitutions every ten years. But for the early years the number was so small that cutting it in half would have created severe limits on testing the reliability of our statistics. Since those early years were the base against which we were going to measure change over a century, it was important for longitudinal analysis to keep that base as large as possible. Moreover, it was apparent that most constitutions were kept in force for very long periods. We therefore decided to study only every twentieth year from 1870 to 1970, but to include in our samples all constitutions in force in the years thus selected. In this way we kept the number of constitutions to be coded within the limits of our staff resources, and we gained the additional advantage of having our periodic counts also contain the entire universe of constitutions extant anywhere in the world at each interval. Finally, we had an interest in keeping to the twenty-year intervals because other attributes of the constitutions and the nations we studied had been independently coded by John Boli,[44] and we wished to be in a position to relate our findings to his.

If we had been studying only one country or a special small sample of countries, the twenty-year intervals separating our sample sets would have made those sets an unreliable basis for judging trends over time. Given that our samples were nearly total, however, we felt that the sample sets provide a reasonable basis for judging long-term worldwide processes of stability and change. In our view, a ten-year interval would not have produced patterns significantly different from those we observed, although this is clearly an empirical question that can only be tested by having someone collect the samples for the years in question. We do not, however, mean to minimize the limitations on the portrait of world change that our sampling procedure, adopted out of necessity rather than by preference, may have imposed on us.

Our operating principle was in effect to take a snapshot of the total company of constitutions that were in force at twenty-year intervals starting in 1870 and ending in 1970, which gave us measures at each of six points in time. Because we focused on only these six time points, a constitution that might have been in the picture two years before would not have been represented in our data set *if* it had been replaced by the time our twentieth year came around, and one that came into force a year later than our target date would similarly not have been counted unless it was still in force at the time of the count on the next twentieth year. For example, Panama had constitutions dated 1868, 1870 and 1873. Our 1870 sample set included only Panama's 1870 constitution. That of 1868 was not considered. The 1873 constitution did not enter our samples either because by 1890, for which year we created our next sample set, the 1873 constitution had been replaced by an 1875 constitution, and since that was the one still in force at the time, it entered into the 1890 sample set.

The problem that some constitutions never got to count in any sample set is matched in significance, perhaps even outweighed, by the fact that some constitutions got to be counted more than once; indeed, under our system the same constitution could be counted in all the panels if it persisted long enough unchanged. The U.S. Constitution is an outstanding example, since, except for its later amendments, it entered all six of our sample sets as fundamentally the same document.

The situation was similar in Uruguay, whose constitution persisted fundamentally unchanged from 1829. In all, there were seven constitutions that, once entered into one of our panels, were basically unchanged as they successively entered the five subsequent sample sets. Others were repeated less frequently but nevertheless persistently. We shall later say more about the effects of this phenomenon.

Locating Constitutions for the Sample Sets

We located constitutions by referring to standard general compilations, to special regional compilations, and where necessary to the series published by individual nations. Collecting and publishing groups of constitutions for comparative study began with Aristotle.[45] Until very recently most compilations reflected the strength of regional interests, with collections of mostly European constitutions beginning to appear around 1800.[46] As more constitutions were written, more specialized collections appeared, either as study guides for those writing new constitutions or as propaganda instruments for those promoting constitutional reform. In this period the standard comprehensive reference was Dareste and Dareste (four editions between 1883 and 1929), which was for us the most useful single source for locating the earliest constitutions. As constitutionalism spread early in the twentieth century and became an object of systematic study, collections of comparative constitutions became quite common in English.[47] The task of publishing and republishing a truly comprehensive collection was not taken up again, however, until the first of three excellent collections by Peaslee appeared in 1950.

With the appearance of the third of the Peaslee collections, however, the limitations of book-format bound editions was becoming obvious.[48] In the 1950s, 1960s, and 1970s constitutions were appearing at a prodigious rate, and keeping up-to-date with the latest constitutions of every nation was a major task. To some extent the Inter-Parliamentary Union's *Constitutional and Parliamentary Information* was useful, but unfortunately it made no attempt to collect constitutions systematically—they were published by the union only as they became available through being submitted by interested nations. Fortunately, Blaustein and Flanz, beginning in the early 1970s, corrected the situation. *The Constitutions of the Countries of the World* is both comprehensive and up-to-date. It is now the standard authoritative source for both current and recent constitutions.

Using Blaustein and Flanz, the researcher may gather data on current constitutions equipped with a knowledge of English only. However, for complete *historical* coverage, French, Spanish, and German are also necessary. French allows access to Dareste and Dareste and Spanish and German are necessary for the few constitutions that have not been gathered in these compilations.[49]

Composition of the Six Sample Sets

Our selection procedures, applied to the sources we have described, generated a total of 391 constitutions, each considered an "entry" in our grand sample. This total reflected the constitutional history of 139 nations of the world, organized in six sample sets, with each set meant to represent *all* constitutions extant at twenty-year intervals.[50] Because the same constitution was sometimes in effect in two or more time periods the number of distinctive separate constitutions was actually only 245. The difference (391 –245 = 146) was accounted for in good part by constitutions repeated only once or twice; indeed sixty-two of the repetitions were of this type.[51] In any event, since our objective was to reflect the state of the world at successive points in time, it is not pertinent, at least with regard to each periodic profile, whether any constitution was old or young, unique or repeated, so long as it was a legitimate entry in the total set of constitutions in effect at a given twenty-year interval. Of course, from a different perspective, the fact that constitutions were repeating from sample set to sample set increased the chances that the amount of apparent change from one set to another might be muted.

The six sample sets ranged in size from thirty-six in 1870 to 132 in 1970, becoming progressively larger as more and more nations came into being as sovereign states. The 1870 set was dominated more or less equally by the countries of Western Europe and Latin America as a result of the efflorescence of constitution writing in the Southern Hemisphere as it freed itself from Spanish domination after 1830. Later sets, particularly those of 1950 and 1970, reflected the great surge of nations becoming newly independent after World War II.

In addition to being grouped in sample sets, each nation became part of a "generation" of nations, representing all those that came into being in a given census year. However, to qualify as part of a generation, a given nation had to persist and have a constitution from the date of its founding forward to 1970, a requirement made necessary by the fact that each generation was treated as a panel in a panel study design.[52]

The first set, for the year 1870, was large in part because it incorporated all the nations that had come into existence at any time before 1870.

Within that set, however, there was only one true generation in our sense, made up of the twenty-four known to have developed their first recorded constitution between 1850 and 1870.[53] The 1890 and 1910 generations were very small, only three and five new nations, respectively, making up those groups, a number so small as to make it reasonable to eliminate them from systematic consideration.[54] By 1930, however, we begin to get generations of more substantial size, in that case with twelve members. The 1950 generation, reflecting the first effects of the end of colonialism, had twenty members. Finally, there came the great surge of nation building of the postwar era that gave the 1970 generation fifty-five members, with a predominance of new nations from Africa. The Appendix to this chapter lists all the countries in the study, the date each entered the sample to identify the generations, and the number of due process rights they offered as of 1970.

Analysis of the Data

With the data in hand we may proceed to its analysis, which we will present in three stages. In the first stage we will seek to ascertain whether there has been a steady movement for constitutions *worldwide* to grant more and more due process rights with the passage of time from 1870 onward. In the second stage we deal with the issue of convergence, testing whether over time the various nations of the world come to have constitutions that are increasingly more like one another in both the number of due process rights they grant and the nature of the particular rights they bestow on their citizens. In the third stage we seek to establish how far the differences that separate and the similarities that link one nation to another can be explained by socioeconomic, political, and cultural similarities and differences among nations. However, this third stage is here treated here only tentatively.

Due Process Guarantees over Time

If the constitutional provision of due process guarantees has been truly a long-term worldwide movement, that fact should be reflected in two measures. First, over the past 100 years, the average number of guarantees provided for by the sets of constitutions extant at twenty-year intervals should have progressively increased at a significant rate. Second, the provision of due process guarantees should have become more widely diffused, not concentrated in a particular set of nations but rather found more or less equally in nations all over the globe. This means that increases in worldwide averages, standing alone, would not permit one to argue that the guarantees had become more widely diffused, because all of the gains could have been accounted for by one subset of countries such as the European.

The Overall Rights Count.   The data presented in Table 10.1 test the hypothesis that national constitutions worldwide have, to a significant degree, come increasingly to offer citizens more due process guarantees. It permits us to assess changes at twenty-year intervals over a 100-year period of potential development, focused particularly on the fourteen individual rights that we consider to constitute the core of the due process guarantees provided by typical national constitutions.

A simple measure that we call the due process rights count (DPRC) records the number of due process guarantees offered in the constitutions of any nation or, on average, in any set of nations. The countries in our sample sets proved to be well differentiated on the DPRC index. For example, in 1870 there were four countries—Austria, Guatemala, France, and Russia—whose constitutions granted none of the basic due process rights, and the rest distributed themselves regularly until the three top scorers came in at nine for Liberia, ten for the United States, and eleven for Mexico.

Looked at over time, however, the world's performance on this measure is not impressive and hardly supports an argument for the existence of a truly forceful social movement on a global scale. As late as 1970 the number of nations that did not constitutionally grant a single due process right had risen to eight, a distressingly large number even allowing for the increase in the total pool of nations having constitutions. Such changes in the number of nations considered can be adjusted for by considering the *averages* for the set of fourteen core personal rights we coded. On average, some 4.7 rights were granted by the thirty-six constitutions extant in 1870. By 1970 the DPRC for all constitutions extant, at an average of approximately 5.2, was barely 11 percent greater. This gain was not statistically significant at even the .05 level.[55] After 100 years the world's collection of constitutions, taken as a whole, granted only about one-half of an additional right, whereas it would have been possible to add up to nine additional personal procedural rights, on average. Moreover, even the modest gain attained over the total span of time was not regular. There were actual declines in the number of rights granted as the world moved from 1910 to 1930, and again between 1950 and 1970. It is clear that humankind, taken as a whole, has not been marching on any high road leading to the universal adoption of the widest range of personal due process rights guaranteed by the national constitutions that are everywhere nominally the highest law of the land.

Even without overall growth the set could have become more homogeneous over time, as measured by the index of agreement or coefficient of variation.[56] A glance at Table 10.1 indicates that this was not the case; the index remained at much the same level, and indeed eventually became larger, as we move across the 100-year span. Clearly the expectations both

Table 10.1   Average number of due process rights affirmed by constitutions worldwide, 1870–1970

Sample Set Date	Average Rights Granted	Standard Deviation	Coefficient of Variation	Number of Countries
1870	4.7	2.8	0.60	36
1890	4.9	2.8	0.57	41
1910	4.9	2.7	0.56	47
1930	4.7	2.8	0.60	59
1950	5.3	2.9	0.55	76
1970	5.2	3.3	0.63	132

of the world polity model and of convergence theory are not met by this first pass at our data.

This failure of due process guarantees to increase is, moreover, in marked contrast to the situation with regard to other kinds of rights, such as social and economic rights, which Boli reported to have increased by 340 percent over the same span of time.[57] By contrast, Boli also reported, this time in agreement with our results, that his index that was focused more narrowly on due process rights alone increased only very slightly.[58] However, apart from noting that fact, Boli offered no explanation and did not hesitate to incorporate his measure of judicial rights into a summary index of citizen rights based on some forty-two different rights. We believe that these two measures—due process rights and citizen rights—are theoretically distinct, and our results make it evident that they are also empirically distinct. Therefore, to throw them together in a summary score, as Boli did, obscures the degree to which the due process guarantees have followed a different path from that taken by other constitutional rights, most notably the political and economic rights. By concentrating on due process rights as such we can obtain a more differentiated, and therefore more accurate, picture of the fate of human rights in the modern era. We also can more meaningfully explore the question of which nations grant more and which grant fewer such rights, and, finally, we can more effectively assess the social forces that advance or retard the diffusion of such rights. But before we get to these tasks we must satisfy ourselves more fully that the apparent failure of due process guarantees to be more frequently manifested in the world's constitutions is a real and not a spurious finding.

An Alternative Approach.   The apparent slow growth of the DPRC may have been a result not only of the failure of the expected diffusion pattern. It could as well be an artifact of our method, and of certain decisions we made in defining the strategy of our study.

The basic score for DPRC that we used earlier was based on a coding of each guarantee as being either "present" or "absent" in some given constitution. The data provided so far do not reflect the *relative emphasis* on a given right, the *amount of attention* given to it, nor the degree to which it might have been *specified in detail* in that constitution. Thus, whether a constitution gave only two lines to habeas corpus in citing it as a guarantee, or elaborated the relevant article into a full page of detailed restrictions on prison officials, prosecutors, and judges, the DPRC still treated both documents equally as a case where the habeas corpus guarantee was "present" in the constitution, without further distinction. Clearly there is a meaning of "growth" that is not captured by such a global measure. The obvious implication is that we need a different kind of coding in which growth is understood to include the expansion of attention and the elaboration of detailed specifications concerning any given due process guarantee. Anticipating this issue, we had developed a measure of the "degree of explicitness" with which each right was treated, and the "degree of prominence" with which each article was featured in any given constitution. These features were coded in a uniform way on a common scale, scored from one to four for each due process right, thus permitting more precise evaluation of the emphasis given to each right and of possible changes in such emphasis over time.

Growth in Explicitness and Prominence.   Briefly, by *explicitness* we meant the clarity and precision with which any constitution expressed its grant of a specific right. We paid particular attention to what we called "discrete details." The details involved explicitly specifying such matters as who did and did not enjoy the right, who granted the right, which agency or organization was bound by the right, the time periods within which the right could be exercised, and so forth. The more such details were mentioned, the higher the score, up to a maximum of four.

By *prominence* we meant the centrality or apparent visibility of a right within the larger clause in which it was granted. If the right took up one-quarter or less of the clause, it was coded one, and so on until the score of four was allocated when the discussion of the given right was the sole content of the relevant clause.[59]

Table 10.2 presents the average explicitness and prominence scores for those rights that were affirmed in each of our six sets of constitutions.[60] Just as was the case with the simple frequency count of rights previously noted, these new measures gave little evidence of growth over the 100-year span we studied. The prominence measure, after an insignificant increase, actually declined, so that the scores in 1950 and 1970 were lower than they had been in 1870. The average explicitness score rose unsteadily and only modestly, so that after 100 years of constitutional development it was only some 13 percent greater than it had been in the 1870 baseline. This increase is very similar in magnitude to that observed when we measured only the absence or presence of the due process rights with the DPRC, the increase

Table 10.2   Average prominence and explicitness of fourteen due process rights

Sample Set Date	Average Prominence Score	Average Explicitness Score	N[a]
1870	3.2	2.3	31
1890	3.3	2.3	34
1910	3.3	2.3	40
1930	3.3	2.4	50
1950	3.1	2.4	71
1970	3.0	2.5	119

[a]At least one right had to be affirmed for prominence and explicitness to be scored. Since some constitutions did not accord even a single due process right, the number of cases included in the average was, correspondingly, reduced below the totals shown in other tables.

on that measure having been, as previously noted, only some 11 percent over the 100-year span. And none of the differences between the sample sets, especially not those at the beginning and the end of the 100 years, was statistically significant at even the .05 level. Again we must conclude that there is no evidence of a *worldwide* movement to adopt more and more constitutional guarantees of due process.

Differential Popularity of Particular Guarantees.   The image of constitutional due process guarantees presented so far suggests little change or dynamism, with the worldwide situation being much the same in 1970 as it was in 1870. But again we must face the possibility that the problem might be less a lack of objective change and more an artifact of the method we have used so far. Our finding a more or less constant number of rights might obscure the fact that while some guarantees or groups of guarantees were indeed rising very rapidly in frequency, others were falling. The outcome would then have been a seemingly static overall count that masked the actual dynamic growth of some types of guarantee.

The data in Table 10.3 do indeed suggest that the growth in the frequency of citation for some guarantees was offset by declines in the frequency of citation of others over the 100-year span of our study. Evidently some rights were represented in a relatively constant proportion of the constitutions over time. This was true, basically, of the right to trial and the right to a jury. Some of the other guarantees followed a U-shaped curve pattern, rising and then falling in the frequency of mentions. There were, however, some instances of dramatic shifts up or down in the relative proportion of constitutions that provided certain guarantees. Thus the right to counsel, mentioned in only slightly more than 8 percent of all constitutions in 1870, became steadily more widespread, until by 1970 it was cited in

Table 10.3   Percentage of constitutions extant affirming each of fourteen due process rights

Due Process Protection	1870	1890	1910	1930	1950	1970
General clause	47	46	45	29	43	36
Warrant for arrest	56	59	55	58	55	46
Arrest time	36	34	32	27	41	39
Documentation of charges	28	27	23	17	20	28
Habeas corpus	22	24	30	34	41	36
Right to trial	36	41	36	36	37	41
Trial time	6	7	6	7	9	19
Right to counsel	8	12	15	14	34	53
Right to jury	14	12	15	17	14	21
Appeal rights	31	27	26	31	34	41
Property confiscation	67	73	77	75	75	72
Injury compensation	28	20	21	29	32	32
Right to petition	67	76	74	71	71	47
Response to petition	25	27	30	27	21	17

some 53 percent of all the world's constitutions. The practice of setting time limits within which a trial must begin also was mentioned more frequently with the passage of time. By contrast, the right to petition lost ground as the years passed. Although it declined only modestly for some sixty years, it went into a rather precipitous decline in the interval between the 1950 and 1970 surveys. We must conclude, then, that there has indeed been a dynamic process of change ongoing, with some guarantees rising in popularity while others come to be mentioned in a smaller fraction of the world's constitutions.

The cause of these fluctuations, however, remains an open question. They might be random. That argument would be supported by the fact that none of the differences observed over the span from 1870 through 1930 were statistically significant. However, comparing the 1970 sample set with the other five yielded fifteen comparisons significant at the .05 level or better.[61] That outcome might be reflecting the process of convergence, with the rise of new standards being widely diffused throughout the world and influencing nations to adjust their constitutions according to that standard by dropping some guarantees and adding others. Alternatively, however, it could be that the observed pattern was produced by the changing composition of the total pool of nations making up the world community, and by the tendency of the newer nations to grant either fewer or more process rights, and different ones at that, as compared to the older nations, which had come on the world scene earlier. In short, it could be that the situation has been dynamic rather than static, but the dynamics have moved the world's nations not to converge on a common standard but rather to diverge in distinctive directions. We turn next, in stage two of our analysis, to examine the data that permit us to assess whether the world's nations have been diverging or converging in their constitutional approach to due process rights.

Testing for Convergence

We now ask whether there is evidence for an international climate of opinion, such that nations have been influenced to provide guarantees in their constitutions merely because such guarantees have been adopted by others extant at the time they wrote their respective constitutions. In short, is there evidence that a process of simple diffusion has been at work here?

Testing Diffusion by the Rights Count. We can test the diffusion or "world culture" hypotheses using either the sheer numerical rights count or by examining the content of the specific rights granted by the constitutions of different nations.

With reference to the simple rights count, the diffusion hypothesis would have to meet two tests to be supported. First, there should be evidence that the number of rights granted worldwide has been increasing steadily and at a statistically significant level with the passage of each twenty-year period. Either in addition or as an independent test, the index of variation would have been getting smaller and smaller with each successive sample. Table 10.1 has already made it clear that neither of these requirements has been satisfied.

The second test requires that we shift the basis of our analysis from the twenty-year interval sets to the "generations."[62] Using the grouping of the constitutions by generation we can test the diffusion-convergence hypothesis in two forms. The strong form makes two related requirements. First, it requires that each new generation of constitutions shows a tendency over time to move toward some common, homogenizing standard, and second, it requires that each new generation come onstream granting approximately the same number of personal due process rights as were granted by the average of the other constitutions in their respective sets. The weaker form of the test would require that each *generation* come onstream granting a number of rights more or less equal to those granted on average by the *panel that preceded it* by some twenty years.

The Strong Form of the Hypothesis. Evidence to test the strong form of the convergence hypothesis is presented in Table 10.4, which shows the number of rights each generation granted when it first appeared on the scene and then follows that generation, as a panel, moving through each of the subsequent twenty-year intervals that were open to it. Table 10.4 makes it clear that growth in the DPRC was a differentiated phenomenon, with

Table 10.4   Average number of due process rights affirmed in constitutions worldwide by each generation across time

Time Sampled	Generations					
	1870	1890	1910	1930	1950	1970
1870	4.4					
1890	4.9	3.3				
1910	5.2	3.3	3.4			
1930	5.4	3.3	3.4	3.2		
1950	5.9	6.0	4.4	3.5	4.7	
1970	6.1	7.3	4.5	4.3	4.5	4.8

different generations showing contrasting patterns, and those differentiated patterns were such as to produce more divergence than convergence in the relevant generations.

The first nations onstream, that is, those making up the generation that wrote its first constitutions before World War II, afforded additional procedural rights to their citizens at a steady pace. By 1970 they were all granting at least one-third more core rights than they had when they first joined the ranks of nations with constitutions. For example, the largest and therefore most reliable set, the 1870 generation, provided more guarantees at an uninterrupted pace over the entire 100-year span, the number of rights granted increasing from 4.4 to 6.1, a gain of some 40 percent. This difference was significant at the .05 level. The 1890, 1910, and 1930 generations gained about as much, and did so over shorter spans of time. Indeed, the 1890 generation had more than doubled the number of guarantees it offered individuals by 1970.[63] By contrast, the 1950 generation actually reduced the average number of rights it affirmed as it moved to 1970.

The evidence as presented in Table 10.4 requires us to reconcile the new data with the pattern of reverses and the evident lack of growth observed earlier when *all* the generations were combined in sets, as in Table 10.1.

One part of the answer, available in Table 10.4, lies with the behavior of the 1950 generation, which departed from the pattern seen in the earlier generations in that it actually gave fewer citizen rights by 1970, twenty years after it had come onstream. By itself this reversal, modest in magnitude, might not have had so much impact except for the fact that the 1950 generation was relatively large, and so its slipping back had a noticeable effect on the total sample as we moved from the 1950 to the 1970 set.

Another way of perceiving the process of historical decline is to read Table 10.4 horizontally from left to right, which permits one to see the relative contribution of the different generations to each sample set. Thus, reading across the 1950 sample, we can see there how the higher scores of the 1870 and 1890 generations, at 5.9 and 6.0 rights, respectively, were off-

Table 10.5   Average number of due process rights affirmed by each new generation's constitutions compared to the rest of its respective sample set

	1870	1890	1910	1930	1950	1970
Number of rights granted by:						
New generation	4.4	3.3	3.4	3.2	4.7	4.8
Rest of sample set	5.2	5.0	5.0	5.1	5.5	5.5
Total sample set	4.7	4.8	4.8	4.7	5.3	5.1
Number of countries in:						
New generation	24	3	5	12	20	55
Rest of set	12	38	42	47	56	77
Total sample	36	41	47	59	76	132

set by the much lower scores of the 1930 and 1950 generations at 3.5 and
4.7 rights, respectively.[64]

Even more important, however, was a more general fact visible in Table
10.5, namely, that each new generation came onstream providing a number
of due process guarantees well below the average granted by the constitutions already in place as parts of the sample set of constitutions extant in
any year. This would obviously pull down the average for the sample set as
a whole.[65] Moreover, such retrogressive effects were greater to the degree
that the new nations coming onstream were numerous compared to the
others already in any sample set. Thus the arrival of the 1970 generation on
the world scene had a great effect, since, by numbering fifty-five cases, it
was almost equal in size to the whole of the first four generations combined. That new 1970 generation granted fewer rights on average, at 4.80,
than the rest of the 1970 set, at 5.5 rights. Given the large number of these
new nations, their arrival inevitably dampened or erased any tendency for
the worldwide average to show an increase over the set representing the
preceding twenty-year period.

Testing the Weak Form of the Convergence Hypothesis.   Clearly our data
failed to support the strong form of convergence hypothesis, but perhaps
they will support the weak form. The weak form, it will be recalled, would
require that each generation come onstream granting a number of rights
more or less equal to those granted on average by the set that preceded it by
some twenty years. This pattern, if observed, would suggest convergence
because newly formed nations would be shown to follow the standard established by the generation that had immediately preceded it.

To make this test one must compare the first number entered for each
generation in Table 10.4 with the score for the preceding *twenty-year set* in
Table 10.1. For example, we see in Table 10.4 that the *1890 generation*
came on with an average rights score of 3.3, which was well below the
score for the *1870 set,* which Table 10.1 shows to have been 4.7. Continu-

ing this process of comparing the score of each *generation* with that of the *set* that preceded it by twenty years, we find that only the 1950 generation passed the test, since it came onstream granting 4.7 rights, which made it the equal of the 1930 set.[66] The relevant numbers are listed in the first and third lines of Table 10.5.

It is clear, then, that the data also fail to support the weak version of the hypothesis that the rights count shows evidence of convergence among the world's nations. Indeed, all the new generations except one came onstream granting *fewer* rights than had been common among the nations established before the arrival of the new generation. In other words, each new generation was not converging on an existing standard but rather was retreating from it.

Testing Convergence by the Rights' Content. The diffusion-convergence hypothesis can be tested by considering not only the number of rights granted but also the *content* of the rights involved. If at each historical moment there existed a worldwide standard that was compelling as a model for all nations, but especially for those newly shaping their basic institutions, then new nations adopting their first constitutions should have introduced in their constitutions basically the same *content* found in the typical constitution extant worldwide at the time these new constitutions were written. We can test how far this actually happened at any historical moment by dividing each of our sample sets into two groups, one representing the "old" established nations who at a given point in time were already on the scene, some for a long time, and the "new" nations that had just come onstream in the same period.[67] If there were indeed a worldwide standard expectation of what a proper constitution should include, then the nations that were new to any given period should grant basically the same array of specific due process rights as had the typical nation already established at the time these new nations wrote their constitutions. This did not happen.

The available evidence clearly indicates that the new nations that came onstream just before 1950, and particularly those formed in the next twenty years, thus constituting the 1970 generation, produced constitutions with quite a different profile of due process rights from that which applied in the constitutions of the older nations. Table 10.6 shows the proportion of constitutions affirming a given right, dividing the constitutions into those we call "new" nations—those that came onstream for the first time as part of the respective sets for 1950 and 1970—as against those that came onstream earlier, which we call, collectively, "old" nations. Although the definition of the "new" is fairly unambiguous, that is not so for the "old." In particular, nations that were "new" in 1950 had become part of the "old" by the time the 1970 set was constituted. To deal with this problem we use two definitions of old as criteria, one applying to those nations that came

Table 10.6   Percentage of constitutions "new" and "old" in 1950 and 1970 affirming each of fourteen due process rights

	Nations			
Rights	1 "Old" in 1950	2 "New" in 1950	3 "New" in 1970	4 "Old" in 1970
General clause	45	40	22	45
Warrant for arrest	63	35	36	73
Arrest time	45	35	35	43
Documentation of charges	16	30	36	22
Habeas corpus	39	45	35	36
Right to trial	39	30	47	36
Trial time	9	10	35	8
Right to counsel	29	50	64	45
Right to jury	20	0	5	17
Appeal rights	36	30	51	34
Property confiscation	77	70	67	75
Injury compensation	34	25	25	36
Right to petition	75	60	18	68
Response to petition	27	5	4	27

onstream before World War II, labeled "'Old' in 1950," and those that were old only from the perspective of the new in 1970, and these are labeled "'Old' in 1970."

We start by using as our criterion the "'Old in 1950" nations, those formed before World War II, and compare them with nations newly formed in two periods, those new in the 1950 panel, and those new in the 1970 panel. Columns one to three in Table 10.6 show the percentage of all constitutions in the three groups of nations that provided a given due process guarantee.

Constitutions from the countries that were old by 1950 were much more likely to grant certain rights than were the nations that came onstream either in the 1950 group or in the 1970 group, and they did so by a large margin, indeed at times a margin of two to one or better. For example, comparing those new in 1950 (column two) with those already old at that time (column one), we find the right to a jury granted by 20 percent of the old and none of the new, and the right to response to one's petition granted by 27 percent of the old constitutions and only 5 percent of the new.

Those nations that were new in 1970—column three—show equally striking contrasts with those—in column 1—that were old in 1950, that is, the constitutions carried forward from the period before World War II. Whereas 75 percent of the old-nation constitutions granted the right to petition, only 18 percent of the 1970 newcomers did so, and while 45 percent of the older constitutions offered a general due process clause, only 22 percent of the 1970 new nations did so. Other differences, though less dramatic, were nevertheless substantial. Thus, in the comparison using the 1950 old as the criterion, the 1950 new showed six substantial differences in fourteen comparisons, and the 1970 new nations had ten such differences in fourteen comparisons with those nations carried over from before World War II.[68]

Additional evidence that the new nations joining the world polity after World War II went their own way rather than following an established standard as to what to offer in the way of due process rights is provided by a comparison of the nations newly arrived in 1970 as against those already on the scene from earlier waves of constitution writing. This can be done by comparing column three with column four in Table 10.6. This yields ten substantial differences by our rule, seven of which were by the t-test standard significant at the .05 level or better. Clearly there was something quite distinctive about the way in which this 1970 generation went about writing its constitutions.

Another way of judging from Table 10.6 whether the sets of constitutions became more alike in their content after World War II is to consider the average across all fourteen rights of the percentage differences separating the nations compared. For the 1950 old versus 1950 new comparison, the average difference was twelve percentage points; comparing 1970 old and new, it was seventeen percentage points. Again this suggests, if anything, divergence rather than convergence.

Role of Political Ideology

The world polity theory argued that it was particularly the period after 1945 that saw the emergence of an international standard that all nations felt compelled to follow. The evidence just presented with regard to due process indicates just the opposite. Far from simply emulating the advanced nations that had developed their constitutions in earlier times, the new nations that joined the world community after World War II evidently had their own special agenda in mind in writing their constitutions. They argued, as in the Proclamation of Tehran, that it was "impossible" to achieve full civil and political rights until social, economic, and cultural rights had been attained. As one analyst described the situation, "The control of individual rights (especially property) in the interests of the whole has become generally accepted in the Third World."[69] Another reported that "the conventional wisdom of the sixties and early seventies held that . . . in many cases the exercise of human rights . . . tended to interfere with economic growth and development . . . therefore . . . many, even most, must be temporarily suspended."[70] The prevalence of this political ideology must be assumed to have played a considerable role in the tendency of the nations created after World War II to eschew following the model of the nations established earlier and instead to reduce the number of due process rights their constitutions offered. Their leaders very often intended to strengthen the state by subordinating the individual,[71] and that objective was not consonant with the granting of due process rights that citizen could then use in an effort to curb the exercise of centralized and authoritarian political power.

Conclusion

If the century after 1870 was a period of burgeoning democracy and the efflorescence of individual citizen rights, as proposed and documented by Boli,[72] that fact was not noticeably expressed through the gaining of due process rights in the national constitutions under which most citizens lived, at least when those constitutions were viewed as a worldwide set. Moreover, this failure of procedural rights to be more frequently and fully specified in constitutions clearly cannot be attributed to some presumed conservative influence exerted by the older nations that were the first to develop written constitutions. On the contrary, the older nations did continue to offer more rights as time passed. It was rather the new nations coming onstream, in particular those formed after World War II, that put fewer due process guarantees in their constitutions than were in the constitutions of the nations already on the scene. As a result, one of our basic theoretical assumptions was not supported. With regard to the expectation of general and common growth in the granting of due process rights, the data give support neither to Inkeles's convergence theory nor to the world polity model developed by Meyer and his associates. If anything, it seems we must acknowledge the disturbing fact that the worldwide trend over a 100-year span has been one of retrogression rather than of progression in the granting of constitutional due process guarantees.

But historical time, whether measured by successive sets or by generation, is not the only form of potentially relevant differentiation in the world of national constitutions. It seems reasonable, for example, to assume that constitutions would differ significantly in their treatment of procedural rights depending on distinctive features of national origins and history. In this connection it is interesting to cast a glance back at Table 10.6, to compare the nations new in 1950 with those new in 1970 (columns two and three). While these two sets have in common their background as being mainly former colonies, they are nevertheless sharply differentiated geographically. The nations new in 1950 came predominantly from Asia, and none were from sub-Saharan Africa, whereas the 1970 generation came overwhelmingly from the latter region. It is clear that being new, in the sense of acquiring independence and one's first constitutions in the period after World War II, did not imply sharing preferences with regard to due process guarantees. There clearly was no general standard that all newcomers had to adopt. On the contrary, each generation followed its own standard. Most striking is the fact that 60 percent of the nations new in 1950 granted the right to petition, whereas only 18 percent of those new in 1970 did so. Overall, the nations new in 1950 showed substantial differences in comparison with those new in 1970 in nine of fourteen comparisons. In other words, nations new in 1950 and 1970 were about as different from each other as either set was from the nations that had been established before World War II.[73]

These differences in emphasis in the constitutions of new nations predominantly from Asia as contrasted with those from Africa challenge the world polity model's assumption about the increasing worldwide dominance of "standardized models of society,"[74] and seems to confirm convergence theory's acknowledgment that "one of the most important brakes on the process of homogenization lies in the distinctive cultural traditions which different national populations bring to the contemporary situation, and in the array of historically determined institutional arrangements with which they enter the contemporary era."[75] Unfortunately, we can find no basis for assuring all national populations that some process like imitation, or some general law of social development, will, with the mere progress of time, bring them more protection of their basic human right to due process.

Appendix: Nations in 1970 sample set, by generation and number of due process rights granted

Country	Generation[a]	Rights Granted[b]
Afghanistan	1930	5
Albania	1930	5
Algeria	1970	2
Argentina	1870	5
Australia	1910	1
Austria	1970[d,e]	3
Barbados	1970	9
Belgium	1870[c]	7
Benin (Dahomey)	1970	0
Bolivia	1870	7
Botswana	1970	10
Brazil	1870[c]	8
Bulgaria	1890	6
Burma	1950	5
Cambodia	1950	6
Cameroon	1970	1
Chad	1970	3
Chile	1870[c]	8
China	1930	4
Colombia	1870	7
Congo	1970	3
Costa Rica	1870	8
Cuba	1910	9
Cyprus	1970	13
Czechoslovakia	1930	4
Denmark	1870	4
Dominican Republic	1910[d]	6
Ecuador	1870	8
Egypt	1950	3
El Salvador	1870	10
Equatorial Guinea	1970	0
Ethiopia	1950	8
Fiji	1970	9
Finland	1930	1
France	1870	0
Gabon	1970	2
Gambia	1970	7
Germany (Dem. Rep.)	1950	8
Germany (Fed. Rep.)	1950	4
Ghana	1970	11
Greece	1870	8

(*continues*)

Appendix   *(continued)*

Country	Generation[a]	Rights Granted[b]
Guatemala	1870	10
Guinea	1890	1
Guyana	1970	8
Haiti	1870	8
Honduras	1870	10
Hungary	1950	1
Iceland	1950	3
India	1950	7
Indonesia	1950	0
Iran	1910	2
Iraq	1930	3
Ireland	1930	5
Italy	1970[d]	5
Ivory Coast	1970	1
Jamaica	1970	9
Japan	1890	9
Jordan	1950	3
Kenya	1970	9
Korea (North)	1950	3
Korea (South)	1950	10
Kuwait	1970	4
Laos	1950	0
Lebanon	1950	2
Lesotho	1970	9
Liberia	1870[c]	9
Libya	1970	3
Liechtenstein	1870	6
Luxembourg	1870	5
Malagasy Republic	1970	2
Malawi	1970	2
Malaysia	1970	6
Maldive Islands	1970	2
Mali	1970	0
Malta	1970	9
Mauritania	1970	2
Mauritius	1970	9
Mexico	1870	13
Monaco	1930	5
Mongolia	1930	4
Morocco	1970	1
Nauru	1970	9
Nepal	1950	5

(continues)

Appendix   *(continued)*

Country	Generation[a]	Rights Granted[b]
Netherlands	1870[c]	4
Nicaragua	1870	9
Niger	1970	1
Nigeria	1970	0
Norway	1870[c]	2
Pakistan	1950	6
Panama	1910	9
Paraguay	1910	7
Peru	1870	6
Philippines	1870	7
Poland	1930	6
Portugal	1870[c]	6
Qatar	1970	3
Romania	1870	6
Rwanda	1970	4
Saudi Arabia	1930	0
Senegal	1970	2
Sierra Leone	1970	9
Singapore	1970	0
Somalia	1970	8
South Africa	1910	1
Spain	1870	3
Sudan	1970	8
Swaziland	1970	7
Sweden	1870[c]	4
Switzerland	1870	2
Syria	1950	2
Taiwan	1950	2
Tanzania	1970	1
Thailand	1950	5
Togo	1970	0
Tonga	1970	4
Trinidad/Tobago	1970	5
Tunisia	1970	3
Turkey	1890	7
Uganda	1970	10
United Arab Emirates	1970	3
Uruguay	1870[c]	11
USA	1870[c]	10
USSR	1870	1
Venezuela	1870	5
Vietnam (PDR)	1970	3

(continues)

Appendix   (*continued*)

Country	Generation[a]	Rights Granted[b]
Vietnam (Rep.)	1970	7
Western Samoa	1970	7
Yemen Arab Rep.	1970	3
Yemen, PDR	1970	3
Yugoslavia	1930	10
Zambia	1970	9
Zimbabwe	1970	8

[a]Date entered Sample Set. This date also identifies the generation to which the country was assigned except as noted below.

[b]Number of Due Process Rights granted as of 1970.

[c]One of ten countries included in the 1870 sample set whose constitutions were adopted earlier than 1850 and were therefore excluded from the 1870 generation.

[d]These countries in the 1970 sample set were eliminated from the generational analysis due to discontinuities in their status as autonomous nations or to our inability to locate all relevant constitutions.

[e]The following countries not in the 1970 sample set were, however, in the sample set for some earlier periods, and all were excluded from any generational analyses: Austria-Hungary, Orange Free State, Serbia, Montenegro, Latvia, Lithuania, Estonia.

Part Five

INDIVIDUAL LEVEL RESPONSES

eleven

PATTERNED RESPONSES TO INDUSTRIAL LIFE

Ever larger segments of the world's population are living and will come to live in what is now commonly called "industrial society." The standard complex of institutions—most notably the factory—associated with this system daily becomes more widely diffused into a variety of traditional and even "primitive" cultural contexts. These institutions rather rigorously prescribe a set of norms, with regard to such matters as dress, time, order, and authority, which must be conformed to, at least during the time that individuals are engaged in their industrial and related occupations. This aspect of the diffusion of the industrial order is easily recognized.

It is less evident that the distinctive roles of the industrial system also foster typical patterns of perception, opinions, beliefs, and values that are not institutionally prescribed but arise spontaneously as new subcultures in response to the institutional conditions provided by the typically differentiated role-structure of modern industrial society. This chapter reports a comparative study of the influence of these standard environments on attitudes, which yielded considerable evidence that the process is effective and pervasive.

In this investigation I take the institutional pattern or setting as given and the responses to it, particularly those not explicitly required by the institutional forms, as the dependent variable. The individual and groups of indi-

Reprinted with permission from Alex Inkeles, "Industrial Man: The Relation of Status to Experience, Perception, and Value," *American Journal of Sociology,* Vol. 66, No. 1 (July 1960), 1–31.

viduals, not institutions, are the central concern, and we study variation not in formal institutional arrangements but in individual and collective social perception and action. Only one institutional complex is considered here, namely, that which characterizes the modern, large-scale, bureaucratic industrial system. What is not given, namely, the response to it, will be sought in a number of different realms but in each case will be measured through reported experiences and expressed attitudes and values.

The underlying theory is very simple. It is assumed that people have experiences, develop attitudes, and form values in response to the forces or pressures that their environment creates. By "environment" I mean, particularly, networks of interpersonal relations and the patterns of reward and punishment one normally experiences in them. They include not only access to facilities and items of consumption, necessary and conspicuous, but also such intangibles as prestige, the comforts of security, respectful treatment, calculability in the actions of significant others, and so on. The theory holds that, within broad limits, the same situational pressures, the same framework for living, will be experienced as similar and will generate the same or similar response by people from different countries. This is of course not a denial of individual variation, of personality as a determinant of perception, cognition, or affect. Neither is it meant to deny the effect of traditional cultural ways on behavior. These will mute the independent effect of the industrial institutional environment, but it is assumed that they cannot eliminate it. Rather, its force is sufficiently great to assert itself clearly despite the countervailing influence of personal idiosyncrasy and traditional cultural ways of thinking and feeling. Insofar as industrialization, urbanization, and the development of large-scale bureaucratic structures and their usual accompaniments create a standard environment with standard institutional pressures for particular groups, to that degree should they produce relatively standard patterns of experience, attitude, and value—standard, not uniform, pressures. The situation of worker and manager may be relatively standard in the factory, wherever it is located, but relative to each other these positions are by no means uniform.

The test of the assumption is very simple. It is made by comparing the perceptions, attitudes, and values of those in comparable positions in the typical hierarchies of modern society, in particular the occupational, educational, and socioeconomic. If the "foreign" (read: "industrial"), externally introduced institutional environment plays no role, there should be no pattern or similarity in the response of incumbents of a given type of position from country to country. If there is such a pattern—if, for example, workers are everywhere less "happy" or "optimistic," or more insistent on obedience in children, than are engineers—this can come only from the similarity of their situation in the hierarchical setting of occupation, income, or education, since on the basis of their nationality alone they should obviously differ.

To discern this influence of the industrial environment is of course not the same as determining either its extent or its intensity. The pressure generated by the institutional setting of industrialism may affect only a narrow range of experience and attitude—possibly only that relating to work experience. It may exert only a moderate influence, producing only a small part of the variance, the main part being accounted for by other factors, such as traditional cultural orientations. These are important problems for further elucidation. For now, I restrict myself to a statement of the main proposition—*that people's environment, as expressed in the institutional patterns they adopt or have introduced to them, shapes their experience, and through this their perceptions, attitudes and values, in standardized ways that are manifest from country to country, despite the countervailing randomizing influence of traditional cultural patterns.* I trust it will be understood without great elaboration that this proposition is stated so unequivocally only to facilitate clear exposition. The hypothesis is tentative, a guide to the exploration that this chapter reports, and not a dictum or an empirically established fact. We are equally interested in proof and disproof and must expect to find both supporting, negating, and ambiguous evidence.

I can hardly claim novelty for the proposition. The idea that the institutions in which people live shape their character and their views is old indeed. So is the more refined notion that a person's distinctive standing and role within the social structure will influence not only his or her perspective on the world but his or her wishes, beliefs, and values as well. Probably very few will argue that any people can indefinitely, or even for very long, utilize the material and institutional forms of industrial society without also absorbing some of its culture. At the same time, very few will argue that the industrial system is indeed so standardized or its influence so compelling as to permit no variation in the culture of those who share it. The obvious task of serious investigation, therefore, is to determine with some degree of precision where and how far the institutions of industrial society impose or foster the development of new subcultures wherever they are introduced, and in what realms of life and to what degree traditional patterns maintain a relative independence from or immunity to the influence of the industrial institutional system.

There are two main avenues open to us. The first would be to designate certain attitudes or values as indexes of the industrial "subculture," and then to test the degree of association between these indexes and the level of industrialization in various countries. This is essentially the path taken by Kingsley Davis and Seymour Martin Lipset in their comparative studies. Both used the percentage of males engaged in nonagricultural pursuits, and the per capita consumption of energy, as indexes of industrialization. For his dependent variable, Davis studied the degree of urbanization, and Lipset, the extent and stability of democratic political processes.[1] If we were to follow this path, our dependent variable would be the proportion of the population in each country holding a certain belief or sharing a particular value presumed to be fostered by the industrial milieu—for example, the belief that most human problems can ultimately be solved by technological advances.

There are several reasons for not adopting this procedure. Indexes of industrialization tend to generalize to the population as a whole characteristics that may in fact be intensely developed in only one segment. An outstanding example would be the Soviet Union, which was highly and intensely industrialized by 1960, yet in which about half of the population was still engaged in agriculture. In such cases a nationwide index of the industrial subculture might be low, not because the industrialized segment of the population failed to show the expected characteristic but because so large a part of the population was not integrated into the industrial structure. Our theory applies only to those segments of the population whose life conditions are standardized through industrial or other large-scale bureaucratic organizations.

Another reason for not focusing on national populations as a whole is that the average level of response for a nation may so heavily reflect traditional cultural orientations, or recent events, as to mask the independent influence of the industrial environment. To control this would require matching countries sharing the same traditional culture but varying in the degree of industrialization. On the face of it, many would deny the possibility of meaningfully accomplishing this, even if the pool of countries available for matching were much larger than it is.

The most compelling reason for not relying on a single national average as an index of the industrial subculture, however, lies in the nature of the theory being tested. The idea that the industrial institutional order carries with it a distinctive industrial culture does not necessarily mean that the culture is the same for all who live in industrial society. This commonly made assumption can be quite misleading. We should rather expect that, in accord with the differences among positions in the modern occupational hierarchy, the different occupational groups will have differentiated attitudes and values. What is likely to be common to industrial societies, therefore, is not a single idea or a set of commonly held ideas but a particular *structure* of experience, attitude, and value that takes its form from the occupational structure.

My expectation that the distinctive feature of the industrial culture is a structure of response characteristic of the occupational hierarchy as a whole also accounts for my not adopting the simple alternative of studying just one distinctive group, such as factory workers. From country to country the proportion of factory workers giving a particular answer might be quite different, yet in each country the workers might stand in a fixed relation to the other strata. This regularity would not be evident at all if we studied only one typical occupational group in different societies. I therefore take as my unit of analysis not a national average or a score for a particular group, but the *structure of response* in some status hierarchy representing the entire nation or, at least, its industrialized segment.

I will speak of the existence of a *structure of response* when the proportion in each stratum (occupation, prestige, income, or educational group) reporting certain experiences or holding particular views rises or falls more or less regularly as we ascend or descend the hierarchy. I will speak of a cross-national *pattern,* with which we are most concerned, when the structure of response is more or less the same as we move from country to country—that is, when the direction and, to some degree, the magnitude of the changes in proportion are similar in different national populations.

I assume that the industrial order fixes the situation of different groups relative to one another in a more or less invariant fashion. I also assume that occupational groups, as units, respond distinctively to their occupational environment and the world outside it according to their situation and the characteristic pressures it generates. Insofar as these assumptions are correct, we should expect to find a cross-national pattern of response on many issues directly and indirectly related to the typical pattern of experience in the roles common in industrial society. The similarity in the structure of response as we move from country to country may exist, even though the average response varies widely from one nation to another. The typical response of any population may be strongly shaped by its traditional culture, and that of any particular group in some country may be influenced by a unique local situation. But by focusing on the occupational hierarchy as a whole, country by country, we at once control both the effect of traditional culture at the national level and the special circumstances affecting one or another occupational group at the "local" level.

To test these assumptions, we should, ideally, have data gathered for this specific purpose. Our samples should come from a variety of countries selected to represent diverse cultural traditions, and the sample from each country should be restricted to those holding strictly comparable positions in each respective society's industrial sector. The questionnaires would be carefully translated to ensure comparability of meaning. But what is actually available is very far from meeting the optimum requirements. I have had to rely on already completed studies drawn from a file of reports of various national survey agencies,[2] the one major international compilation edited by Hadley Cantril,[3] the few, more systematic comparative studies such as those undertaken by the United Nations Educational, Scientific, and Cultural Organization (UNESCO)[4] and International Research Associates, Inc. (INRA),[5] and sundry other scattered sources. None of these studies were designed for the purpose for which I wish to use them. The selection of countries is highly variable. The sample subgroups are frequently not equivalent from country to country, and it has been necessary to use criteria of stratification other than occupational status, which is most relevant to my theory. The questions used in different countries are often only very approximate equivalents. Under the circumstances, failure to find the expected patterns would be somewhat inconclusive as a test of my hypothesis. On the other hand, the presence of so many potentially randomizing influences in the data means that the emergence of the expected pattern, even if weakly manifested, may be taken as highly suggestive of the probable predictive power of the theory.

The Realm of Work

If my theory holds at all, it should be most effective in ordering information in the realm in which it has most direct and immediate applicability, namely, within the industrial enterprise. Wherever the factory of the large-scale organization exists, there will be a clearly stratified hierarchy of authority and of technical competence. A hierarchy of income, prestige, and other rewards will also be found following the main lines of the hierarchy of authority and technical competence. There is naturally a great deal of variation, but the general pattern is seldom departed from in fundamentals.

Our problem, then, is this: In what ways and to what extent does this objective hierarchy, this standardization of external conditions of work and pay, shape the attitudes and feelings of the incumbents of the commonly differentiated positions? We may begin with the simplest and perhaps most obvious of examples—that relating to job satisfaction, or the sense of pleasure or gratification a person finds in his or her work. Since those in certain positions, such as managers and engineers, are almost always better paid, given more security, granted more respect, and perhaps allowed more freedom and autonomy, we may reasonably expect that they will more often express satisfaction.

As Table 11.1 reveals, this expectation is indeed borne out. We have in hand fairly good data on job satisfaction in six countries, covering a fair range of situations. There is a definite and unmistakable structure in the responses manifested from country to country.

Those standing at the top are, as a rule, more satisfied than those in the lower positions. Indeed, in every country the proportion who report job satisfaction decreases quite regularly as we descend the steps of the standard occupational hierarchy. Even the departures from the strict step pattern appear to be the same, at least in those countries where the data permit a comparison. Thus in each of the three countries for which we have more refined data (United States, USSR, Germany), the skilled manual workers are slightly more often found among the satisfied than the rank-and-file

Table 11.1 National comparisons of job satisfaction, by occupation: percentage satisfied

U.S.S.R.		United States		Germany		Italy		Sweden		Norway	
		Large business	100								
		Small business	91								
Administrative, professional	77	Professional	82	Professional	75			Upper class	84	Upper class	84
Semiprofessional	70			Upper white collar	65						
White collar	60	White collar	82	Civil servants	51			Middle class	72	Middle class	88
				Lower white collar	33						
Skilled worker	62	Skilled manual	84	Skilled worker	47	Skilled worker	68				
Semiskilled	45	Semiskilled	76	Semiskilled	21	Artisan	62	Working class	69	Working class	83
Unskilled	23	Unskilled	72	Unskilled	11	Unskilled	57				
Peasant	12			Farm labor	23	Farm labor	43				

Percentage satisfied with their jobs was determined for each country as follows: *U.S.S.R.*—percentage answering "Yes" to: "Did you like the job you held in 1940?" (Soviet refugee data, Russian Research Center, Harvard University). *United States*—percentage answering "Satisfied" to: "Are you satisfied or dissatisfied with your present job?" (Richard Centers, "Motivational Aspects of Occupational Stratification," *Journal of Social Psychology*, Vol. 27 [1948], 100). *Germany*—percentage who would choose present occupation in response to: "If you were again 15 years old and could start again, would you choose your present occupation or another one?" (from German poll data, courtesy of S. M. Lipset). *Italy*—percentage "satisfied" or "fairly satisfied" with work (*Doxa Bolletino*). *Sweden and Norway*—percentage answering "satisfied" to: "Are you satisfied with your present occupation, or do you think that something else would suit you better?" (Hadley W. Cantril, ed., *Public Opinion 1935–1946* [Princeton: Princeton University Press, 1951], 535).

white-collar workers. This presumably reflects the fact that, generally, the pay and often the prestige accorded to the skilled worker exceeds that of ordinary white-collar personnel.

There are of course some other departures from the standard pattern that could not so easily be explained. Note, for example, that in Germany the group with the smallest proportion satisfied are the unskilled workers, whereas the farm laborers are twice as often satisfied. The latter are disgruntled only as often as the semiskilled workers. By contrast, in the Soviet group the situation is reversed. The one least often satisfied is the peasant.

Such variations, or departures from a standard, point to quite important differentiation in the relative positions of particular occupational groups in different countries. Consequently, our method, far from covering up or glossing over the differences between countries, can serve as a definite pointer for locating precisely what is distinctive in the situation of a particular group in a given country.

The data on job satisfaction illustrate well the appropriateness of the model of analysis sketched in the preceding section. Although all the countries are advanced, well-to-do representatives of the West European complex of industrial nations, the *average* level of satisfaction in each is markedly different. For example, in the United States the national average would clearly be over 80 percent satisfied, whereas in Germany it would be closer to 40 percent. Similarly, if only one particular occupational group, such as the semiskilled workers, were considered, one would be led to conclude that their shared status by no means produced a shared or standard effect, regardless of nationality. On the contrary, the proportion satisfied among the semiskilled ranges from 21 percent in Germany to 76 percent in the United States. Yet, as we have seen in Table 11.1, there *is* a definite, unmistakable, and obviously quite meaningful pattern in the experience of job satisfaction that is uniform from country to country. But that, to repeat, emerges only when the unit of analysis is the occupational hierarchy as a whole and when attention is on the pattern of response within it rather than on the data taken country by country or group by group.

It may seem obvious that in all the countries for which we have data, job satisfaction is structured, with those higher in the hierarchy of occupations more often satisfied. Of course those who are not ready to take a close look at the obvious have little need for science. Certainly it is less pejorative to say that the example is striking rather than obvious. In any event, it is not presented as definitive proof of the theory but rather because it so clearly illustrates the mode of analysis to be used later in assessing reactions that are not so "obviously" derivable from the external conditions of the individual's situation at work.

A more serious criticism is that this mode of analysis unduly emphasizes the regularity in the pattern across national lines while slighting the impressive differences in the absolute proportion satisfied in the several countries. Choice of emphasis is largely a consequence of one's purpose; the concern here is to discover regularity in human social behavior in response to standard stimulus conditions, something that seems rather more difficult to find than examples of diversity. This is not to say that for some purposes the location and analysis of differences is not more important. For example, if you wished to predict whether unskilled workers in Europe were more likely to vote communist, or for whatever was the legal party of the far left, it would be quite important to know that compared to unskilled workers in the United States, they are seldom satisfied on the job. But even here it is only when you have the comparative data that you are alerted to take special notice of the German or Italian workers' response. Furthermore, the signal does not rest mainly on comparing German and American *workers*. The striking nature of the German response is evident only when we realize that German professionals and business people were satisfied about as often as were their American counterparts, whereas this is *not* true of workers. If Germans in all occupational groups characteristically reported job satisfaction less often than their opposite numbers in other countries, we would have to assume that some economic or cultural factor common to all Germans, or something peculiar or distinctive in the question put to them, accounted for the difference. Indeed, if we found such homogeneity *within* nations existing simultaneously with substantial differences *among* nations in the response to questions that, on theoretical grounds, we expected to show the predicted step pattern, then that would constitute evidence refuting our hypotheses.

Finally, in assessing average or typical responses from country to country, we should keep in mind the possibility that these differences may be not so much a reflection of real differences in sentiments as an artifact of technique. We must take account of the marked effect produced by changes in question wording, differences in meaning introduced through translation, and variations in the conventions used for reporting answers to a question. In many of the comparisons made in this chapter the questions used were only approximate equivalents. Thus, to assess job satisfaction, we might for one country have the question, "Do you like your job?" for another, "Do you enjoy your work?" and for a third, "Would you take the same job again if you started over?" Each may legitimately be taken as a measure of job satisfaction. Yet, if asked of a single population in one country, they would probably yield quite different proportions of "satisfied" workers. Nevertheless, the underlying structure of response would undoubtedly be similar for all three measures, with each showing the professional managerial groups most satisfied, the workers and farm laborers least so. This is not a purely hypothetical example. It can clearly be demonstrated on the basis of data available for the United States, the USSR, and other countries. Even in more systematic international polls the translation of the questions often gives them special meanings that influence the level of response in different countries. In one case the alternatives offered may be only "I like my job" or "I don't like my job." But another study may include a third alternative, such as "I like it somewhat." These variations can obviously have a marked effect on the absolute proportion considered "satisfied" in one or another country.

If job satisfaction is a response to the "objective" factors that characterize the job as a whole, it should also respond to variations in the individual factors that make up the job complex. One of the most obvious determinants of job satisfaction, therefore, should be the salary or wage it carries. Data for the United States and the Soviet Union suggest a very direct connection. The higher the job in the hierarchy of power and prestige, the more often will the incumbents be satisfied with their pay. This is in good part, though not exclusively, because the pay is generally greater for jobs higher in the hierarchy. Yet pay alone is not sufficient to account for reported job satisfaction. If it were the step pattern shown in Table 11.1, it should be fairly uniform for all the countries. In fact it is not.

In both the Soviet Union and Germany, as against the United States, there are sharp breaks and discontinuities. For example, the proportion satisfied falls off precipitously between the skilled and the semiskilled. There is another sharp drop in going from semiskilled to unskilled, and again in going from semiskilled to peasants. An initial exploration suggests that the cause is not a difference in the structure of the wage scales, which are relatively similar in these countries. It seems instead to have to do with the "absolute" meaning of the very low pay received by those at the bottom in Germany and the USSR as against the standard of living possible to the unskilled American worker even when he or she *is* at the bottom. In addition, differences in the absolute levels of prestige and self-respect that those at the bottom can command also seem to play a role.

Values About Jobs

It may be obvious that position in the occupational hierarchy, because it determines income and psychic reward, should influence the sense of job satisfaction. But what about *values?* Should the things people want from jobs also be so determined? We might reasonably make any one of three assumptions. Since values are presumably what is "shared" in any culture, we might expect that in each country everyone would want pretty much the same qualities in a job, with more or less the same intensity. Alternatively, if we assume that what people want is determined by what their life situation induces them to desire, we will expect systematic variation in the values reflected in job evaluations made by those at different levels of the occupational hierarchy. A third possibility would be that what people will want in a job will be determined by the kinds of people they are, that is, by their personality or training.

These three theories are not necessarily totally independent of one another, and only a full-scale analysis with data of good quality could settle the issue by revealing the relative weight of the factors and their interrelations. The scattered data in hand suggest that there are definitely some common values about the occupational realm shared not only within particular countries but also in all modern, large-scale, more or less industrial societies, without much differentiation within the population by occupational group. This has been documented in Chapter 8, in which we located and analyzed the relative standing of lists of occupations in six industrial countries.[6] To an extraordinary degree the occupations were ranked in the same order. More important for us, we found very little variation in the evaluation of these occupations from one subgroup of the population to another. In other words, whether a worker or a professor does the rating, both place the doctor, lawyer, and engineer very near the top of the list, the ordinary worker about two-thirds of the way down, and the shoe-shine boy or garbage man at the bottom. This seems to be true for all countries, although there are some interesting variations.

In the light of these findings, are we not forced to restate the theory with which we started? The evaluation of occupations seems not to be influenced by differential situational pressures. At least the rater's own position in the occupational structure seems to make no fundamental difference in how he or she evaluates the standing or prestige of occupations. It might be objected that, after all, a person's standing in the community is a pretty "objective" thing. Anyone can see how much respect a doctor gets from everyone else. The fact that people agree on his or her standing is therefore "natural." But even so, this requires that we reformulate our theory to say that a rater's own position or situation can be expected to influence only his *subjective* judgments—those statements in which he reports what *he* feels, or what he wants or likes. This is, however, a very confining assumption and more conservative than is strictly necessary. We will see that certain estimates made by people about situations that are as "objective" and "external" as the standing of an occupation *are* influenced by the position of the observer, just as the experiments of Solomon Asch have shown that interpersonal situations can have a marked effect on the reported perception of such objective physical facts as the length of a line. But it may be that situationally determined perceptions of "objective" facts are not common and partake of a special nature. For the present, then, let us make the more conservative assumption that only intrinsically "subjective" reactions will be shaped by one's position in the social structure.

The qualities one desires in one's job certainly may be regarded as personal and subjective choices. Such desires may be assumed to reflect deeper values. Do those in different positions in the occupational hierarchy then wish for different qualities in a job? The relevant question has been asked in a number of countries, but I have located appropriate cross-tabulations for only two. The results suggest that there are some patterns that hold up across national lines. But there is also substantial variation, an absence of pattern, with regard to certain classes and dimensions, which obviously reflects very important differences in the general state of affairs within the two countries and in the relative position of certain special groups within each.

We may begin with the more regular patterns, as presented in Table 11.2. In both the United States and the Soviet refugee sample, those who hold jobs of higher status are much more likely to be concerned about having a job that is "interesting," stimulating, challenging, permits self-expression, and so on. The proportion of professionals desiring this quality, as against the proportion of unskilled workers citing it, produces a ratio of about three to one in both countries.

But the role of a large income is quite different in the two countries. In the United States it is a factor in the "free choice" of a *job* for only 3 to 8 percent, and there is no step pattern. In the Soviet Union, by contrast, the responses are highly patterned. Large earnings are the primary consideration for 57 percent of the peasants and only 8 percent of the intelligentsia. This may be striking evidence that in the United States, at least in 1948 and perhaps beyond, pay was no longer so desperately problematical an issue for the working class as it was in many other countries. Americans seem sure that if they have work their pay will be decently adequate. Additional evidence for this conclusion lies in the fact that when Americans cited their reasons for being dissatisfied with a job, low pay accounted for only one-fifth of the complaints and was actually cited more often by white-collar than manual workers, whereas in the Soviet sample more than two-thirds of the dissatisfied workers and peasants cited low pay as the reason for dissatisfaction and did so much more often than ordinary white-collar workers.

Our impression—that workers are generally concerned to increase their pay, while those more highly placed care more about interesting work[7]—must be tempered by the consideration of security. As between still more pay or still more interesting work, it seems that those higher in the scale will vote for increased interest, the worker for more pay. But what about security, or certainty, *as against* more pay linked to uncertainty? A number of questions asked in different countries bear on this issue. They all suggest that workers, more often than the middle classes, will choose certainty of income, or security, over more money with less security.

Thus in the Soviet-American comparison (Table 11.2) it is evident that security is much more a concern for the American workers than it is for professional-administrative people. Unskilled workers cited security as the basis for choosing a job in 29 percent of the cases as against 2 percent

Table 11.2 Quality most desired in a work situation, by country and occupation (in percent)

Occupation	Preferences of Sample of Soviet Refugees[a]				
	Adequate Pay	Interesting Work	Free of Fear	All Others	N
Intelligentsia	8	62	6	24	95
White collar	23	31	13	33	62
Skilled workers	22	27	15	36	33
Ordinary workers	48	20	13	19	56
Peasants	57	9	17	17	35

Occupation	Preferences of Sample in United States[b]				
	Adequate Pay	Interesting Work[c]	Security	Independence	Other
Large business	6	52	2	7	33
Professional	3	50	3	12	32
Small business	6	41	5	22	26
White collar	7	42	12	17	22
Skilled manual	4	36	13	22	25
Semiskilled	6	20	26	24	24
Unskilled	8	19	29	15	29
Farm tenant and laborer	12	21	20	18	29

[a]Based on coding of qualitative personal interviews from the Harvard Project on the Soviet Social System.

[b]Based on R. Centers, "Motivational Aspects of Occupational Stratification," *Journal of Social Psychology,* Vol. 23 (November 1948), 187–218, Table 11.

[c]Includes: "A very interesting job" and "A job where you could express your feelings, ideas, talent, or skill."

among those in more favored occupations. The Soviet data are not strictly comparable, since, in that context, security meant mainly freedom from fear of the secret police. Even so, it is striking that the intelligentsia, which experienced by far the highest rate of political arrest, nevertheless cited freedom from fear as the quality "most desired" in a job only one-half as often as did the ordinary workers.

In Australia, people were asked to choose between a straight raise or an incentive award. Among employers, 76 percent chose the riskier incentive award, but only about 50 percent of the workers did so.[8] The issue of security is only indirectly raised here. But in a number of cases the choice between more money and less security, or the reverse, has been put more directly, although the results are unfortunately not always reported with a breakdown by class.[9] In three of four cases in which this breakdown is available, the choice of security over earnings is favored by workers more often than by those higher in the occupational or income hierarchy. The question has been asked in the United States a number of times in slightly different form. In 1940 the choice was between "a steady job earning just enough to get by on, with no prospect for advancement," as against "a job that pays a high wage, but with a fifty-fifty chance of getting promoted or fired." Forty-five percent of factory labor as against a mere 8 percent of executives chose the low-income–high-security alternative![10] On another form of the question, 64 percent of professionals and executives were willing to risk all their savings on a promising venture, whereas only 40 percent of the unemployed workers inclined to this course as against sticking to "a good steady job."[11]

These results are congruent with those from the Soviet Union. Here the alternatives offered were: "A job that pays fairly well and is secure, but offers little opportunity for advancement," as against "A job that pays less well and is not secure, but offers good opportunities for advancement." In the Soviet refugee sample, among men under forty, the proportion preferring advancement over security was 50 percent among the intelligentsia and about 23 percent among workers and peasants. The ratio of preference for security over advancement is about four to five in the intelligentsia, but the preference for security is three to one among workers.

The evidence seems strong that when offered the incentive of promotion or success at the risk of security, those in high-status occupations are willing to take risks that are shunned by the manual classes, who favor security above all else. But we are brought up short by the fact that in both Britain and Australia the same occupational differentiation is not noted in response to a seemingly similar question: "Which is more important in a job—as high wages as possible or security with lower wages?" In the British sample security was chosen over high wages at the rate of at least two to one *in all groups*. Indeed, the preference for security was strongest among salaried clerical and professional executive groups.[12] For Australia we do not have the exact percentage but are told that "all occupational groups have similar ideas" in overwhelmingly preferring security to better-paying but presumably insecure jobs.[13]

The conflict between these results and those reported for the United States and the USSR may be less glaring than appears at first glance. It should be observed that in both the American and Soviet studies there was an added element not present in the British and Australian question, namely, the prospect of promotion or "advancement." It may be that our initial formulation was too sweeping or too imprecise. Perhaps we should have said that where there is a prospect of advancement, a promise of special success, then those in the occupations of higher status will more readily take risks, but where security is balanced against high earnings alone, they will act like most others in preferring security. Formulated thus, our expectation is more congruent with relevant psychological theory treating "need achievement" as a risk-taking propensity,[14] and with the evidence that is much more common among those higher in the occupational hierarchy.[15]

This formulation is also more in line with our earlier finding that in judging the qualities of a job those in the positions of higher status were not particularly preoccupied with higher earnings. Fortunately, we have a partial test of the soundness of our shift in emphasis, since an American sample was also asked a question similar to the one used in Britain and Australia.[16] Under this condition, *with no mention of advancement,* the response was markedly different from that reported in the preceding discussion. Although there was still some structured occupational differentiation, it was very slight compared to that observed when the hope of advancement was one of the conditions. With the question in this form the overwhelming majority of Americans at all occupational levels chose the secure job, as had their opposite numbers in Britain and Australia.

That seemingly so slight a difference in wording a question can produce so marked a difference in the structure of the response must give us real pause about this whole enterprise. It warns against too casually accepting all the scattered and limited findings we have and demonstrates the great importance of doing carefully designed, focused, informed, special studies of our own. But it should not discourage us. It does not cast serious doubt on the basic theory. In the case just discussed, for example, we did not refute the general proposition that the higher status groups respond in a different way than those of lower status when confronted with certain alternatives in the job realm. But we did see the need for refinement in delineating precisely what has special appeal to these groups and wherein they share values in common. The theory therefore becomes less global, less "omnipredictive," but in the long run, more interesting and more suggestive.

To sum up our findings in the realm of work: We see striking confirmation of the differential effect of the job situation on the perception of one's experience in it. The evidence is powerful and unmistakable that satisfaction with one's job is differentially experienced by those in the several standard occupational positions. From country to country, we observe a clear, positive correlation between the overall status of occupations and the experience of satisfaction in them. This seems to hold as well for the relation between satisfaction and the components of the job, such as the pay, but the evidence is thinner here. We may expect that the relationship will hold for other components, such as the prestige of the job and the autonomy or independence it affords. Job situation appears also to pattern many values germane to the occupational realm, such as the qualities most desired in a job and the image of a good or bad boss.[17]

At the same time, we note that there are certain attitudes that position in the occupational hierarchy does not seem to influence. For example, all occupational groups agree on the relative ranking of the status or desirability of different jobs. And they seem to agree in favoring job security at less pay over a better-paying but less secure job. Yet in the latter realm we discover an interesting fact. When we add the special ingredient of a promise of success, promotion, or advancement, we trigger a special propensity to risk-taking in those in more esteemed occupations, whereas those in the manual classes remain unmoved and stick to security. This alerts us to the importance of precision and refinement in seeking the exact nature of the values and beliefs that differentiate the social groups on the basis of position in the occupational hierarchy, as against those that they share in common with all of their nationality or all who participate in modern society.

On Happiness

Granted that happiness is a very elusive thing, we may yet make so bold as to study it and to do so through so crude a device as a public-opinion poll. Of course we should not naïvely accept what a person says when we ask, "Are you happy?" But neither is it reasonable to assume that whatever he or she says means the opposite. That would be all too regular and a sure key to the truth. Some will be truly cheerful but suspect our purpose; fear of the "evil eye," or a trait of personality, may lead them to deny publicly their true feeling. If everyone answered the question in a random and, in that sense, meaningless way, we would expect by chance that 50 percent in any population would say "Yes," 50 percent "no," and that no control variable such as age, sex, or income would reveal anything but this fifty-fifty division.

Common sense tells us that some groups produce more people who feel they are happy than do others, and with reason. Those about to commit suicide tell their friends, doctors, or diaries that they are miserable; those who are about to get divorced are likely to report that their marriage is unhappy. Admittedly, where there are pressures that make people disguise their true feelings, their more or less public report of how they feel will certainly reduce the clarity of relationship between the objective situation and their true inner feeling. If, despite this built-in and essentially uncontrollable distortion, we still find strong and meaningful connections between people's situations and what they say about their happiness, then we must assume that the "real" connection is, if anything, not weaker but stronger than the one that emerges in our data.

Both direct and indirect questions have been used in an effort to assess individual happiness. An identical direct question was put to people in the United States, England, France, and Canada in 1946. In contrast to the Anglo-Saxon trio, the French emerge as dour indeed: In the other countries a third or more were "very happy," but in France only 8 percent. Forty per-

Table 11.3   Laughing and crying in England, by class and sex

Economic Class	Percentage Who Laughed in Last 24 Hours (Men Only)	Percentage Who Cried in Last 24 Hours (Women Only)
Well-to-do	47	12
Average	50	11
Below average	41	16
Poor	26	27

Source: Doxa Bolletino, Vol. 5, No. 6 (April 1956).

cent of the French said that they were "not very happy," as against a maximum of 10 percent elsewhere.[18] Much the same question was asked in 1949 by at least six of the Gallup affiliates, with similar results. Only 11 percent of the French were "very happy," as against a range from 26 percent in Norway to 52 percent in Australia.[19] Unfortunately, we do not have cross-tabulations by stratification variables for either of these two studies, but comparable data from Italy and Britain leave little doubt that when these are made, we will find in each society that such happiness as anyone cares to admit will be found most often among those in the more advantaged strata of society.

In the British study men were asked: "In the last twenty-four hours, have you had a hearty laugh?" Women were asked whether they had had a "good cry," an effort being made to disarm them by prefacing the question with the statement: "Many doctors say it is good to give vent to your feelings by crying once in a while." Although the questions do not deal directly with happiness, they very probably measure much the same thing. The proportion who had laughed in the last twenty-four hours decreased, and the proportion who had cried increased, as one descended down the socioeconomic scale (see Table 11.3). The differentiation was sharp, however, only in the case of the very poor, who had laughed only half as often and had cried twice as often as did those in the middle and upper economic classes.

I have asked many people, including several large audiences, to predict the outcome of this poll. The great majority invariably expected the working class to laugh more often. They express surprise at the findings and generally question me closely as to the time and country involved.[20] On learning that the study was done in England, they invariably offer an ad hoc explanation, based on assumptions about the character of English society, and regularly volunteer the opinion that certainly in Italy the results would be different. Unfortunately the same question seems not to have been asked in sunny Italy. But its smiling workers and singing peasants have been asked two other questions that should serve our purpose. The first was simple and straightforward: "Just now do you feel happy or unhappy?" The second was more complex: "Could you summarize in a few words the state (or balance) of your life today?" The respondents were then offered a choice of six sentences suggesting various combinations and degrees of pain and joy ranging from "Life has given me only joys and satisfactions," to "Life has given me only pain and disillusionment."

The results were fairly unambiguous but, as is so often true of such data, by no means completely so. For example, on the first "test" the lowest proportion of happy people is found among one of the more favored groups—the managers (dirigente), a category that seems to include free professionals. On the other hand, this group is quite "normal" on the second test, reporting life to be full of pain and disillusionment less often than any other group. Leaving aside such complications, however, we may conclude on the whole, in Italy no less than in Britain, that happiness is much more commonly reported by the advantaged strata of society, and sadness and despair are more standard in the manual and depressed classes. Of course the well-to-do have no monopoly on happiness, nor does a majority of the working class report itself miserable. In all classes the central tendency is toward some mixture of happiness and pain. But at the extremes the general pattern we have found elsewhere is manifested in Italy as well. As we ascend the occupational ladder, the proportion who are "very" or "fairly" happy is 29 percent among farm laborers and ordinary workers and 47 percent among employers.[21] Similarly, at the other extreme, workers report themselves as unhappy two and a half times as often as do the employers and managers. Among the manual classes the ratio of happy to unhappy is as low as one to one, whereas in the more advantaged group it is almost five to one.

Much the same pattern is shown in the second test. The life of much pain and little joy is claimed by about 50 percent of workers and farm laborers, by as few as 23 percent of the managers and professionals, and by about one-third of employers and farm owners (see Table 11.4).

To assess happiness in a number of countries simultaneously we must unfortunately use a question that can at best be taken as only a rough approximation of those dealing directly with happiness, namely, one inquiring about "satisfaction." What happiness is may be somewhat ambiguous, but we are generally clear that it deals with an *emotional* state. "Satisfaction" is a much more ambiguous term, and when not further specified, it can mean satisfaction with one's financial situation, social or political advancement, family life, or any of a number of things. Furthermore, "happiness" may be translated fairly well from one language to another, but "satisfaction" changes its meaning. In addition, in the available comparative study the question on satisfaction came immediately after one on security, and this probably led people more often to respond in terms of financial criteria rather than of general satisfaction in life. Consequently, to check the reasonableness of using the question on satisfaction in life as an index of hap-

Table 11.4   Balance of joy and pain in life in Italy, by occupation (in percent)

Occupation	More Pain than Joy[a]	More Joy than Pain[b]	A Balance of Joy and Pain[c]	No Answer
Employer	32	20	45	3
Manager	23	23	56	–
Farm owner and operator	33	20	46	1
White collar	28	15	55	2
Artisan	36	12	51	1
Worker	48	11	41	–
Farm laborer	51	11	38	1

[a]Includes the response "Life has given me *only* pains and disillusionment."

[b]Includes: "Life has given me *only* joys and satisfactions."

[c]Includes: "Many pains but also many joys" and "Few pains and few joys." Among workers and farm laborers and employees the choice of "few joys" predominated markedly; among managers, the reverse; and by the remainder the two alternatives were equally chosen.

Source: Doxa Bolletino, No. 12 (April 1948).

piness, I compared the results (for Italy) of two different polls, one asking directly about happiness (described in the preceding discussion), the other using the question on satisfaction from the available cross-national study. The structure of the answers was very similar (see Table 11.5). On both questions business and farm owners and managers reported themselves either dissatisfied or unhappy only half as often as did manual and farm workers, with clerks and artisans falling in between. The correlation was not perfect, but there was quite a close association.

Allowing, then, for many necessary reservations, let us look at the responses to the question, "How satisfied are you with the way you are getting on now?" which was asked simultaneously in nine countries. The results (see Table 11.6) are certainly less sharp and clear-cut than those obtained for job satisfaction. There are numerous irregularities and ambiguities. For example, Germany produces not our familiar step pattern but a U-shaped curve, and Australia yields an inverted U of sorts. These cases suggest what the table as a whole hints, namely, that the question is ambiguous and people respond to it in terms of different criteria. Nevertheless, there seems to be an underlying cross-national pattern. The higher positions held at least rank one (lowest proportion dissatisfied), two, or three in seven of nine countries, whereas the workers held that high a rank in no country and farm laborers in one. The occupations were originally listed in a rough approximation of their standing in the hierarchy of power and rewards. It is interesting, therefore, that when we sum the rank orders for each occupation we emerge with a regular progression that follows the

Table 11.5 Comparison of Italian results on questions of "happiness" and "satisfaction with situation" (in percent)

Occupation	"Dissatisfied" with Present Situation[a]	Occupation	"Unhappy" at This Moment[b]
Business owners	31	Employers	10
Salaried managers	35	Managers	10
Farm owners	32	Farm owners	10
Artisans	43	Artisans	16
Clerks	55	Employees	14
Manual workers	64	Workers	26
Farm workers	63	Farm laborers	20

[a]From William Buchanan and Hadley Cantril, *How Nations See Each Other* (Urbana: University of Illinois Press, 1953), 176. The question was the same as that reported in Table 11.6 for nine countries including Italy.

[b]From *Doxa Bolletino*, No. 12 (April 1948).

original ordering. Except for the owners, whose score of twenty-seven is strongly affected by the deviant response in Britain, there is a steady increase from managers (twenty), through professionals (twenty-four), white collar (thirty-three), artisans and skilled workers (forty-five), and workers (fifty), to farm laborers (fifty-three). That a comparable cross-national pattern emerges when either socioeconomic status or education is used as the independent variable strengthens our conviction that the underlying structure is real. The fact that the relationship holds more firmly when occupation or economic status rather than education is the independent variable suggests that, as we anticipated, the answers more strongly reflect satisfaction with economic than with spiritual welfare.

Whatever their weakness as a guide to the cross-national pattern we seek, these data also point to the usefulness of our procedure for identifying groups with special problems or distinctive responses to more general problems. It is striking, for example, that in Britain the owners formed the group whose members were *most* often dissatisfied with the way they were "getting on." But this was 1948, when they were threatened by the highest level reached by the wave of nationalization sentiment in England, and so the result is not surprising.

Some of the difficulty raised by the question on "satisfaction with getting on" could be avoided if the respondent were asked to disregard his financial condition. An international poll meeting this requirement is, unfortunately, not at hand. We should, however, examine an International Research Associates study in which the wording of the question and its location in the questionnaire may have reduced somewhat the role of economic referents. The question was: "Do you feel that you have gotten as far ahead as you should

Table 11.6 Percentage dissatisfied with how they are "getting on," by country and occupation

				Occupation			
Country	Owners	Managers	Professionals	White Collar	Artisans	Workers	Farm Labor
Australia	11	18	15	22	31	17	17
Britain	41	21	14	36	40	36	26
France	38	29	55	56	56	67	63
Germany	46	39	50	35	37	48	52
Italy	31	35	46	55	43	64	63
Mexico	58	57	50	55	67	65	75
Netherlands	26	15	22	23	37	43	41
Norway	7	4	2	11	12	11	22
United States	20	22	26	24	28	31	39

Adapted from data in Appendix D of William Buchanan and Hadley Cantril, *How Nations See Each Other* (Urbana: University of Illinois Press, 1953), 125–216.

Table 11.7   Percentage satisfied with progress in life, by country and status

Country	Occupational Group			Socioeconomic Group		
	Executive, Professional	White Collar	Wage Earner	Upper	Middle	Lower
Australia	70	64	66	73	70	65
Austria	61	60	47	64	59	60
Belgium	37	36	21	43	41	34
Brazil[a]	74	60	63	81	71	54
Britain	79	66	70	73	68	71
Denmark	77	78	68	81	75	64
Germany	73	71	68	73	72	65
Japan	52	42	33	50	40	13
Netherlands	61	57	59	67	58	66
Norway	89	79	70	87	71	60
Sweden	71	58	67	80	67	60

[a]Rio de Janeiro and São Paulo only.

Source: Tabulations from a study conducted by International Research Associates.

at this stage of your life, or are you dissatisfied with the progress you have made so far?" Here again, unfortunately, the question would probably be understood by many to mean mainly economic or material "getting ahead" or "progress." This assumption is greatly strengthened by the fact that the responses are more regular and the differences sharper when socioeconomic status rather than occupation is used (see Table 11.7). Using socioeconomic status to classify the respondents, we find the step structure present in eight of eleven cases, markedly so in four. There is no instance in which the result is the complete reverse of our expectation, but in three countries the group classified as "middle" has the lower proportion satisfied. Using occupation as the independent variable, we again have four strong cases and a fifth that is up to standard, but now six fail to qualify. In five of these instances the difficulty arises again from the fact that a higher proportion of the middle level of white-collar workers are dissatisfied than is the case among workers. If we compare the executive-professional and worker groups alone, the pattern is very clear-cut in all eleven cases.[22]

In sum, no very "pure" measure of feelings of happiness or of spiritual or psychic (as against material) well-being, applied cross-nationally and fully reported, is at hand. Taking the available evidence together, however, we cannot entertain any other hypothesis but that the feeling of happiness or of psychic well-being is unevenly distributed in most, perhaps all, countries. Those who are economically well off, those with more education or whose jobs require more training and skill, more often report themselves to be happy, joyous, laughing, free of sorrow, satisfied with life's progress. Even though the pattern is weak or ambiguous in some cases, there has not been a single case of a *reversal* of the pattern, that is, a case where measure of happiness is inversely related to measures of status, in studies involving fifteen different countries—at least six of which were studies on two different occasions, through the use of somewhat different questions. There is, then, good reason to challenge the image of the "carefree but happy poor." As one angry man wrote to me after he had read a news report of a speech I had made reporting the relation of laughter to social status: "And what the hell do you think the poor have to laugh about, anyway?"

Plausible as this contention may be on the surface, it is obviously not the end but only the beginning of a study. If those who are better placed and more fortunate more often report that they are happy, can we test the validity of this report by such other measures as their rates of suicide, homicide, and mental illness?[23] If the proportion satisfied rises with income, will better-paid workers in any country be happier than those less well paid at the same occupational level? Will raising the incomes of all increase the happiness of all, or does it require an unequal gain to bring happiness to some? What of the man who is well educated but poorly paid, or rich but poorly educated? Some questions of this kind can be answered by further cross-tabulation of the data.[24] Some will require new cross-national studies clearly focused on these issues.

The Mastery-Optimism Complex

Those lower in the occupational hierarchy bring certain important personal characteristics or propensities to their typical "assignments" in life, which tendencies are reinforced by conditions of their characteristic setting. Their education is limited, they generally will not have benefited from travel, and they confront most of the challenges of the outside world with minimum training or skill. Their home environment, particularly the example of the father, will probably have taught blind obedience to authority, if not as a virtue, at least as a necessity.[25] Even before he goes to work, the factory will have been described to the working-class boy: its great power, its vast size, the impersonality of its processes, and the mystery of the forces that move within it. On arriving at the plant, the young worker will find many of his images and expectations confirmed. Personnel clerks will treat him as something to be fitted into impersonal categories. If there is a doctor who passes on his fitness, the worker may well sense that he is treated as an object assessed, not as a person examined. The foreman will probably be a tough character who makes it clear who is boss, what is expected, what happens to those who step out of line. All the force and power that the lowly employee sees around him will appear to be under the control of people distant and not highly visible who are controlled by others more distant, more powerful, and still more invisible. The other workers, if not initially suspicious, perhaps will immediately begin a briefing on how to stay out of trouble, replete with accounts of unpleasant things that happened to people who could not stay out of trouble, and other tales that make evident the workers' helplessness. If he is too energetic, the new worker will soon be taught by the others, by force if necessary, to restrict his output, to "play it safe," and to be cautious.

These forces conspire to impress upon the worker a particular view of himself and his relation to the world of work and beyond. His image of the world is, as a result, likely to be that of a place of great complexity whose workings are not too easily comprehended by the common man. He has rights, but he needs friends who are more powerful or knowledgeable, who can explain things, tell him where to go, or help him by putting a good word in the right place, like a key in a special lock that opens closed doors. For his own part, he feels he should stick to his job, not ask too many questions, and stay out of trouble. Part of staying out of trouble involves keeping one's work mates assured of one's sense of solidarity with them; group loyalty must be placed above personal ambition and self-aggrandizement. But the requirement to conform to orders from above and, at the same time, to pressures from one's equals encourages his impression of other people as unreliable, untrustworthy, and out to do for themselves first. The one thing a man can really count on are his own sensations, and this fosters a certain hedonism: "Eat, drink, (fornicate) and be merry." These impulses, however, can be gratified only sporadically because of one's dependency, insecurity, and liability to punishment by powers that do not favor too many riotous good times.

A comparable profile for someone at the other end of the occupational hierarchy would presumably be quite different, if not always polar. It is this relative polarization, and the steady gradations as we move from one extreme to the other, that cause the step pattern of experiences and reactions that we have observed and on the basis of which we could generate a host of specific propositions and predictions. For nine-tenths of the propositions there would be no data with which to test them. It will be more economical, therefore, to assemble all the seemingly relevant comparative materials available and to select the topics for investigation in accord with them. We have good comparative data on feelings of personal competence, on images of human nature and malleability, and on several questions that may be taken as alternative measures of optimism.

Personal Competence

Lacking skills, education, and training, directed by people who have more power than he has and who exercise it effectively over him, the member of the lower classes may be expected less often than others to have self-confidence, that is, a favorable assessment of his competence and capacity. This feeling could presumably be tapped by a single general question. More specific questions, separately testing self-confidence about technical or managerial ability in, say, hospitals, courts, or schools, would presumably produce sharper differentiation. At the same time, there might be some areas where those of lower status typically felt more competent or at least less in conflict. For example, the staff at the University of Michigan Survey Research Center reports in an informal communication that their data suggest that middle-class men are more often insecure in their performance as husbands than are lower-class men.

Asked point-blank: "Are you troubled with feelings that you can't do things as well as others can?"—most people in most countries said "No." But the proportion who said they were troubled by feelings of inadequacy rose as high as 59 percent (in the lower class in Brazil). The question is clearly worth examining. The only breakdown available is by socioeconomic status.[26] It provides some, but only modest, corroboration of our expectation. Of twelve countries reporting, the expected pattern is clear-cut and moderately strong only in Denmark and Brazil. In the latter the proportion who feel less competent is 43 percent in the upper class, 52 percent in the middle class, and 59 percent in the lower class. But these cases are offset by Australia, which clearly reverses the predicted direction. Even if we adopt the crude standard of qualifying all countries in which the lower class had the highest proportion troubled by feelings of inadequacy, only seven of the twelve countries qualify.

This is hardly impressive support for our theory. One reason for this outcome may be the ambiguity of the referent "others." The theory predicts mainly that those in the lower strata will feel less competent than "others" who are above them. But many answering the question undoubtedly took as their referent "others" on the same level. Insofar as this was the case, it would obviously reduce the differentiation between classes. The results may also have been influenced by ambiguity as to the types of competence the questioner had in mind. There are of course some areas where lower-class people may generally feel quite competent, or at least not disposed to question their own competence. If they had such areas in mind, they would be less likely to say "yes" to the question.

We may then say that there is some slight evidence that groups of lower status tend in many countries to be the least often assured about their own general competence. Very rarely are they the group with the most pervasive feeling of adequacy. But the issue is not simple, and the response depends on the area of life. Our main gain here, then, is perhaps increased awareness of the complexity or subtlety of the issue.

Child-Rearing Values

Not only is the horizon restricted for the individuals themselves of lower status; they also tend to ensure their self-perpetuation by restricting the horizon of their children and others who share their disadvantaged status. Less well equipped with education and experience than those in more favored positions, they learn that a little bit of security is a good thing and that it is wiser to choose what is certain than to strive for the perhaps unattainable. Consequently, we may expect such individuals to be much less likely than persons of middle or upper status to urge young people to strive for an occupation with high status that may not be easily obtained, and much more likely to urge them to go after a well-paid, secure job at the working-class level. This is true not only in everyday practice but also holds even under the stimulus of a white-collar interviewer who saves the interviewee further embarrassment by offering him conditions free of the objective restrictions he may know actually exist. In one International Research Associates poll in nine countries, the question was put: "If an *intelligent young man who seemed suited for almost any line of work* asked your advice, what occupation would you be most likely to recommend for him?" (Italics added.) Rather consistently from country to country, people of lower socioeconomic status chose the modest goal of "skilled labor" for such a boy much more often than did the more advantaged classes (see Table 11.8). Very similar results were obtained with comparable questions in the United States, in Italy, and with Soviet refugees.

We might again say that this is obvious. It is, furthermore, objective and realistic to advise the working-class boy to set his job sights low. But should we assume that a father's occupational position influences his values in child rearing only in regard to the "objective" realm of job choices? The influence of the father's life situation may be expected to flow over into other areas; ambition itself may be affected. And not only ambition but also a number of other values that guide child rearing may well fall into class-determined patterns.

An International Research Associates study inquired which value is the most important to teach to children and offered as choices: "To be ambitious and get ahead," "To obey parents," "To enjoy themselves," "To place their trust in God," and "To be decent and honest." Since in our Soviet refugee study we had already investigated very similar values and had found patterns broadly congruent with the theory underlying the thinking in this report,[27] I undertook to predict the outcome of the INRA inquiry. The main assumption, following from general theory and supported by the earlier study, was that traditional, restrictive, cautious, conventional values are much stronger among manual workers, whereas the belief in effort, striving, energetic mastery, and the sacrifice necessary to those ends is much stronger in the middle class. On the basis of this fundamental assumption, I predicted for the INRA study that ambition would be more stressed by the middle class, obedience to parents by the working class. A secondary prediction was that the values focused on personal qualities produced by care-

Table 11.8   Occupations recommended to young men, by country and occupation (in percent)

Country and Occupation Recommended	Respondent's Occupation		
	Executive, Professional	White Collar	Wage Earner
Australia			
Engineering, science	24	26	20
Skilled labor	10	11	28
Belgium			
Engineering, science	43	52	28
Skilled labor	8	11	33
Britain			
Engineering, science	54	50	48
Skilled labor	7	6	9
Denmark			
Engineering, science	8	15	8
Skilled labor	7	7	17
France			
Engineering, science	20	30	19
Skilled labor	8	5	11
Japan			
Engineering, science	24	22	26
Skilled labor	1	–	2
Netherlands			
Engineering, science	33	39	22
Skilled labor	7	5	13
Norway			
Engineering, science	11	17	19
Skilled labor	15	18	16
Sweden			
Engineering, science	12	19	15
Skilled labor	8	8	15

Source: Adapted from data made available by International Research Associates through courtesy of Dr. Elmo Wilson.

ful training, such as decency and honesty, would be more stressed by the middle classes. Although predicting emphasis on religion was obviously complicated, I assumed that trust in God, taken as an *external* source of authority and power, would be stronger among manual workers. Finally, I anticipated that stress on enjoyment would be more evident in the working class, presumably as a compensation for past and present frustrations and anticipated future deprivations.

These predictions are generally, but not consistently, borne out by the data (see Table 11.9). The working class does have the lower proportion

Table 11.9 Values in child rearing, by country and socioeconomic status (in percent)

Country and Child-rearing Values	Socioeconomic Status		
	Upper	Middle	Lower
Australia			
Ambition	5	3	8
Obedience to parents	13	17	23
Enjoyment	–	–	1
Trust in God	26	33	25
Decency; honesty	60	51	45
Don't know	5	4	3
No. of respondents	94	313	367
Austria			
Ambition	17	14	11
Obedience to parents	21	21	27
Enjoyment	8	10	8
Trust in God	13	13	14
Decency; honesty	53	51	50
Don't know	2	2	1
No. of respondents	273	581	161
Brazil[a]			
Ambition	9	9	6
Obedience to parents	13	21	23
Enjoyment	2	1	1
Trust in God	22	26	37
Decency; honesty	55	41	34
Don't know	2	2	1
No. of respondents	188	292	320
Britain			
Ambition	7	14	7
Obedience to parents	8	10	17
Enjoyment	1	2	–
Trust in God	26	21	20
Decency; honesty	60	53	52
Don't know	3	1	4
No. of respondents	175	170	152
Denmark			
Ambition	11	13	9
Obedience to parents	14	18	15
Enjoyment	2	1	3
Trust in God	16	9	10
Decency; honesty	54	56	61
Don't know	3	3	2
No. of respondents	167	390	129

(*continues*)

Table 11.9   (*continued*)

Country and Child-rearing Values	Socioeconomic Status		
	Upper	Middle	Lower
Germany			
Ambition	16	17	12
Obedience to parents	24	21	22
Enjoyment	_	1	2
Trust in God	17	10	11
Decency; honesty	61	62	61
Don't know	2	2	2
No. of respondents	120	595	270
Italy			
Ambition	22	13	17
Obedience to parents	22	21	31
Enjoyment	5	2	5
Trust in God	29	31	31
Decency; honesty	53	56	45
Don't know	2	2	2
No. of respondents	148	435	712
Japan			
Ambition	20	24	22
Obedience to parents	6	9	19
Enjoyment	4	3	1
Trust in God	4	4	6
Decency; honesty	64	58	46
Don't know	2	2	6
No. of respondents	368	422	69
Netherlands			
Ambition	8	4	3
Obedience to parents	4	9	12
Enjoyment	1	2	2
Trust in God	40	41	37
Decency; honesty	46	48	50
Don't know	4	2	2
No. of respondents	214	147	142
Norway			
Ambition	23	13	11
Obedience to parents	8	15	11
Enjoyment	1	–	–
Trust in God	11	17	26
Decency; honesty	51	50	46
Don't know	6	5	6
No. of respondents	142	519	72

(*continues*)

Table 11.9   (*continued*)

Country and Child-rearing Values	Socioeconomic Status		
	Upper	Middle	Lower
Sweden			
Ambition	12	16	18
Obedience to parents	15	24	38
Enjoyment	3	3	12
Trust in God	12	9	26
Decency; honesty	76	72	59
Don't know	2	1	1
No. of respondents	156	307	91

[a]Rio de Janeiro and São Paulo only.

Source: Data provided by International Research Associates, from a release of March 13, 1958.

stressing ambition in six of eleven countries and is tied in a seventh, a position held only twice each by the middle and upper socioeconomic groups. Only three countries show the usual step pattern, however, and there are two clear-cut reversals to offset them. The absence of pattern is largely a result of the tendency, perhaps not surprising, of the middle class to exceed the upper classes in stressing ambition in rearing children.

Our prediction with regard to emphasis on obedience is more firmly supported. The lower class has the highest proportion stressing it in eight of eleven cases, and it took no less than second place in the remaining three countries. In six the expected step pattern is clearly manifested, and there are no reversals.

Among the second-line predictions, the estimate with regard to decency and honesty was relatively correct. In seven of eleven countries, the higher the socioeconomic status, the greater the proportion emphasizing it. In an eighth case the lower class behaves as expected, but the middle class is out of line. In addition to one unpatterned case, however, there were two clear reversals. The prediction with regard to trust in God was not confirmed: The lower class did most often have the highest proportion, but it also was most often in last place; in general, there was almost a complete lack of pattern from country to country. We may note, finally, that not much can be said about the theme of enjoying oneself, since it was mentioned by only 1 or 2 percent in most countries.

In general, the class patterning in which we are interested manifests itself again, but the patterns are not strong. In most cases only a few percentage points separated one class from the next. In values in child-rearing, cultural forces—particularly those deriving from ethnic and religious membership—play a powerful role and may indeed be the prime movers. Yet the fact that in this initial and unrefined procedure we can see a definite patterning of values that fit the expectations derived from our general theory is encouraging and recommends us to further and fuller explorations.

Changing Human Nature

People's conceptions of the nature of human nature reveal much of their overt ideology, but questions that delve deep are unfortunately not at hand. However, in nine countries national samples were asked whether they thought their compatriots' "national characteristics" were due to the way they were brought up or were born in them and, also, whether "human nature" can be changed.

Our theory leads us to predict that the more advantaged classes will more often hold upbringing rather than heredity to determine national characteristics and will more often express belief in the malleability of human nature. This outcome is not assumed to be merely a function of intelligence and knowledge. Indeed, when people are grouped by education rather than by socioeconomic level, the strength of the association between social position and the belief that national characteristics are a product of training becomes much smaller and the patterning more confused and ambiguous. Rather, it follows from differences in training and life situation; those in the professional and managerial classes will more often have grown up in an environment that stressed training and character development, and in their work they will have learned the importance of mastering and transforming things by disciplined will and effort. By contrast, those in the working and peasant classes will have grown up in an atmosphere of more conventional beliefs and will have been taught to see important events as largely independent of the individual's will or effort. The manual worker enjoys less opportunity to assess the evident variability of behavior in different situations, and his life at work will foster the impression of an unchanging life order. When it is changed "from above," he will be less able to assess the shifting pressures and forces at work and therefore is more likely to see change as a product of some powerful person's fixed character.

We must allow for certain forces that will, however, operate to push the results in the opposite direction. In the upper, and particularly the aristocratic upper, classes, obvious forces encourage the notion that character is inborn and immutable, the finest of these inborn character types of course being concentrated in the aristocratic classes. This sentiment, often quickly adopted by the *nouveaux riches,* might act sharply to increase the proportion among the well-to-do, taken as a whole, who believe character to be mainly a product of training and hence subject to change.

Of nine national samples, seven fell into the step pattern in assessing the origins of national characteristics; the proportion who stated that these characteristics result from the way people are brought up rose with each step up the socioeconomic ladder. Three of the seven, however, are not clear-cut, because the highest or "wealthy" group either does not show a higher proportion believing in training or even shows a much lower proportion than does the group average in socioeconomic status. This relates to the point about the aristocratic conception of upper-class status just discussed. In two countries there is no definite pattern, but there are no clearcut reversals. The belief that human nature can be changed is similarly patterned by social class membership. Of nine countries, the step pattern is found in six; the proportion who believe that human nature can be changed again rises as one ascends the socioeconomic scale (see Table 11.10). But again the pattern is marred by the tendency of the wealthy to stress training less often than does the average income group. This was true in four of the seven cases of patterning. Italy, Norway, and the United States show no pattern. Again, there are no reversals.

This outcome definitely supports our hypothesis, even allowing for the fact that the supporting evidence is somewhat weak in the case of estimates of the origins of national characteristics. For example, in one of the clearest manifestations of the structured response, in Germany the proportion who stress training rises by only 5 percent or so on each step up the socioeconomic ladder, with 21 percent of the very poor at one extreme and 36 percent of the wealthy at the other. Bigger ranges are present in opinions about changing human nature, the difference between the wealthy and the very poor being as many as thirty-three percentage points. On both questions the pattern is, furthermore, blurred by the tendency of the wealthy to entertain the belief in the immutability of human nature and the inborn character of national traits. We must particularly regret, therefore, that the responses were not cross-tabulated by occupation.

Optimism and Control of the Atom

Views about the possibility of changing human nature have been treated here as evidence of a belief in the importance of character training and in the possibility of man's control and mastery over himself. Belief in the possibility of changing human nature can also be interpreted as expressing a certain optimism about *social* man and his future progress and a faith in the meaningfulness of efforts to master one's physical and social environment. The superior intellectual equipment that the more advantaged bring to situations, their advanced training and actual experience, encourage and support them in developing and maintaining optimism. To them the world is less a mysterious and threatening place. It presents obstacles, but those are assumed to be controllable by forces at man's disposal so long as he applies skill, motivation, and good will. Evidence for the more frequent oc-

Table 11.10 Percentage who believe in the possibility of change in human nature, by country and class

Socioeconomic Status[a]	Australia	Britain	France	Germany	Italy	Mexico	Netherlands	Norway	U.S.
Wealthy	54	55	70	50	31	59	42	57	54
Average	45	46	63	48	37	37	50	58	50
Below average	42	38	61	51	31	38	43	57	49
Very poor	39	30	50	40	55	26	38	51	50

[a]Judgment of interviewer.

Source: From data by country in Appendix D of William Buchanan and Hadley Cantril, *How Nations See Each Other* (Urbana: University of Illinois Press, 1953).

Table 11.11 Estimates of long-run effects of atomic energy, by country and education (in percent)

Education	More Good than Harm	More Harm than Good	Can't Say or Don't Know
United States[a]			
University	69	20	11
Secondary	55	30	15
Primary	40	40	20
Australia[b]			
Higher	61	18	21
Middle	47	25	28
Lower	31	23	46

[a]*Doxa Bolletino*, Vol. 2, No. 22 (November 1948).

[b]Australian Gallup Polls of Melbourne, *Bulletin*, Nos. 645–661 (January-February 1950).

currence of optimism in the advantaged class is not ample, but a number of very suggestive items come to hand that support the assumption.

The sources of atomic energy present so great a potential threat to man that they often induce visions of the total destruction of civilization and even human existence. But atomic energy also holds the possibility of great benefits. Casual reading of newspapers leads us to assume that fears about the destructive misuse of atomic energy have a particularly strong hold on the better-educated segments of modern society. But our theory also leads us to believe that the same people—because of their greater faith in man's ability to change, adopt, transform, and control natural and social forces—should more often hold the belief that *ultimately* the beneficial effects of atomic energy will predominate. For Australia and the United States there are class data, by education, on responses to the question, "In the long run do you think atomic energy will do more harm than good, or more good than harm?"[28] In both countries the differentiation by education is extremely sharp, and in both cases the differences are in the expected direction, that is, there is greater optimism as one ascends the educational ladder (see Table 11.11).

These striking indications of the greater frequency with which optimism, based on mastery of natural and social forces, is found among the better-educated are further supported, although less dramatically, by the results of a question on war and peace. In the UNESCO study the question was put as follows: "Do you believe that it will be possible for all countries to live together at peace with each other?" Certainly this strains optimism more than does the question on atomic energy. Even so, in four of nine countries the step pattern was clearly manifested, and in no case was the proportion giving the more optimistic answer less among those with university training than among those with only primary schooling (see Table 11.12).

Table 11.12   Belief in possibility of peace, by country and education (in percent)

Country	Educational Level		
	Primary	*Secondary*	*University*
Australia	41	40	33
Britain	45	50	52
France	47	48	54
Germany[a]	59	53	59
Italy	30	31	30
Mexico	16	19	33
Netherlands	41	52	45
Norway	54	57	62
United States	49	47	57

[a]British Zone only.

The table presents the percentages of positive responses to the question: "Do you believe that it will be possible for all countries to live together at peace with each other?" Taken from data in William Buchanan and Hadley Cantril, *How Nations See Each Other* (Urbana: University of Illinois Press, 1953), Appendix D.

Economic Optimism

It may be argued on common-sense grounds that optimism is obviously more to be expected from the well-to-do—after all, they have more to be optimistic about. In this view optimism is just an alternative formulation for happiness, to be explained on the same grounds. This might seem in accord with the theory that one's situation shapes one's perspective. But it is only superficially in accord with the more explicit formulation just developed, that those who are better educated and trained, and hold more responsible positions, will be more optimistic *specifically about those situations where the possibility of man's mastery of himself or his environment is involved.* This is not the same thing as saying that they will be generally and indiscriminately more optimistic, even where definite or precise objective assessments are involved. A judgment about the possibility that man can develop the institutional prerequisites to peace is by no means the same thing as a judgment as to whether there will be a war in the next few years. Fundamental optimism about man's capacity to organize and solve his problems could well lead one to believe that *in the long run* man will develop the means for preserving peace, even while realism prompts the prediction that there may be a war in the next few years. When an estimate of the probability of war *within a fixed time period* was requested, the well-to-do were less optimistic, or, to put it better for our purposes, more "realistic," in virtually all of the studies that reported class breakdowns.

Thus in Great Britain in October 1946, the proportion who felt that there would be a war in the next twenty-five years rose steadily from 30 percent among the very poor to 44 percent among those above the middle class. Numerous other studies in Britain in this period yielded similar findings, as did also a poll in Sweden in April 1945 and in France on January 19, 1946.[29] It is interesting that Buchanan and Cantril also noted, but may have misunderstood, the apparent disagreement of the national totals that affirmed the possibility of peace in their study and the proportions that, in surveys made by others in the same country and in the same year, were reported as expecting another big war in the next ten years. This disagreement led Buchanan and Cantril to feel that responses to these questions lack "validity." They may, but our analysis suggest that if the responses are not highly correlated, it is because the questions often tap quite different dimensions of opinion, even though their wording is superficially comparable. Optimism about man's *ultimate* capacity to master his own nature and his social forms should not be confused with optimism about the immediate chances of war.

Neither should optimism about man's potential for mastering himself and his environment be mistakenly assumed to be the simple equivalent of optimism about general economic development and personal economic prospects. We have a substantial number of studies reporting optimism about the national economy or about individual or personal economic prospects. There is no pattern from country to country, or at least no *consistent* pattern, in the responses to such questions as "How soon do you expect a peace standard of living after the signing of the new peace treaty?" "Do you expect to be better off next year?" "Will there be a depression in the next two years?" Sometimes there is no structure of opinion at all; sometimes the higher classes are more optimistic, in other cases the lower classes. Often in one country a particular group is outstanding in its pessimism, but this is not true for the same group in other countries.[30] This has led us to conclude that specifically *economic* optimism is mainly determined by the unique economic conditions in a nation as a whole or by the distinctive prospects of certain groups in particular countries at different times. The economic optimism of particular groups is apparently not predictable either from their general position as wealthy or poor or by some common characteristic of their situation that prevails across national boundaries.

This is strikingly evident in the UNESCO study, in which the same question on economic expectations was asked in a number of countries in the same year: "When the war ended did you expect you would be getting along better, worse, or about the same, as you actually are getting along at the present time?" The question did not explicitly call for an assessment of economic prospects, but from its context and the response pattern, it evidently was generally taken to apply to economic welfare. It also suffers from the defect of asking people how they had felt some years *earlier,* "when the war ended." This would be a rather indefinite time, not the same in all countries. These considerations must limit our confidence in the distinctive relevance of the answers to the issue discussed earlier. Such ambiguity in a question typically "washes out" patterns that might otherwise be observed. Allowing for it, there is virtually no steady association, country by country, between occupation and the percentage who at the end of the war (presumably 1945) expected to be getting along better than they actually were in 1948 (see Table 11.13). For example, in France, the Netherlands, and the United States, business owners yielded more or less the lowest proportions indicating that they had thought at the end of the war that things would turn out better than they seemed to have done by 1948. But in Britain, Germany, and Italy, the opposite was the case; business owners were outstanding in the proportion who reported that at the end of the war they had been too optimistic—in 1948 they were not getting on as well as they had earlier anticipated. A comparable lack of agreement is shown at other levels, and consequently there is no pattern in the responses by occupation from country to country.

This lack of pattern contrasts very sharply with the findings from a different question on economic prospects put to the same samples, namely, that on job security (see Table 11.14). In this case, the structure of response, by occupation, was very similar from country to country and is particularly clear-cut in the four occupational groups at the bottom of the hierarchy. In seven of the nine countries farm laborers consistently had the lowest proportion, rank eight, reporting job security, and in the remaining two countries, rank seven. By contrast, on the preceding question on expectations of economic outcome, farm laborers held rank eight only once, rank seven once, and were actually in the first rank twice (see Table 11.13). The sum of differences between the average rank and the attained rank for each occupational group in all countries was two or three times larger for most occupational groups when economic welfare rather than job security was assessed.

We may then conclude that the degree of job security remains a fairly fixed quality or attribute of jobs *relative to each other* in the industrial hierarchy. Estimates of job security therefore yield a comparable structure of responses from country to country, rather than being variable in the manner of more general estimates of economic prospects. Even if economic security in a country decreases, it will probably drop for all or most groups, thus ensuring that the cross-national pattern will be maintained. Within limits this will probably be true even when the decrease in security hits one stratum, such as workers, harder than others. To some degree the security pattern is built into the nature of large-scale industrial organization. It therefore produces a similar pattern from country to country.[31] The prospects for economic improvement for any group, especially relative to

Table 11.13 Expectations of personal economic betterment, by country and occupation (in percent)

Country	Business Owners	Farm Owners	Salaried Managers	Professionals	Clerical Workers	Artisans	Manual Workers	Farm Laborers
					Occupation			
Australia	49	66	52	39	49	55	53	42
Britain	61	57	49	49	60	60	56	74
France	67	80	79	89	79	81	81	80
Germany[a]	49	37	45	47	44	39	50	42
Italy	38	37	29	21	37	37	52	54
Mexico	35	14	52	41	34	43	37	38
Netherlands	30	58	53	44	52	56	66	64
Norway	39	36	48	28	58	58	52	57
United States	29	30	38	37	45	45	36	22

[a]British Zone only.

The table presents the percentages of persons who at the end of World War II *expected* to be getting along better than they now actually are. From data in Appendix D of William Buchanan and Hadley Cantril, *How Nations See Each Other* (Urbana: University of Illinois Press, 1953), 125–216.

Table 11.14 Job security compared to average, by country and occupation (in percent)

				Occupation				
Country	Business Owners	Farm Owners	Salaried Managers	Professionals	Clerical Workers	Artisans	Manual Workers	Farm Laborers
Australia	60	53	70	79	57	50	48	33
Britain	47	43	52	56	31	30	32	29
France	24	27	43	28	20	16	10	11
Germany[a]	29	28	26	24	28	42	20	12
Italy	39	22	18	34	31	18	15	6
Mexico	59	100	74	80	62	50	46	38
Netherlands	48	20	51	51	36	19	11	7
Norway	4	18	48	24	21	14	29	9
United States	53	42	47	65	37	37	28	22

[a]British Zone only.

Source: From data by country in Appendix D of William Buchanan and Hadley Cantril, *How Nations See Each Other* (Urbana: University of Illinois Press, 1953), 125–216.

others, are by no means "structurally given" to anything like the same degree. Nothing in the nature of large-scale economic organization dictates what progress any stratum, relative to other strata, may or should make in the next year or the year after.

At first glance the fact that position on the socioeconomic ladder does not make possible prediction of the pattern of economic optimism from country to country may seem to impugn our original general theory. But the theory does not predict that the well-off will be uniformly optimistic about economic affairs. It states rather that the opinions and attitudes of people in all countries will be similarly shaped or patterned to the degree that they face similar objective conditions or situations and are located in comparable positions in networks of power, influence, and interpersonal relations. Insofar as economic conditions held varying promise of good or bad outcomes for particular economic strata in the individual nations, to that degree we would expect to find the local expressions of economic optimism more or less distinctive. Such lack of pattern is exactly what we do find. But the variation observed is probably not random. We would take ourselves far afield, however, if we endeavored to discover the rational or objective basis for each variation in response, group by group and country by country.

Summary and Conclusions

There are many other areas into which we might look—politics, religion, recreation, family life.[32] But the purpose of this study is to open a discussion, not to settle an issue. The following statements seem justified by our experience:

There is substantial evidence, over a wide attitudinal and experiential range, that perceptions, opinions, and values are systematically ordered in modern societies. The proportion of people who give a particular response increases or decreases fairly regularly as we move up or down the typical status ladders of occupation, income, education, and prestige. These patterns emerge not only in realms that are obviously closely related to status pressures but also in areas seemingly far removed. In every country the average or typical response may be distinctive, but the same order or structure is manifested within *each*, even though they vary widely in their economic and political development and have unique cultural histories. This similarity in the patterning of response seems best explained by assuming that, in significant degree, perceptions, attitudes, and values are shaped by the networks of interpersonal relations in which individuals are enmeshed and particularly by rewards and punishments.

It follows that a careful study of the specific external situation of the major subgroups in any country would enable one to deduce the distinctive internal life—the perceptions, attitudes, and values—of those groups relative to each other. This makes the very large assumption, however, that one is equipped with a great battery of subtheories that specify the probable psychological outcome of a very wide range of diverse external situations, taken alone and in numerous combinations. With or without the requisite battery of subtheories, this is, in effect, what historians, anthropologists, and sociologists frequently attempt to do when they analyze life in some one nation or culture. However, the uniqueness of the external situation studied in each case and the ad hoc nature of the theory used make it difficult to test and refine theory and on this basis to accumulate firm empirical knowledge.

The cross-national or comparative approach permits concentration on a few widely present situational forces and facilitates the systematic testing and validation of theory. This chapter's concentration on modern industrial society should not be understood, however, as suggesting it to be the only realm in which the theory sketched here is applicable. On the contrary, we expect that, whenever any set of nations places major social strata in a structure highly comparable from society to society, a cross-national attitudinal pattern similar to the one we observed will also be found. Theoretically, a parallel analysis could be made for the various strata of medieval European societies, of the traditional monarchies of the eighteenth century, or of the underdeveloped nations of the earlier twentieth century. In fact any such effort would probably founder, either because we could not secure adequate information on the specific distribution of attitudes or because we could not satisfy the requirement that the situation of the subgroups, and the hierarchies in which they were organized, be strictly comparable from one society to the next.

The choice of industrial society as a field of investigation is therefore not based solely on grounds of methodological expediency or political interest. It is the only setting that relatively unambiguously satisfies the conditions to which the theory has critical relevance. Modern society, most notably in the factory system, and secondarily in large-scale bureaucratic organizations in business, government, and other fields, is more or less unique in the extent to which it produces standardized contexts of experience. These are exportable and are sought after to a degree that far exceeds the exportability of most other culture complexes. And to an extent far beyond what is true of other complexes, they resist being reformulated, changed or adapted to suit the larger sociocultural environment into which they bluntly intrude or are invited or accepted.

The patterns of reaction we have observed are to be expected, however, only insofar as the hierarchies in the different countries are equivalent, not merely in the positions recognized, but also in the conditions of existence they provide for the incumbents of those statuses. Departures from the standard pattern (as distinguished from differences in the average response for any country) must in all cases be assumed to arise from empirically discoverable variations in the conditions of existence, by status. It follows, therefore, that to the degree a nation's social structure approximates the model of a full-scale primary industrial society, to that degree will it more clearly show the differentiated structure of response I have delineated, and do so over a wider range of topics, problems, or areas of experience. There are of course many theoretical and methodological difficulties in developing a model of industrial society. Suffice it to say that England before World War I, the United States between World Wars I and II, and the Soviet Union and West Germany after World War II all can be shown to have approximated the model in important respects. My anticipation is that all the currently developed nations, and all those on the verge of developing, will at some point approximate the model and will at that point show most clearly the patterns I have described.

This brings us to the often cited tendencies toward homogenization of experience in the most advanced industrial countries, notably the United States. If our general theory is valid, then to the extent that the conditions of life, the network of interpersonal relations in which people work, the patterns of reward and punishment, come to be more and more alike regardless of status and situs, to that degree should their perceptions, attitudes, and values become similar. In other words, the typical step pattern we observed would become less and less evident and might eventually disappear altogether. Furthermore, to the degree that similar conditions come to prevail in other countries, the same process of homogenization could be expected to manifest itself there as well. Indeed, although it seems far off and far fetched, it could very well be that we will in the future come to have a fairly uniform world culture, in which not only nations but also groups within nations will have lost their distinctive subcultures. In important respects—exclusive of such elements as language—most people might come to share a uniform, homogeneous culture as citizens of the world. This culture might make them, at least as group members, more or less indistinguishable in perceptual tendency, opinion, and belief not only from their fellow citizens in the same nation and their occupational peers in other nations but from all people everywhere.[33]

Such speculation of course goes far beyond what our data can at present support even remotely. The data are, furthermore, by no means unambiguous. The questions put in different countries, for one thing, are not comparable. But it is highly improbable that ambiguity in the stimulus would generate agreement in the response pattern. On the contrary, the likelihood is vastly greater that any consistent pattern that is actually present would be muted or muffled by questions that put, in effect, a randomly varying stimulus to respondents in the different countries. There is also the substantial problem that *within* any country a question in the same language may have quite different meaning for people with markedly dissimilar education. We obviously need to develop methods that ensure that our questions, *as understood* by respondents of different countries and classes, are more strictly equivalent. We have methods that can satisfy this requirement in substantial degree. They are moderately costly, and they require time, but the advantage of using them in scientific, as contrasted with the commercial, studies is great enough to warrant the cost.

Another difficulty arises with regard to the criteria to be used in determining when opinions are structured in any country and patterned across national boundaries. The usual statistical tests are not automatically applicable. In any event, for the purposes of this exploratory study I have adopted a liberal and flexible definition. But in more systematic studies we must be prepared to specify our criteria more precisely and to apply them more rigorously.

A more imposing challenge to our findings is that in a great many items the *absolute difference* in the average or typical response for different countries is so great as to dwarf into insignificance the *similarity in pattern* from nation to nation. The occupation or other hierarchy, in other words, often explains only a small part of the variance, at least as compared to dimensions like nationality, citizenship, or ethnicity. We should, perhaps, be pleased to have discovered *any* regularity in human behavior that persists across national boundaries, even if it is only "minor." It is also possible that often the seemingly great size of these differences among nations is more spurious than real, and arises mainly from the fact that the questions used are not really comparable stimuli for the various respondents. The differences may, however, be very real indeed. If they are, then we will still have to choose between alternative explanations—the distinctive cultural tradition of a nation, on the one hand, and its level and style of economic and political development, on the other. Undoubtedly both factors exert major influence, and often they will be so intertwined as to make it impossible to assign separate weights to them. But careful selection of the countries to be studied—perhaps even matching countries with similar traditions but different economic or political development, and vice versa—would yield interesting results. It will be particularly important to seek to discover those realms of perception, opinion, and value that seem most influenced by the industrial social order, as against those that are relatively more tightly integrated in an autonomous pattern of traditional culture, and hence more immune, or at least resistant, to change even in the presence of the standard industrial environment.

One last reservation is the claim that these data are subject to quite different explanations from those here offered. For example, the pattern can be explained as arising mainly from educational differences—not an alternative explanation, but really an integral part of my argument. The theory stresses that people are ordered in modern society in hierarchies of power, responsibility, prestige, income, and education. The amount of education a person receives is part of the structure of rewards. It also is a major element in determining his or her occupational status. As such it can be seen as merely an integral, although alternative, *index* of the person's *situation* rather than as independent and alternative *explanation* of his or her *behavior*. But, quite apart from this, the theory holds that situational pressures exert an influence independent of the education of the incumbents of the position. To test this assumption and to discover how great is the independent influence of education, we would of course need to compare the responses of people with comparable education who occupied systematically different positions, and vice versa.

We obviously need more and better research on the important problem this initial exploration has barely opened up. It is to be doubted, however, that merely by collecting more data of the type now in hand we can settle many of these issues. But through carefully designed studies, building on the experience of this exploration and sharply focused on some of the issues raised by it, we may expect to make substantial progress. We would hope to ensure comparability in the meaning of the questions from country to country and from class to class. Instability and unreliability in the findings could further be greatly reduced by the use of scales to measure important attitude domains, in place of the single question that has been the standard in the past. Rather than gathering scattered bits and snippets of information from numerous different samples, we should aim to secure a rich set of responses from the *same* set of respondents in each country, thus providing the basis for studying patterns of interrelation among sets of perceptions, opinions, and values. To aid in resolving some of the difficult problems of interpreting the findings we have so far accumulated, the countries studied should represent a wide range of stages and forms of economic development and cultural type. And the samples drawn from each should be not the bare minimum representative sample but rather carefully stratified and, where necessary, extensively overrepresented to permit complex internal comparisons. With sufficient resources we could reasonably hope to make substantial strides toward developing a respectable social psychology of industrial society.

twelve

INDUSTRIALIZATION, MODERNIZATION, AND THE QUALITY OF LIFE

Effectively to discuss the relation of industrialization, modernization, and the quality of life we must have some common understanding of the meaning of those terms, including, indeed, the term relation itself.

In the narrowest technical sense, industrialization refers to the process of increasingly shifting the composition of all goods produced by any society in two major respects: First, the share of all products resulting from manufacture rather than from agriculture increases markedly, and second, there is a major shift in the share of all fabrication that is undertaken not by craft hand-labor but by machine processes, especially as driven by inanimate sources of energy. Evidently inherent in this second shift is a propensity vastly to increase the total volume of all goods produced.[1] Looking to England as the first industrializer, we note that the share of agriculture in the national income fell from an estimated 45 percent in 1770 to a mere 15 percent by 1870, and over the next hundred years the proportion was driven down to a mere 3 percent.[2] In that same century the United States, coming later to industrialization, reduced the proportion of the labor force

Reprinted with permission from Alex Inkeles, "Industrialization, Modernization, and the Quality of Life," *International Journal of Comparative Sociology*, Vol. 34, No. 1-2 (1993), 1–23.

engaged in agriculture from close to 50 percent to less than 5 percent as machines replaced horses and mules and then, in turn, men and women.[3]

The shift out of agriculture, however, was by no means into manufacturing alone, nor into industry more broadly conceived. Thus the century that saw such precipitous decline in the importance of agriculture in the United States witnessed an increase in the weight of manufacturing personnel as part of the total labor force from about 18 percent to only about 25 percent.[4] This was due to the fact that people moved more and more into services, and of these the most significant in their implications for development were education, science, and engineering. Profound changes in the mode and capacity of transportation and communication followed, often in a prodigious surge. Thus the railroad network of Europe was increased by seventy times in the half century from 1850 to 1890, and in one decade in the United States, from 1870 to 1880, the number of railroad miles was almost doubled.[5]

No less important were changes in the character of the population's education and residence. In 1870 no one in the United States lived in a city of a million population, but by 1970 almost 19 million people lived in such metropolitan conglomerations.[6] In education, Canada moved from spending only approximately 1 percent of its gross national product (GNP) for schooling in 1867 to allocating more than 7 percent of its national income for this particular form of investment in human capital by 1967.[7] Even countries that started from a relatively high level of education linked their industrialization to increasing education for the population. Thus Japan, although already educating some 30 percent of the five-to-nineteen age group by 1880, nevertheless more than doubled that percentage by 1915.[8]

For such reasons it is much too restrictive to limit oneself to measures of industrialization only, and much more appropriate to speak of modernization, a broad process of technological, economic, and social change in which even countries that continued to draw more heavily for their production on agriculture or extraction could and did participate. Argentina, for example, while remaining overwhelmingly agricultural nevertheless expanded its railway network from a mere fifteen miles in 1860 to almost 6,000 miles by 1890.[9]

The potential indicators of a nation's industrialization and modernization are numerous, but they are also highly consistent. A set of those elements subjected to factor analysis will yield a strong principal component explaining a large amount of variance and characterized by factor loadings for the participant elements in the .8 and .9 range. So tightly structured is this syndrome that a simple index based on a set of some ten indicators chosen to be representatives of different realms will stand in quite well for the 100 or so measures various scholars might nominate. Indeed, it is often quite serviceable to use a single, readily available number, namely, the per capita GNP of a nation, as an indicator of industrialization and modernization.[10]

The Meaning of Quality of Life

To judge the quality of life we have several alternative modes available. The first critical choice is between subjective and objective measures. Within each of these sets a second set of choices can be made, providing us with four basic types of potential indicator.

Objective Indicators

Objective indicators are those that can be ascertained and rated by an outside observer without reference to the inner states of persons presumably affected by the conditions observed. The objective measures are themselves divided into those for which there is a clear physical or material referent, such as how many square feet of housing each person enjoys, and those that reflect a social or political condition, such as the legal right to join any church of one's choice.

Among the physical and material factors that are commonly identified and measured we can identify at least nine categories of goods and services that are of actual or potential concern to the typical individual. These include: food; housing and associated amenities such as piped water and sewage; medicine and health; education; communications and information; free time available, as for leisure; physical security of the person; the social security of the person, usually represented by the flow of welfare expenditures; and, increasingly, environmental and ecological conditions. Each of these categories can and often is represented by a subset of specific indicators. Health, for example, is often assessed by considering infant mortality rates and doctor-to-patient ratios; physical security by rates of victimization from various crimes, such as armed assault or robbery; and communications conditions by newspapers published per capita.[11]

Governments and international agencies have a long-standing interest in measures of this type, and they have been systematically and assiduously collected for most nations over decades. From this experience we know that most of these diverse indicators tend to be closely related to each other and form a syndrome readily summed up in a general index of the physical quality of life for any population.[12]

Objective measures of the sociocultural and sociopolitical variety can be established by studying laws and their implementation, but also by systematic observation of social behavior. In either case, the measurement does *not* involve asking people how they feel about an issue. I propose six broad categories: *freedom of movement,* as in moving from the countryside to the city or from one job to another; *freedom of belief,* as in choosing your religion or political ideology; *freedom of association,* as expressed in the right to form and join organizations of common interest; *freedom of political de-*

termination, as expressed in the right to choose your political leaders in meaningfully contested elections; *economic freedom,* as expressed in the employee's freedom to work at a job of his or her own choosing, the consumer's choice of what to buy, and the saver's choice of what to do with his savings; and *freedom from discrimination and denigration,* as when black children in the United States are no longer forced to use segregated schools, or, looking to India, when low-caste persons are allowed to draw water from the same well as high-caste persons. Under each of these six major headings, of course, numerous subcategories can be suggested.

Objective indicators of sociocultural and sociopolitical conditions have been less systematically collected than the physical and material variety, partly because they are less easy to measure, but possibly also because many governments find that they raise sensitive and even embarrassing issues. Private organizations, however, have been quite active in this realm. Perhaps best known are the Freedom House ratings, developed by Raymond Gastil and annually applied to all countries worldwide since 1973. By considering the status of some eleven political rights and twelve civil liberties a summary "freedom rating" is developed for each country on a scale from one to fourteen.[13]

Subjective Indicators

Subjective indicators, as the term suggests, are accessible to us only by asking people to express an evaluation, judgment, opinion, or belief about their own condition, or the condition of others and the world around them. The main indicators that have been worked with extensively are expressions of personal satisfaction with one or another realm of life. Typically the interview confronts the individual with the question: "Now considering your job, are you very satisfied, only somewhat satisfied, or not satisfied at all?" The same sort of question is regularly put with regard to one or more additional realms of life such as marriage, family life, one's education, friendships, health, finances, housing, leisure time, community, and nation.

It will be apparent that this list closely approximates the categories dealt with by the objective measures, only in this case it is not the *facts* that are at issue but rather the *perception* of them, and the *feelings* such perceptions elicit. Clearly, the same approach could be and is taken with regard to the *subjective evaluation* of the more or less objective measures of sociopolitical conditions. Thus while the objective measures will tell us whether individuals have the legal freedom to select their place of residence, the subjective evaluation will tell us how far people feel they really are free to move from one place to another.

For many purposes one would obviously wish to focus on a measure of satisfaction limited to one particular realm, such as housing or the job.[14]

And indeed, such specialized lines of analysis, as, for example, on the quality of urban living, are well developed.[15] Nevertheless, it is the case, as with other measures we have examined, that the set of subjective satisfaction measures tend to be well, although not tightly, correlated, and to constitute a syndrome, so that when satisfaction is expressed with one realm it is likely to be expressed in other realms as well.[16] As a result, it generally proves meaningful to develop a summary index by adding the scores for satisfaction felt in each of several different realms. As with the objective measures it is also possible, and indeed quite practical, to rely on the subject himself or herself to provide a summary judgment, as in response to the question: "Now, taking life as a whole, would you say that you are very satisfied, only somewhat satisfied, or not at all satisfied?"[17] Asking about whether a person is happy or not provides a similar and equally serviceable summary judgment.[18]

There is a second category of subjective measures of the quality of life whose theoretical status is less well established but that nevertheless deserves serious attention. In this category are the subjectively felt conditions, states, attributes, or qualities of the person—if you like, "psychosocial" indicators. Perhaps the best example is anxiety. It would seem obvious, for example, that a society that induces the majority of its citizens to be constantly suffering intense anxiety is providing them with a lower quality of life than is one that permits them to enjoy freedom from such noxious feelings.

In this realm there is no agreed-on set of themes or measures, and the research on it has been less systematic and comprehensive. Nevertheless, there have been good studies on a cross-cultural basis of quite a variety of personal properties relevant to evaluations of the quality of life in psychosocial terms. These include measures of trust; personal efficacy and fatalism; self-esteem; cognitive flexibility; a sense of control over one's life; and measures of practical and general knowledge.[19]

Relating Quality of Life and Modernization

What can we now say about the relations of physical, material, and psychological well-being, on the one hand, and the processes of industrialization and, more broadly, of modernization, on the other? The conditions of life can of course be the cause of industrialization, driving a people to overcome their lack of natural resources or numbers and to strive to enhance their power, prestige, or wealth by adopting a highly concentrated program of industrialization. This model has been utilized to explain the rapid industrialization of Japan, and sometimes is also applied to the forced industrialization that Stalin pressed upon the Russian and other Soviet peoples. For most of us, however, the more compelling question is likely to involve a different direction in the causal sequence. We want to know whether industrialization and modernization bring about an improvement or a deterioration of the quality of life.

Getting an answer involves us in some complex analysis because the answer depends in part on which indicators we use, on what historical time period we have in mind, and to which groups of the population we pay attention. To anticipate my conclusion, however, let me state my belief that, on the whole, industrialization and modernization, in the overwhelming majority of the cases where they have been produced, have meant an improved, often vastly improved, quality of life for most people in most places in most historical periods including the present. I know this is a statement that many would challenge and, indeed, be prepared to dismiss out of hand. I am well aware of the complexities of the argument, and to deal with them with the seriousness they deserve would require a big book rather than merely a chapter-length treatment. But even in one chapter there is enough space to marshal considerable evidence bearing on my conclusion.

Contemporary Contrasts

Focusing initially on objective indicators of the material and physical kind, we may seek an answer to our question by contrasting the condition of people in the so-called advanced countries, those that the World Bank classifies as "industrial market economies," and those it places in the category of "low-income countries." In terms of our critical differentiating criterion, the latter usually have 70 percent or more of their labor force in agriculture, the former typically have only 7 percent so engaged. The World Bank, the United Nations, the International Labor Organization, the World Health Organization, and other international organizations offer us dozens of measures that make it painfully clear how much the physical and material condition of life in the poorer countries is inferior to the quality of life of those in the more advanced nations.

For me, the most dramatic and compelling of such contrasts concerns women dying in childbirth. In the low-income countries as of about 1990, for every 100,000 live births the number of women dying was 607, whereas in the so-called market economies it was eleven. In other words, when she entered her labor a woman in a less developed country was fifty-five times more likely to lose her life in the process of giving birth than was a comparable woman in one of the advanced industrial countries.[20]

Many other measures tell a similar story. Infant mortality per 1,000 live births ran 106 for the less developed versus nine for the advanced; correspondingly, life expectancy in the former was only fifty-two years, whereas it was seventy-six in the latter. Behind these statistics lie other facts. Those in the least developed countries got, on average, 1,200 fewer calories per day; they suffered many times over the most debilitating and destructive contagious diseases; and to deal with these conditions they had to share each physician with some 17,500 other persons as compared to the advanced country ratio of one physician per 550 persons. Similar contrasts prevail in most other realms. In education, for example, the chances of getting to a university for the typical person of college age was one in 100 for a resident of a less developed country, versus thirty-nine in 100 for those living in the industrialized countries. Summing it all up is the contrast in the per capita income available to average citizens in the two sets of countries, standing at about US$200 for the least advantaged as against some $13,000 for the most advanced, yielding a ratio of one to sixty-five.[21]

Industrial and Industrializing Countries Across Time

It may be objected that the type of analysis just presented does not satisfy our purpose because we well know that the rich and the poor live very differently and, in any event, there is no guarantee that in the future the currently poor nations, even if they were to industrialize, would attain the same advantages enjoyed by the now advanced countries. The appropriate response to this challenge is to review the experience of the now advanced countries to assess how far they were always advantaged, rather than having actually improved in the quality of physical life over time. Useful also, and perhaps even more relevant because it gets us out of the cultural frame of a Eurocentric analysis, would be an examination of the experience of countries that have only recently experienced a surge of industrialization and modernization, such as Taiwan, Korea, and Malaysia.

Turning first to the United States as an example of historical development, and selecting medical and health conditions as an appropriate realm to test the effects of economic growth, we may note that despite the seemingly unlimited resources available to the settlers in a virtually virgin land, the conditions of life experienced by the population before the period of industrialization were those of a typically rural, agrarian, and less developed nation. Many diseases were of course only brought under control as a result of breakthroughs in the development of new medicines and vaccines, although even these depended on the science and technology that is an integral part of the modernity syndrome. Nevertheless, I have selected for examination those common scourges that had their roots mainly in poor conditions of life, that is, in inadequate diets and lack of sanitation.

The best data are available for the State of Massachusetts, surely not one of the poorest. In 1861, at the start of the greatest industrial expansion, for every 100,000 of Massachusetts's population there were 365 cases of tuberculosis, whereas a hundred years later, after a long-term and steady decline, the number was down to fewer than six. In parallel fashion, infant mortal-

ity declined in the same hundred years from 143 per 1,000 live births, a figure comparable to that for the very poorest countries today, to about
twenty-two.[22]

Comparable data for the United States as a whole do not go so far back,
but those available from 1900 on for the diseases most conditioned by limits on diet, shelter, and sanitation tell a similar story. Thus the rates per
100,000 from 1900 to 1970 fell as follows: for influenza and pneumonia,
from 202 to thirty-one; for gastroenteritis and related conditions, from 143
to less than one; and for malaria, from close to 200 to less than two.[23]

Among the late industrializers the case of Japan is most dramatic from an
economic point of view. It is especially notable, therefore, that in 1940 the
infant mortality rate there was ninety deaths per 1,000 live births, higher
than in most developing countries today, whereas by 1986 it had fallen to
5.5, one of the lowest rates in the world.[24] Other nations that started their
industrialization and modernization still later showed comparably rapid
rates of decline in infant mortality, the shift between 1960 and 1986 of
deaths per 1,000 live births being: for Korea from eighty-five to twenty-
five; for Malaysia from seventy-three to twenty-seven; and for Thailand
from 103 to forty-one. While these countries were generally cutting infant
mortality by two-thirds or more, the nations that were failing to advance
economically reduced infant mortality much more modestly.[25]

Relating Life Conditions to Satisfaction with Life

Let us assume that I have established clearly and unambiguously that the
physical and material conditions of existence for the average citizen of the
economically less developed countries are generally much worse than those
in the industrially advanced nations, and this is so by very wide margins,
with the ratios of disparity typically in the range from one to five up to one
to thirty.[26] This puts us in a position to address the next, and for some the
most, critical issue of what difference, if any, these objective physical and
material contrasts make in how people perceive their condition and how
they feel about it. We ask the question: How much more satisfied, content,
and happy are people when their physical and material condition is of the
highest standard, and how much more frustrated, anxious, fearful, and
worried when their condition is the poorest in the world?[27]

To many, I am sure, the answer to this question will seem obvious, allowing no latitude of opinion. To others, the issues will be seen as inherently
intractable and the answer inevitably obscure because they make different
assumptions about human nature and espouse a different philosophy of living. In their view, the Chinese poet Lao Tsu was closest to the truth when
he wrote: "As want can reward you, so wealth can bewilder."[28] More con-
temporaneously, in one of the strongest affirmations of such views, d'Iri-

barne has argued that "objective indicators as currently constructed rest on implicit assumptions bearing little relationship to reality."[29] Our own experience indicates that this position is too sweeping, for, as we shall see, the data show that at least some subjective assessments closely mirror physical and material conditions and support some rather clear-cut conclusions, which I shall attempt first. But the data also reveal ambiguities, present apparent contradictions, and raise some challenging conundrums, to which I shall turn subsequently.

First I present, in Table 12.1, data on the evaluation of a set of life conditions as judged by representative samples from five continental areas studied in what the Gallup organization claimed to be "the first global public opinion survey covering sixty nations with 90 percent of the population of the free world."[30]

It is clear from these data that the people in the less advantaged countries recognize that they are deprived, worry much more about managing the demands of everyday living, and, in general, are much less likely to have a sense of satisfaction with life or to see their life as a happy one. Perhaps most clear are the progressions in the proportion of people who say yes to the question: "Have there been times during the last two years when you did not have enough money to buy food (or medicine, or clothing) for your family?" Typically, only some 15 percent of the population in North America and Europe had this experience, whereas it was the norm for 50 to 60 percent in Latin America and the Far East, with a high of 81 percent in sub-Saharan Africa reporting lack of sufficient resources to clothe their families.[31]

Making more summary judgments of their condition, less than 8 percent in North America were "not too happy," whereas this was true of 28 percent in Latin America, 31 percent in sub-Saharan Africa, and half the population in the Far East. Forty-four percent of East Asians felt that they were at the bottom of the ladder representing "the worst possible life you can imagine," whereas only 6 percent of North Americans saw their situation in such negative terms. This survey provides numerous additional contrasts in the perception by rich and poor peoples of their respective condition of life, with disparities in the proportions dissatisfied or worried often in the range of one to five. Taken together, they give grounds for supporting the Gallup study's conclusion that "nearly half the people of the world are engaged in an unending struggle for survival. Only in the advanced industrial states of the Western world can the inhabitants engage in anything akin to a 'pursuit of happiness'."[32]

Pressing the argument further, that same report concluded that it was "most striking that the gulf which separates the advanced societies from the developing nations in respect to *material* well-being is just as wide in respect to *psychological* well-being."[33] However, they did not specifically test this proposition in the way that the argument about physical and material

Table 12.1 Regional patterns in evaluations of quality of life (percentage reporting condition)

	North America[a]	Western Europe	Latin America	Sub-Saharan Africa	Far East
Worry a lot	34	42	61	43	60
Satisfied with health[b]	73	64	62	45	30
Satisfied with housing[b]	67	64	51	23	19
Satisfied with living standard[b]	59	53	48	30	44
Not able to meet expenses[c]	26	22	69	69	68
No money for food[c]	14	8	40	71	58
No money for medicine[c]	15	5	40	57	48
Life in general "not too happy"	9	18	28	31	50
Life near worst possible[d]	6	8	13	28	44

[a]Calculated from tables in Kettering and Gallup 1977. North America is represented by the United States. Canada is represented in Table 12.2. See text for explanation.

[b]The figure for those "satisfied" equals the cumulative percentage who placed themselves on the top four rungs of a ten-step ladder of satisfaction.

[c]Represents those who said they lacked money for various needs "all the time" or "most of the time."

[d]Proportion placing themselves on lowest four rungs on the ladder of possible life satisfaction.

conditions was tested. We may then ask: How strong is the association between objective advantage and subjective feelings of deprivation?

More than a decade before the Gallup global survey, Hadley Cantril, working with outcome measures very similar to those later used by Gallup, elaborated a "development index," based on eleven objective measures including GNP per capita, and compared national scores on the index with those on the ladder of life. The rank-order correlation between the standing of the fourteen national samples on the index of development and where their populations stood in satisfaction on the ladder of life, was .67.[34] Much later, for the period around 1984, Inglehart correlated national average "satisfaction with life scores" with the GNP per capita for twenty-four countries, mostly in Europe, and obtained a comparable level of a .67 correlation.[35]

It seems clear from these results that knowing the level of a nation's economic development tells us a good deal about how the population will rate its conditions of life. But it is also apparent that the association is very imperfect, since we are predicting only some 45 percent of the variance even with such highly aggregated data. It is time, then, to look to the anomalies, conundrums, and apparent contradictions. We should also enlarge our explanatory scheme to take account of other factors, among which two are critical. First comes the role of cultural traditions that may strongly mute or intensify the expression of satisfactions and discontents, and second, we must take account of the psychology of adjustment, which apparently leads people to bring their aspirations so far into line with the realities of their situation as to greatly diminish the extent to which expressed satisfaction exactly mirrors objective disadvantage.

Cultural Sensitivities and Distinctive National Response Propensities

In his pioneering study *The Pattern of Human Concerns*, Hadley Cantril long ago called attention to the fact that populations in generally *comparable* social and economic conditions nevertheless showed markedly *different* preoccupations when asked what they were most concerned about. At the same time, one could point to instances in which national populations *differing* markedly in their economic condition nevertheless expressed certain concerns in *equal* degree. Thus when West Germany and the United States were paired as two well-developed nations, the latter showed almost twice as many people worried about family life as did the former. And when two very poor countries such as India and Egypt were paired, the Egyptians proved to be worried about ill health twice as often as the Indians. Cantril also noted that "in the 'rich' United States economic aspirations and fears were mentioned almost as frequently as they were in 'poor' India."[36]

Similar distinctive national patterns were later reported in the Gallup world poll. The French, for example, were outstanding among developed countries in the proportion who worry a lot, but they were much like the European average in the satisfaction they found in family life, whereas the Japanese were only half as often worried as the French, but very seldom took pleasure in family life.[37]

Of course it might be argued that such variation in the sensitivities and satisfactions of national populations will tend to be randomly distributed and thus would cancel themselves out when peoples came to assess their *overall* condition. But there is strong evidence (assembled in Table 12.2) to suggest that the response to one's objective condition is strongly influenced by cultural propensities to see most things in either a positive or negative light. Thus, it is clear (from the data in Table 12.2) that Brazilians have a strong propensity to see things more positively, expressing much more satisfaction in their health and educational attainments than their objective condition would seem to justify. Indeed, on many dimensions the proportion of people well satisfied with life conditions in Brazil equals or exceeds that in the most advanced countries of Europe and North America. By contrast the French as well as the Italians repeatedly showed markedly smaller proportions satisfied, and larger proportions worried and discontented, than was the case with their comparably advanced European partners.

The pattern observed in the evaluation of the various specific domains of life was manifested in the summary judgments as well. The English-speaking world, represented by the United States and most of Canada—but also the United Kingdom and Australia—is populated by individuals who tend to be well above the European average in the frequency with which they report themselves as happy and as satisfied with life in general. The French and the Italians are fairly consistently well below average in this respect. The Brazilians, on the other hand, seem impervious to the reality of their objective situation, and report levels of general satisfaction equal to those found in the most advanced countries in the world. At the other end of the continuum, the Japanese, despite their great economic success, seem remarkably unable to muster any but the smallest number ready to place themselves in the category of the most satisfied and most happy. All this should make it apparent why efforts to relate GNP per capita or other indexes of economic development to life satisfaction do not yield strong correlations. It is because national groups display a response propensity—evidently an aspect of their cultural orientation—to see most things in either a positive or a negative light.

Differences Within Countries

Another great challenge to the idea that objective differences in people's material and physical life situation ought to determine their level of happi-

Table 12.2 Qualify of life as perceived in different nations (percentage expressing certain views)

	Canada	United States	West Germany	France	Italy	European Economic Community	Brazil	Japan
Worry a lot	36	31	31	50	45	39	58	25
Very satisfied with family[a]	47	43	39	37	34	39	57	14
Very satisfied with health[a]	44	40	23	28	28	31	42	22
Very satisfied with housing[a]	37	27	32	24	20	28	37	35
Very satisfied with standard of living[a]	24	16	18	7	14	15	22	8
Not able to meet expenses[b]	15	22	10	22	29	19	50	41
No money for food[b]	6	8	7	6	15	8	26	14
No money for medicine[b]	4	1	1	8	9	5	36	5
Generally very happy	36	38	12	22	9	22	36	9
Very satisfied with life in general[a]	18	17	11	8	8	12	14	5

[a]The very satisfied in these cases represent all those who had placed themselves on the top two steps of a ten-step ladder of possible satisfaction.

[b]Percentages represent those who reported lack of sufficient money "all the time" or "most of the time."

Source: Calculated from Tables in Kettering and Gallup 1977.

ness and satisfaction comes from the analyses comparing individuals with differing degrees of objective advantage *living within the same country.* Logically, if we assume that the average person in a poor country will be less satisfied with his or her life than an average person in a rich country, then it should be true that *within* any country the rich, those with the prestigious jobs, and those who have garnered the most education, would also be more satisfied and that there would be a regular progression of such satisfaction as one moved up the several different ladders of lifetime achievements.

As it turns out, this proposition does hold, broadly speaking, but the statistical association is so weak as to seem quite counterintuitive. Thus in a regression analysis that I applied to a joint index of satisfaction and happiness for each of the countries covered by the Eurobarometer survey, the eight most powerful objective variables—including income, education, and occupation—could explain only an extremely small proportion of the variance, at worst a mere 1.2 percent in the Netherlands and at best 8.5 percent in Italy. Within country after country I found the proportion happy and satisfied among the rich and the poor to be much the same, as it was when I compared those with prestigious jobs and those who do society's dirty work. Moreover, this outcome is not unique to my research, nor to the Eurobarometer nations but rather has been well documented in independent investigations in other places.[38]

In contrast with the socioeconomic status variables such as income and occupation, entering "country" as a variable into the regression made a much more appreciable difference. Putting all the national samples in the Eurobarometer survey together in a single pool, and then using eight objective explanatory variables such as income, we found that we could explain almost 14 percent of the variance in our summary scale of well-being. Of this total, however, the other seven objective variables together could explain only 2.6 percent of the variance, whereas the country variable explained 9.3 percent, three and one-half times the impact of the other variables in the equation combined.[39]

This again provides strong evidence for the relative importance of the cultural factor in explaining differences in expressed well-being. But even though the cultural factor is a much more powerful predictor of satisfaction in life than are the usual socioeconomic measures, it too leaves a great deal unexplained. In particular, we are challenged by the implication that whatever government may do, and however much we improve objective standards of living, people will be no more satisfied than they were before their economic situation improved. We must therefore turn to such measures as we have available to assess how far *changes* in the condition of individuals and communities may be reflected in their perceived and expressed sense of satisfaction and well-being.

The Effect of Changed Conditions

Expressions of well-being are not immutable. On the contrary, there is considerable evidence to support the argument that they are intelligibly responsive to changed circumstance. People who experience an improvement in their financial condition in any year respond by expressing much more satisfaction with their standard of living in the immediately subsequent period.[40] Divorced women express strongly negative assessments of the state of their interpersonal relations almost six times more often than do all married women and thirteen times more often than former widows who have experienced the gratification of being newly married.[41] Black men in America show their feelings about being economically disadvantaged and socially discriminated against by reporting themselves "not too happy" twice as often as do whites.[42] Unemployed persons, but especially men, have markedly lower scores on indices of well-being than do those who still have jobs at comparable levels of skill and training.[43]

Given such responsiveness of the life satisfaction measures to changed conditions of existence, it would seem reasonable that at the national level we should find rising standards of living—especially of the kind associated with successful industrialization and modernization—to be reflected in increasing proportions of the populations in the more successful nations declaring themselves happy and expressing general satisfaction with life. But this assumption must meet some stiff challenges. Indeed, the predominant opinion, largely shaped by Richard Easterlin's pathbreaking study, holds that improving the living standards of a nation does not lead to increases in the sense of well-being in the population.[44]

It is notable that most countries, most of the time, report levels of satisfaction that are remarkably stable over periods of a decade or longer. For example, for the ten countries covered in the Eurobarometer, the absolute percentages of those reporting themselves as "very happy" fluctuated very little over the decade from 1976 to 1986, and the relative standing of each country in relation to all the others was remarkably stable.[45] A decade is of course a short span of time, but data for longer spans of time suggest the same kind of stability. Thus Gallup showed thirty-nine percent of the U.S. population claiming to be "very happy" in 1946, and a virtually identical proportion of 40 percent thirty years later.[46] Much the same kind of stability over thirty years was manifested by Canada and Great Britain.[47]

France, however, showed considerable improvement in this thirty-year period, with its proportion "very happy" rising from 8 percent to 22 percent. In 1946 France was of course barely freed from German occupation and was still reeling from the shock of the wartime destruction of its economy. The observed change can therefore be interpreted as showing that general improvements in a nation's condition, at least in part economic, can produce a considerable increase in the proportion of satisfied or happy individuals. To test this idea we should have data for longer periods and for more countries that have undergone industrialization and modernization in recent decades. And it would be helpful to have the indicators include a score for satisfaction with life, which might serve our purpose better than the measure of happiness, which is considered more volatile.

Taiwan, Korea, and Thailand, among others, would be ideal candidates, but, at least to date, I have not located the necessary data for these countries, and they might not exist. However, appropriate data are available for five nations whose populations placed themselves on the ladder of life around 1960 and then again some seventeen years later in 1977. All but one enjoyed vigorous economic growth in the period in question,[48] and all but that one showed marked increases in the proportions well satisfied with their lives. The percentage placing themselves on the top four rungs of the ladder of life in West Germany rose from 25 percent to 50 percent; in Brazil, from 22 percent to 42 percent; and the United States from 52 percent to 75 percent. Cantril also presented data for Japan, although in somewhat different form, and there too our calculation suggests a strong upward movement in the proportion placing themselves on the top rungs of the ladder, with the number rising from 17 percent to 32 percent. India's economy was growing much more slowly in this period, and that seems to have been reflected in a much more modest increase in the proportion of those placing themselves on the top four rungs of the ladder, starting at slightly over 4 percent around 1960 and still at a low 7 percent in 1976.[49]

Our findings must meet the challenge of seemingly contradictory evidence.[50] We must also allow for the real possibility that these results are an artifact of our method.[51] But if they are not such an artifact, then the conclusion seems warranted that as economic conditions improve in particular countries, especially as reflected in per capita income, then the proportions of the population who express satisfaction with the general condition of their lives also increases.[52]

Of course we must entertain some caveats with regard to this conclusion. First, there must surely be ceiling effects, such that increases in the percentage of people content with life become harder and harder to achieve as the average proportion satisfied moves into the range of 70 percent and higher. Secondly, regardless of the absolute level of satisfaction, there are probably comparison and "diminishing returns" effects, so that a given economic gain won against a background of economic deprivation will bring larger increments in satisfaction than will a gain of the same magnitude, absolute or proportional, won at higher absolute levels of affluence. Many other constraints on raising the levels of satisfaction in contemporary communities may be suggested, not least among them the fact that increasing affluence, especially that based on industrial expansion, brings with it a host of new discouragements. Roads become choked with cars whose occupants, and others in turn, choke on smog-filled air; people find fish laced with toxic substances and meat larded with chemicals; they boat on, or stroll along, rivers that have been turned into open sewers; they worry that their housing may have been built over hidden poisonous waste dumps; and on vacation they find it harder and harder to locate pristine forests to camp in before all the trees are either lumbered or die of acid rain exposure.

So here we rest. We have some evidence that national levels of expressed well-being may be relatively constant despite rising levels of economic wealth and an increasing flow of goods and services, a constant that could be explained either by deep-seated cultural propensities or by the tendency of the new problems faced and burdens imposed on modern populations to offset the positive effects of material prosperity and social and political freedom. We also have some evidence, more limited and possibly less reliable, that nevertheless supports the reasonable proposition that in countries experiencing marked increases in the standard of living and in general economic and social development, the populations do show increasing proportions satisfied with what their lives bring them from day to day.

To come much closer to a resolution of the disagreement among these positions we must hope to find data for key countries such as Taiwan, Korea, Thailand, Singapore, Hong Kong, and Malaysia over the period of their most vigorous economic growth. If those countries can be shown to have been following the pattern that I suggested may have earlier characterized Brazil, Japan, and West Germany, then that will provide less discouraging evidence for policymakers and a more encouraging prospect for those seeking to improve the physical conditions they live in, since in that case they may assume that the increases in the flow of goods and services that industrialization and modernization bring will also gain for the population a heightened sense of psychological well-being. However, we must also assume from experience that such gains will be constrained by two counter forces. First, cultural propensities seem to determine the general range within which any national population falls in expressing happiness and life satisfaction. And second, we may expect sharp increases in the levels of expressed satisfaction to be followed by a stabilization of each national population at a new level as people become accustomed to their prosperity, and new improvements come to have little or no effect on satisfaction because of the continually heightened expectations that develop.

thirteen

CONTINUITY AND CHANGE IN POPULAR VALUES ON THE PACIFIC RIM

In the heart of the Brazil's rain forest, near the city of Manaus, two great streams come together in a distinctive, perhaps unique, way. One branch, the Amazon, arrives a muddy, sand-colored, churning river. The other branch, flowing equally strongly, is more nearly brown, close to the color of tobacco, noticeably clear and even translucent.[1] At the point where the two rivers come together, they do not immediately blend but rather run side by side within common banks for several miles, so sharply delineated at their common margin that one could easily imagine that there was a great glass wall separating the two. But gradually the swirling and eddying effect of the river becomes manifest. The two streams begin to run together at the edges and then gradually blend into a new, more uniform consistency. A few miles farther on the Amazon becomes one uniform stream, once again a predominantly muddy sand color. Perhaps a scientific test of the waters could identify the separate elements that had been carried into the mixture of the two great tributaries. But to most observers the new river would seem to reflect the original Amazon more than the stream that had so recently joined it.

Presented as the keynote address at the conference "Diffusion of Core Values Through Formal and Informal Education in Asia and the Pacific," jointly sponsored by the Pacific Basin Research Center, Soka University of America, and the University of Hong Kong, held in Hong Kong, January 12–14, 1997.

Just so in Asia, and especially on the Pacific Rim, we see the confluence of two great streams of culture operating under the vast and powerful stimulus of industrialization, urbanization, modernization, and globalization. As in my geographic account, these two streams—Asian and Western—manage for a period to run side by side, preserving remarkably intact their distinctive identities. But as time elapses, and as they become increasingly entangled with each other, a vast blending ensues. Both great sources contribute in significant ways to the new melded stream. But, I believe, the nature of the forces at work ensures that one of the streams will predominate and that the emergent new river will reflect the long-standing properties of the one more than the other.

The river metaphor, and the model it suggests of modernization as a dominant force in the contemporary world, certainly has imperfections and surely can operate only within certain parameters. Although acknowledging these limitations, I believe that the metaphor and the model capture the essence of the great transformation that many societies and cultures on the Pacific Rim are currently experiencing.

Conceptual and Methodological Issues

If we are making a case for change, we need to agree on the character of the entities whose change we purport to document and on some common standards that will enable us to judge whether or not change has occurred.

One great strand in the web of change girdling the Pacific Rim may be broadly characterized as organizational or structural. One example might be the development of a modern system of law and its supporting institutions and professions—courts, barristers and solicitors, wardens and prisons—under British rule in Hong Kong. At the same level of importance is the development of the political structure in Taiwan, with its system of legislative bodies, effective administrative apparatus, and ultimately freestanding and competitive political parties. Along similar lines, varying by place and time, a whole panoply of institutional change and innovation in social structure, especially in the economic and political spheres, has spread over the Pacific Rim. Profound changes have been introduced in education, in the occupational structure, in urbanization, and in transportation and communication. These changes may be thought of as the main force producing the shifts in attitude and behavior that I have taken as the focus of my investigation. I here note in passing how aware I am of this process of structural transformation and commit myself, as I come to my conclusions, to return to those structures and their influence.

Apart from structural change, there are at least two great realms of human response that may be seen as the proper foci of our attention. Those realms may be thought of as broadly divided into the cognitive and the behavioral. As manifestations of the cognitive I have particularly in mind attitudes and values, images of the good life, personal aspirations, and ideas about interpersonal relations both formal and intimate. Such mental sets and ways of thinking about the world are properly separated from, and understood to stand in a problematic relationship to, actual behavior. Thus people may affirm the virtue of charity but give little to private welfare organizations; they may stress the moral obligation for filial piety without necessarily providing for the suitable maintenance of their aged parents.

A Methodological Excursus

As we get closer to our subject matter, a number of challenges, or perhaps cautions, confront us, stemming in part from differences in style of various investigators but also arising from experience, sometimes bitter experience, in the pursuit of the issue at hand.

Measures over Time.   If we take seriously the idea that we are looking for evidence of *continuity* and *change* in attitude, value, and behavior, we must acknowledge that the form in which most data will be available to us does not provide a compelling basis for judging the relative stability over time of popular sentiments in the Pacific Rim countries. Unfortunately, a large number of the most interesting questions have been asked only once. We are thus usually left with an *absolute* datum taken at a single point in time rather than having the preferable *relative* fact for several points in time. To get around this limitation, we must evaluate the single observation we have for the current situation against the condition we *assume* existed at an earlier time. That assumption, in turn, is based on historical and cultural analysis.

Consider, for example, what happens if current research finds some 75 percent of young women in an Asian population saying that they expect to select their own mate rather than have their parents make the selection. If our historical and cultural analyses of that population suggest that in earlier times it was standard for parents to select spouses for their children, then we may *assume* that our current information reflects a substantial change in norms and probably in behavior. But we cannot know for *certain* that there was such a change because our reading of the historical and cultural record, and the assumptions based on it, may simply have been in error.

Given the risk of being misled by such assumptions, we should wherever possible seek to build our case on measures applied at more than one point in time.[2] Even having data for two points in time can put us at risk of premature closure. For example, we may be tempted to make a good deal of a shift of ten percentage points in the popularity of a given attitude, neglecting the fact that with the kind of sample used in the study, we must assume a margin of error of at least 6 percent.

Lack of measures over time will surely tempt us to substitute what is often assumed to be reasonably equivalent, namely, the analysis of age groups within the *same* sample. A steady progression of attitude change as one moves across the age range within a national sample may certainly indicate real *cohort* or *generational* change, but, alas, it may also merely reflect the influence of aging. This kind of evidence should therefore always be closely scrutinized to ascertain to what extent we can assume that the observed shifts across age groups are unlikely to be an artifact of the mere process of aging.[3] Much less ambiguity attends this issue when, as in the studies by Martin Whyte, different *generations* within the same families constitute the sample.[4]

Ideally, therefore, we should have measures for the same or broadly comparable populations over two or more points in time. As I have noted, some studies meet this demanding criterion, and insofar as they confirm the impressions from other sources, they greatly strengthen our confidence in the conclusions. In general, however, we must accept a lesser standard of rigor in the quality of the data we have available. That, in turn, requires us to acknowledge the tentativeness of our conclusions, at least as concerns any single trend or tendency.

The General Versus the Specific.   There is a great, and at times seemingly unresolvable, tension between those who stress the distinctiveness, indeed even the uniqueness, of the change process in a particular setting and culture and those who believe in and seek to find comparatively general processes across nations and cultures. I cannot resolve this tension, and candor requires that I acknowledge that I have a disposition to search for the general. Fairness of course obliges me to be ready, as I think I have been, to acknowledge the many instances that my locally rooted colleagues have offered showing how, in their particular microcosm, the presumably general forces I deal with have operated differently from the way they operated elsewhere, thus challenging the validity of some too-sweeping generalization. Although gladly accepting this caution, I hold that it is nevertheless intellectually appropriate to search for the more general and to insist as well that exceptions, within certain limits, do not invalidate generalizations so long as these are stated in less than absolute or universal terms. Generalizations, however basically sound, cannot in themselves deny the validity of what seem to be exceptions, but neither should exceptions, even if well documented, be assumed to disprove the validity of generalizations that have been properly stated with clear limits.

A comparable tension, encouraging a similar type of challenge and caution, involves generalizing across the elements within a single, broadly defined realm of human activity such as the system of kinship and marriage. Evidence that a considerable number of the elements of such a system have changed, indeed changed profoundly, does not constitute proof that all elements of the given realm have changed in equal degree or even have changed at all. As we shall see, there are communities in which the virtually universal selection by parents of their children's mates has been almost totally replaced by individual choice, yet in those same communities commitment to the support of aged parents remains undiminished. Global images of change sweeping across each and every aspect of some complex system of human relations may easily fail to differentiate and discriminate among those elements of a system that change and those that persist in the face of seemingly general change. There is a parallel here with the analysis of cultures. Change in most aspects of a social subsystem, such as that regulating marriage and family life, cannot be taken as proof of change in all aspects of that subsystem. But it is equally true that well-documented exceptions to a general pattern of change across some broad range of elements of a sociocultural system, however notable, do not in themselves prove that a generalization, properly circumscribed, is in error. They only prove that it has limits, limits we are happy to acknowledge. Indeed, in locating the limits of our generalizations, and in seeking to explain the exceptions, we find some of the most interesting and challenging tasks for the student of social change.

The Evidence for Continuity and Change

I present evidence to illustrate four processes, which I designate as (1) the strengthening of tradition, (2) the persistence of tradition, (3) the adaptation of tradition, and (4) the abandonment of tradition and the substitution of new attitudes and values.

I cannot at this point claim to have done an exhaustive survey or, indeed, one that is rigorously systematic in its search for evidence. Rather, I have searched for studies that meet high standards with regard to sampling, design, and data analysis. One consequence of this selection procedure has been to limit the number of nations represented in my survey. As of this writing I have found the kind of data I consider relevant to my purpose only for Hong Kong, Taiwan, mainland China, and Japan, with some modest representation of the former East Pakistan (now Bangladesh) as well as India. Adequate representation of the Pacific Rim as a whole requires that I find comparable data for nations including Singapore, Indonesia, Malaysia, and the Philippines. At the same time, in deciding which issues to discuss, I have cast my net rather widely since evidence on many issues of theoretical and practical importance is not abundant. Taken together, however, there is a considerable weight of available evidence that, as I read it, is notable in its consistency across populations and study topics. It satisfies me that the peoples of the Pacific Rim have been and are undergoing a remarkable reorientation and transformation of values and lifestyles that, in their depth, scope, speed, and intensity, closely matches the extraordinary economic development that those same populations have been enjoying over recent decades.

The Strengthening of Tradition

In a world in which various kinds of religious fundamentalism are burgeoning on every hand as a response to the perceived threats of modernization and Westernization, it seems appropriate to inquire whether the nations on the Pacific Rim may be experiencing some of the same tendencies. Indeed, Lau and Kuan envisioned the possibility of an "erosion of modern elements by traditional concerns" and "a reinvigoration of traditional forms."[5] I see little evidence that the Pacific Rim is anywhere generating the kind of intense reassertion of tradition that is evident in many parts of the Muslim world, but there are indications that some Asian populations are in some ways reinvigorating traditions that had been slipping away under the impact of forces for change. In some cases the pattern seems to be one in which an externally forced process of change, such as that imposed by the cultural revolution in China, has been lifted, permitting the expression of value commitments that had never fully died out. At least this is the interpretation I put on the data from Baoding, where the now adult offspring are more likely than their elderly parents, who lived through the Maoist era, to *disagree* with the modern idea that obligations to children or careers should come ahead of obligations to parents.[6]

Ancestor Worship.   Ancestral worship is a widespread and deep-seated element of many Asian cultures. Yet it is also something one might expect has been eroded by the acids of the modernizing experience. It is therefore notable that in Taiwan there seems to have been a resurgence of commitment to this ancient tradition. Between 1963 and 1991 the proportion of Taiwanese who claimed to have attended an ancestor worship ceremony increased from 39 percent to 75 percent.[7] Something similar, although less dramatic, may have occurred in Shanghai.[8] These developments can perhaps be explained as exemplifying a principle I first enunciated in my research on individual modernity in six developing countries: Contrary to popular expectation, the more modern individuals claimed to be fulfilling the practice requirements of their religion more often than the nominally more "traditional" individuals in our samples. We reasoned about this outcome as follows: To fulfill the practice obligations of one's religion requires that one be reasonably integrated and functioning effectively in one's environment. In addition, such practices often require the outlay of some moneys. Both these conditions were more likely to be met by individuals who had fully joined the modern economy. Following this logic, we might argue that on the Pacific Rim as well, the more individuals increased their incomes and sought the outward signs of social respectability, the more they might be expected to participate in selected religious practices and rituals that earlier they felt they had neither the free energy nor the discretionary income to expend on such gestures.[9]

Filial Piety.   One additional example of the strengthening of tradition comes to us from the long-term studies of the national character of Japan mounted by Professor Hayashi and his collaborators every five years from 1953 on. In their assessment of *giri-ninjo,* which they identified as a key element of Japanese culture, they asked their national samples to select two values, from a set of four, to which the respondents felt most committed. One of the four was "filial piety."[10] Contrary to expectations, the preference for filial piety rose year by year. In 1963, the first year this question was asked, filial piety was selected by 61 percent of the respondents, but by 1983 it had risen in popularity to 73 percent; it held its rank as the number-one value in subsequent surveys through 1993.

Clearly there is some evidence that on the Pacific Rim, much as in other parts of the world, the response to the forces of modernization may be an actual recommitment to, and a strengthening of, some traditional values and behaviors. At the same time, it must be acknowledged that in this region of the world such reaffirmations seem modest in number.

The Persistence of Tradition

If we expected traditions to be reaffirmed and strengthened beyond the historical norm, we may have set too high a requirement. Perhaps it should be enough if traditions persist at roughly the level of commitment they experienced before the countries of the Pacific Rim were washed over by the tides of industrialization and modernization. To assess this, I especially searched for evidence over time. I found that despite changes in the economy and the opening of society to Western influences, many traditions managed to hold steady in their support from the populations on the Rim.

I begin with an item about which I believe those who know the Pacific Rim are least likely to take exception. Most are aware of the reputation of those of Chinese origin for hard work, steadfastness of effort, and readiness to sacrifice and save. These characteristics are shared by many of the peoples on the Pacific Rim. One can easily imagine, however, that some forty years of Chinese socialism may have deeply eroded these tendencies in a population long organized in communal enterprises and encouraged to become totally dependent on their *danwei* (local production unit), at close hand, and on the communist state, at greater remove. But this seems not to have happened. In 1990 the population in and around Shanghai was asked to rate some eighteen basic values. The score for each value was given as the percentage affirming a value minus the percentage of those opposed to it. At the top of the list stood the values diligence and frugality with a score of +86, indicating that virtually everyone was for this value and that few denied its relevance. Further supporting the claim that in the population of China the old value of hard work persisted despite forty years of communism, the same survey showed that 72 percent of the people of Shanghai considered that failure in life was a result of "not working hard enough," even though the question offered them the alternative of blaming such an outcome on "fate."[11]

Filial Piety. I turn next to a topic already introduced, namely, filial piety, but I excuse the repetition because this sentiment is so often cited as distinctive to many of the cultures of Asia. My evidence, which comes from Baoding on the mainland, has the advantage that both the elders and their adult children in the same family were asked the same question. If there were a movement across generations this would surely be the ideal design for identifying a value shift. Instead, across the generations the value of filial piety was affirmed with a remarkable consistency, with approximately 95 percent of both the elders and their adult children stressing their absolute commitment to this value.

Supporting evidence comes from a survey of the people of Hong Kong. In this case I have neither a generational survey nor a survey over time to assess stability, but since a striking 88 percent of the respondents agreed with the idea that "government should punish the unfilial," it seems reasonable to interpret the result as evidence of the persistence of a traditional value. There seems every reason to accept Martin Whyte's conclusion that "filial obligations are robustly intact, with little sign that parents and children are separated by a 'generation gap' when it comes to these attitudes."[12]

Dominant Opinion in Japan. Turning to Japan, I assess the persistence of traditional views by examining the stability over time of a set of so-called dominant opinions. In the Japanese national character research, a view of the world was defined as a "dominant opinion" if 75 percent or more of the population held that view. Because they win such high consensus, these orientations might be broadly interpreted as defining the essential elements of the national culture, ethos, or belief system.

In the forty-year period from 1953, when the first survey was done, to 1993, the latest year reported, some opinions readily recognized as characteristically Japanese held steady as dominant opinions despite the many forces for change that might have been expected to erode their support. I cite here, to illustrate the pattern, four such persistent attitudes:[13]

1. Giving a job to the person who scored higher on a test rather than to a qualified relative who scored lower[14]

2. Preferring a boss who will sometimes demand extra work from you,
   despite rules to the contrary, but who looks after you personally in
   matters not connected with the work, over a boss who sticks to the
   rules and makes no unreasonable demands but never does things for
   you in matters not connected to the work[15]
3. Preferring to work in a firm with a family-like atmosphere, even if it
   means accepting lower wages[16]
4. Preferring a picture of an attractive Japanese-style garden over an attractive English-style garden[17]

Data to test for such persistence in other settings on the Pacific Rim are
not readily available because it is rare that studies are done over time using
the same standard questions. However, when a traditional value readily
identifiable as a characteristic element of Asian belief systems wins virtually
unanimous support from a population as thoroughly modernized in its economic life and as totally open to Western influence as is the population of
Hong Kong, it seems reasonable to interpret the result as evidence of the
persistence of values. It is in this way we interpret the fact that in Hong
Kong in 1987 some 91 percent of the people supported the principle that
"officials should set a moral example."

Continuity in Chinese Thought Patterns.   A different kind of evidence for
the persistence of cultural patterns in the face of extensive economic, social,
and political change is offered by Thomas Metzger. His reading of a wide
range of recent and contemporary philosophical, political, and sociological
Chinese writing leads him to assert that there exists a major Chinese cultural strand, made up of a broad range of intellectual writing, whether the
writer is a communist or a member of the Kuomintang, on the left or the
right, a conservator or a modernizer. Across these otherwise critical divisions, he argues, there is a shared style of intellectual discourse, which he
characterizes as "an optimistic, transformative, Napoleonic belief that intellectuals can grasp the ultimate nature of reality and control history."
Further elaborating on the common features of this type of discourse,
which, he argues, can be traced far back in the history of Chinese thought,
Metzger delineates four characteristic elements:

1. *Utopianism* as a way of defining the goal of human life
2. *Epistemological optimism,* "holding that a total, objective, systematic understanding of human life can be obtained to guide action"
3. *History as a teleological process* moving inexorably toward the ultimate goals of humankind
4. *Agency* of a socially visible group, usually seen as the intellectuals,
   who can grasp the right theoretical system *(t'i-hsi)* and use it to in-

fluence the course of development of China and perhaps the whole world[18]

The Adaptation of Tradition

Some traditions truly persist. Others, however, may only seem to persist, maintaining their external form or their obedience to the religious or ritual calendar but nevertheless in actual content are transformed into something quite different. It is a moot point whether such phenomena should be counted as additional evidence of how persistent tradition can be or, on the contrary, should be weighed as evidence of how economic and social change engender change in a culture. I take no stand on the issue but feel it necessary to note that my survey of continuity and change in Asian values identified a number of instances of the seeming persistence of traditions that on closer examination proved to have been profoundly adapted, so that they were quite different from the tradition they presumably continued. The phenomenon warrants further and fuller exploration, but I can only pause in my exposition for a single illustration.

My example again involves the phenomenon of ancestor worship, with the evidence coming from the population of Shanghai, where 44 percent of the people surveyed in 1990 felt that it was a moral obligation to visit and sweep tombs. Given the long history of communist opposition to this idea and the associated practice, it might be argued that having so relatively high a proportion of Shanghai citizens still affirming the importance of tomb sweeping is evidence of the persistence of tradition. But Chu and Ju note the anomaly that tomb sweeping is stressed in the face of the fact that in Shanghai today there are few tombs one could visit and sweep. Moreover, according to Chu and Ju, what people are here talking about and doing has little to do with ancestor worship in the sense in which it was practiced in earlier times. Rather, the practice has been transformed into a kind of social occasion and a way of expressing solidarity with living relatives. Instead of being true ancestor worship, the event has now become the occasion for a family gathering, "usually meaning having a small family dinner with relatives on the birthday of a deceased parent."[19]

The Abandonment of Tradition

We come now to the main part of the story. Although one can find some evidence of the strengthening, the persistence, and the adaptation of tradition, the frequency with which one can document such occurrences is modest compared to the mountain of evidence that in numerous Pacific Rim nations traditions are being massively abandoned in one realm of life after another. The Pacific Rim is being inundated by a flood of forces exposing it to industrialization, modernization, and globalization. Occupational systems are being transformed, mass communication of all kinds is washing over every shore and reaching every distant corner, transportation and associated human movement are being extended, deepened, and greatly speeded up, knowledge is being redefined and revalued. In the process, many fundamental values are being challenged and reformulated, basic human relationships are redefined and reordered, and numerous traditional ways of thinking and behaving are undergoing a great transformation.

To document fully this massive abandonment of tradition is beyond the scope of this chapter. A modest selection of the evidence across a series of realms, however, may serve to suggest the depth, the scope, and the force of the argument.

Family, Marriage, and Kinship. Few aspects of human relations can claim to be more fundamental than those grouped under the rubric of family, marriage, and kinship. Yet few realms exceed this in the degree of change in tradition that they manifest.

Continuing the Lineage. Continuity of the family name in Japan has for centuries had the status of an almost sacred responsibility. When the head of a family produced no male heir, it was essential that an appropriate male be adopted to carry forward the family name. In the years immediately after World War II, despite the great upheaval Japan was experiencing, a striking 73 percent of a national sample affirmed the idea that it was necessary to adopt a child to continue the family line "even if there was no blood connection." In every subsequent five-year period, however, fewer and fewer people supported this idea. After twenty years, in the 1973 survey, the proportion taking this position had been cut in half to 36 percent, and at the latest report, from the 1993 survey, it had sunk to 22 percent, considerably less than one-third its original strength.[20]

Surveys taken in Taiwan indicate that there too the population was responding in a manner similar to the way people were responding in Japan. In this case we do not have numerous periodic reports, but we do have information for two relatively widely separated points in time. In 1963, 70 percent of the Taiwanese considered it "very important" that one have a male heir "to transmit the lineage"; by 1991 the proportion was down to 32 percent.[21]

Choosing a Marriage Partner. Perhaps no decision in life is more important than determining whom one will marry, and all the more so in societies in which divorce is infrequent and difficult to obtain. From Chengdu, on mainland China, comes evidence of a virtually total transformation in the practice of finding a mate.

Martin Whyte divided his sample from Chengdu according to the year in which individuals were married. For each event he knew from his informants whether it had followed the tradition of arranged marriages or whether the individuals had found their mates in some other way. The oldest cohort consisted of people who had married between 1933 and 1948. Thereafter they were grouped in five-year intervals, except for the last cohort, which included all those whose marriages had occurred between 1977 and 1987.

It is hard to imagine a more profound shift in fundamental human values and behavior than that reflected in the reports of the residents of Chengdu. In the cohorts married before the communist victory, 68 percent reported that their marriages had been "arranged," but in the last cohort the proportion of arranged marriages had dwindled to a mere 2 percent! Almost equally dramatic was a shift in the proportion affirming the importance of being in love as a condition for marrying. In the oldest cohort love had been a factor in 17 percent of the cases, but by the 1977–1987 cohort it was an important consideration in 67 percent of the marriages. Given both Chinese cultural mores and the puritanism of the communist regime, it is also notable that having sex with one's affianced before the wedding rose from 4 percent in the marriages occurring in the earliest period to 18 percent of those entered into during the 1980s.[22]

The striking pattern that Whyte reported for Chengdu was also manifested in Taiwan, although the data there covered a somewhat shorter span of time, with the sample made up of six cohorts starting with those married in 1955 and ending with those married between 1980 and 1984. As on the mainland, in Taiwan marriages in which the parents decided on the marriage partner fell over time from 53 to 11 percent of the cases; marrying without have first gone through a period of dating fell from 51 percent to a mere 4 percent; and having had sex before the actual marriage rose from 13 percent to 37 percent. In short, the patterns of change in Taiwan were, broadly speaking, identical with those observed in Chengdu.[23]

This evidence from Taiwan makes it clear that the shift reported for Chengdu was not merely an artifact of communist control of every aspect of life. Rather we are led to conclude that broad forces of social change—occupational, educational, and spiritual—were at work in both places and that they had the same effect despite the differences in the socioeconomic and political systems governing these two settings.

Basic Values and Life-Guiding Principles. In perhaps in no other realm is the evidence for a fundamental shift in values more extreme or more visible than in the basic values for living, in the goals and aspirations one holds out for oneself and one's children, and in the perception of the good and bad in human relations. In place of the dominance of the clan, the community, and the family, the individual and the self come increasingly to be the key points of reference for both the society and the person. In place of subordination of the self to common interests, and the enthronement of some collective goals and collective good, we increasingly find a concern with self-fulfillment, with personal gratification, and with the assertion of individual rights.

The Shanghai Story. I begin my exploration of the evidence with data from Shanghai. Unfortunately, measures over time are not available, and we must content ourselves with differences among age groups as a proxy. For a number of the topics covered, however, a true shift across the generations is a more likely explanation of the observed differences than is one based on the presumed effects of aging alone.

Chu and Ju asked their Shanghai sample to make a series of choices about their basic hopes, aspirations, and fundamental goals in life. The proportion choosing the modern idea of seeking "true love" as a life goal rose from 11 percent among those over fifty years of age to 49 percent among those under twenty-nine years. This difference might be interpreted as merely reflecting a characteristic of the aged, who may be assumed to feel that the search for true love is past for them. I, however, see these statistics more as an expression of new values. To support my interpretation, I note certain other results from the same survey that cannot so easily be explained by the mechanisms of aging yet that also suggest the rising *general* importance of personal satisfaction—as against community harmony—as a central goal in life. For example, the proportion who chose "living happily" as the key to meaning in life rose from a mere 7 percent among those over fifty to 35 percent among those under twenty-nine.[24]

Perhaps the most important evidence from Shanghai, however, comes from a different phase of the study. To interpret it, I use as a standard the general acceptance that some value is presumed to have enjoyed earlier and compare that with the level of support for that value expressed by a contemporary sample. The values tested by Chu and Ju were selected on expert advice as those that the Chinese people had "cherished for thousands of years" and had "nearly universally accepted in the past." On that basis, a list of some eighteen values were presented to the sample in Shanghai, preceded by the question, "Of these elements of traditional Chinese culture . . . which ones do you feel proud of, which ones should be discarded, and which ones are you not sure of?"

Initially, for the total sample, the scoring system used an index based on the percentage who were proud of a value minus the percentage who said it should be discarded. By this method "diligence and frugality" earned a top score of +86 percent. The lowest score was -64 percent, indicating that the great majority voted to discard the venerable value called "the three obediences and the four virtues."[25] Other low scores, indicating a predominant opinion that the principle should be discarded, were earned by "the way of the golden mean," at -60 percent on the index; "differentiation between men and women," at -60 percent; and "discretion for self-preservation," at

−56 percent.[26] The authors found such a high level of rejection of these values, which for centuries had been the core of Chinese culture, to be "*nothing short of phenomenal*," which must have played a major role in their entitling their book *The Great Wall in Ruins*.

This rejection of key traditional values by the Shanghai population certainly may reflect conscious and intense efforts by the communist regime to inculcate new values in the Chinese population. This study, however, was based on the people of a city generally recognized as the most international and cosmopolitan and the most subject to modernizing influences in all of China. Note that the responses of the younger generation, which had been much less exposed to concentrated communist propaganda efforts directed against these values, showed one-half to two-thirds rejecting them, albeit not quite so strongly as the older generation.[27]

Life Goals in Japan. By turning to Japan for further evidence regarding changes in life goals, we escape the issue of systematic government pressure raised for the Shanghai data. But we find again the same pattern, namely, that self-centered values have come to outweigh the commitment to group morality and public service.

In the Japanese national character survey, respondents were given a list of six "attitudes toward life" and were asked to select the one that "comes closest to your feeling." The design of the question meant that no value was likely to command a majority because the total vote was divided across so many choices. Nonetheless, the pattern that emerged was fairly clear-cut, with the more self-centered, hedonistic values rising in strength over time, and the more moralistic and public service goals losing support. Thus the attitude "don't think about money or fame; just live a life that suits your own taste" more than doubled its support over the years, being endorsed by only 21 percent in 1953 but becoming the single most popular attitude by 1993, with 41 percent of the respondents casting their single vote for this way of life. By contrast, the value "resist all evils in the world and live a pure and just life" steadily lost ground over the same period, from being the most selected attitude in 1953, at 29 percent, to being one of the least favored in 1993, chosen by a mere 6 percent.

Taken together, the two community service and public morality items dominated the selection in 1953, jointly accounting for 39 percent of all the choices, but by 1993 they had progressively declined in popularity, accounting for only 10 percent of all first choices. By contrast, the two attitudes that suggested a self-centered and hedonistic approach to life doubled their support over time, together accounting for 32 percent of all choices in 1953 and increasing steadily to command 66 percent of all first choices by 1993.[28]

Leisure Activities and Popular Tastes. I conclude my survey of the abandonment of tradition with some evidence concerning the use of leisure time and personal preferences for different kinds of popular entertainment. It is by now commonplace to note the worldwide diffusion of certain movies and the music of some bands and singers. Madonna, for example, is recognized worldwide and has an audience in virtually every country. But some countries, among which communist China is perhaps most notable, sought for decades to seal off their populations from such influences, considering them not only foreign but also "polluting." It is therefore particularly revealing to discover how massive the shifts in popular taste have been across the generations in the provincial city of Baoding on the Chinese mainland.

Martin Whyte asked his respondents to indicate their first and second choices in entertainment, providing them a list that included traditional opera and Hong Kong–Taiwan pop. As might be expected, the older generation gave 68 percent of their votes to Chinese opera, but their adult children, only 13 percent. By contrast, the older generation voted for pop music only 13 percent of the time, but their mature children gave 71 percent of their votes to this variety of entertainment.[29]

Sources of Influence: Cause and Effect

All the countries of Asia are subject to a number of influences that have the potential for eroding tradition and fostering new attitudes, values, and behaviors. These different streams of influence sometimes act independently, but usually they combine in a great confluence, a whole sea of forces for change that washes over everyone and everything. Hong Kong perhaps exemplifies the most extreme case, where, according to Lau and Kwan, "economic growth and the ensuing rise in the standard of living . . . in turn fuel the inexorable process of Westernization and modernization, the pervasive effects of which are evident in almost all spheres of life . . . discernible even among people in the lower strata, thus testifying to their penetrative potency."[30]

It is of course a moot point whether the rise of industry and commerce should be considered Western in the same sense as certain films, music, and literature are more or less unambiguously identifiable as Western. Much is to be gained if we carefully *disaggregate* the different concrete forms of influence and study separately their *differential* impact on society, culture, and the individual. Moreover, we need to take into account the substantial cultural, economic, and political variety of the nations and peoples in the Pacific Rim countries.

Educational Effects

The spread of modern education may well be the most pervasive and profound source of influence on many of the attitudes and behaviors we have assessed. As Lau and Kuan noted for Hong Kong:

The more educated had a more "modernist" orientation toward society. . . . They had a stronger sense of personal efficacy, and believed much less in fatalism. They were more tolerant of social conflict, and more likely than the less educated to believe that conflict was a natural and integral part of social life. . . . They were less traditional in that they placed less emphasis on filial piety and kinship relations. They were more likely to give freedom of speech to others, less likely to ban newspapers that published false news, and less likely to prohibit meetings for an unorthodox cause. . . . The more educated believed in competition and individual effort, and they would oppose any organizational efforts to thwart the competitive process.[31]

Among the striking differences separating the more educated from the less educated in Hong Kong, I note the response to the idea that the kind of government you have is immaterial, a view to which an overwhelming 81 percent of the least educated agreed, whereas this idea was affirmed by only 22 percent of the most educated.[32] The effects of education were manifest not only under conditions of relative freedom, as in Hong Kong, but also under the more controlled conditions of life in communist-dominated Shanghai. For example, the idea that one should plan to live with one's parents after marriage was favored by 57 percent of the less educated, but the proportion was about half that, at 27 percent, among the more educated.[33]

The Role of Changing Occupational Structures

The transformation of Pacific Rim societies in the recent past began, in most cases, not with political regime or social policy changes but rather with economic development.[34] In particular they have experienced rapid industrialization, burgeoning trade and commerce, vast expansions of their transportation networks, and great declines in the proportion of the national income accounted for by agriculture. Vast numbers moved from the countryside and agricultural employment to take up city residence and nonagricultural work. These shifts in the composition of the labor force and in the nature of the work performed seem especially relevant to our concerns.

First, the shift of the place and type of work from traditional agriculture to industrial labor has substantial effects in inducing more modern attitudes and values, including a greater sense of efficacy, a heightened openness to new experience, increased tolerance for departures from tradition, and a greater appreciation and respect for the nature and rights of socially less powerful groups such as children and women. In my research on individual modernity I demonstrated these effects in six developing countries, two of which were in Asia, and there is every reason to believe that similar processes have been at work in the developing countries of the Pacific Rim.[35] These effects, furthermore, are not dependent on the fact that most industry is located in urban settings. The six-nation study of individual modernity and more recent work on factories in the countryside in mainland China,[36] demonstrate conclusively that industrial work in modern factories has a significant impact in fostering modern attitudes independent of the contribution of urban living.

Perhaps as important as the general growth of industrial employment, has been the massive movement of women out of the home and into the paid labor force. For example, in Taiwan, even after the first spurt of industrialization, only 16 percent of the respondents in the 1963 sample of men reported their wives to be in the paid labor force, those of the remainder working at home. But by 1991 the proportion having wives in paid employment had risen to 48 percent. Comparable and even more dramatic shifts in the extent of formal employment by women have been reported for other countries on the Pacific Rim. I believe the impact to have been profound, but my sources have paid less attention to the effects of female employment than they might have.[37]

Other Sources of Influence

Urban Experience.   The urban setting as such seems to exert an influence on attitudes, values, and behaviors independent of the modernizing impact of employment itself, especially on those who do not find work there. In the six-nation study of individual modernity, I showed that in East Pakistan (now Bangladesh) and India, as in the other nations studied, the longer men of rural origin lived and worked in urban areas, the higher their scores on the overall measure of attitudinal modernity (OM) scale. Moreover, this effect of urban living was clearly independent of the impact of factory experience in the Indian case and was independent of mass media exposure in both countries.[38]

In his study of Taiwan, Robert Marsh also took into account the extent of rural living and later urban contact that his respondents had experienced. He found that a number of attitudes and values were influenced by the scores on his index of rural-urban exposure. For example, in response to the question of whether physical punishment is necessary in raising children, the urban index showed a modest but consistent effect, even with occupation held constant, those with more urban contact being less likely to believe in the necessity of physical punishment.[39]

Exposure to Mass Media and Western Culture.   In the six-nation study, exposure to the mass media was generally second only to education as a force moving people toward modern attitudes and behaviors. Even with occupation and education controlled, the β weight for mass media exposure in a regression on the OM score stood at .20 in both India and East Pakistan.[40]

Although the mass media have been bringing indigenous material to the populations of the Asian-Pacific nations, much of their material may reasonably be dubbed Western. It is of special interest, therefore, that several relevant studies have sought to disentangle the effect of mass media exposure in general from the specific influence of Western culture. In Shanghai, Chu and Ju found many instances in which the degree of contact with Western culture played a substantial role in shaping attitudes and behavior to a degree equal to, and sometimes greater than, the mere fact of exposure to the mass media. For example, the view that divorce is acceptable if the couple involved does not have children was affirmed by only 27 percent of those with low exposure to Western influence, whereas this view was manifested by 57 percent of those under high Western influence. Fifty-one percent of those with high exposure to the West said that if given the opportunity they would retire if they could live comfortably, whereas only 27 percent of those with little Western exposure said that they would take that option, claiming that they would continue working instead.[41]

The Next Step

All the sources of influence we have examined are interrelated,[42] and they often produce their effects in complex interactions. Regression analyses, which a number of the key investigators I cite have used extensively, can help to identify the general realms and the particular issues that are more or less sensitive to one or another source of influence. To understand in any depth the complex response of cultures, communities, and individuals to the sources of influence to which they are exposed, however, would require a more fine-grained analysis with a battery of techniques to assess each important question separately. Such analysis is the next step required to move us beyond the stage to which this chapter has brought us. I have shown conclusively, I believe, that a number of the nations on the Pacific Rim have in the last decades of the twentieth century experienced great, often profound, shifts in values, attitudes, and behavior in various realms of life. But even in the realms of greatest volatility, some attitudes change and some values shift but others do not. Attitudes may change but behavior may not, and the reverse pattern is also observed. Moreover, many traditions persist unchanged, and some seem to enjoy a resurgence of commitment and support. A comprehensive, coherent, and convincing account of the complex and important process of social change currently being experienced by perhaps as much as one-third of the human race awaits our discovery.

NOTES

Notes to Chapter 1

Original paper presented at the International Political Science Association meeting at Montreal, August 20–23, 1973. The creative research assistance of Dean Nielsen is gratefully acknowledged.

1. There is another related and currently very popular use of the term dependence, which gives prime emphasis to the ability of a nation-state to make decisions about its internal development relatively free of the dominant and/or domineering pressure of more powerful states or economic systems. Thus contemporary radical political economists make a great deal of the "dependence" of the Latin American and other less developed countries on the greater political and economic power of the U.S. government, on "international capital," and on multinational corporations. The concept is also used to describe cultural phenomena, epitomized by the dominance of products like Coca-Cola, which displaces indigenous beverages, or systems of American empirical social research, which are charged with inhibiting the development of distinctive national systems of social analysis. See Suzanne Bodenheimer, "Dependency and Imperialism: The Roots of Underdevelopment in Latin America," in K. T. Fann and Donald D. Hodges, eds., *Readings in U.S. Imperialism* (Boston: Porter Sargent, 1971); James D. Cockcroft, André Gunder Frank, and Dale L. Johnson, eds., *Dependence and Underdevelopment: Latin America's Political Economy* (New York: Anchor, 1972); Arghiri Emmanuel, *Unequal Exchange* (New York: Monthly Review Press, 1972); John D. Esseks, "Economic Dependence and Political Development in the New African States," *Journal of Politics*, Vol. 33 (November 1971); Irving L. Horowitz, *The Three Worlds of Development* (New York: Oxford University Press, 1966); and Harry Magdoff, *The Age of Imperialism* (New York: Monthly Review Press, 1969).

2. The diversity of basic materials to be found within the boundaries of the United States is well known. It is helpful, however, also to see the contrast expressed in statistical terms. For the United States, foreign trade (in 1965) was only 7.3 percent of GNP, whereas for Japan it was 20 percent and for Singapore 238 percent. See Charles L. Taylor and Michael C. Hudson, *World Handbook of Political and Social Indicators*, 2d ed. (New Haven: Yale University Press, 1972), 372–377.

3. The water mill was one of the few, and certainly one of the most important, mechanical inventions introduced in Hellenic times. Yet Gordon Childe reports that a century after Christ such mills were hardly more common than a century before. See Childe, *What Happened in History* (Baltimore: Penguin Books, 1942), 235,

251–253. I am indebted to Keith Hopkins for the distinction between Roman invention and Roman innovation, that is, the adoption and adaptation of the inventions of others.

4. Nathan Keyfitz of Harvard University estimates that 69 billion people have lived on the Earth since the beginning of the human species. Of this total, roughly 18 billion, or 26 percent, have lived on Earth during the past 300 years; 3 billion, or 4 percent, are living on Earth now. See Keyfitz, "How Many People Have Lived on the Earth," *Demography*, Vol. 3, No. 2 (1966), 581–582. For our purposes here the span of human habitation on earth is estimated to be 300,000 years, which yields the calculation that the modern era, covering some 300 years, equals 0.1 percent of the span of human occupancy of the globe. Keyfitz took the period of human habitation to cover 1 million years. Using that base would of course make the modern era an even smaller fragment of the span of human habitation on earth.

5. Donella H. Meadows et al., *The Limits of Growth* (New York: Universe Books, 1972).

6. The figures for the percentage of annual increase given in this paper were almost all computed by the author and his research assistant from relatively crude time series, and should therefore be considered only approximate. In most cases only summary figures for two points in time were available to us, sometimes thirty or more years apart. Obviously within so great a span the actual annual rate could have varied greatly from year to year and decade to decade. In cases where we could obtain more detailed time series, we checked to verify that the rates of increase had been more or less uniform over the longer span before computing a per annum rate of increase. Hence we did not compute such a rate-of-increase figure for direct U.S. investment abroad for the *total period* from 1946 to 1971, because the years from 1946 to 1952 were relatively stable, whereas there was a sharp upturn from 1963 to 1971.

The formula used to calculate annual rates of increase takes beginning year and ending year figures and derives the yearly rate of growth in the following manner:

$$r = \frac{I}{T \log_e} \frac{f(t)}{f(o)}$$

T = total time elapsed
$f(t)$ = figure at ending year
$f(o)$ = figure at beginning year

This formula has been checked by use after the fact where appropriate and in most cases has proven to be quite accurate. In fact, there is a slight conservative bias in our growth rate statistics. Discrepancies probably do arise because (1) the table we have been using gives natural logarithms ($\log_e$) to five significant figures only and thus contains a certain amount of statistical error; (2) the assumption behind the use of the natural log is that "interest" is compounded constantly, that is, the number of times per year that the interest is compounded is taken to the mathematical limit; (3) there is an assumption that the value of the variable increases at a constant rate over the time period.

7. *United Nations Statistical Yearbook, 1971* (New York: Statistical Office of the United Nations, 1972), 78; United Nations Educational, Scientific, and Cultural Organization (UNESCO), *Statistics of Students Abroad, 1962–1968* (Paris: UNESCO 1972), 19–21.

8. Figures are from forty countries listed in the *United Nations Statistical Yearbooks* for 1955 and 1971 for which there were data for the years 1938 and 1970. More recent data and a discussion of these trends may be found in Chapter 9 of the present volume.

9. Figures were computed on the basis of data found in *United Nations Statistical Yearbooks* for 1955 and 1971.

10. Between 1963 and 1970 the number of overseas telephone calls from the United States increased by about 25 percent per year (*World's Telephones* [New York: American Telephone and Telegraph, January 1970]). Data for other countries are not at hand but it seems reasonable to assume that, at least for the other developed countries, rates of increase have not been much lower. Moreover, the United States alone accounts for a very large share of all the world's telephonic communication. To assume a worldwide increase in international telephonic communication of 15 percent therefore seems conservative. For further discussion, see Chapter 9.

11. Figures were computed on the basis of data found in *United Nations Statistical Yearbooks* for 1955 and 1971. The countries considered in estimating the annual increase of tourists used in these calculations include Belgium, Denmark, France, Germany, Ireland, Italy, Netherlands, Switzerland, and the United Kingdom as countries of origin. The omission of some European countries results in an underestimation of the absolute numbers of tourists going from Europe to the United States. This omission, however, is not likely to affect the percentages of change reported.

12. *United Nations Statistical Yearbook, 1970,* 402.

13. Calculated from data in *United Nations Statistical Yearbook, 1972,* Table 12, p. 43, for the years 1938–1971.

14. Figures taken from U.S. Department of Commerce, Bureau of Economic Analysis, *Survey of Current Business* (Washington, DC, 1973).

15. Kjell Skjelsbaek, "The Growth of Nongovernmental Organizations in the Twentieth Century," *International Organization,* Vol. 25 (Summer 1971), 420–443. Additional data and a discussion of these trends may be found in Chapter 9.

16. Percentages computed on the basis of data reported in Moshe Y. Sachs, ed., *World Encyclopedia of the Nations* (New York: Harper and Row, 1960 and 1971).

17. The measures of increasing interconnectedness presented here are almost all absolute rather than relative or proportional. They indicate the number of ties extant, rather than the proportion of all countries, institutions, or individuals having such ties. Since world population is increasing substantially, even holding constant the average degree of connectivity would obviously yield a significant increase in the absolute *number* of connections to be observed year by year. Therefore, some downward adjustment of our figures on interconnectedness should be made on a systematic basis. Nevertheless, the adjustment would not lead to a dramatic reinterpretation of the facts, since world population has grown at a rate of only some 2 percent per annum, whereas most of the interconnections we noted increased at a rate of more than 7 percent per annum.

18. Based on figures reported in Taylor and Hudson, *op. cit.,* 372–377. By our calculation, the percentage of GNP represented by trade falls regularly as the population of a country increases. Median percentages are as follows: less than 1 million population, 78 percent of GNP; 1 to 10 million, 43 percent; 10 to 50 million, 33 percent; 50 to 100 million 26 percent; more than 10 million, 10 percent.

19. Based on figures from *United Nations Statistical Yearbooks* for 1955 and 1971. Developed countries in these calculations included most European countries, the United States, Canada, Japan, Australia, and New Zealand. Less developed countries included the following few for which complete data were available: Angola, Morocco, Mozambique, Tunisia, India, Indonesia, Lebanon, Syria, Turkey, Argentina, and Paraguay.

20. All data on student exchanges are from United Nations sources, especially UNESCO, *op. cit.*

21. For example, the reason less developed countries are gaining on the more developed ones in the use of the telegraph can probably be explained by the fact that the more advanced are switching to the long-distance telephone, a more modern, rapid, and flexible form of communication. That would certainly seem to be indicated by the fact that the number of foreign telegrams sent out from the United States remained more or less the same in most years between 1963 and 1970, whereas the number of telephone calls abroad placed from the United States increased by more than 25 percent per year. (See *United Nations Statistical Yearbook, 1972*, and *The World's Telephones, op. cit.*)

22. See UNESCO, *op. cit.*, 30. If we assume a condition in which *all* young people went as far as the university, and make the further unlikely assumption that all university students would customarily be sent outside their own country for advanced training, we have designed a situation such that in time no further increase in the number of students studying abroad could be attained unless the population of young people could be expanded by a rapid rise in births. Moreover, such expansion of the supply of young people could hardly occur at a rate of more than 2 or 3 percent per year, whereas the current and recent past rate of expansion in foreign study has run at 7 or 8 percent per year. Thus, with a stable rate of population growth, the *rate of increase* in students studying abroad could be brought as low as zero even though the frequency of interchange of students was at 100 percent, that is, saturation, with all students studying outside their home country. This hypothetical example may give some satisfaction to our need to find some way of showing that exponential growth has clearly definable limits; we must nevertheless acknowledge that it is improbable that the conditions specified will be reached in the near or even the distant future, or indeed ever.

23. The percentages of all foreign students enrolled in medicine and engineering in the period 1962–1968 are as follows

	1962	1966	1968
Medicine	16.2	13.5	12.7
Engineering	19.5	18.1	17.8

Source: Excerpted from UNESCO, *op. cit.*, Table 21, p. 47, which gives the field of study of all students studying abroad from 117 countries.

24. For example, UN statistics show the following: In foreign mail received, twenty less developed countries show an average annual gain of 7.3 percent from 1938 to 1970. In comparison, twenty developed countries show an average annual gain of only 3.7 percent during that period. In foreign telegrams sent, twelve less de-

veloped countries show an average annual increase of 4.3 percent from 1938 to 1970, and twenty-two developed countries averaged only 2.0 percent. These statistics are complemented by telephone use data. Between 1967 and 1971 telephones in use increased 61.4 percent in Asia as compared to only 37 percent in Europe.

25. This is of course not to gainsay the fact that some countries are relatively heavily dependent on foreign universities to train their specialists in certain fields. Some evidence is presented later, in the section on *dependence*.

26. The *United Nations Statistical Yearbook* for 1972 shows that in 1953 tourists from Japan to the United States numbered about 17,000. By 1971 the figure was 313,000. The 1953 figure included tourists from Korea, which, if omitted, would probably leave us a figure closer to the 15,000 mentioned in the text. The press reports an enormous surge of additional Japanese tourists to Hawaii in 1973. Some estimates place that flow at an increase of over 100,000 in a single year.

27. This subset of seventy-nine countries was selected from the full set of 124 presented by Taylor and Hudson, *op. cit.*, in order to facilitate a comparison with figures for 1959 that had been presented by Bruce M. Russett et al., *World Handbook of Political and Social Indicators* (New Haven: Yale University Press, 1964). Results of the comparison are presented later. The full set of 124 countries presented by Taylor and Hudson shows the median proportion of trade to GNP to be 39 percent. The figures on trade as a percentage of GNP just cited are not meant to reflect total world trade as a proportion of total world GNP. Since many small countries in the set have high ratios of trade to GNP and relatively *small* GNPs, the median percentage figure given here is bound to be considerably greater than the ratio of total world trade to world GNP. This is especially true when one considers that the countries with the highest GNPs (U.S., USSR) show figures for the proportion of trade to GNP that are below 10 percent. World trade as a proportion of world GNP can be roughly estimated from UN statistics. Considering market economies only, the proportion of worldwide imports to worldwide GNP in 1963 was roughly 10 percent. By 1970 this figure had risen to nearly 12 percent. Figures based on *United Nations Statistical Yearbook, 1972*, Tables 146 and 188.

28. *United Nations Statistical Yearbook, 1971*, 460–463.

29. One basis for this conclusion is the fact that trade *within* the set of industrialized countries is much more intense than is trade either *between* industrialized and nonindustrialized sets or *within* the subset of the nonindustrialized. A more direct test of the hypothesis presented requires that we compare the increases in trade with the increase in industrialization for specific countries. To do this, we selected eleven countries on the basis of availability of data, geographic spread, and variation in the degree to which their industrialization increased between 1948 and 1970. For those eleven we then compared the increase in industrialization with the increase in the value of exports over the same period. The rank-order correlation of the two sets of figures was .67, indicating a close correspondence between the two types of growth. At the top of the list, Japan's industrialization index increased 25.8 times (1963 = 100), and its trade increased by 20 percent per year; at the bottom of the list, Algeria's industrialization index increased only 1.1 times, and its exports by only 4 percent per year.

30. Figures for countries found in Russett, *op. cit.*, as well as in Taylor and Hudson, *op. cit.*

31. Again we call attention to the fact that thus approaching the association of trade with GNP by country gives an impression of greater interdependence than one would derive by considering only the fact that the value of worldwide exports as a proportion of worldwide GNP is in the much more modest range of 10–12 percent.

32. Childe, *op. cit.*, 239.

33. It is fascinating to apply this notion of potential autarky in trade and science to the realm of art. Some critics would assert that all the important sources of real creativity in art are found outside these giants, and that if they were not interconnected with the rest of the world, they would soon become artistic wastelands.

34. These assertions are confirmed by the fact that in 1970 tourism accounted for 8.1 percent, 5.6 percent, and 4.5 percent of the national income in Jamaica, Spain, and Mexico, respectively. By comparison, in the same year foreign tourism receipts accounted for a mere 0.3 percent of the national income of the United States and 0.1 percent of that of Japan. (Based on *United Nations Statistical Yearbook, 1972,* Tables 157 and 187.)

35. If the point was not obvious when this sentence was first written in August 1973, it must surely have become obvious since then as a result of the Arab oil embargo and the resultant worldwide energy crisis.

36. UNESCO, *op. cit.*, 33.

37. Ibid., 30.

38. Ibid., 55.

39. Ibid., 57.

40. Philippe de Seynes, "Prospects for a Future Whole World," *International Organization,* Vol. 26 (Winter 1972), 6.

41. See William J. Goode, *World Revolution and Family Patterns* (New York: Free Press, 1963).

42. Reinhard Bendix and Seymour Martin Lipset, eds., *Class, Status, and Power: Social Stratification in Comparative Perspective,* 2d ed. (New York: Free Press, 1966); see especially in that volume Robert W. Hodge, Donald J. Treiman, and Peter H. Rossi, "A Comparative Study of Occupational Prestige."

43. See Alexander Szalai, ed., *The Use of Time: Daily Activities of Urban and Suburban Populations in Twelve Countries* (The Hague: Mouton, 1973).

44. Alex Inkeles, "Industrial Man: The Relation of Status to Experience, Perception, and Value," *American Journal of Sociology,* Vol. 64 (July 1960).

45. Alex Inkeles and David H. Smith, *Becoming Modern: Individual Change in Six Developing Countries* (Cambridge, MA: Harvard University Press, 1974).

46. Alex Inkeles, *Social Change in Soviet Russia* (Cambridge, MA: Harvard University Press, 1968); see especially chapter 20, "Russia and the United States: A Problem in Comparative Sociology," and Chapter 3 in this volume.

47. It may be argued that increasing affluence has actually had the effect of greatly increasing freedom of choice for the average individual in the United States. The issue is certainly debatable, but it is not the one I address here. Rather, I refer to the ever-widening regulation by the state of matters previously left to individual resolution. For example, we started with each person obliged to look to his retirement as best he could, but in time we have arrived at government social security payments obligatory for most people and increasing government regulation of previously private retirement plans worked out by corporations, unions, and other organizations. Under these

new conditions, individuals may be more secure financially, but they also operate within a wider and more penetrating network of regulation and control.

48. The nature of the "postmodern" man is a challenging subject that unfortunately I must bypass here.

Notes to Chapter 2

The basic framework for this chapter was initially developed while I was a visiting scholar in London at the Royal Institute for International Affairs, which kindly organized a study group on convergence and divergence in industrial societies during my stay there in the first half of 1978. I am indebted to the members of the study group for their encouragement and criticism, to the institute for its generous hospitality, and to Stanford University, the Guggenheim Foundation, and the Institute for World Order, which underwrote the expenses of my sabbatical leave. On the basis of discussions at the International Sociological Conference on Modernization, convened in Brussels by the University of Pittsburgh, I revised and greatly amplified my original model, thanks to continuing support from the Hoover Institution on War, Revolution, and Peace.

1. Government statistics do occasionally show more than 100 percent of the eligible age group as enrolled in primary school. This comes about because many are repeating a grade. Let us assume that the primary grades include ages six through ten and that there are 1 million children in that age group, all enrolled in primary schools. If in addition 100,000 children of age eleven are also still in primary school because they were repeating a grade, then official statistics will show that enrollment is 110 percent of children of ages six through ten.

2. The failure of further investment in facilities to produce improvements in scholastic performance was notably demonstrated in comparisons of the different school systems within the United States by Coleman et al. 1966. Evidence that the same pattern was manifest in other advanced industrial countries is presented in the various books discussed in Inkeles 1977.

3. The general case is argued and the basic supporting data are presented in Boli 1979.

4. Heidenheimer et al. 1975, 189.

5. Thus in Mexico, Argentina, and Brazil the full array of all twenty-three organizations was in place by 1960, whereas in less developed countries, such as Paraguay, only ten to twelve as yet existed. However, administrative complexity was only imperfectly correlated with economic development. Size also played a role, with nations that had small populations being less likely to install the full array of institutions. See Farrell 1968.

6. Teitelbaum 1975.

7. Teitelbaum 1975; World Bank 1978.

8. By 1870 the industrialization of England was going full scale, while that of the United States was just beginning. The difference in relevant economic development was mirrored in a GNP per capita of US$670 for Great Britain versus only $370 for the United States. Yet the United States was sending to school 187 of every 1,000 in the population, whereas England managed to send only 67. Thus with less than two-thirds

the wealth available per person, the United States was sending almost three times as many individuals to school. Equally precise figures are not available for earlier periods, but apparently these contrasts were already evident at the turn of the century.

9. A similar pattern can be seen in infant mortality rates, which are dropping in all the more advanced countries, but at a similar rate. Consequently, the leaders in 1965 were still the leaders in 1975, although the gap separating them from the laggards had been somewhat narrowed.

10. Johnson 1973.

11. The statement in the text is from Brown 1978, 193. The size of the gap in living standards between the rich and the poor countries depends on which groups one takes into account and on whether money equivalents or real income is measured. The World Bank (1978) classification of low-income, middle-income, and industrialized countries yielded per capita incomes of US$150, $750, and $6,200, respectively, for 1976. At the extreme, then, the ratio of income from the low to the industrialized was a staggering 1:41. But were the middle-income nations added to the set of the less developed, as is customary, the ratio given would obviously be greatly reduced. In addition, the differences expressed in monetary terms would be much smaller—in the extreme case, some say, by half—if the contrast were expressed in terms of "actual consumption" rather than in terms of dollar equivalents.

12. These numbers are based on projections originally made by Kahn and Wiener (1967) and discussed by Rosenstein-Rodan (1972), among others. It should be noted that this large increase in the absolute gap would not at all be matched by an increase in the *ratio* of the income of the two sets of countries. The 1965 ratio was 1:13, and the estimated ratio for the year 2000 is much the same at 1:14. Estimates of the future gap expected to separate the advanced from the less advanced countries vary considerably depending on what one assumes to be the rates at which population and wealth are growing in the two sets of countries. The latest United Nations calculations (Leontief et al. 1977) indicate that the ratio will probably remain about 1:12, but they give an optimistic scenario that could reduce the gap to 1:7. It is a curious anomaly of such statistics that even if the ratio were reduced in this manner, the absolute gap in income by the year 2000 would still be much larger than it was in 1970.

13. UNESCO 1967, 1970, and 1977.

14. Heidenheimer et al. 1975, 191, 207, 258, 280.

15. Cappelletti et al. 1975.

16. Coale 1973.

17. Kuznets 1973, 302–303.

18. In this task it was helpful to be able to follow the trail blazed by William J. Goode (1963).

19. Trewartha 1969.

References to Chapter 2

Baum, Rainer C. 1974. "Beyond Convergence: Toward Theoretical Relevance in Quantitative Modernization Research." *Sociological Inquiry,* Vol. 44, No. 4, 225–240.

Bendix, Reinhard, and Seymour Martin Lipset. 1966. *Class, Status, and Power.* 2d ed. New York: Free Press.

Boli [Boli-Bennett], John. 1979. "The Ideology of Expanding State Authority in National Constitutions, 1870–1970." In *National Development and the World System: Educational, Economic, and Political Change, 1950–1970,* ed. John W. Meyer and Michael T. Hannan, 222–237. Chicago: University of Chicago Press.

Brown, Lester R. 1978. *The Twenty-ninth Day: Accommodating Human Needs and Numbers to the Earth's Resources.* New York: W. W. Norton.

Cappelletti, Mauro, James Gordley, and Earl Johnson Jr. 1975. *Toward Equal Justice: A Comparative Study of Legal Aid in Modern Societies.* Dobbs Ferry, NY: Oceana Publications.

Coale, Ansley J. 1973. "Demographic Transitions." In *[Proceedings of the] International Population Conference,* International Union for the Scientific Study of Population, Vol. I, 53–71. Liège, Belgium.

Coleman, James, Ernest Q. Campbell, Carol J. Hobson, Alexander M. Wood, and Frederick Weinfeld. 1966. *Equality of Educational Opportunity.* Washington, DC: U.S. Department of Health, Education, and Welfare, Office of Education.

Farrell, Joseph P. 1968. *A Cross-National Study of Education and Development Using Scalogram Analysis.* U.S. Department of Health, Education, and Welfare, Office of Education, Bureau of Research report.

Goode, William J. 1963. *World Revolution and Family Patterns.* New York: Free Press.

Hannan, Michael T., and Glenn R. Carroll. 1979. "Dynamics of Formal Political Structure." Unpublished National Science Foundation Grant Technical Report No. 72, Department of Sociology, Stanford University.

Hansen, Roger. 1975. "The Emerging Challenge: Global Distribution of Income and Economic Opportunity." In *The U.S. and World Development,* ed. James Howe and the staff of the Overseas Development Council. New York: Praeger Publishers.

Heidenheimer, Arnold J., Hugh Heclo, and Carolyn Teich Adams. 1975. *Comparative Public Policy: The Politics of Social Choice in Europe and America.* New York: St. Martin's Press.

Inkeles, Alex. 1960. "Industrial Man: The Relation of Status to Experience, Perception, and Value." *American Journal of Sociology,* Vol. 64 (July), 1–31.

_____. 1968. *Social Change in Soviet Russia.* Cambridge, MA: Harvard University Press.

_____. 1975. "The Emerging Social Structure of the World." *World Politics,* Vol. 27, No. 4 (July), 489–495.

_____. 1977. "The International Evaluation of Educational Achievement." *Proceedings of the National Academy of Education,* Vol. 4, 139–200.

Inkeles, Alex, and David H. Smith. 1974. *Becoming Modern: Individual Change in Six Developing Countries.* Cambridge, MA: Harvard University Press.

Johnson, David Gale. 1973. *World Agriculture in Disarray.* London: Macmillan.

Kahn, Herman, and Anthony Wiener. 1967. *The Year 2000.* New York: Macmillan.

Kuznets, Simon. 1973. *Population, Capital, and Growth: Selected Essays.* New York: W. W. Norton.

Leontief, Wassily, Anne P. Carter, Peter Petri, and Joseph Stern. 1977. *The Future of the World Economy: A United Nations Study.* New York: Oxford University Press.

Levy, Marion J. 1972. *Modernization: Latecomers and Survivors.* New York: Basic Books.

McHale, Magda C., and John McHale, with Guy F. Streatfeild. 1979. *Children in the World.* Washington, DC: Population Reference Bureau.

Mitchell, B. R. 1975. *European Historical Statistics, 1750–1970.* New York: Columbia University Press.

Office of Population Research, Princeton University, and Population Association of America, Inc. 1962. *Population Index,* Vol. 28, No. 1 (January). Princeton: Princeton University Press.

Rosenstein-Rodan, P. N. 1972. "The Have's and Have-not's Around the Year 2000." In *Economics and World Order from the 1970s to the 1990s,* ed. Jagdish N. Bhagwati. London: Collier-Macmillan.

Rostow, Walter W. 1978. *The World Economy: History and Prospect.* Austin: University of Texas Press.

Szalai, Alexander, ed. 1973. *The Use of Time: Daily Activity of Urban and Suburban Populations in Twelve Countries.* The Hague: Mouton.

Teitelbaum, Michael S. 1975. "Relevance of Demographic Transition Theory for Developing Countries." *Science,* No. 188.

Trewartha, Glenn T. 1969. *A Geography of Population: World Patterns.* New York: John Wiley.

United Nations Educational, Scientific, and Cultural Organization (UNESCO). 1965. *Statistical Yearbook.* Paris: UNESCO.

_____. 1970. *Statistical Yearbook.* Paris: UNESCO.

_____. 1977. *Statistical Yearbook.* Paris: UNESCO.

World Bank. 1978. "World Development Report, 1978." Washington, DC: International Organization for Reconstruction and Development.

Notes to Chapter 3

1. Pitirim Sorokin, *Russia and the United States* (E. P. Dutton, New York, 1944). Unless otherwise indicated, the page citations given in parentheses all refer to this first edition.

2. There are several excellent standard works on the development and structure of the polity in Soviet society. Generally acknowledged as outstanding is Merle Fainsod, *How Russia Is Ruled* (Cambridge, MA: Harvard University Press, 1953).

3. The system of control of means of communication and the Communist theory underlying that control are dealt with at length in Alex Inkeles, *Public Opinion in Soviet Russia* (Cambridge, MA: Harvard University Press, 1956.)

4. Sorokin, *op. cit.,* p. 173.

5. C. Wright Mills, *The Power Elite* (New York: Oxford University Press, 1957).

6. For the definitive statement on the similarities and differences between the *mir* and the collective farm, see Lazar Volin, "The Peasant Household Under the *Mir* and the Kolkhoz in Modern Russian History," in *The Cultural Approach to History,* ed. Caroline F. Ware (New York: Columbia University Press, 1940).

7. David Granick, *The Red Executive* (New York: Doubleday, 1960).

8. Alex Inkeles and Raymond A. Bauer, *The Soviet Citizen* (Cambridge, MA: Harvard University Press, 1959).

9. The role of the Communist youth organizations in socializing the young for life in Soviet society is dealt with at length in Allen Kassof's *The Soviet Youth Program: Regimentation and Rebellion* (Cambridge, MA: Harvard University Press, 1965).

10. Sorokin did not explicitly mention the schools, but he did discuss the role of the Zemstvo in local government and in supplying medical care (1944, 75, 78, and 149).

11. London, Stevens and Sons, 1950. Page citations for the second edition refer to this source.

12. Sorokin, *op. cit.,* 1st edition, p. 208.

13. Sorokin, *op. cit.,* 2d edition, p. 176.

14. Ibid.

Notes to Chapter 4

1. All data I have identified with the World Bank are from *World Development Report, 1988* (New York: Oxford University Press, 1988).

2. See Alex Inkeles and David H. Smith, *Becoming Modern: Individual Change in Six Developing Countries* (London: Heinemann Educational Books, 1974), and Alex Inkeles, *Exploring Individual Modernity* (New York: Columbia University Press, 1983).

3. For a brief description and general review of the project see Alex Inkeles, "The International Evaluation of Educational Achievement," *Proceedings of the National Academy of Education,* Vol. 4 (1977), pp. 139–200. A version of that publication is reproduced as Chapter 6 in this volume.

4. In addition to the test for science knowledge, the IEA researchers also tested knowledge of English or French as foreign languages, knowledge of the literature of one's own country, and reading comprehension in one's national or native language.

5. The round of studies reported on here was actually the second wave for the IEA. This second wave was launched in 1965 and 1966 and the results began to appear in 1973 and later years. A subsequent wave of studies was to include many more developing countries because many ministries of education were becoming more interested in this kind of comparative test.

6. It should be kept in mind that in Israel we studied not the people who came from Europe to Israel, but rather those who came mainly from North Africa. Therefore, their cultural background was not so different from that of our samples from the other countries as it might have seemed to be. But their exposure to the modern society that Israel represents was probably a major factor in shifting their attitudes and values in the modern direction.

Notes to Chapter 5

Original paper prepared for the conference "Perspectives on the American Study of Contemporary China," Asia Program, Woodrow Wilson International Center for Scholars, held at the Wye Plantation, July 20–23, 1988.

1. The title initially suggested for my paper was "The Generalists and the China Specialists: Dialogue of the Deaf?"

2. See Alex Inkeles and Raymond A. Bauer, *The Soviet Citizen: Daily Life in a Totalitarian Society* (Cambridge, MA: Harvard University Press, 1959).

3. Martin K. Whyte, "From Arranged Marriages to Love Marriages in Urban China," in *Family Formation and Dissolution: Perspectives from East and West,* ed. Chin-Chin Yi (Taipei: Academica Sinica, 1995). The same technique was used in collecting samples in Baoding, as reported in Martin K. Whyte, "The Persistence of Family Obligations in Baoding," manuscript, George Washington University, 1996.

4. See Alex Inkeles and Peter H. Rossi, "National Comparisons of Occupational Prestige," *American Journal of Sociology,* Vol. 61, No. 4 (January 1956), 329–339, reprinted as Chapter 8 of this volume. Also see Donald Treiman, *Occupational Prestige in Comparative Perspective* (New York: Academic Press, 1977).

5. See Alex Inkeles and David H. Smith, *Becoming Modern: Individual Change in Six Developing Countries* (Cambridge, MA: Harvard University Press, 1974).

6. See A. Inkeles, C. M. Broaded, and Z. Cao, "Women, Men, and the Construction of Individual Modernity Scales in China," *Cross-Cultural Research,* Vol. 28, No. 3 (August 1994), 251–286, and A. Inkeles, C. M. Broaded, and Z. Cao, "Causes and Consequences of Individual Modernity in China," *China Journal,* No. 37 (January 1977), 31–59.

7. See Chapter 2 in this volume, which is based on Alex Inkeles, "Convergence and Divergence in Industrial Societies," in *Directions of Change,* ed. Mustafa O. Attir et al. (Boulder: Westview Press, 1981).

8. Reported in Alex Inkeles, "Modernization and Family Patterns: A Test of Convergence Theory," *Conspectus of History,* Vol. 1, No. 6, ed. Dwight W. Hoover and John T.A. Koumoulides (Muncie, IN: Department of History, Ball State University, 1980), 31–62; reprinted as Chapter 7 of this volume.

Notes to Chapter 6

We are indebted to the Spencer Foundation for a research grant which made this study possible. Special thanks are due to the Foundation's President Thomas James for his encouragement of our efforts. Additional support provided by the Hoover Institution on War, Revolution, and Peace, and by its director, Dr. W. Glenn Campbell, is also gratefully acknowledged.

1. Inkeles 1981.

2. To make a reliable judgment requires that we observe a standard set—that is, the exact same set—of cases over time. Wherever possible we do this. However, frequent poor statistical accounting by the reporting agencies confronts us, and rather than accept a severely reduced number of cases we relax the rule by requiring only that no new cases confound our observations at later points in time. Thus, even though a few cases observed earlier may be missing at one point later, a relatively stable set is achieved. To ensure that our findings are not artifacts of this strategy, we have replicated each analysis with a constant number of cases only, and we note throughout the text any differences we may have found.

3. We have experimented with other measures and tests of convergence, including the variance ratio test. We believe, however, that the properties of the coefficient

of variation make it well suited for the purposes of this chapter, designed mainly to describe and illustrate our general strategy of research.

4. Nations classified as "Rich" are those located within the upper 40 percent of the worldwide distribution of GNP per capita at the start of the specific observation period. Nations classified as "Poor" are located within the lower 60 percent of the cases on the same distribution. Depending on whether the start of the observation period is 1955, 1960, or 1965, the cutoff value for classifying nations as "Rich" is US$285, $278, or $288. GNP per capita data are from the International Bank for Reconstruction and Development (IBRD).

5. Meyer 1981, 4.

6. The countries and the time at which they established public responsibility for elementary schooling, are as follows: Germany (Prussia) (1763), Austria (1770s), the Netherlands (1806), Denmark (1814), France (1833), Portugal (1834), Switzerland (1830s), Sweden (1842), Belgium (1842), Turkey (1846), Norway (1848–1860), England (1870), Scotland (1872), Spain (1857), Italy (1859), and Finland (1866).

7. Certainly all of the sixteen had converged on adopting legal provisions for compulsory education that were of common symbolic worth; what was more variable was their organizational worth, that is, the extent to which they preceded or followed higher enrollments and the extent to which authorities enforced the provisions specified by the law.

8. Ramirez and Boli 1982.

9. Craig 1981.

10. UNESCO, *Statistical Yearbook,* 1981.

11. Williamson and Fleming 1977. The ten were Germany, Italy, Japan, New Zealand, Norway, Sweden, United Kingdom, Austria, Belgium, and France.

12. The data for these calculations are found in UNESCO, *Statistical Yearbook,* 1981.

13. Aries 1962.

14. Perry 1912.

15. UNESCO 1958.

16. Gimenso and Ibanez 1981.

17. Friesen et al. 1980.

18. Ramirez and Rubinson 1979.

19. Adams and Farrell 1967.

20. Clark 1978.

21. These figures are based on seventy-two cases for 1955 and fifty-five for 1979. The c.v.'s for the Rich set were 0.19 ($N = 34$) in 1955 and 0.08 ($N = 29$) in 1979, and the corresponding figures for the Poor group were 0.52 and 0.29. These figures were found to be nearly identical when the analysis was performed for a constant set of cases only. Data are from UNESCO, *Statistical Yearbook,* various years.

22. These figures did not significantly differ when only a constant number of cases was used. Data are from UNESCO, *Statistical Yearbook,* various years.

23. Bray 1981.

24. For the Poor set of countries in 1965 the mean proportion repeating was 21.7 percent ($N = 18$) with a c.v. of 0.45, and by 1979 the mean had dropped to 16.1

percent (N = 12) while the c.v. had risen to 0.55. The corresponding figures for the
Rich set were 16.8 percent (N = 19) and a c.v. of 0.59 in 1965, and 8.2 percent (N =
13) and a c.v. of 1.01 in 1979. The findings were nearly identical when the analyses
were replicated for a set of cases with a constant N. Data for the dimension are
from UNESCO, *Statistical Yearbook,* various years.

25. Pryor 1968.

26. The respective figures for the Rich set in 1955 were a mean of 30.3 (N = 38)
and a c.v. of 0.21. By 1979 the mean was 22.0 (N = 27) and the c.v. 0.28. The figures for the Poor set of countries were a mean of 36.6 percent (N = 37) and a c.v. of
0.29 in 1955, and mean of 34.4 percent (N = 22) and a c.v. of 0.26 in 1979. These
figures were nearly identical when the analysis was performed for sets of constant
cases. The data are from UNESCO, *Statistical Yearbook,* various years.

27. Levin 1978.

28. The figures for the Rich and Poor sets (both excluding Eastern European
countries) were as follows

		1955	*1975*
Rich	Mean	27.3%	24.4%
	N	27	22
	c.v.	0.49	0.57
Poor	Mean	20.6%	12.2%
	N	30	26
	c.v.	0.74	0.86

Figures for all sets of nations are nearly identical to those found when the analysis was based on constant cases only. Data are from UNESCO, *Statistical Yearbook,*
various years.

29. OECD 1974.

30. Friesen et al. 1980.

31. The countries were the United States, England, West Germany, Canada, Brazil,
Australia, Japan, Chile, the Netherlands, Nigeria, France, Sweden, India, and Israel.

32. National scores were determined by averaging the separate score for five areas of decisionmaking. The possible scores for each area were 0—none, 1—consul-
tative role, 2—advisory role, 3—determining voice, 4—veto power, or N—nobody.
The areas were: salaries, curriculum design, education reform, building construction, and instructional materials selection and adoption. For further details, see Passow et al. 1976, p. 248.

33. This scheme for differentiating degrees of centralization in public educational
systems rather oversimplifies a complex reality. For instance, two nations could be
scored as being alike with respect to the relative domination of states and provinces, as
against local communities, as are the United States and Japan, while beneath the surface the two are clearly distinct. This comes about because the local communities in
each country, while having considerable responsibility, have *different kinds* of responsibility. In Japan they look after only primary schooling, whereas in the United States
they attend to postprimary schooling as well. Thus, given the same absolute level of
centralization, we should further differentiate systems by whether responsibility for
given elements of the school ladder are shared between levels or are level-specialized.

34. UNESCO 1971.

35. Coombs and Merritt 1977.

36. Beattie 1978.

37. Ramirez and Boli 1982. Their measure was developed by examining and coding the government level that had control over each of five areas of primary education. These areas were admission policies, curricula, examination procedures, degrees, and funding. The procedure was repeated for secondary education. See also Ramirez and Rubinson 1979.

38. Characteristically the proportions of all students enrolled in public (rather than private) schools around 1965 were 90, 72, and 90 percent for the primary, secondary, and tertiary levels, respectively. These figures were calculated for a set of nations that were independent in 1955. Data are from UNESCO 1966.

39. A few cases can be cited in which there was a long gap between the introduction of compulsory education and of free elementary education, such as Austria, with a gap of ninety-five years, and Germany with a gap of 125 years. It appears, however, that as the nineteenth century proceeded the gap considerably lessened, as it logically and equitably should have. For example, in England it was twenty-one years, and in France, one year.

40. Countries were included in this analysis only if they were independent in 1955 and provided data for the initial 1955 observation period. The corresponding figures for the Poor set of nations were 1.7 percent ($N = 20$) with a c.v. of 0.40, and 3.1 percent ($N = 13$) with a c.v. of 0.48. These results are comparable to those produced by an analysis resting on a constant number of cases. Data are from UNESCO, *Statistical Yearbook,* various years.

41. Friesen et al. 1980; IBE 1955.

42. The distribution of *financing* responsibility closely corresponds to the distribution of *control* already discussed.

43. Edding and Berstecher 1969.

44. IBE 1955; UNESCO 1971.

45. Edding 1966, 56.

46. OCSR (Organization for Comparative Social Research) 1954.

47. Monroe 1913.

48. Ramirez and Meyer 1981.

49. Howard points out an issue that the reader should keep in mind when considering coeducation and the mixed school, especially from a historical perspective. The presence of a mixed-sex school does not necessarily mean that it is a school in which boys and girls are treated alike or one in which they follow identical courses of study.

50. Lange 1890.

51. UNESCO 1969.

52. The mean female share at the primary level was stable at 49 percent across the period for the "Rich" subset of countries, and at the secondary level the figure was around 45 percent.

53. Hans 1934.

54. Although the available data are not strictly comparable, coming as they do from the different sources, they do reflect what seems an obvious trend. Female shares at the secondary level, for selected countries were:

	1888	1934	1955
United States	50%	50%	50%
Austria	16	30	37
France	10	32	50
Germany	30 (Prussia)	35 (Germany)	45 (W. Germany)
Italy	28	40	40
United Kingdom	50	50	50

The figure "50 percent" in the table should be interpreted as an estimate of sexual parity. Data for the dates 1888, 1934, and 1955 are from Lange 1890; Hans 1934; and UNESCO, *Statistical Yearbook*, 1955, respectively.

55. Hans 1934.

56. These seventeen more industrialized nations were Canada, the United States, Japan, Austria, Belgium, Denmark, Finland, France, Germany, the Netherlands, Italy, Norway, Sweden, Switzerland, England and Wales, Australia, and New Zealand. The corresponding figures for the other sets of countries were as follows

		1955	1975
World	Mean	24.9%	37.1%
	c.v.	0.43	0.26
	N	59	49
Rich	Mean	29.5%	41.5%
	c.v.	0.31	0.16
	N	32	30
Poor	Mean	18.6%	30.4%
	c.v.	0.53	0.31
	N	25	18

These figures were calculated for only those countries that were independent in 1955 and that had figures available for the 1955 observation point. A replication of this analysis for a constant number of nations yielded no significant differences. Data source was UNESCO, *Statistical Yearbook,* various years.

57. The index of segregation by area of study developed by Boulding et al. (1976) should prove useful for this purpose.

58. OECD 1975.

59. The countries studied were Belgium, France, West Germany, Greece, Italy, Luxembourg, the Netherlands, Norway, Spain, the United Kingdom, and the United States ($N = 11$).

60. Hastings and Hastings 1980.

References to Chapter 6

Adams, Don, and Joseph P. Farrell, eds. 1967. *Education and Social Development.* Syracuse, NY: Syracuse University, Center for Development Education.

Aries, Philippe. 1962. *Centuries of Childhood: A Social History of Family Life.* Translated by Robert Baldick. New York: Knopf.

Beattie, N. 1978. "Formalized Parent Participation in Education: A Comparative Perspective (France, German Federal Republic, England and Wales)." *Comparative Education*, Vol. 14 (March), 41–48.

Boulding, Elise, Shirley A. Nuss, Dorothy Lee Carson, and Michael A. Greenstein. 1976. *Handbook of International Data on Women*. New York: Wiley.

Bray, M. 1981. "Policies and Progress Towards Universal Primary Education." *Journal of Modern African Studies*, Vol. 19, No. 4, 547–563.

Clark, B. R. 1978. "Academic Differentiation in National Systems of Higher Education." *Comparative Education Review*, Vol. 22, 242–258.

Coombs, F. S., and R. L. Merritt. 1977. "The Public's Role in Educational Policy-Making: An International View." *Education and Urban Society*, Vol. 9 (February), 167–196.

Craig, J. E. 1981. "The Expansion of Education." In *Review of Research in Education*, Vol. 9, ed. David C. Berliner. American Educational Association.

Edding, F. 1966. "Expenditure on Education: Statistics and Comments." In *The Economics of Education*, ed. E.A.G. Robinson and J. E. Vaizey. Macmillan.

Edding, Friedrich, and Dieter Berstecher. 1969. *International Developments of Educational Expenditure, 1950–1965*. UNESCO.

Friesen, David, Avigdor Farine, and J. Collins Meek. 1980. *Educational Administration: A Comparative View*. Department of Educational Administration, University of Alberta, Edmonton.

Gimenso, Jose Blat, and Ricardo Marin Ibanez. 1981. *The Education of Primary and Secondary Schools*. UNESCO.

Hans, N. 1934. "The Educational Systems of Foreign Countries." In *The Year Book of Education*, ed. Lord Eustace Percy. London: Evans Brothers.

Hastings, Elizabeth H., and Philip K. Hastings, eds. 1980. *Index to International Public Opinion, 1978/79*. Westport, CT: Greenwood Press.

Howard, B. A. 1928. *The Mixed School*. London: University of London Press.

Inkeles, A. 1980. "Modernization and Family Patterns: A Test of Convergence Theory." *Conspectus of History*, Vol. 1, No. 6, ed. Dwight W. Hoover and John T.A. Koumoulides (Muncie, IN: Department of History, Ball State University), 31–62.

_____. 1981. "Convergence and Divergence in Industrial Societies." In *Directions of Change: Modernization Theory, Research, and Realities*, ed. Mustafa O. Attir, Burkart Holzner, and Zdenek Suda, 3–39. Boulder: Westview Press.

Inkeles, A., and L. Sirowy. 1979. "Cross-National Comparison on Students-to-Teacher Ratios: An Example in Convergence Theory." Project Report No. 79-A10, Institute for Research on Educational Finance and Governance, School of Education, Stanford University.

International Bank for Reconstruction and Development. 1971. *World Tables*. Washington, DC: IBRD.

International Bureau of Education. 1955. *Financing Education*. Geneva: IBE.

Lange, Helene. 1890. *Higher Education of Women in Europe*. Translated by L. R. Klemm. Appleton.

Levin, H. M. 1978. "The Dilemma of Comprehensive Secondary School Reforms in Western Europe." *Comparative Education Review*, Vol. 22 (October), 434–451.

Meyer, J. W. 1981. "Organizational Factors Affecting Legalization in Education." Program Report No. 81-B10, Institute for Research on Educational Finance and Governance, School of Education, Stanford University.

Monroe, Paul, ed. 1913. *A Cyclopedia of Education.* Vol. 5. Macmillan.

Organization for Comparative Social Research. 1954. "Cross-National Research: A Case Study." *Journal of Social Issues,* Vol. 10, No. 4, 1–68.

Organization for Economic Cooperation and Development. 1974. *Towards Mass Higher Education.* Paris: OECD.

_____. 1975. *Education, Inequality, and Life Chances.* Paris: OECD.

Passow, A. Harry, Harold J. Noah, Max A. Eckstein, and John R. Mallea. 1976. *The National Case Study: An Empirical Comparative Study of Twenty-one Educational Systems.* Stockholm: Almqvist & Wiksell.

Perry, Arthur C. 1912. *Outlines of School Administration.* Macmillan.

Pryor, Frederic L. 1968. *Public Expenditures in Communist and Capitalist Nations.* Homewood, IL: Irwin.

Ramirez, F. O., and J. Boli [Boli-Bennett]. 1982. "Global Patterns of Educational Institutionalization." In *Comparative Education,* ed. Philip G. Altbach, Robert F. Arnove, and Gail P. Kelly. New York: Macmillan.

Ramirez, F. O., and J. Meyer. 1981. "Comparative Education: Synthesis and Agenda." In *The State of Sociology: Problems and Prospects,* ed. James F. Short Jr. Beverly Hills: Sage.

Ramirez, F. O., and R. Rubinson. 1979. "Creating Members: The Political Incorporation and Expansion of Public Education." In *National Development and the World System: Educational, Economic, and Political Change, 1950–1970,* ed. John W. Meyer and Michael T. Hannan. Chicago: University of Chicago Press.

United Nations Educational, Scientific, and Cultural Organization (UNESCO). 1958. *World Survey of Education,* Vol. 2, *Primary Education.* United Nations.

_____. 1966. *World Survey of Education,* Vol. 4, *Higher Education.* United Nations.

_____. 1969. *Study of Co-education.* United Nations Economic and Social Council, Commission on the Status of Women.

_____. 1971. *World Survey of Education,* Vol. 5, *Educational Policy, Legislation, and Administration.* United Nations.

_____. 1965–1981. *Statistical Yearbook.* UNESCO.

Williamson, J. B., and J. J. Fleming. 1977. "Convergence Theory and the Social Welfare Sector: A Cross-National Analysis." *International Journal of Comparative Sociology,* Vol. 18 (September-December), 242–253.

Notes to Chapter 7

The essential elements of this chapter were presented as the Robert La Follette Lecture at Ball State University on March 28, 1979, under the title "Modernization and the Family." Its scope was expanded, and the evidence it contains was considerably augmented and amplified, thanks to the continuing support of my research by the Hoover Institution on War, Revolution, and Peace.

1. Goode 1963, 7–10, 13–18, 70.

2. Lenero-Otero 1977.

3. The propositions so far tested against the evidence were selected largely on the basis of my knowledge as to whether data were readily available to conduct any given test. Whether this opportunistic approach masked some underlying bias, I cannot tell. My preliminary excursions into topics not reported here suggest that, in the final set of thirty tests, the proportion of propositions clearly supporting the convergence hypothesis will be about the same as in the subset reported here.

4. Data are from World Bank 1978, 506–509. Even when the reproduction rate is at unity, and, in effect, each woman is replacing only herself, the total population may continue to grow. The time elapsing between the point at which a country achieves a stable reproduction rate and the point at which growth ceases may be thirty or more years.

5. U.S. Bureau of the Census, *Current Population Reports,* 1975, Series B, 42–48.

6. World Bank 1978, 506–509.

7. To evaluate fertility levels and their decline, Cutright and Kelly (1978) used an indicator of "structural modernization"—based on education, urbanization, and living standards. It proved to be much more important than measures of the land available per capita or the legalization of abortion. It is an important task, beyond the scope of our effort here, to ascertain the separate contribution of each of these as well as of other elements of the modernization syndrome, especially attitudinal and valuational, to the declining gross reproduction rate.

8. See Bogue and Tsui 1979. They attribute the rapid movement of the less developed toward the standard of the industrialized mainly to the adoption of family planning programs. They are so impressed by the sharpness in the recent decline in fertility in less developed countries that they predict that by the year 2025 the entire world will have nearly achieved zero population growth.

9. Goode 1963, 43. The data Goode presents, however, are by no means consistent in support of his conclusion. Thus in Finland the male marriage age went down from 27.3 in 1900 to 24.9 in 1955, but by 1940 it had climbed back up to 27.2 after having been as low as 26.0 in 1901. In Sweden the average remained essentially the same from 1900 to 1955 but rose and fell in the intervening years. The same was true for Norway, England, and Wales. Of the data for eight countries in Goode's Table 11-6, only one country seems unambiguously to follow the pattern stated in his conclusion.

10. These computations are based on data for the pre-1955 period given in Hajnal 1965 and in Glass and Eversley 1965, and for the post-1955 period in United Nations 1977.

11. This earlier U.S. marriage age could have been produced by forces other than the modernization processes mentioned. A large part of the massive waves of immigration to the United States came from Eastern Europe, and the cultural preference in Eastern Europe was for early marriage.

12. Data are from U.S. Bureau of the Census, *Current Population Reports,* 1975, Series P-20, No. 323.

13. Hajnal 1965, 110.

14. Trost (1977) recognized that the crude marriage rate is not as good a measure as the percentage married at given ages, but he chose the former measure to increase the number of cases available.

15. Trost 1977, 198. The percentage "married" in Sweden does not necessarily define the percentage living as couples in a nominally permanent relationship. There is a long history in Sweden of postponing "marriage" until a child comes along. More recently in the 1970s many young people are not formalizing or registering their relationship even after children have been born.

16. For example, in the decade from the mid-1960s to the mid-1970s, both the United States and Sweden experienced a sharp increase in the proportion of young women aged twenty to twenty-four who had not yet married. Despite these dramatic shifts, the United States clearly continued to be a country favoring earlier marriage than did Sweden, and the gap separating them had been only very slightly reduced.

17. Using Goode's data for Norway, Sweden, Finland, the United States, and England and Wales, we note that in 1900 the five nations had an average age at first marriage of 26.9; fifty-five years later the average had declined slightly to only 26.2. One nation was at exactly the same point, two saw the average rise, and two saw it fall. But the gap separating the highest from the lowest age at marriage among the five increased from three years to five years over that span. In other words, the set of five became more divergent over time! (See Goode 1963, 47, Table 2-6). For a more precise measure using a larger set of countries, see Hajnal 1965.

18. Hajnal 1965.

19. Ibid. Increasing convergence or divergence may be measured by an index of dispersion, obtained by dividing the standard deviation by the mean of a series. If the index increases, the set is becoming more divergent, that is, there is more variation around its average. For our fifteen countries of Western Europe the index rose from 1900 to 1970. For males at age twenty-four it went from 0.05 to 0.11, and for females from 0.13 to 0.17. These figures indicate that the countries have diverged even though, as noted above, almost all have experienced parallel change in the direction of earlier marriage for men and women. We recognize that comparing only two points in time may not truly reflect the long-term trend.

20. Davis 1962, 348.

21. Indeed, Hajnal goes so far as to say that marital status data for Latin America and the Caribbean are almost useless because so many people who by common definition ought to be treated as married are counted as legally unmarried (1965, 105).

22. In Ireland 28 percent of men at age fifty were still single, whereas the median for the other countries of Western Europe was about 9 percent (United Nations 1977).

23. Goode 1963, 49.

24. Calculated from data for 1900 in Hajnal 1965 and for 1970 in United Nations 1977. Data given earlier by Goode (1963, 49, Table 2-7) for only five "European" countries had suggested that there was a modest long-term trend in Europe for larger proportions of the population to have been "ever married." His data on five "European" countries, going back to 1890, show a greater proportion of the "ever married" by 1950 in all five countries. The average ever married among those aged forty-five to fifty was 88.8 percent in 1890 and had risen to 90.8 percent by

1950, although the intervening years witnessed some fluctuations in the recorded rates.

25. In 1970 Korea, despite its considerable modernization, still had only 0.1 percent of women as "never married" before age fifty. Although they were much less modernized, Pakistan, Nepal, Iran, and Indonesia, among others, also reported 1 percent or less in that category. There was, however, some evidence of change. In Japan there was an increase in the percentage of never-married women from 2 to 4 percent between 1920 and 1970 (United Nations 1977).

26. The main contribution to this line of analysis has been made by Robert Winch and his associates and is summarized in Winch 1977.

27. Goode 1963, 6.

28. Blumberg and Pilar 1977, 188–220.

29. Wrigley 1977.

30. Davis 1977.

31. Yamane 1977, 81.

32. To continue the family line by adoption when one had no son has traditionally been a fundamental principle of Japanese family organization. In 1953, long after much modernization and urbanization, 73 percent of the Japanese said that they would adopt someone under the circumstances. But the proportion who held to that view fell steadily from then on. By 1973 only 36 percent would still adopt merely to continue the family line. It must be acknowledged, of course, that other attitudes more than held their own. For example, having a "grand affair" for weddings and funerals fluctuated somewhat, but about one-third of all respondents were in favor in both 1953 and 1973 (Sakamoto 1974, 49).

33. Yamane 1977, 81.

34. Turowski 1977.

35. Wagatsuma 1977

36. These are approximate figures based on data given in Bane 1976, Table A-13. The figures given represent the totals of all persons over sixty-five whose relationship to the head of the household was described as either "parent" or "other relative"; the latter I presume to mean mainly a son-in-law or a daughter-in-law. If we combine men and women we have 22.5 percent of older men and women living with their grown children. Without citing a source or a year, Turowski (1977) said that 25 percent of old people in the United States lived with their children.

37. Yankelovich, Skelly, and White 1977.

38. Wagatsuma 1977.

39. Yamane 1977, 94.

40. Haranne and Allardt 1978, 54.

41. The contrasts in Libya were comparable but much less marked (see Haranne and Allardt 1978, 54).

42. Ornauer et al. 1976, 655.

43. The "parents" were sampled in 1976/77 and the college youth in 1973, and the "parents" in the one study were not the actual parents of the college students in the other. The difference in emphasis could be generational, but it seems more likely explained by the stage of the life cycle that each sample found itself in. In other words, we may assume that the college youth will give greater emphasis to the family as a value once they too are married and have children. The difference between

the samples could also be produced by differences in average level of education; the parent sample obviously had a much lower average than the college students (see Yankelovich, Skelly, and White 1977, 73.)

44. Bane 1975.

45. Goode 1963, 75.

46. Schneider, in Szalai et al. 1972, 330–331.

47. Yankelovich, Skelly, and White 1977, 119.

48. Form 1976.

49. Shorter 1975, 244.

50. Goode 1963, 75.

51. My account here paraphrases the succinct account in Hiroshi Wagatsuma 1977.

52. Wagatsuma 1977.

53. Yankelovich, Skelly, and White 1977, 80.

54. Shorter 1975, 327.

55. Of women born in the United States between 1870 and 1910, generally 20 percent came to the end of their period of fertility without ever having had a child. The proportion thus childless fell steadily starting with the cohort born in 1915. In the cohort born in 1925, only half as many women, some 10 percent, reached the end of their productive years (around 1970) without having had a child. A number of forces could have brought about this condition. Fewer women may have remained unmarried; those who got married may have done so earlier; improvement in health may have contributed to fertility; attitudes may have changed (U.S. Bureau of the Census, *Current Population Reports,* 1975, Series P-23, No. 70, and Series B, 42–48).

56. Employed men who were single spent an average of 29 minutes per day, married men with children, 26 minutes, averaging the time spent across all the days of the week. The term "total housework" includes not only cooking and laundry but also other household tasks in which men more often specialize—such as animal care and house maintenance. The data came from forty-nine U.S. cities sampled during the 1960s (Szalai et al. 1972, 643).

57. These "participation" ranges apply to working days only, for both employed men and employed women, with distinction as to whether or not they were married (Szalai et al. 1972, 584 and 588).

58. The numbers I have given in the text are the median across twelve countries. The numbers for each country, however, are averages. That is, they took into account the time of nonparticipants, equal to zero. In computing these medians across twelve countries, I represented each country by the same subgroup of the population (Szalai et al. 1972, 643).

59. For example, the ratios of time spent per day by employed men with children versus employed women with children was: for Jackson, U.S.A., 1:5.9 and for Pskov, U.S.S.R., 1:6.3. Comparing Osnabruk in the Federal Republic of Germany with Kragujevac in Yugoslavia, we obtain ratios of 1:11.5 and 1:9.4, respectively.

60. Allardt and Wesolowski 1978.

61. Szalai et al. 1972, 599.

62. See Lenero-Otero 1977.

63. The rabbi is thus quoted in the Pirke Aroth. I am in debt to Daniel Bell for calling this injunction to my attention.

References to Chapter 7

Allardt, Erik, and Wlodzimierz Wesolowski, eds. 1978. *Social Structure and Change: Finland and Poland—Comparative Perspective.* Warsaw: Polish Scientific Publishers.

Bane, Mary Jo. 1975. *Here to Stay: American Families in the Twentieth Century.* New York: Basic Books.

Blumberg, Rae L., and Maria G. Pilar. 1977. "The Political Economy of the Mother-Child Family." In *Beyond the Nuclear Family Model: Cross-Cultural Perspectives,* ed. Luis Lenero-Otero. Beverly Hills: Sage Publications.

Bogue, Donald J., and Amy Ong Tsui. 1979. "Zero World Population Growth?" *The Public Interest,* No. 55 (Spring), 99–113.

Coale, Ansley J. 1973. "The Demographic Transition." In *The International Population Conference, Liège 1973.* Liège, Belgium: International Union for the Scientific Study of Population.

Cutright, Phillips, and William R. Kelly. 1978. "Modernization and Other Determinants of National Birth, Death, and Growth Rates: 1958–1972." *Comparative Studies in Sociology,* Vol. 1, 17–46.

Davis, Kingsley. 1963. "The Theory of Change and Response in Modern Demographic History." *Population Index,* Vol. 29 (October), 345–365.

Davis, Natalie Z. 1977. "Ghosts, Kin, and Progeny: Some Features of Family Life in Early Modern France." *Daedalus* (Spring), 87–114.

Form, William H. 1976. *Blue-Collar Stratification: Autoworkers in Four Countries.* Princeton: Princeton University Press.

Glass, D. V., and D.E.C. Eversley. 1965. *Population in History.* London: Edward Arnold.

Goode, William J. 1963. *World Revolution and Family Patterns.* New York: Macmillan.

Hajnal, J. 1965. "European Marriage Patterns in Perspective." In *Population in History,* ed. D. V. Glass and D.E.C. Eversley. London: Edward Arnold.

Haranne, Markku, and Eric Allardt. 1978. "Attitudes Toward Modernity and Modernization: An Appraisal of an Empirical Study." Unpublished paper presented at International Sociological Conference "Socio-Economic Systems and Modern Orientations," Brussels, December 1978.

Lenero-Otero, Luis, ed. 1977. *Beyond the Nuclear Family Model: Cross-Cultural Perspectives.* Beverly Hills: Sage Publications.

Ornauer, H., H. Wiberg, A. Sicinski, and J. Galtung, eds. 1976. *Images of the World in the Year 2000.* Atlantic Highlands, NJ: Humanities Press.

Sakamoto, Yosiyuki. 1974. "A Study of the Japanese National Character." Part V, Fifth Nationwide Survey, *Annals of the Institute of Statistical Mathematics,* Supplement 8, 1–57.

Shorter, Edward. 1975. *The Making of the Modern Family.* New York: Basic Books.

Szalai, Alexander, ed., with Philip E. Converse, Pierre Feldheim, Erwin K. Scheuch, and Philip J. Stone. 1972. *The Use of Time: Daily Activities of Urban and Suburban Populations in Twelve Countries.* The Hague: Mouton.

Thompson, E., and J. Peretz, eds. 1979. *Social Trends,* No. 9. Government Statistical Service. London: H. M. Stationery Office.

Trost, Jan. 1977. "Married and Unmarried Cohabitation: The Case of Sweden with Some Comparisons." In *Beyond the Nuclear Family Model: Cross-Cultural Perspectives,* ed. Luis Lenero-Otero. Beverly Hills: Sage Publications.

Turowski, Jan. 1977. "Inadequacy of the Theory of the Nuclear Family: The Polish Experience." In *Beyond the Nuclear Family Model: Cross-Cultural Perspectives,* ed. Luis Lenero-Otero. Beverly Hills: Sage Publications.

United Nations, Department of Economics and Social Affairs Statistical Office. 1977. *Demographic Yearbook, 1976.* New York: United Nations.

United States Bureau of the Census. *Current Population Reports.* Washington, DC: U.S. Government Printing Office. Series P-20, No. 323.

_____. 1975. *Historical Statistics of the United States: Colonial Times to 1970,* Vols. 1 and 2. Washington, DC: U.S. Government Printing Office.

Wagatsuma, Hiroshi. 1977. "Some Aspects of the Japanese Family." *Daedalus* (Spring), 171–210.

Winch, Robert F., with the collaboration of Rae Lesser Blumberg, Maria-Pilar Garcia, Margaret Gordon, and Gay C. Kitson. 1977. *Familial Organization: A Quest for Determinants.* New York: Free Press.

World Bank. 1978. *World Development Report, 1978.* Washington, DC: World Bank.

_____. 1976. *World Tables, 1976.* Baltimore and London: Johns Hopkins University Press.

Wrigley, E. Anthony. 1977. "Reflections on the History of the Family." *Daedalus* (Spring), 71–85.

Yamane, Tsuneo. 1977. "The Nuclear Family Within the Three Generational Household in Modern Japan." In *Beyond the Nuclear Family Model: Cross-Cultural Perspectives,* ed. Luis Lenero-Otero. Beverly Hills: Sage Publications.

Yankelovich, Skelly, and White, Inc. 1977. *Raising Children in a Changing Society.* Minneapolis: General Mills Consumer Center.

Notes to Chapter 8

1. Additional studies of occupational prestige are available for the United States and Australia. The authors decided to restrict the U.S. data to the most comprehensive study available. The Australian case (Ronald Taft, "The Social Grading of Occupations in Australia," *British Journal of Sociology,* Vol. 4, No. 2 [June 1953]) was not included in this report because it was felt that little was to be gained by the inclusion of another Anglo-Saxon country.

2. (1) A. A. Congalton, "The Social Grading of Occupations in New Zealand," *British Journal of Sociology,* Vol. 4, No. 1 (March 1953) (New Zealand data); (2) John Hall and D. Caradog Jones, "The Social Grading of Occupations," *British Journal of Sociology,* Vol. 1, No. 1 (January 1950) (Great Britain); (3) National Opinion Research Center, "Jobs and Occupations: A Popular Evaluation," in Reinhard Bendix and Seymour Martin Lipset, *Class, Status, and Power* (Glencoe, IL: Free Press, 1953) (United States data); (4) the Schleswig-Holstein data are taken from an article published in *Der Spiegel,* June 30, 1954, reporting a study by Pro-

fessor Karl-Martin Bolte, of Christian-Albrecht University, in Kiel, Germany, to be published early in 1955; (5) Research Committee, Japan Sociological Society, "Report of a Sample Survey of Social Stratification and Mobility in the Six Large Cities of Japan" (mimeograph, December 1952) (the authors are grateful to Professor Kunio Odaka, of the University of Tokyo, for bringing this valuable study to their attention); and (6) the Soviet materials were collected by the Project on the Soviet Social System of the Russian Research Center at Harvard University.

3. Note that the correlation coefficients are all product-moment correlations, with the exception of the five coefficients involving the German study, which are rank-order correlations. With the exception noted, these coefficients represent the degree of similarity between the prestige *scores* given to the occupations.

4. Since the correlations involving Germany are rank-order correlations, it is difficult to make comparisons of such coefficients with others in Table 8.1. However, the relationship between rank-order correlations and product-moment correlations is rather high in the upper ranges, and it can be taken for granted that if prestige scores were available for the German ratings, the analysis shown in Table 8.2 would not be materially altered.

5. Table 8.5 will be found a useful aid in this connection, since by reading across the rows of the table one can tell quickly how many times a particular occupation was evaluated and by which national samples.

6. See the note to Table 8.4 for examples of occupations included in each type.

Notes to Chapter 9

The authors express their appreciation to Edward A. Tiryakian for his voluntary services as research assistant and to Alice S. Rossi for a critical reading.

1. My definition excludes the activities that *create* knowledge, symbols, and values, such as science, religion, and art. It also excludes transportation, in the usual sense of moving goods *physically*. Much of electronic communication is, in a sense, a form of transport, but it is nevertheless included in, indeed it is central to, my inquiry.

2. Mitchell 1975, 652; Euromonitor Publications 1987, 1346.

3. Data are from Universal Postal Union 1984, Tables 16 and 18. Worldwide data for later years were not available as of 1987. Newspaper and small packet mail, not included in these figures, equals the volume of letter and postcard mail but involves less international traffic.

4. For the period 1977–1981 I calculated the share that international mail constituted of all mail worldwide, letters and packages combined, and found that the role of the international fell off steadily, with the percentages each year being, respectively 2.78, 2.74, 2.70, 2.65, and 2.58 percent. This decline, however, was accounted for almost entirely by a sharp decrease in the flow of international mail from the more developed countries. Over this same period the less developed countries, not so able to acquire electronic means of communication, were increasing their international mailings at a steady rate of about 7 percent each year. See Universal Postal Union 1984, 200–205.

5. Calculated from data given in International Telecommunication Union 1977 and 1986. Despite their more rapid rate of growth, international calls were still a modest proportion of domestic calls. For example, in Germany in 1984 calls going abroad equaled less than 1.5 percent of domestic calls.

6. The International Telecommunications Union (ITU) credits the United States with placing 773,000 foreign calls in 1950 (MacBride et al. 1980, 55), and with 419.7 million such calls in 1984 (ITU 1986, 138). One should note, however, that there was a tremendous surge in the report of such calls from 1981 to 1982. As reported by the ITU, in that one year the calls escalated from 127 to 310 million. It may be that much of this traffic was not in the form of conversations but rather reflected the increasing tendency to send computer and other electronic information along phone lines.

7. Data are from ITU 1986, 38, 138. The seeming anomaly that Germany, with one-fourth the population of the United States, might account for almost as many international calls appears in a different light if one allows that in geographical spread the nation-states of the European Community are analogues to the several states of the United States. A call from New York to San Francisco conducted in a foreign language counts as a domestic call; one from Paris to Brussels carried only in French, or from Milan to Lugano spoken in Italian, will be scored as international. The conventions for defining different types of calls, which vary considerably from country to country, also play a role in confusing efforts to compare the phone traffic of nations.

8. *The World's Telephones: A Statistical Compilation of January 1982*, published by AT&T, reports on the basis of total international "conversations," thus taking account of incoming as well as outgoing calls. As of 1982 they credited the United States with 530 million international conversations, presumably for the calendar year 1981. In that year the Federal Communications Commission reported to the ITU only 127 million outgoing calls, but as noted earlier, the figure was revised sharply upward for 1982.

9. U.S. Department of Commerce 1987, 31ff.

10. Ploman 1984, 31.

11. See MacBride et al. 1980, 55; Firestone 1985, 146–150; Mosteshar 1986, 1; Martinez 1985, 1–2. Not all the telephone circuits available on a satellite are used for strictly international communication. National telephone systems may also rent satellite channels to use for communication within a single country. However, the dominant mode for carrying telecommunications overland, and within nations, is by point-to-point microwave transmission, which accounts for as much as 80 percent of all long-distance traffic revenue (see Electronic Industries Association 1986).

12. Demac 1985, 7; U.S. Department of Commerce 1987, 31–39; *New York Times,* September 16, 1987; *Business Week,* November 9, 1987.

13. Quoted in Martinez 1985, xvii.

14. INTELSAT, *Annual Report 1976/77,* 198ff.; Martinez 1985, 3–4.

15. MacBride et al. 1980, 54–55. The figure for the number of phones is my estimate for 1988. Calculating the world's stock of phones is made problematic by national differences in how *phones* as against *phone lines* are counted, and by the imprecision of many of underlying national surveys. The latest estimate of the

worldwide total I could find was for 1984, at which time AT&T placed the number just under 500 million. The U.S. Department of Commerce's *U.S. Industrial Outlook*, 1987, credits the United States alone with 220 million phones. Since in recent times the United States has consistently had close to 40 percent of the world's phones, it seems highly likely that in 1988 there will be 600 million sets in the world.

16. Smith 1980, 5.

17. Merrill 1983, 14–15.

18. Ibid., 48.

19. Demac et al. 1985, 7.

20. Gertner and Pay 1987, 639.

21. Katz 1981.

22. Savit 1980, 19–22.

23. Electronic Industries Association 1986, 56.

24. Ibid., 55. VANs are private data networks that, while transmitting data, offer related services beyond what the regular long-distance carriers normally provide. Their market was estimated to be US$310 million in 1985, expected to rise to $1.5 billion in 1988 and to 2.25 billion in 1993.

25. See U.S. Department of Commerce 1987, No. 31, pp. 1–9. Just a year before this business service was established, another went into operation under the name INMARSAT to link all vessels at sea with each other and the land. In this case the Soviet Union actually became a member, and indeed, it took a share, at 14 percent, second only to that paid by the United States, with the rest divided among some forty maritime nations. See Martinez 1985, 1–2.

26. Hudson 1985, 36.

27. Firestone 1985, 37. Of course such cost reductions at the macro level depend in good part on reductions effected at the micro level. Thus the Intel Corporation reported in *Business Week,* November 9, 1987, that in ten years it had brought the cost of programmable memory chips down from 1,000 millicents per bit to a mere 1 millicent per bit.

28. Much of what was incorporated in this equipment was of course a product of the electronic components industry, which in that same year made shipments valued at over $43 billion. We should also note that a significant portion of the communications equipment shipped was meant for use by the military. See Electronic Industries Association 1986, 35–39; U.S. Department of Commerce 1986, pp. 32-2, 28-7.

29. U.S. Department of Commerce 1986, pp. 31ff.; Electronic Industries Association 1986, 35, 57. To arrive at these totals only four media were considered: telephone, data communications, mobile radio and paging, and satellite and broadband communications. For an earlier period, approximately 1980, Loomis (1983, 175), put the total "information market" at US$250 billion, and the telecommunication element within that market at $100 billion, with an annual growth rate of 20 percent, which would cause it to double every 3.5 years. She did not, however, indicate what subcategories were combined to arrive at this estimate.

30. The 1987 figures are estimates based on data for earlier years given in *Survey of Current Business,* March 1986, and *National Income and Product Accounts,* September 1986, Table 6.1. The narrow definition includes only the industries designated printing and publishing, telephone and telegraph, radio and television broadcasting, and motion pictures (lines 32, 47, 48, and 66 in Table 6.1). A broad

definition would include some fraction of electronic equipment manufacture (line 21), but more important, it would take account of education, which is mainly based on communication, and which alone accounts for some 6 percent of GNP.

31. U.S. Department of Commerce 1986, p. 27-10, and 1987, p. 27-10.

32. Sauvant 1986, 82.

33. *Mondo Economico*, March 1985.

34. The latest data on consumer expenditures available was for 1984, as reported in *Survey of Current Business,* March 1986, 71. To arrive at the total for mass communication expenditures I followed the convention of combining expenditures in five categories and lines as follows: book, etc. (83); magazines, etc. (84); radio and television receivers (87); radio and television services (88); admissions (90). The total for 1984 was $64.7 billion, and to reach the 1987 figure I assumed an annual increase of 8.5 percent, which has been characteristic for recent years.

35. See Haigh et al. 1981, 218; H. Schiller in Haigh et al. 1981, 183, quoting a prediction made in *Advertising Age* (U.S. Department of Commerce 1986, p. 59-4), put the total U.S. advertising expenditures at $66.5 billion for 1982, the latest date available, and I arrived at the 1987 estimate by applying a compound growth rate of 11.5 percent.

36. This points to one of the limits on sign language, since its international form has only some 2,500 signs, at least as of 1975. See British Deaf Association 1975.

37. See UNESCO, *Statistical Yearbook,* 1965, 1975, 1985. The totals for the latest years reported were 1978, 57,000; 1979, 54,000; 1980, 53,000. The books translated in recent years equal approximately 7 percent of all titles published worldwide in any given year.

38. For example, the number of translations in 1971 versus 1980 was: for the Federal Republic of Germany, 4,200 vs. 6,700; for France, 1,900 vs. 5,600; and for the United Kingdom, 727 vs. 1,300. By contrast, Israel went from 579 down to 330; Turkey from 801 to 694; India from 739 to 655. Of course some more advanced countries also slowed down or declined, and some less developed countries increased their translations, but there does seem to be a clear trend.

39. UNESCO, *Statistical Yearbook* 1985, Table 7.15.

40. These figures are from Barrett 1987 and information provided by the American Bible Society, November 16, 1987. Also see *Guinness Book of World Records* 1986.

41. *Guinness Book of World Records* 1986; UNESCO, *Statistical Yearbook,* 1985, Vol. 8, 130–132.

42. This information can be found reproduced in many editions of *The Reader's Digest.*

43. Merrill 1983, 142.

44. See UNESCO, *Statistical Yearbook,* 1985, Table 7.19 compared with Table 7.18.

45. Fenby 1986, 90–91.

46. Ibid., 91–92.

47. Ibid., 97–101. The five agencies covered were: Reuters Europe North, Reuters West Africa, AP Europe, AP Middle East/Africa; and UPI Europe. The survey covered three days in May and dealt with 2,459 news items totaling 574,530 words.

48. See, for example, Rachty 1978 on the wire services input to nine Arab countries, and Schramm 1978 on the wire services in Asia.

49. Fenby 1986, 94.

50. McQuail 1977, pp. 29, 248. Variations in such estimates result from the different conventions and rules about how to calculate both the base and the subject matter that is part of it. McQuail took as his base only "news" space, which meant he excluded financial and business news and feature stories. If those had been included the observed proportions might have been different.

51. Merrill 1983, 277.

52. For explication of the concept of the "prestige" newspaper and a discussion of such papers' performance, see Pool et al. 1970.

53. Pinch (1978) analyzed four leading U.S. newspapers in 1978 and found them to give about 25 percent of their space to foreign news, without much variation. The sixteen newspapers from less developed countries he examined gave an average of 35 percent of their space to events abroad. There was, however, very great variation from country to country. For example, *The Indian Express* gave only 12 percent of its news space to matters foreign, whereas the *Singapore Straits Times* turned over an astonishing 62 percent to such material. The most frequent pattern, however, was to give about 25 percent to this realm.

54. Fenby 1986, 96.

55. In the classic study of the newspapers of thirteen representative countries, reported in Schramm 1964, Figure 1, p. 60, the share of the space dealing with the United States was found generally to be 30 to 40 percent of that given to all foreign countries. France and the Soviet Union each captured 15 to 20 percent of the attention. Obviously that left little room for other countries to be featured.

56. Pinch 1978, Table 1. Rachty (1978, 8), working with eight Arab countries, found a similar ratio, assigning 60 percent of foreign news to the Third World and only 34 percent to the First World.

57. McQuail 1977, 254. In evaluating these results it should be kept in mind that events in the Third World may more often get attention because of great-power involvement in their affairs, as would be the case for Nicaragua as it confronts U.S. policy.

58. Seventy-seven percent of the space in these newspapers was given over to the home country, much as is the custom worldwide. Beyond that, they gave 17 percent of their space to the Third World and only 10 percent to the First World, something less than but close to the 2 to 1 ratio (Pinch 1978, 5).

59. For relevant breakdowns, see McQuail 1977 for Great Britain; Rachty 1978 for the Arab press; and Schramm 1978 for newspapers in Asia.

60. On the Arab countries, see Rachty 1978, and on the Asian countries, Schramm 1978. Note that in the Arab countries all foreign news items were scored, whereas in the Asian press study only the items dealing with the Third World were further classified by subject.

61. McQuail 1977, Table E1, 248.

62. UNESCO, *Statistical Yearbook,* 1986, VI-19, VI-20; Katz and Wedell 1977, 59; Smith 1980, Table 2.

63. The UNESCO *Statistical Yearbook,* 1986, Table 6-9, reported that for 1983 the developed countries had 835 sets per 1,000 of population, and less developed countries 113. Also see MacBride et al. 1980, 128.

64. MacBride et al. 1980, 132.

65. UNESCO, *Statistical Yearbook,* 1985, Table 10.2.

66. Merrill 1983, 222.

67. Katz and Wedell 1977, Table 5.1.

68. Cowlan and Love 1978. The stations surveyed were located in Egypt; Argentina and Colombia; Ghana and Nigeria; India; and Jamaica.

69. As reported by Head (1985), whose source was evidently *World Radio-TV Handbook.* The 1987 edition of the *Handbook* lists 174 "countries" as having television, but many of those listed are territories or dependencies, such as the Virgin Islands and the Galapagos Islands.

70. The UNESCO *Statistical Yearbook,* 1986, Table 6.10, gave the number of transmitters as of 1983 as 45,370. Extrapolating on the basis of recent rates of growth, this figure would have grown to almost 52,000 as early as 1986.

71. Data are from UNESCO, *Statistical Yearbook,* 1986, Table 6.11. Also see MacBride et al. 1980, 128.

72. Merrill 1983, 48.

73. Varis 1984, Table 2.

74. Katz and Wedell 1977, 156.

75. Ibid., 161–162.

76. See Smith, 1980, which is subtitled "How Western Culture Dominates the World." A succinct and moderate summary of the argument about cultural imperialism will be found in MacBride et al. 1980, especially in Part III. The perceptive comments of Elie Abel, appended to the report, serve as a useful critical challenge to some of the main assumptions on which this argument rests.

77. Varis 1984, 273, and Table 2.

78. Antola and Rogers 1984, 186.

79. Ibid., 186; Wirth 1984, 157.

80. UNESCO, *Statistical Yearbook,* 1985, Tables 6.5 and 9.1.

81. Calculated from Table 9.2 in UNESCO, *Statistical Yearbook,* 1985.

82. According reports applying to 1983, Cuba had 880 mobile film units as against 525 fixed locations, and the attendance at the mobile showings was 41.6 million compared to 44.7 million in the regular cinemas. UNESCO, *Statistical Yearbook,* 1985, Table 9.3.

83. MacBride et al. 1980, 128; UNESCO, *Statistical Yearbook,* 1985, Table 9.3.

84. Data are from UNESCO, *Statistical Yearbook,* 1985, Tables 9.3 and 6.7. UNESCO set the total for 1983 at just over 14 billion, exclusive of China. If we assume that a billion Chinese go to the cinema on average only twice a year, that brings the world total to at least 16 billion attendances.

85. As reported by Primo Levi in *The Drowned and the Saved* (New York: Summit Books, 1988), 92.

86. Merrill 1983, 258.

87. Figures are from *Inside Recording* 1986. This source did not explicitly distinguish classical from other forms of recorded music, but we may assume that the greater part of what the European Community exported to the United States was of that type.

88. *Rolling Stone,* September 10, 1987.

89. *Rolling Stone,* September 24, 1987.

90. *Rolling Stone,* September 10, 1987.

91. Briggs 1981, 208.
92. On the emerging structure of world society, see Inkeles 1975, reproduced as Chapter 1 in this volume.
93. Quoted in Firestone 1985, 299.

References to Chapter 9

Antola, Livia, and Everett M. Rogers. 1984. "Television Flows in Latin America." *Communications Research,* Vol. 11, No. 2, 183–202.

Astrain, Santiago. 1975. "'Early Bird' to INTELSAT IV-A (A Decade of Growth)." *Telecommunications Journal,* Vol. 42, No. 11.

AT&T Communications Overseas Marketing Department. 1982. *The World's Telephones: A Statistical Compilation as of January 1982.* Atlanta: R. H. Donnelley.

Barrett, David B. 1987. "Status of the Global Mission, 1987, in Context of the Twentieth Century." *International Bulletin of Missionary Research* (January).

Briggs, Asa. 1981. "Looking Back from the Twenty-first Century." In *Communications in the Twenty-first Century,* ed. Robert W. Haigh, George Gerbner, and Richard B. Byrne. New York: John Wiley & Sons.

The British Deaf Association. 1975. *Gestuno—International Sign Language of the Deaf.* Carlisle, England.

Cowlan, Bert, with Lee M. Love. 1978. *A Look at the World's Radio News.* Medford, MA: Edward R. Murrow Center of Public Diplomacy, The Fletcher School of Law and Diplomacy, Tufts University (March).

Demac, Donna A., et al. 1985. "Equity in Orbit: The 1985 ITU Space WARC." Background Paper, World Administrative Radio Conference on the Use of the Geostationary Satellite Orbit and the Planning of Space Services Utilizing It. London: International Institute of Communications (June).

Electronic Industries Association. 1986. *1986 Edition Electronic Market Data Book.* Washington, DC: Electronic Industries Association.

Elias, Norbert, and Eric Dunning. 1986. *Quest for Excitement: Sport and Leisure in the Civilizing Process.* Oxford: Basil Blackwell.

Euromonitor Publications Ltd. 1987. *European Marketing Data and Statistics, 1987/88.* London: Euromonitor Publications; Detroit: Gale Research Co.

Fenby, Jonathan. 1986. *The International News Services: A Twentieth Century Fund Report.* New York: Schocken Books.

Firestone, Charles M., ed. 1985. *International Satellite and Cable Television: Resource Manual for the Fourth Biennial Communications Law Symposium.* Los Angeles: University of California Regents.

Gertner, Richard, and William Pay, eds. 1987. *International Television and Video Almanac.* 32nd ed. New York: Quigley Publishing Company.

Guinness Book of World Records. 1986. New York: Sterling Publishing Company.

Head, Sydney W. 1985. *World Broadcasting Systems: A Comparative Analysis.* Belmont, CA: Wadsworth Publishing Co.

Haigh, Robert W., George Gerbner, and Richard B. Byrne, eds. 1981. *Communications in the Twenty-first Century.* New York: John Wiley & Sons.

Hudson, Heather E., ed. 1985. *New Directions in Satellite Communications: Challenges for North and South.* Dedham, MA: Artech House.

Inkeles, Alex. 1975. "The Emerging Social Structure of the World." *World Politics,* Vol. 27, No. 4 (July), 467–495.

INTELSAT. 1977. *Annual Report to the Secretary General of the United Nations by the Executive Organ of INTELSAT.* Washington, DC: INTELSAT.

International Telecommunication Union. 1977. *Yearbook of Common Carrier Telecommunications Statistics (Chronological Series, 1966–1975)* and *Radiocommunication Statistics (Year 1975).* Geneva: ITU Press.

_____. 1982. *Yearbook of Common Carrier Telecommunication Statistics (11th ed., Chronological Series, 1973–1982).* Geneva: ITU Press.

_____. 1986. *Yearbook of Common Carrier Telecommunication Statistics (13th ed., Chronological Series, 1975–1984).* Geneva: ITU Press.

Katz, Elihu, with Daniel Dayan and Pierre Motyl. 1981. "In Defense of Media Events." *Communications in the Twenty-first Century,* ed. Robert W. Haigh, George Gerbner, and Richard B. Byrne. New York: John Wiley & Sons.

Katz, Elihu, and George Wedell, with Michael Pilsworth and Dov Shinar. 1977. *Broadcasting in the Third World: Promise and Performance.* Cambridge, MA: Harvard University Press.

Loomis, Mary E.S. 1983. *Data Communication.* Englewood Cliffs, NJ: Prentice-Hall.

MacBride, Sean, et al. 1980. *Many Voices, One World: Communication and Society Today and Tomorrow.* Report by the International Commission for the Study of Communication Problems. New York: Unipub.

Martinez, Larry. 1985. *Communication Satellites: Power Politics in Space.* Dedham, MA: Artech House.

McQuail, Denis. 1977. *Analysis of Newspaper Content.* Royal Commission on the Press Research, Series No. 4. London: H. M. Stationery Office.

Merrill, John C., ed. 1983. *Global Journalism: A Survey of the World's Mass Media.* New York: Longman.

Mitchell, B. R. 1975. *European Historical Statistics, 1750–1970.* New York: Columbia University Press.

Mosteshar, S. Alexander. 1986. *Satellite Communications.* London: Longman.

Pinch, Edward T. 1978. "A Brief Study on News Patterns in Sixteen Third World Countries." *Murrow Reports: Occasional Papers of the Edward R. Murrow Center of Public Diplomacy.* Medford, MA: The Fletcher School of Law and Diplomacy, Tufts University (April).

Ploman, Edward W. 1984. *Space, Earth, and Communication.* Westport, CT: Quorum Books.

Pool, Ithiel de Sola, et al. 1970. *The Prestige Press: A Comparative Study of Political Symbols.* Cambridge, MA: MIT Press.

Rachty, Gehan. 1978. "Foreign News in Nine Arab Countries." *Murrow Reports: Occasional Papers of the Edward R. Murrow Center of Public Diplomacy.* Commissioned by The Fletcher School of Law and Diplomacy, Tufts University, Medford, MA, and the Faculty of Mass Communication, Cairo University, Cairo, Egypt.

Sauvant, Karl P. 1986. *International Transactions in Services: The Politics of Transborder Data Flows.* Boulder: Westview Press.

Savit, Carl H. 1980. "A Quadrillion Geophysical Data Bits Per Year." In *Electronic Communication: Technology and Impacts,* ed. Madeline M. Henderson, and Marcia J. Macaughton, 19–27. AAAS Selected Symposium. Boulder: Westview Press, 1980.

Schramm, Wilbur. 1964. *Mass Media and National Development: The Role of Information in the Developing Countries.* Stanford: Stanford University Press.

Schramm, Wilbur. 1978. "International News Wires and Third World News in Asia." *Murrow Reports: Occasional Papers of the Edward R. Murrow Center of Public Diplomacy.* Medford, MA: Tufts University Press; and Hong Kong: Chinese University of Hong Kong, Centre for Communications Studies (June).

Sennitt, Andrew G., ed. 1987. *World Radio TV Handbook.* New York: Billboard Publications.

Smith, Anthony. 1980. *The Geopolitics of Information: How Western Culture Dominates the World.* London: Faber and Faber.

United Nations Educational, Scientific and Cultural Organization (UNESCO). 1985. *Statistical Yearbook.* Paris: UNESCO.

United States Department of Commerce. 1986. *U.S. Industrial Outlook, 1987.* Washington, DC: U.S. Department of Commerce.

_____. 1987. *U.S. Industrial Outlook.* Washington, DC: U.S. Department of Commerce.

Universal Postal Union. 1984. *Five-Yearly Report on the Development of the Postal Services, 1977–1981.* Bern: International Bureau of the Universal Postal Union.

_____. 1984. *Postal Service Statistics.* Bern: International Bureau of the Universal Postal Union.

Varis, Tapio. 1984. "The International Flow of Television Programs." *Journal of Communication,* 269–278. (Reproduced in Firestone 1985).

Wirth, John. 1984. "Preface." *Communication Research,* Vol. 11, No. 2 (April).

Notes to Chapter 10

The research on which this paper is based was initially supported by a grant from the Russell Sage Foundation. At a later stage in the work the Hoover Institution on War, Revolution, and Peace provided ample assistance. The contribution of both organizations is gratefully acknowledged. Creative assistance was provided by Thomas Oscherwitz, Saori Kamano, and Diana Khor.

1. See Meyer et al. 1979; Inkeles 1980a,b; Inkeles and Sirowy 1983; Inkeles and Usui 1988; Benavot et al. 1991; and Thomas et al. 1987.

2. This statement was made in his decision in *McNabb v. McGrath* and is quoted in Bayles 1990.

3. In the instance of social security the decisive case is *Goldberg v. Kelley,* which is extensively discussed in Mashaw 1985; for student discipline issues, the landmark case is *Goss v. Lopez,* dealt with in Price, Levine, and Cary 1988; and for the mentally ill the watershed cases were *Wyatt v. Stickney* and *Dixon v. Jacobs,* concerning which see Friedman 1976 and Shah and Sales 1991.

4. Marshall 1964.

5. The distinction has a long history. Daniel Bell notes (in a personal communication) that the procedural/substantive distinction in modern legal philosophy is grounded in Kant and was taken up by Weber in an effort to expand the private sphere and to provide a basis for liberalism.

6. Mashaw 1985, 5. Mashaw's pessimism on this score is in marked contrast to that of the legal philosopher Michael Bayles (1990), who is persuaded that "most people have a common sense grasp of the difference."

7. This guarantee is provided in Article 23. We are aware, of course, of the fact that the substantive rights guaranteed in constitutions are seldom granted in absolute or unrestricted form but rather are hedged about with conditions, limitations, and exceptions. Thus the Irish constitution in effect in 1970, while granting citizens in Article 40 the right "to express freely their convictions and opinions" goes on to say that this liberty may not be "used to undermine public order or morality or the authority of the state."

8. To us the term "negative rights" verges on being an oxymoron. Moreover, the distinction between positive and negative rights becomes blurred because substantive rights are often affirmed in the negative, as when the U.S. Constitution states that "Congress shall make no law . . . abridging the freedom of speech," a negative sanctioning, rather than simply specifying free speech as a "positive" right. We find it clearer to maintain the substantive/procedural distinction rather than to speak of positive and negative rights.

9. The limitations on government action described here are not purely hypothetical. Rather, our description tracks the elaboration of the due process rights of the mentally ill as they evolved in the United States through a series of court decisions and legislative enactments. For a review of this process, see Brooks 1974; Golann and Fremouw 1976; Friedman 1976; Shah and Sales 1991; and Mechanic 1989.

10. In the case of handicapped children, the rights here described do not derive directly from the constitutional guarantee in the Fourteenth Amendment but rather rest on Public Law 94-142, known as the Education for All Handicapped Children Act, and on Section 504 of the Rehabilitation Act of 1973. We believe that handicapped children might have obtained comparable treatment if their case had been pressed on constitutional grounds alone, but with the passage of these acts that question became moot.

11. The landmark case in establishing the due process rights of prisoners in the United States was the 1974 Supreme Court decision in *Wolff v. McConnell,* in which the Court declared that "there is no iron curtain drawn between the Constitution and the prisons of this country." See Rudovsky, Bronstein, and Koren 1983, especially pp. 93–96.

12. Davis 1965.

13. United Nations 1983.

14. Emery and Smyth 1986.

15. Mashaw 1983; Schwartz 1987.

16. For a succinct and sobering account of the failure of the Fourteenth Amendment to protect the rights of African-Americans, see Franklin 1991/92.

17. The Court saw this as an issue of freedom, in this case the freedom to enter willingly into a contract, however disadvantageous that contract might seem to some.

18. The cases cited are described and discussed in Mashaw 1985.

19. For a description of the issues and discussion of this case *(Franklin v. Minister of Town and Country Planning)*, see Schwartz 1987.

20. The idea of the shift from subject to citizen is developed in Almond and Verba 1963. For a description and analysis of the expansion of constitutionally specified citizen rights and obligations see Boli 1987b.

21. We say "nominally" because we are well aware that many governments systematically deny their citizens the exercise of the due process rights inscribed in their constitutions and laws. However, as we explain more fully later, the fact that rights may be violated does not completely alter the significance of their having been enshrined in a national constitution.

22. Quoted in Nwabueze 1973, 50.

23. Hughes 1985.

24. Scarman 1987.

25. Andrews 1963, 24.

26. Nwabueze 1973, 2.

27. Martin and George 1923.

28. Baker 1891.

29. Zaide 1970.

30. Friedrich 1967, 5.

31. For example, the American Council of Learned Societies (1990), with the aid of the Ford Foundation, initiated a project on comparative constitutionalism in 1987, and over the next several years organized regional "institutes" for the comparative study of constitutions in Europe, Asia, and Latin America. The debates in these meetings indicated that even among specialists in the study of constitutions there are profound disagreements. Although some argued that there could be a single, universal standard of rights that could be protected by the rule of law, others stressed ethnic, national, and political grounds for challenging what they saw not as a universal but rather as an essentially parochial American and European constitutionalism "which owes its existence to an historical experience quite alien, even antagonistic to the cultures and societies of Asia and Africa, as well as some of those in Latin America."

32. Stalin 1950, 55–65.

33. Triska 1968; Simons 1980.

34. Lee 1977, 8.

35. *New York Times,* February 2, 1990.

36. Kornblith 1991.

37. Inkeles 1975.

38. Meyer et al. 1979, italics added. Whether a given form and practice are truly common can be the subject of considerable uncertainty and disagreement, and establishing the facts requires detailed and meticulous research. At the most general level the diffusion and convergence argument require only that all nations, or all industrial nations, develop systems such as social security or general education, but that level of commonality is hardly likely to impress. However, when the thrust towards the common comes to include arrangements as specific as teacher-pupil ratios or the allocation of time within the school curriculum—as documented in Inkeles, 1975, and in Benavot, *et al.* 1991—then the case becomes more compelling.

39. Benavot et al. 1991; Meyer 1987; Meyer et al. 1979.

40. Inkeles 1975, 1980.

41. Blaustein, in *New York Times*, February 2, 1980.

42. We also coded the constitutions' provision of procedures for the indictment and trial of legislators and other officials as well as for suspending the constitution itself. Because such procedures fall well outside what is conventionally included in the set of generally recognized procedural guarantees for the citizen, and because we have reason to believe that those procedures are determined by different forces, we have not included them in this study.

43. John Boli (1987b) developed a comparable and partially overlapping due process scale based on only seven elements that he coded in the world's constitutions. These were: arrest only by law; innocent until proven guilty; civilians tried in civil court only; bail, and bail not excessively high; habeas corpus; no incommunicado detention; imprisonment only by law, in designated place; trial—public, by jury, adequate defense. Scores ranged from 0, in the case of complete absence of all elements, to 4, one half point being assigned for each element except that a maximum of one point could be assigned for the trial element.

44. Boli 1976, 1979, 1987a, 1987b.

45. Aristotle and his pupils evidently collected information on some 158 states, mostly Greek city-states, in the form of a set of descriptive memoranda on government structure and function. There is reason to believe that the material was collected as a basis for the writing of the *Politics*. What has come down to us, and is known as Aristotle's *Constitution of Athens*, surveys the history of constitutional change and describes the Athenian constitution of Aristotle's own time, with emphasis on the franchise, legislation, administration, and the judiciary. See Rhodes 1984 and Moore 1975.

46. E.g., Delacroix 1792; Politz 1817; Dufau 1821.

47. E.g., Rodriguez 1907; Dodd 1909; Wright 1919.

48. Peaslee and Xydis 1965.

49. We recognize risks of error built into the translation process. Words and phrases that in the original language might have been recognized by our coders as proper examples of due process rights may not have been so recognized in the translation of a constitution into another language. Similarly, words that in the original might not be considered proper examples of due process rights might inadvertently be transformed into such by translation. We tried to sensitize ourselves to this risk but can offer no assurance that some errors in our coding did not arise from the fact that we worked mainly with translated constitutions. We very much doubt, however, that these errors introduced systematic distortions of our results.

50. To represent *all* constitutions extant at each twenty-year interval was our ambition, but it set a goal we could not consistently achieve. There were more nations in existence in each period than there were constitutions in our sample set. In some cases, this came about because there were sovereign nations without written constitutions, as was the case for Great Britain for all six of our time periods and for Israel in the 1950 and 1970 periods. In other cases, however, the nations in question evidently had a constitution, but we were unsuccessful in locating a copy.

51. There were 169 constitutions that entered our sample sets only once; thirty-eight were repeated once again, which means that they appeared in two sample sets

and thus contributed seventy-six entries or observations; twenty-four appeared in three sample sets, thus contributing seventy-two entries. Appearing in four, five, or all six sample sets occurred for three, four, and seven constitutions, respectively, yielding a total of eighty-four observations. The 169 single-use constitutions plus all of those with multiple entries, which numbered seventy-six, yields a total of 245 distinct constitutions. Adding the 146 repetitions yields the total number of 391 entries.

52. This required that we eliminate ten countries from the generational panel analysis, each of which, however, could still qualify to be part of one or more twenty-year sample sets. Examples of countries that we had to drop from the generational analysis because of the discontinuity of their constitutional history were Serbia and Estonia.

53. In the 1870 sample only ten of the entries were constitutions written before 1850, but since their origins stretched back to 1789 they could not be grouped to form a generation on the same basis as was used to constitute the other generations in our study.

54. A further complication in the case of these generations arose because they included nations not truly new to the period, but new only in the sense that it was in the given period that we first located one of their constitutions. This was true of two of the three cases in the 1890 generation and in two of the five entries in the 1910 generation. For this reason a cautious reader will be justified if inclined not to give much weight to any conclusions heavily dependent on the data for those years, *so long as this reservation is limited to the generational analysis only.*

55. This was true for the set of averages as a whole, tested by the more conservative Scheffe procedure, and in separate two-tailed t-tests comparing even the largest average differences between 1870 and 1950 or 1970, respectively.

56. The index of agreement, also know as the index of variation, is obtained by dividing the standard deviation by the mean. A rising mean with a constant standard deviation, or a constant mean with a declining standard deviation, will give a smaller index, retreating all the way to zero. The smaller the index, the more the nations in a set may be considered to be homogeneous. Most comparisons of sets of nations seem to generate an index between 0.2 and 0.6. An example of steady and strong convergent movements was provided by Williamson and Fleming (1977), who show that in industrial countries the compulsory schooling requirement moved from an average of 6.1 years in 1900 to 7.7 years in 1969 while the coefficient of variation declined dramatically from 0.40 to a mere 0.07, indicating that most of the nations surveyed had come to adopt more or less the same exact standard. See Inkeles and Sirowy 1983.

57. Boli 1987b.

58. On our measure, as noted, the average number of rights constitutionally guaranteed by the world's constitutions rose by 11 percent; on Boli's index it rose by 17 percent (see Boli 1987b, Table 6.1).

59. For both of these codings numerous intercoder reliability checks were made, with regular meetings devoted in part to coding articles for both prominence and explicitness. Because the coding system was easily understood, with practice near complete unanimity between coders was achieved on these measures.

60. To have indicated the average scores for all rights, rather than only for those actually affirmed, would have produced a distortion, because some constitutions

mentioned few rights, and in the case of rights not affirmed it was meaningless to ask how explicit or prominent they were.

61. Three rights accounted for this result. The right to petition, to counsel, and to a reasonably speedy trial differentiated the 1970 sample set in comparison with each of the other five sets. Typically the differences were significant at the .01 level or better. This process of differentiation was already manifested, but less strikingly, in the 1950 sample set. In that set, the proportion citing the right to counsel was cited more often at a significant level in comparisons with three of four earlier samples.

62. It will be recalled that the nations in our sample were grouped into genera-tions, each generation representing all the nations whose constitution first entered the sample in a given twenty-year period. This does not necessarily mean that the nations involved first achieved independence in a given twenty-year period but rather that we first identified them as having a constitution by the end of that pe-riod. Each generation, once defined, was then followed, as a separate self-contained group, through all the subsequent periods of the study. The 1870 generation has been rendered comparable to the other generations by limiting it to those nations in the 1870 set that had their first constitutions identified by us in the twenty years be-tween 1851 and 1870.

63. These differences, however, were not statistically significant, except for the 1890 generation. Within that generation the averages for 1890, 1910, and 1930 were signif-icantly different from the 1970 average at the .01 level. As we noted earlier, caution is required in judging this result because the 1890 generation had only three entries.

64. In this series the difference between the 1870 average and that for 1930 was significant at the .01 level.

65. Looking back to Table 10.1, it will be seen that the 1950 set granted an aver-age of only 5.3 rights, reflecting the retrogressive effect of the newly arriving 1950 generation on the total 1950 sample set. This point is clearly established in Table 10.5, which shows that the nations already in the pool by 1950 granted an average of 5.5 rights, whereas those newly arrived in 1950 granted only 4.7.

66. This result comes only after rounding. Before rounding the 1950 generation also failed to meet the test, since it came on with 4.65 rights, whereas the preceding (1930) set had 4.69 rights.

67. It will be recognized that these nations "new" to any sample set are the same nations that make up the generation associated with each twenty-year period, plus any nations that came onstream in the period in question but that, for lack of conti-nuity, were excluded from the strict generational analysis.

68. We defined a difference as "substantial" if the gap was ten percentage points or more, except that in the case of absolute percentages of ten or less we required that the larger number be at least twice the smaller. For those who might prefer the more conventional criterion of a t-test, we note that of the comparisons of the 1950 old with the 1950 new, three of the fourteen paired comparisons were significant at the .05 level or better, and in the comparison of the 1950 old with the 1970 new, seven of the fourteen comparisons met that test. Hence we may conclude that the 1950 generation was considerably different from the nations on the scene earlier, and the 1970 generation was *markedly* different.

69. Shepherd 1981.

70. Donnelly 1984.

71. Boli 1987a.
72. Boli 1987a,b.
73. Here again the definition of a "substantial" difference was that given earlier. Using the t-test as a standard, only two of these differences were significant at the .05 level or better.
74. Benavot et al. 1991.
75. Inkeles 1975, 495.

References to Chapter 10

Almond, Gabriel, and Sidney Verba. 1963. *The Civic Culture: Political Attitudes and Democracy in Five Nations*. Princeton: Princeton University Press.

American Council of Learned Societies. 1990. *The ACLS Comparative Constitutionalism Project*. Final Report, Occasional Paper No. 13. New York: American Council of Learned Societies.

Andrews, William G. 1963. *Constitutions and Constitutionalism*. Princeton: D. Van Nostrand Co.

Baker, Richard C. 1891. *A Manual of Reference to Authorities for the Use of the Members of the National Australian Convention Which Will Assemble at Sydney on March 2, 1891, for the Purpose of Drafting a Constitution for the Dominion of Australia*. Adelaide, Melbourne, and Sydney: E. A. Petherick & Co.

Bayles, Michael D. 1990. *Procedural Justice Allocating to Individuals*. Dordrecht, Boston, and London: Kluwer Academic Publications.

Benavot, Aaron, Yun-Yung Cho, David Kamens, John W. Meyer, and Suk-Ying Wong. 1991. "Knowledge for the Masses: World Model and National Curricula, 1920–1986." *American Sociological Review*, Vol. 56, No. 1 (February), 85–100.

Blaustein, Albert P., and Gisbert H. Flanz. 1971. *Constitutions of the Countries of the World: A Series of Updated Texts, Constitutional Chronologies, and Annotated Bibliographies*. Dobbs Ferry, NY: Oceana Publications.

Boli [Boli-Bennett], John. 1976. "The Expansion of Nation-States, 1870–1970." Ph.D. diss., Stanford University.

Boli, John. 1979. "The Ideology of Expanding State Authority in National Constitutions, 1870–1970." In *National Development and the World System: Educational, Economic, and Political Change, 1950–1970*, ed. John W. Meyer and Michael T. Hannan, 222–237. Chicago: University of Chicago Press.

Boli, John. 1987a. "World Polity Sources of Expanding State Authority and Organization." In *Institutional Structure Constituting State, Society, and Individual*, ed. George M. Thomas, John W. Meyer, Francisco O. Ramirez, and John Boli. Newbury Park, CA: Sage Publications.

Boli, John. 1987b. "Human Rights or State Expansion? Cross-National Definitions of Constitutional Rights, 1870–1970." In *Institutional Structure Constituting State, Society, and the Individual*. Newbury Park, CA: Sage Publications.

Brooks, Alexander D. 1974. *Law, Psychiatry, and the Mental Health System*. Boston: Little, Brown & Co.

The Constitution of the United States. 1988. With introduction by Warren Burger, Chairman of the Commission on the Bicentennial of the United States Constitution. Washington, DC: U.S. Government Printing Office.

Dareste, Pierre, and François Rudolphe Dareste. 1929. *Les Constitutions Modernes: Europe-Afrique-Asie-Océanie-Amérique.* 4th ed. Vols. 1–6. Paris: Librairie du Recueil, Sirey.

Davis, G.R.C. 1965. *Magna Carta.* London: Trustees of the British Museum.

Delacroix, Jacques V. 1791–1801. *Constitutions des principaux Etats de l'Europe et des Etats Unis de L'Amérique.* 2 vols. Paris: Buisson.

———. 1792. *A Review of the Constitutions of the Principal States of Europe and of the United States of America.* Vols. 1–2. Translated by Elizabeth Ryves. London: Paternostra-Row.

Dodd, Walter Fairleigh. 1909. *Modern Constitutions: A Collection of Fundamental Laws of Twenty-two of the Most Important Countries of the World, with Historical and Bibliographical Notes.* Vols. 1–2. Chicago: University of Chicago Press.

Donnelly, Jack. 1984. "Human Rights and Development: Complementary or Competing Concerns?" *World Politics,* Vol. 36, No. 2, 255–283.

Dufau, Pierre Armand. 1821–1823. *Collection des constitutions, cartes, et lois fondamentales des peuples de L'Europe et des deux Amériques.* 6 vols. Paris: J. L. Chanson.

Emery, C. T., and B. Smyth. 1986. *Judicial Review.* London: Sweet and Maxwell.

Fox, Karla H. 1988. "Due Process and Academic Misconduct." *American Business Law Journal* (Winter), 671–700.

Franklin, John H. Winter, 1991/92. "Unequal Protections Under the Bill of Rights in the Early Days." *The Key Reporter,* 5–8. Washington, DC: Phi Beta Kappa.

Friedman, Paul R. 1976. *The Rights of Mentally Retarded Persons: The Basic ACLU Guide for the Mentally Retarded Person's Rights.* New York: Avon Books.

Friedrich, Carl Joachim. 1967. *The Impact of American Constitutionalism Abroad.* Boston: Boston University Press.

Golann, Stuart, and William J. Fremouw. 1976. *The Right to Treatment for Mental Patients.* New York: Irvington Publishers.

Hughes, Graham. 1985. "Review of Michael A. Graham, *Tightening the Reins of Justice in America: A Comparative Analysis of the Criminal Jury Trial in England and the United States.*" *New York Review of Books,* March 14, 17–18.

Inkeles, Alex. 1975. "The Emerging Social Structure of the World." *World Politics,* Vol. 27, No. 4 (July), 467–495.

———. 1980a. "Convergence and Divergence in Industrial Societies." In *Directions of Change: Essays on Modernization Theory and Research,* ed. Zdenek Suda and Burkart Holzner, 3–39. Boulder: Westview Press.

———. 1980b. "Modernization and Family Patterns: A Test of Convergence Theory." *Conspectus of History,* Vol. 1, No. 6, ed. Dwight W. Hoover and John T.M. Koumoulides (Muncie, IN: Department of History, Ball State University), 31–62.

Inkeles, Alex, and Larry Sirowy. 1983. "Convergent and Divergent Trends in National Educational Systems." *Social Forces,* Vol. 62, No. 2, 303–333.

Inkeles, Alex, and Chikako Usui, 1988. "Retirement Patterns in Cross-National Perspective." In *Age Structuring in Comparative Perspective,* ed. David I. Kertzer and K. Warner Schaie, 227–262. Hillsdale, NJ: Lawrence Erlbaum.

Inoue, Kyoko. 1991. *MacArthur's Japanese Constitution.* Chicago: University of Chicago Press.

The Inter-Parliamentary Union. 1950–. *Constitutional and Parliamentary Information.* "New Series." Geneva: Association of Secretaries General of Parliaments [called 1948–1959: Autonomous Section of Secretaries General of Parliaments] First Series, 1 vol. including period 1939–1947, 1948; Second Series, 1 vol. 1949; Third Series.

_____. 1936–1947. *Informations constitutionnelles et parlementaires.* Geneva: Association of Secretaries General of Parliaments.

Kornblith, Miriam. 1991. "The Politics of Constitution Making." *Journal of Latin American Studies,* Vol. 23, 61–89.

Lee, T.S.Y. 1977. "Japan." In *Constitutions of the Countries of the World,* ed. Albert P. Blaustein and Gisbert H. Flanz. Dobbs Ferry, NY: Oceana Publications.

Marshall, T. H. 1964. *Class, Citizenship, and Social Development: Essays by T. H. Marshall.* Garden City, NY: Anchor Books.

Martin, Charles E., and William H. George. 1923. *Representative Modern Constitutions.* Los Angeles: Times-Mirror Press.

Mashaw, Jerry L. 1985. *Due Process in the Administrative State.* New Haven: Yale University Press.

Mechanic, David. 1989. *Mental Health and Social Policy.* 3d ed. Englewood Cliffs, NJ: Prentice-Hall.

Merryman, John. 1969. *The Civil Law Tradition: An Introduction to the Legal System of Western Europe and Latin America.* Stanford: Stanford University Press.

Meyer, John W., Francisco O. Ramirez, Richard Rubinson, and John Boli [Boli-Bennett]. 1979. "The World Education Revolution, 1950–1970." In *National Development and the World System: Educational, Economic, and Political Change, 1950–1970,* ed. John W. Meyer and Michael T. Hannan. Chicago: University of Chicago Press.

Moore, J. M. 1975. *Aristotle and Xenophon on Democracy and Oligarchy.* Berkeley: University of California Press.

New York Times. 1990. "Constitutions Anyone? A New Cottage Industry." February 2.

Nwabueze, Benjamin O. 1973. *Constitutionalism in Emergent States.* Rutherford, NJ: Fairleigh Dickinson University Press.

Peaslee, Amos Jenkins, and Dorothy Peaslee Xydis. 1965. *Constitutions of Nations.* 3d ed. Vols. 1–4. The Hague: Martinus Nijhoff.

Politz, Karl H.L. 1817–1825. *Die Constitutionen der Europaischen Staaten seit den Letzten 25 Jahren.* Vols. 1–4. Leipzig and Altenburg: Brodhaus.

Price, Janet T., Alan H. Levine, and Eve Cary. 1988. *The Rights of Students.* 3d ed. Carbondale: Southern Illinois University Press.

Rhodes, P. J., transl. 1984. *Aristotle: The Athenian Constitution.* Harmondsworth: Penguin Books.

Rodriguez, A. I. 1907. *A Compilation of the Political Constitutions of the Independent Nations of the World.* Washington, DC: U.S. Government Printing Office.

Rudovsky, David, Alvin J. Bronstein, and Edward I. Koren. 1983. *The Rights of Prisoners.* Revised ed. Toronto and New York: Bantam Books.

Scarman, Leslie George. 1987. "The Constitution: A British View." *American Philosophical Society News,* Vol. 2, No. 2 (June).

Schwartz, Bernard. 1987. *Lions over the Throne: The Judicial Revolution in English Administrative Law.* New York and London: New York University Press.

Shah, Saleem A., and Bruce D. Sales, eds. 1991. *Law and Mental Health: Major Developments and Research Needs.* Rockville, MD: National Institute of Mental Health. (U.S. Department of Health and Human Services Publication No. [ADNM] 91-1875.)

Shepherd, George W. 1981. "Transnational Development of Human Rights: The Third World Crucible." In *Global Human Rights,* ed. Ved P. Nanda et al. Boulder: Westview Press.

Simons, William B., ed. 1980. *The Constitutions of the Communist World.* Alphen aan den Rijn, the Netherlands, and Germantown, MD: Sijthoff and Noordhoff.

Stalin, Joseph. 1950. *On the Draft Constitution of the U.S.S.R.* Moscow: Foreign Languages Publishing House.

Thomas, George M., et al. 1987. *Institutional Structure: Constituting State, Society, and Individual.* Newbury Park, CA: Sage Publications.

Triska, Jan F. 1968. *Constitutions of the Communist Party-States.* Stanford: Hoover Institution Press.

United Nations. 1983. "Universal Declaration of Human Rights." In *International Human Rights, Instruments of the United Nations: 1948–1983.* Pleasantville, NY: UNIFO.

Williamson, J. B., and J. J. Fleming. 1977. "Convergence Theory and the Social Welfare Sector: A Cross-National Analysis." *International Journal of Comparative Sociology,* Vol. 18 (September-December), 242–253.

Wright, W. F. 1919. *The Constitution of the States at War, 1914–1918.* Washington, DC: U.S. Government Printing Office.

Zaide, Gregorio F. 1970. *Philippine Constitutional History and Constitutions of Modern Nations.* Manila: Modern Book Company.

Notes to Chapter 11

The original article was a revised and somewhat abridged version of a report prepared for the Conference on Political Modernization that met in June 1959 under the auspices of the Committee on Comparative Politics of the Social Science Research Council. I am particularly indebted to the Committee's chairman, Professor Gabriel Almond, for support and encouragement. The data were assembled with the aid of a grant from the Ford Foundation, supplemented by the Russian Research Center at Harvard University. Dr. Elmo C. Wilson generously made available special tabulations from studies undertaken by International Research Associates, Inc. Jay Greenfield rendered creative research assistance.

1. Kingsley Davis and Hilda H. Goldern, "Urbanization and the Development of Pre-industrial Areas," in *Cities and Society* (rev. ed.), ed. Paul K. Hatt and Albert J. Reiss Jr. (Glencoe, IL: Free Press, 1957), pp. 120–140; Seymour M. Lipset, "Some Social Requisites of Democracy: Economic Development and Political Legitimacy," *American Political Science Review*, Vol. 53 (March 1959), pp. 69–105.

2. Particularly useful were the Italian agency *Doxa Bolletino,* published in Milan (hereinafter cited as *Doxa*); the releases of the Netherlands Institute of Public Opinion in Amsterdam (hereinafter cited as NIPO); and the bulletins of the Australian Gallup Polls of Melbourne (hereinafter cited as AGP).

3. Hadley W. Cantril, ed., *Public Opinion, 1935–1946* (Princeton: Princeton University Press, 1951).

4. William Buchanan and Hadley Cantril, *How Nations See Each Other* (Urbana: University of Illinois Press, 1953).

5. During 1958 International Research Associates undertook a substantial number of comparative surveys, released through the *New York Herald Tribune.* Additional tabulations were made available through the courtesy and cooperation of Dr. Elmo Wilson. Although the Gallup affiliates in various countries often ask the same question at more or less the same time, detailed consolidated results suitable for comparative study are generally not available. Some reconstruction is possible from the bulletins released by the individual affiliates.

6. Originally published as Alex Inkeles and Peter H. Rossi, "National Comparisons of Occupational Prestige," *American Journal of Sociology*, Vol. 61, No. 4 (January 1956), 329–339. These values may also be shared between countries not so highly industrialized but already incorporated into or influenced by currents of modernization (see E. Tiryakian, "The Prestige Evaluation of Occupations in an Underdeveloped Country: The Philippines," *American Journal of Sociology*, Vol. 63 [1958], 390–399).

7. In the Netherlands (NIPO, Ballot 118, November 1948) the question was asked: "Could you tell me for what purpose you work?" A breakdown by socioeconomic standing revealed little patterning. "For family and children" was the chief reason given by all groups, and "money" next. The relative importance of money as against family and children was actually greatest among the well-to-do. Whether this is mainly a result of the difference in the question or is evidence that there is no pattern here that can be expected cross-nationally cannot be said on the basis of present evidence.

8. Reported in *Doxa*, IV, Nos. 23–24 (December 1950). The size of the plant in which the worker is employed seems to play a role here. In smaller plants (fifty or fewer employees) 56 percent chose the incentive pay, but in larger plants only 45 percent would take the risk. Size of plant seems an important factor in shaping the workers' perceptions and attitudes, and we should give it more systematic treatment in future studies. Seymour M. Lipset and Juan Linz, in their unpublished study "The Social Bases of Political Diversity in Western Democracies," noted several German studies that reveal that the larger the factory, the more radical will be the workers in it.

9. In Denmark, NIPO, Ballot of April 11, 1943, for example.

10. Cantril (ed.), *op. cit.,* p. 530.

11. *Public Opinion Quarterly,* Vol. 14 (Spring 1950), 182.

12. Cantril (ed.), *op. cit.,* p. 1016.

13. AGP, Nos. 579–589 (March-April 1949). This issue also reports that at that time Gallup asked the same question in a number of other countries, but the results are not reported with breakdowns by class. The proportion of the total samples choosing the steady job is so high in Canada (85 percent), Holland (79 percent),

and Sweden (71 percent) that we must assume that in those countries as well the steady job was the overwhelming favorite in all groups.

14. See J. W. Atkinson, "Motivational Determinants of Risk-taking Behavior," *Psychological Review*, Vol. 64 (1957), 359–372.

15. This is suggested by a number of the studies in J. W. Atkinson, ed., *Motives in Fantasy, Action, and Society* (Princeton: D. Van Nostrand, 1958). Definitive evidence based on a national sample has been collected by the Survey Research Center at the University of Michigan in a study directed by Gerald Gurin and Joseph Veroff.

16. It was worded as follows: "Some people prefer a job which pays very well even though it may not be so secure (permanent). Other people prefer a steady job even though it may not pay so much. Which would you, yourself, prefer—the steady job or the better-paying one?" (*Public Opinion Quarterly*, Vol. 13 [Fall 1949], 553).

17. To conserve space, the relevant evidence with regard to images of the good and bad boss has not been presented here.

18. Cantril (ed.), *op. cit.*, p. 281.

19. AGP, Nos. 569–578 (February-March 1949). The other countries were Holland (43 percent), the United States (43 percent), and the United Kingdom (39 percent).

20. These audiences were generally composed of faculty and students, supplemented by people in the college or university community who attend lectures "open to the public"—safely characterized as solidly middle class. Despite their high average level of education, they seemed to harbor a stereotype of the working class that in important respects is analogous to that held by Southern whites about the poor, irresponsible, but "happy" Negro.

21. There is, however, not much to choose between the lowest categories, who are clustered around the 30 percent level (cf. *Doxa*, No. 12 [April 1948]).

22. A twelfth case, France, was a strong instance of the expected relationship. Since socioeconomic status classifications were not available for France, it was excluded from Table 11.7 to make both parts strictly comparable.

23. Suicide rates rise with socioeconomic status, but their absolute frequency is quite low in all groups. Homicides, many times more common than suicide, and psychopathic illness, which is incomparably more frequent, are both markedly commoner in the lower classes. Insofar as these states, when combined, provide an index of misery, the pattern observed would be congruent with that already described.

24. The Roper Center for Public Opinion Research at Williams College plans to collect the raw data from studies conducted since World War II in some twenty countries. This will open exceptional opportunities for comparative research.

25. But not necessarily respect. Indeed, the experience of the harsh and peremptory demands for obedience experienced by those at lower status levels more often breeds surface conformity and, beneath that, a smoldering hatred or disrespect for authority, except when so strong as to compel or win blind allegiance.

26. Table not shown. I am indebted to Dr. Elmo Wilson and the International Research Associates for the data.

27. Alex Inkeles, "Social Change and Social Character: The Role of Parental Mediation," *Journal of Social Issues*, Vol. 11, No. 2 (1955), 12–23.

28. The question was apparently also asked in 1950 in other countries with Gallup affiliates, but I do not have the results cross-tabulated by any stratification variable.

29. See Cantril (ed.), *op. cit.*, pp. 785–788. Comparable questions were asked in Australia and the Netherlands, but breakdowns by class were not reported (AGP, Nos. 578–579 [March-April 1949]; Ballots 141, 145, 148 [April, May, July 1949]). There were many technical problems raised by such questions, and the results remain ambiguous (see Buchanan and Cantril, *op. cit.*, p. 62).

30. See AGP, Nos. 529–536 (July 1948); NIPO, Ballot 129 (February 1949), question 7B; and studies in the United States, Great Britain, and Hungary reported in Cantril (ed.), *op. cit.*, pp. 63 (question 29), 66 (questions 48 and 50), 141 (question 19), and 147 (question 6).

31. Perhaps an exception should be made for communist or socialist countries, but I think not. At least in the Soviet Union, if there is reorganization in industry the professional personnel are, I believe, actually more assured of continuing employment than are the ordinary workers. Of course the communist countries have experienced chronic labor shortages while attempting rapid industrialization, and this has tended to eliminate insecurity about unemployment at all levels, except where political circumstances excluded a person from the right to work.

32. The previously cited work in progress by Seymour M. Lipset and Juan Linz parallels this analysis in its application to political belief and action.

33. For a forceful—indeed extreme—argument of this position, including an exposition of the forces working to bring it about, see Roderick Seidenberg, *Post-historic Man: An Inquiry* (Boston: Beacon Press, 1957).

Notes to Chapter 12

This is an expanded version of a paper presented at the Plenary Session at the Thirtieth International Congress of the International Institute of Sociology, Kobe, Japan, August 5, 1991, as keynote address.

1. A simple but striking indicator of the great surge in the production of goods is given by the consumption of cotton in the United Kingdom. In 1750 the consumption of cotton was 1,000 metric tons. By 1850 it had increased by 267 times, and by 1900, 788 times. Imported for the mills that were a central part of the early growth of manufacturing, the cotton went into a flood of cloth partly consumed in the United Kingdom and in great part sent off to Europe and other parts of the world. See Mitchell 1975, 427–433.

2. Cipolla 1962, 74.

3. U.S. Bureau of the Census, *Historical Statistics*, 1975, 1:240.

4. Ibid.

5. Rostow 1978, 152, Table III-21.

6. U.S. Bureau of the Census, *Historical Statistics*, 1975, 1(Series A), 57–72.

7. Rostow 1978, Table N-7.

8. Ibid., Table N-32.

9. Ibid., Table III-21.

10. Though the measure of GNP per capita may be serviceable, it is not necessarily preferable as an indicator. GNP may reflect spending on massive construction and defense that contribute little to the flow of goods and services to individuals, which was the pattern in the communist countries of Eastern Europe. And oil-exporting nations may be recorded as having high per capita GNP even though they are little industrialized and not at all modernized. Per capita income measures also do not describe the inequalities of distribution within a nation. Nevertheless, for many purposes GNP per capita may serve as a useful rough measure of the flow of goods and services to a nation's population, and the general pattern of results obtained using it will be found to be very similar to the pattern obtained with more refined or detailed measures.

11. Probably the most extensive effort to measure the overall physical and social quality of life for a single country was undertaken in West Germany. Ten different realms were identified, including social mobility, health, and "participation," and 196 specific measures were included. See Zapf 1980 and 1984. This project in West Germany closely followed a model that had been elaborated for the larger community of nations in the Organization for Economic Cooperation and Development (OECD) through its Social Indicator Development program (see OECD 1976). The West German project, however, was exceptional in the thoroughness with which the data were collected and evaluations made of progress on different indicators. The OECD continues to publish a "Compendium of Social Indicators" under eight major headings ranging from health to wealth and including thirty-odd separate measures (see OECD 1986).

12. The Physical Quality of Life Index developed by Morris (1979) has become something of a standard in work with less developed countries. It is based on three elements: literacy rate, life expectancy at age one, and infant mortality rate. An alternative Physical Standard of Living Index developed by Williamson (1987) is based on four components: caloric consumption per day per capita, protein consumption per day per capita, infant mortality rate, and life expectancy at birth. Evidence that these elements formed a single coherent syndrome was reflected in the fact that all four showed very strong factor analysis loadings, in the range of .80 to .91. An effort to measure the physical quality of life using the Morris criteria applied to a wider range of countries, including the advanced, will be found in Cereseto and Waitzkin 1986. This source gives incidental evidence that other measures, such as number of physicians per capita or school enrollments, also form part of the more general syndrome of physical quality of life.

13. For a succinct summary of the characteristics evaluated and of the scoring procedures for the scale, see Gastil 1991, 25–50.

14. For example, see the publications of the European Foundation for the Improvement of Living and Working Conditions, especially the annual *Programme of Work*.

15. For example, see the papers collected in Fried 1974 on behalf of the Council of European Studies, and in Frick 1986.

16. This pattern tends to be manifested within any one realm as well as across different realms. For example, in a study specifically focused on the quality of consumption in the Detroit and Baltimore areas of the United States, Pfaff (1976) found consistent correlations around .3 between satisfaction with standard of living

and with job, savings, housing, and automobile. Campbell et al. (1976) cross-correlated seventeen different domains of life in their U.S. study and concluded: "Almost without exception there are positive correlations between all the domain satisfaction measures. People who say they are satisfied with one aspect of life are likely to report relatively high satisfaction where other domains are concerned." They also reported that the experience of the Social Science Research Council of the United Kingdom, working with nine domains, was similar to that of the American researchers (see Campbell et al. 1976, 68–75).

17. The reasonableness of using such summary indices of happiness and satisfaction was definitively established by Campbell et al. (1976) in their finding that the set of seventeen different domain satisfaction scores, taken together, could explain 54 percent of the variance in their general index of well-being, which was based in good part on responses to the question about overall satisfaction with life (see p. 80).

18. I make this statement with full awareness that general affirmations of happiness and declarations of satisfaction with life in general are not overpoweringly correlated. Cantril (1965, 415, Table 52) reported for his U.S. sample around 1960 that the correlation of a question on satisfaction with life and where people placed themselves on the "ladder of life" was .36. Campbell et al., in their 1971 U.S. sample, found the correlation of the single-item general happiness measure and the single-item general satisfaction measure to be .50. The suggestion that either item can be substituted for the other is based on research experience that indicates the pattern and structure of the interrelations of each of these measures with other measures either of socioeconomic background or of attitude and value. For a systematic and nearly exhaustive discussion of the interrelation of various global measures of well-being see Andrews and Withey 1976. Ruut Veenhoven of the Erasmus University, Rotterdam, maintains a world database on the measurement of happiness.

19. The U.S. sample in Cantril 1965 was asked to rate itself on self-confidence and respect for oneself. Campbell et al. (1976) included measures of anxiety and of personal competence in the instruments used in their sample. The Baltimore-Detroit Area Study of 1971–1972 included measures of personal control. Using ten psychosocial measures ranging from "trust" to "feeling down," Krebs and Schuessler (1989) developed a "Life-Feelings Scale" for the U.S. and West German populations. Although the combined scales were unidimensional in both samples, the authors were left with some doubt as to "whether the feelings underlying the scales are identical in both populations."

20. World Bank 1988, 286–287, Table 33.

21. Data are from World Bank 1988, 222–223, Table 1; 278–279, Table 23; 280–281, Table 30; pp. 286–287, Table 33. Data for the less-developed countries are for thirty-five countries, excluding China and India, and are weighted by population size. Data for the industrial market economies cover nineteen countries and are also weighted for population size. Because of the influence of exchange rates and other difficulties in measuring GNP it might be reasonable, in order to assess actual living standards, to weight the GNP per capita cited for the least developed countries by a factor of three, which would reduce the ratio indicated to a still resounding 1:32.

22. Data are from U.S. Bureau of the Census, *Historical Statistics,* 1975, 1:63, Table B193-200, and 1:57, Table B148.

23. Data are from U.S. Bureau of the Census, *Historical Statistics*, 1975, 1:58, Table B149-160, and 1:77, Table B291-304.

24. UNICEF 1988, 40.

25. UNICEF 1988, 64, Table 1. One of the benefits of worldwide development is that even countries that are not advancing economically at a rapid rate can nevertheless experience considerable improvements on important indicators such as the infant mortality rate. This comes about partly from direct aid and from technology transfer from the more advanced countries. It also results from the stimulation and support by international agencies of local government programs to aid pregnant women and young mothers and their infants. Nevertheless, the countries developing most slowly are much less able to reduce infant morality than those that are accelerating industrialization and general economic development. While the countries in Asia and Africa that developed more rapidly during the past three decades had typically brought their infant mortality rate down from 1960 levels to the point where their 1986 rates were only 30 percent of the former, the less rapidly growing nations in the same regions typically had rates in 1986 that were still about 70 percent of the former rate.

26. There are of course many reasons to object to the use of averages, as my presentation does, because they may not only conceal gross disparities in distribution but also disguise situations in which the average may rise but in which some major groups suffer actual deterioration of their condition. I limit myself here to declaring that the more common pattern is for most, indeed, often all, segments of society to benefit from rising levels of national productivity, although certainly not in equal degree, nor in all realms. Using income distribution as a rough indicator of what is at issue, we certainly can say that it tends to be more equal in advanced industrial countries than in low-income nations. Whether or not most steps along the way from underdevelopment to industrialization and modernization bring a general movement toward greater equality in the material and physical condition of life requires detailed analysis. I offer only my impression that the process does occur. Certainly it is the case that some medical improvements have a totally equalitarian distribution. Today no one in the entire world, no matter how wretchedly poor and neglected, can contract smallpox, once one of the greatest scourges of human kind.

27. I am thus again brought face to face with a question I first raised more than thirty years ago when, in a paper that was more widely cited than most, I raised the question: "Will raising the incomes of all increase the happiness of all, or does it require an unequal gain to bring happiness to some?" See Inkeles 1960, p. 18, also reproduced as Chapter 11 in this volume.

28. As translated in Bynner 1978, 359, poem no. 22.

29. d'Iribarne 1974, 34.

30. Kettering and Gallup 1977, 41. In conducting this world poll the Gallup organization was not able to include the countries of North Africa, nor the communist nations of Eastern Europe. Nations from both those areas, however, have been included in other quality-of-life surveys. Cantril (1965), for example, included Cuba, Poland, and Yugoslavia in his set of fourteen nations. Certainly these nations manifest some distinctive patterns, some of which have been peculiar either to the kind of communist country they were or to other national particularities. In general, however, there is little convincing empirical evidence to indicate that either the pat-

terns of response or the levels of satisfaction in socialist countries markedly distinguishes them from other nations at comparable levels of economic development.

31. In most of its tables the Gallup world poll summary did not give a continent-based average for North America but rather listed the data for the U.S. and Canadian samples separately. The Canadian results were, however, consistently very close to those for the United States, and given the vastly greater population of the latter any continental average would have mainly reflected the outcomes for that colossus. I have therefore arbitrarily used the figures for the United States to represent North America in Table 12.1. Comparable data for Canada alone are reproduced in Table 12.2.

32. Kettering and Gallup 1977, 56.

33. Ibid.; italics added.

34. Cantril 1965, 193–199. Cantril's fourteen nations were selected to give wide representation of the world's regions. Their standing on his index of development, based on data for the years 1957–1961 was: United States 1.00; West Germany .71; Israel .67; Japan .60; Poland .45; Cuba .35; Panama .31; Yugoslavia .19; Philippines .17; Dominican Republic .16; Brazil .16; Egypt .14; Nigeria .02; and India .00.

35. Inglehart 1990, 32, Figure 1-2. Each person expressed overall satisfaction with life on a ten-point scale, and the correlation used the mean score for each country to relate to GNP per capita. Intermediate to these periods, in the Gallup world poll data for 1976–1977 life satisfaction was correlated with GNP, and with an N of seventeen countries yielded a correlation of .74 (see Veenhoven 1984, 149).

36. Cantril 1965, 170.

37. Fifty percent of the French worried a lot, well above the average for most industrial countries, whereas only 25 percent of the Japanese gave that response. Being on the highest step of the ladder of satisfaction with family life was true of 18 percent of the French, close to the European average, but that condition held for only 8 percent of the Japanese (Kettering and Gallup, 1977, 137–138 and 177–178).

38. For example, in their exhaustive analysis of the measures of general life satisfaction reported by a representative sample of the U.S. population, Campbell et al. (1976) found that a larger set of objective circumstances, including even race, could explain no more than some 7 percent of the variance in their index of well-being, and the subset of family income, education, and personal income explained only 2.5 percent of the variance (1976, 368). A large Canadian sample showed income and age to be among the strongest predictors of a measure of general life satisfaction, but together they accounted for only 2.4 percent of the variance (see Blishen and Atkinson 1980, 30).

39. The country variable was entered in the regression as a dummy variable.

40. Persons who reported that this year they were better off than last year were more likely to express general satisfaction with their standard of living, as described by Pfaff (1976), in the Baltimore-Detroit study of economic well-being. The correlation was .29 as reported in Pfaff's Table 8-4. No degrees of improvement were specified in the question used. We may assume that a sharp rise in income would produce a much stronger change in the sense of satisfaction.

41. Campbell et al. 1976, 332, Table 10-5; the results for men were broadly similar.

42. Ibid., 447.

43. Campbell et al. (1976, 313–314) report that the average score for unemployed men was a full standard deviation lower than that for men with full-time jobs, and the

differences remained substantial even with adjustments for lower income. This finding is particularly notable because on most measures such as income the differences separating the more advantaged from those less favored were generally quite small fractions of a standard deviation. My reanalysis of data from Eurobarometer 9, the only one with a reasonably reliable measure of unemployment, in general confirms the results obtained earlier for the United States. For the Netherlands, for example, when we compared the happiness and life satisfaction of those who had experienced unemployment at some point in the preceding three years and were currently unemployed, with that of those who also had previously experienced being out of work but were now employed, we obtained a gamma of .68, significant at the .01 level despite a very small N. In Australia, Feather (1990) collected relatively rare longitudinal data and found considerable differences in life satisfaction among school leavers who had found steady work as compared to those who had failed to find it or who found it and lost it (see especially pp. 180 and 186, Tables 8-1 and 8-2).

44. Easterlin (1990, 90) argued that the appropriate conclusion was "skepticism of a positive correlation between output and welfare." He reanalyzed Cantril's data and concluded that Cantril had specified too high a correlation between his index of development and the measures of popular satisfaction. As to the critical issue of whether national levels of satisfaction rise in response to rapid increases in economic development, he presented a national time series for the United States only. In that case, he found a fluctuating pattern between 1946 and 1970 rather than the long-term increase one might have expected if happiness reports were tracking improvements in income. There is of course good reason to expect a stable level of satisfaction in a nation such as the United States, which reached the stage of a mature industrial society many decades ago. This does not settle the questions as to whether marked increases in popular satisfaction might not result from sudden spurts of growth from either depressed conditions, such as those of France and Germany after World War II, or from low levels of development in newly industrializing countries such as Taiwan. These specific conditions and the data for evaluating them were not dealt with by Easterlin.

45. Inkeles 1990/1991, especially 92–95, Tables 1 and 2. Over the ten surveys the Netherlands, which always ranked number one, reported variation in the percentage "very happy" from a low of 38 percent to a high of 49 percent. There was no visible long-term trend, however. Italy, always in the rank of nine or ten and outstanding in the frequency with which people reported themselves "not too happy," had proportions in that category ranging from 27 percent to 44 percent, with the second half of the decade more likely to reveal negative affect. With reference to Italy, it is worth noting that in an analysis I presented in 1960, based on data going back as far as 1948–1950, I reported levels of happiness and satisfaction in Italy and France that were substantially lower than those for comparable European countries (see Inkeles 1960, reproduced as Chapter 11 in this volume).

46. The stability of measures for the years cited masks a certain amount of fluctuation from year to year. Thus Campbell et al. (1976) describe six studies of the happiness of the U.S. population from 1957 to the fall in 1972, noting fluctuations in the percentage claiming to be "very happy" ranging from a high of 35 percent in 1957 to a low of 22 percent in 1972 (1976, 26, Table 2-1). It is not clear how much of this variation was connected with a long-term decline, how much to differences

in the study design and sampling, and how much it may have reflected current events at the time the surveys were taken. We now have long enough series of data with questions of this type to make it meaningful to attempt to explain the year-to-year fluctuations on the basis of economic and political events. Thus the General Social Surveys for the United States conducted by the National Opinion Research Center have asked about general happiness every year since 1972. In 1986 the proportion "very happy" stood at 33 percent.

47. Data for 1946 from Cantril 1951; data for 1976 are from Kettering and Gallup 1977. The percent "very happy" in 1946 and 1976, respectively, were: Canada, 32 and 36 percent; Great Britain, 36 and 38 percent; and France, 8 and 22 percent.

48. Average annual growth in GNP per capita for the years 1960 to 1976 were: Brazil, 4.6 percent; West Germany, 3.4 percent; United States, 2.3 percent; and India, 1.3 percent. For Japan the figure was 5.2 percent (World Bank 1978, 76–77, Table 1).

49. Ladder ratings for 1976 are from Kettering and Gallup 1977, obtained by adding the percentage on each of the top four steps of the ladder as presented on pp. 129–130. Ratings for 1960 are from Cantril 1965, p. 378, Table 21, weighting male and female scores equally and taking the average. For Japan, Cantril did not have the original data but relied on information provided by the Central Research Agency of Tokyo. However, Figure IV-8 permits a reasonably accurate calculation of the cumulative percentage on the top steps of the ladder. Cantril did not present the data for Japan in the same form as for the other countries. The precise figure he did report was a mean rating, which stood at 5.2. Applying the standard method of calculating the score to the data for Japan in Kettering and Gallup yields a 1976 mean of 5.9. The difference of 0.7 is significant well beyond the .01 level and is, by my rough estimate, considerably larger than one standard deviation.

50. Over roughly the same span of time as our ladder ratings measured, the happiness measure for the United States showed a decline rather than a parallel increase. In 1963, 32 percent of Americans reported themselves as "very happy," but by the spring of 1972 that proportion was down to 26 percent. In addition to the passage of time, these comparisons saw a shift from a nationwide quota sample to a nationwide probability sample (see Campbell et al. 1976, 26). By 1977 Gallup showed the proportion of the U.S. citizens who were "very happy" back up to 40 percent, seeming to reverse what had appeared to be a long-term decline in the happiness ratings Americans assigned themselves (see Campbell et al. 1976, 26; Kettering and Gallup 1977, 129–130). Such fluctuations might of course reflect a number of influences, not merely economic. International conflict and domestic tensions can also play a role. In his analysis of national differences in life satisfaction, Inglehart (1990, 32–33) reached the same conclusion, stating that "economic development is not the only explanatory variable; other historical factors must also be involved."

51. The question put to the respondents was similar but was not phrased in exactly the same way in the studies compared. In Cantril's case the stimulus was: "Here is a picture of a ladder. Suppose we say that the top of the ladder (pointing) represents the best possible life for you and the bottom (pointing) represents the worst possible life for you. Where on the ladder (moving finger rapidly up and down ladder) do you feel you personally stand at the present time?" (Cantril 1965,

23). In the Gallup survey the respondent was shown a picture of a mountain rather than a ladder, although one also having ten steps, and was asked the question: "Suppose the top of the mountain represents the best possible life you can imagine, and the bottom step of the mountain represents the worst possible life you can imagine. On which step of the mountain would you feel you personally stand at this time—assuming the higher the step the better you feel about your life and the lower the step the worse you feel about it? Just point to the step that comes closest to how you feel." There were also some differences in the size and quality of the samples for particular countries collected in the two studies. Cantril sought for representative probability samples. The Gallup survey for the Kettering Foundation was based on sampling world regions, but to permit reporting on individual nations the national samples of certain countries were augmented to reach a minimum of 300 cases. For the countries discussed, the N figures for the Cantril and for the Kettering/Gallup data, respectively, were: Brazil, 2,739 and 383; West Germany, 480 and 303; India, 2366 and 354; and the United States, 1,549 and 1,014.

52. This assumption is supported by Inglehart. Thus in comparing the situation of Belgium and Germany he states (1990, 31): "Despite a predominant pattern of stability, life satisfaction among the Belgian public declined, while that of the German public rose slightly, in response to their respective experiences from 1973 to 1987." However, he did not specify what the differences in experience were, and it is clear in the context that this conclusion is quite tentative.

References to Chapter 12

Andrews, Frank M., and Stephen B. Withey. 1976. *Social Indicators of Well-Being: American's Perceptions of Life Quality.* New York: Plenum Press.

Blishen, Bernard, and Tom Atkinson. 1980. "Anglophone and Francophone Differences in Perceptions of the Quality of Life in Canada." In *The Quality of Life: Comparative Studies,* ed. Alexander Szalai and Frank M. Andrews, 21–39. London: Sage Publications.

Buhman, Brigitte, et al. 1988. "Equivalences Scales, Well-Being, Inequality, and Poverty: Sensitivity Estimates Across Ten Countries Using the Luxembourg Income Study (LIS) Database." *Review of Income and Wealth,* Vol. 34, No. 2, 115–142.

Bynner, Witter. 1978. *The Chinese Translations.* New York: Farrar, Straus, Giroux.

Campbell, Angus, Philip E. Converse, and Willard L. Rodgers, eds. 1976. *The Quality of American Life: Perceptions, Evaluations, and Satisfactions.* New York: Russell Sage Foundation.

Cantril, Hadley, ed. 1951. Prepared by Mildred Strunk. *Public Opinion, 1935–1946.* Princeton: Princeton University Press.

———, ed. 1965. *The Pattern of Human Concerns.* New Brunswick, NJ: Rutgers University Press.

Cereseto, Shirley, and Howard Waitzkin. 1986. "Capitalism, Socialism, and the Physical Quality of Life." *International Journal of Health Services,* Vol. 16, No. 4, 643–659.

Cipolla, Carlo M. 1962. *The Economic History of World Population.* Harmondsworth: Penguin.

Converse, Philip, et al. 1980. *American Social Attitudes Data Sourcebook, 1974–1978.* Cambridge, MA: Harvard University Press.

Davis, James Allan, and Tom W. Smith. 1986. *General Social Surveys, 1972–1986.* Machine readable data file, ed. National Opinion Research Center (NORC). Chicago: National Opinion Research Center, producer; Storrs, CT: The Roper Center for Public Opinion Research, University of Connecticut, distributor.

d'Iribarne, P. 1974. "The Relationships Between Subjective and Objective Well-Being." In *Subjective Elements of Well-Being: Papers Presented at a Seminar of the Organization for Economic Cooperation and Development, Paris, May 15–17, 1972,* ed. Burkhard Strumpel. Paris: Organization for Economic Cooperation and Development.

Easterlin, Richard A. 1974. "Does Economic Growth Improve the Human Lot? Some Empirical Evidence." In *Nations and Households in Economic Growth: Essays in Honor of Moses Abramovitz,* ed. Paul A. David and Melvin W. Reder, 89–125. New York: Academic Press.

European Foundation for the Improvement of Living and Working Conditions. 1990. *Programme of Work for 1990–1992 and Beyond: New Opportunities for Acting to Improve Living and Working Conditions in Europe.* Luxembourg: Office of Official Publications of the European Communities.

Feather, Norman T. 1990. *The Psychological Impact of Unemployment.* New York: Springer-Verlag.

Frick, Dieter, ed. 1986. *The Quality of Urban Life: Social, Psychological, and Physical Conditions.* Berlin: Walter de Gruyter.

Fried, Robert C., and Paul M. Hohenberg, eds. 1974. For Council for European Studies. *The Quality of Life in European Cities.* Pittsburgh: University of Pittsburgh.

Gallup, George. 1978. *The Gallup Poll: Public Opinion, 1972–1977.* Vol. 1, *1972–1975.* Wilmington, DE: Scholarly Resources.

Gastil, Raymond D. 1991. "The Comparative Survey of Freedom: Experiences and Suggestions." *Studies in Comparative International Development: On Measuring Democracy,* Alex Inkeles, guest editor, Vol. 25, No. 1, 26–50.

George, Linda K., and Lucille B. Bearon. 1980. *Quality of Life in Older Persons: Meaning and Measurement.* New York: Human Sciences Press.

Haller, Max, Hans Hoffmann-Nowottny, and Wolfgang Zapf, eds. 1989. *Kultur und Gesellschaft: Verhandlungen des 24. Deutschen, soziologentags, des 11. Osterreichischen Soziologentags und des 8 Kongresses der Schweizerischen Gesellschaft für Soziologie in Zürich 1988.* Frankfurt and New York: Campus Verlag.

Hofstede, Geert. 1980. *Culture's Consequences: International Differences in Work-Related Values.* Beverly Hills: Sage Publications.

Inglehart, Ronald. 1990. *Culture Shift in Advanced Industrial Society.* Princeton: Princeton University Press.

Inkeles, Alex. 1960. "Industrial Man: The Relation of Status to Experience, Perception, and Value." *American Journal of Sociology,* Vol. 66, 1–31.

———. 1990/1991. "National Character Revisited." *Tocqueville Review,* Vol. 12 (Spring 1991), 81–117.

Kettering, Charles F. Foundation, and Gallup International Research Institutes. 1977. *Human Needs and Satisfactions.* Summary Volume. Princeton: Gallup International Research Institutes.

Krebs, Dagmar, and Karl Schuessler. 1989. "Life-Feeling Scales for Use in German and American Samples." *Social Indicators Research,* Vol. 21, 113–131.

Kurian, George T. 1979. *The Book of World Rankings.* New York: Facts on File.

Mitchell, B. R. 1975. *European Historical Statistics, 1750–1970.* New York: Columbia University Press.

Morris, D. M. 1979. *Measuring the Conditions of the World's Poor: The Physical Quality of Life Index.* New York: Pergamon Press.

Organization for Economic Cooperation and Development (OECD). 1976. *Measuring Social Well-Being: A Progress Report on the Development of Social Indicators.* Paris: OECD.

_____. 1991. *Historical Statistics, 1960–1989.* Paris: OECD.

Pfaff, Anita B. 1976. "The Quality of Consumption." In *Economic Means for Human Needs: Social Indicators of Well-Being and Discontent,* ed. Burkhard Strumpel, 187–217. Ann Arbor: University of Michigan Press.

Rokeach, Milton. 1973. *The Nature of Human Values.* New York: Free Press.

Rostow, Walt W. 1978. *The World Economy: History and Prospect.* Austin: University of Texas Press.

Stoetzel, Jean. 1982. *Que Pensamos Los Europeos?* Madrid: Editorial MAPFRE.

Szalai, Alexander, ed., in collaboration with Philip E. Converse, Pierre Feldheim, Erwin K. Scheuch, and Philip J. Stone. 1972. *The Use of Time: Daily Activities of Urban and Suburban Populations in Twelve Countries.* The Hague: Mouton.

United Nations Children's Fund. 1988. *The State of the World's Children, 1988.* Oxford: Oxford University Press.

United States Bureau of the Census, U.S. Department of Commerce. 1975. *Historical Statistics of the United States, Colonial Times to 1970.* Bicentennial edition. Washington DC: U.S. Government Printing Office.

Veenhoven, Ruut. 1984. *Conditions of Happiness.* Dordrecht, Holland: D. Reidel Publishing Company.

Verwayen, Henri. 1980. "The Specification and Measurement of the Quality of Life in OECD Countries." In *The Quality of Life: Comparative Studies,* ed. Alexander Szalai and Frank M. Andrews, 235–247. London: Sage Publications.

Williamson, John B. 1987. "Social Security and Physical Quality of Life in Developing Nations: A Cross-National Analysis." *Social Indicators Research,* Vol. 19, 205–227.

World Bank. 1978. *World Development Report, 1978.* Washington, DC: World Bank.

_____. 1988. *World Development Report, 1988.* Oxford: Oxford University Press.

Yuchtman, (Yaar) Ephraim. 1976. "Effects of Social-Psychological Factors on Subjective Economic Welfare." In *Economic Means for Human Needs,* ed. Burkhard Strumpel, 187–217. Ann Arbor: Institute for Social Research, University of Michigan.

Zapf, Wolfgang. 1980. "The SPES Social Indicators System in Comparative Perspective." In *The Quality of Life: Comparative Studies,* ed. Alexander Szalai and Frank M. Andrews, 15–269. London: Sage Publications.

Zapf, Wolfgang, and Wolfgang Glatzer. 1984. *Lebensqualität in der Bundesrepublic: Objektive Lebensbedingungen und subjektives Wohlbefinden.* Frankfurt and New York: Campus Verlag.

Notes to Chapter 13

1. This branch of the Amazon is called the Rio Negro.

2. Of the studies I have relied on most heavily, the goal of having data for at least two points in time was met in two instances. For Taiwan, a survey taken in 1963 could be compared with one completed in 1991, as reported in Robert M. Marsh, *The Great Transformation: Social Change in Taipei, Taiwan Since the 1960s* (Armonk, NY: M. E. Sharpe, 1996). For Japan we have surveys using the same questions asked every five years from 1953 through 1993, as reported in Chikio Hayashi and Tatsuzo Suzuki, *Beyond Japanese Social Values* (Tokyo: Institute of Statistical Mathematics, 1990), 63–118, supplemented by Research Committee on the Study of the Japanese National Character, *A Study of the Japanese National Character: The Ninth Nationwide Survey* (in Japanese), Research Report No. 75, General Series (Tokyo: Institute of Statistical Mathematics, 1994).

3. In the sources I have relied on heavily, differentiation by age is strongly emphasized in the report on Shanghai and that for Hong Kong. On Shanghai, see Godwin C. Chu and Yanan Ju, *The Great Wall in Ruins: Communication and Cultural Change in China* (Albany: State University of New York Press, 1993). On Hong Kong, see Siu-Kai Lau and Hsin-Chi Kuan, *The Ethos of the Hong Kong Chinese* (Hong Kong: Chinese University of Hong Kong, 1988).

4. Whyte used this method of sampling for his study of marriage and family patterns in Chengdu, as reported in Martin K. Whyte, "From Arranged Marriages to Love Marriages in Urban China," in Chin-Chin Yi, ed., *Family Formation and Dissolution: Perspectives from East and West* (Taipei: Academica Sinica, 1995). The same technique was used in collecting samples in Baoding, as reported in Martin K. Whyte, "The Persistence of Family Obligations in Baoding," manuscript, 1996.

5. Lau and Kuan, *Ethos of the Hong Kong Chinese,* 3.

6. Whyte, "Persistence of Family Obligations in Baoding." The proportions *disagreeing* with the idea that obligations to their children should come ahead of obligations to parents was 50 percent for elders and 65 percent of their adult children. In judging whether obligations to one's career should come ahead of obligations to parents, the proportions *disagreeing* were 23 percent of elders and 49 percent of their adult children. That the elders would respond thus, seemingly contrary to their interest, can be explained by assuming that they absorbed this ideology under communist influence, an influence much diluted for their adult children, who spent more of their formative years in the post-Mao atmosphere.

7. Marsh, *Great Transformation,* Table 7-2.

8. Chu and Ju, *Great Wall in Ruins.*

9. A more cynical, although not necessarily contradictory, interpretation of the phenomenon is offered by Godkin, who is quoted by Marsh as seeing the increase of extended kin gathering for ancestor worship as "the deliberate, conscious, social construction of tradition" (Marsh, *Great Transformation,* 139). Marsh notes that

religious behavior at temples and other manifestations of folk religion declined on Taiwan between the 1960s and the 1970s but has been reviving since the 1980s. He believes the cause, curiously enough, to be modernization. Precisely because social change has been so rapid, he suggests, the Taiwanese need some "return to their roots."

10. The other alternatives were repaying moral indebtedness *(On-gaeshi)*, respecting individual rights, and respecting freedom.

11. Chu and Ju, *Great Wall in Ruins,* 260.

12. Whyte, "Persistence of Family Obligations in Baoding," 8.

13. Details of question wording and descriptive statistics will be found in Hayashi and Suzuki, *Beyond Japanese Social Values,* and Research Committee, *Study of the Japanese National Character.* For a full-scale application of this approach to defining the basic ethos of the population of the United States, see Alex Inkeles, "National Character Revisited," *Tocqueville Review,* Vol. 12 (Spring 1991), 83–117.

14. Presumably this response is derived from the Confucian tradition, which placed heavy emphasis on test performance as a criterion for holding office. This question, numbered 5.1c-1, was first used in 1963, when 75 percent said that they would hire the person with the higher score rather than the relative. Over time support for this view fell somewhat, with only 67 percent taking the same position in 1993.

15. This is question number 5.6. The more demanding boss who nevertheless looks out for you was selected by 85 percent in 1953 and forty years later, in 1993, by a similarly overwhelming majority of 82 percent.

16. This is question number 5.6b, and it was first asked in 1973, when 74 percent chose the firm with the family-like atmosphere. By 1993 the preference for this type of firm over one with higher wages had decreased somewhat to 65 percent.

17. This is question number 9.3. Chosen by 79 percent in 1953, the popularity of the Japanese garden increased until it accounted for 90 percent of all votes in 1973.

18. Thomas A. Metzger, "Hong Kong's Oswald Spengler: H.K.H. Woo (Hu Kuo-heng) and Chinese Resistance to Convergence with the West," *American Journal of Chinese Studies,* in press. Support for Metzger's assumption about the long-term continuity of this pattern of thought will be found in Leo Ou-fan Lee, "In Search of Modernity: Some Reflections on a New Mode of Consciousness in Twentieth-Century Chinese History and Literature," in Paul A. Cohen and Merle Goldman, eds., *Ideas Across Cultures: Essays on Chinese Thought in Honor of Benjamin I. Schwartz* (Cambridge, MA: Council on East Asian Studies, Harvard University Press, 1990).

19. Such adaptations, of course, are not peculiar to the nations of Asia. One may well ask how much of the original meaning of the Fourth of July remains for the millions of Americans who stream to beaches, or gather their families for backyard barbecues, without a mention or a thought of the significance of the date as a celebration of the founding of their nation. One may equally wonder how many Christians who at Easter roll eggs and dress as bunnies have in mind the significance of the day as celebrating the resurrection of Jesus.

20. This is question number 4.10. See Hayashi and Suzuki, *Beyond Japanese Social Values,* 104, and Research Committee, *Study of the Japanese National Character,* 56.

21. Marsh, *Great Transformation,* Table 6.5.

22. Whyte, "From Arranged Marriages to Love Marriages in Urban China," Table 2.

23. Ibid., Table 3.

24. Chu and Ju, *Great Wall in Ruins,* chapter 8, especially Table 8.10.

25. This value set the standard of behavior for women, including obedience to father before a woman got married and to husband after marriage, while among the virtues it stressed morality, proper language and manners, and diligent work.

26. The way of the golden mean" is part of Confucian ethics. It counsels avoiding extremes and encourages moderation in all things. The principle of "differentiation between men and women" holds that because men and women are different they should be treated differently. The value called "discretion for self-preservation" urges avoiding the false and sinful but at the same time urges one to avoid getting in trouble. For a fuller account of the meaning of these values and others in the set of eighteen tested, see Chu and Ju, *Great Wall in Ruins,* 222–244.

27. The proportions voting to "discard" the most rejected values, among the young and the old, respectively, were as follows: "way of the golden mean," 62 and 68 percent; "three obediences and four virtues, 64 and 87 percent; "discretion for self-preservation," 51 and 76 percent. See Chu and Ju, *Great Wall in Ruins,* Table 10.1. This pattern can be interpreted as another example of the resurgence of tradition, since the young reject these venerable traditions less often than their elders do.

28. Hayashi and Suzuki, *Beyond Japanese Social Values,* 101, and Research Committee, *Study of the Japanese National Character,* 39. This is question number 2.4.

29. Whyte, "Persistence of Family Obligations in Baoding."

30. Lau and Kuan, *Ethos of the Hong Kong Chinese,* 1.

31. Ibid., 161–162.

32. Ibid., Table 5.1.

33. Chu and Ju, *Great Wall in Ruins,* Table 9.3.

34. This was, of course, least true of the largest entity, namely, communist China.

35. See Ales Inkeles and David H. Smith, *Becoming Modern: Individual Change in Six Developing Countries* (Cambridge, MA: Harvard University Press, 1974), and Alex Inkeles, *Exploring Individual Modernity* (New York: Columbia University Press, 1983).

36. See Alex Inkeles, C. M. Broaded, and Z. Cao, "Causes and Consequences of Individual Modernity in China," *China Journal,* Vol. 37 (January 1997), 31–59.

37. For evidence that the qualities that define the modern individual are basically the same in women as in men and that the experiences that contribute to making women more modern are similar to those that produce modern attitudes and behavior in men, see C. Montgomery Broaded, Z. Cao, and A. Inkeles, "Women, Men, and Construction of Individual Modernity Scales in China," *Cross-Cultural Research,* Vol. 28, No. 3 (August 1994), 251–286, and Inkeles, Broaded, and Cao, "Causes and Consequences of Individual Modernity in China."

38. The zero-order correlation of years of urban experience and the OM score for both East Pakistan and India was .23, significant at the .001 level. Taking into account years of factory experience brought the figure to a nonsignificant .07 for East Pakistan, but for India it remained at the highly significant level of .21. Controlling for mass media exposure brought the correlation down to .18 in East Pak-

istan but raised it to .29 in India; in both cases still significant at .001. Inkeles and Smith, *Becoming Modern,* Table 15.2.

39. This effect was more apparent in 1963, when the contrast between the countryside and the city was still sharp. In 1963 the regression weight for urban exposure was .17 and for occupational status .16, both statistically significant at better than .05. Although Marsh did not present a strictly comparable regression for 1991, the data he did report suggest that the effect of urban exposure, while still positive, had slipped below the level of statistical significance. See Marsh, *Great Transformation,* Table 12.3.

40. Inkeles and Smith, *Becoming Modern,* Table 19.2.

41. Chu and Ju, *Great Wall in Ruins,* Tables 3.1 and 5.5. The interaction of exposure to the media—which in the case of the Shanghai sample meant the official communist sources—and exposure to Western influences is quite complex and warrants being looked at issue by issue before any general conclusions, if any, can be reached.

42. On Taiwan, for example, occupational status was correlated with education at .58 and with household income at .48 in the 1963 sample; in the 1991 sample the respective coefficients were .55 and .37. See Marsh, *Great Transformation,* Table 3.3.

INDEX